THE

Force of Fantasy

RESTORING THE AMERICAN DREAM

Ernest G. Bormann

SOUTHERN ILLINOIS UNIVERSITY PRESS

CARBONDALE AND EDWARDSVILLE

89   88   87   86   85   5   4   3   2   1

Library of Congress Cataloging in Publication Data

Bormann, Ernest G.
   The force of fantasy.

   Bibliography: p.
   Includes index.
   1. Revivals—United States. 2. Rhetoric—Social
aspects. 3. Restorations, Political. 4. Communication—Social aspects—United States. I. Title.
BV3773.B67   1985   302.2'4   84-10539
ISBN   0-8093-1185-2

❧ Contents

❧ Preface

The Force of Fantasy: Restoring the American Dream began as a part of a project at the University of Minnesota to establish a Center for the Study of Religion in American Society. A number of scholars from such disciplines as history, philosophy, English, and speech-communication planned to bring an interdisciplinary approach to the scholarly study of the impact of religion upon a number of aspects of the culture of the United States. We took as our theme "From the Sacred to the Secular," and I began to fashion the materials in my lectures in a course in the history and criticism of American public address to relate to that theme. Subsequently the promise of funding for the Center fell through but my project had by that time taken on a life of its own.

I found myself mulling over a vast and disparate body of materials from scholars in intellectual, social, and religious history, in sociology of religion, and in the critical analysis of speeches and mass communication that covered a large span of years and a very diverse set of communication practices. Since there were no previous studies which surveyed the history of mass communication in America, the diversity of materials and the volume of studies which alluded to or made tangential comments about what was my central concern made the task of finding some unifying explanatory structure most difficult.

Comments in various studies by historians, philosophers, and rhetorical critics hinted at a connection between religious and secular speaking, so I began to search for connecting links. I found the most direct link in the move from religious to reform speaking in the decade of the 1830s. Finally, I was able to document an unfolding rhetorical tradition from the time of the Puritan preachers to the present which exhibited characteristics similar to those traditionally referred to as *romanticism* and *pragmatism*. Crude and unlettered as many of the rhetoricians were who practiced communication in the tradition I had discovered, they still had a basic distinctive communication style which, to me, seemed best characterized as *the rhetoric of romantic pragmatism*.

For much of my work I could rely on secondary sources by a host of scholars on the trail of other matters who had nonetheless documented the occurrence of speeches and other communications, described their content, and portrayed their context. Certainly historians, rhetorical and literary critics, and sociologists had studied and restudied the Puritan preachers and their sermons from many different viewpoints. Much of the communication practice associated with the Great Awakening of 1739–1740 was part of the record established by previous scholarship. Scholars had also documented the details of Abraham Lincoln's career including his speaking practices. But when I began to get hints of connections stemming from religious speakers and reformers who were unlettered, uneducated, circuit-riding preachers or lawyers, the secondary sources ran out.

With the help of research grants from the Graduate School of the University of Minnesota and a grant from the Minnesota Foundation, I was able to spend a sabbatical year gathering information from primary sources where previous scholarship left important gaps in the move from the sacred to the secular in the rhetorical tradition of romantic pragmatism. Much of what I needed I found in manuscript collections at the Boston Public Library, in the archives of the New England Methodist Historical Society, in the Baptist Historical Society at the University of Richmond, in the archives of the Massachusetts Historical Society and the Virginia Historical Society, in the archives of the Williamsburg, Virginia Corporation, and in the manuscript division of the Alderman Library at the University of Virginia.

I found a unifying structure in the move from sacred to secular reform speaking from the beginnings of the antislavery movement to the time of the Civil War. The speaking of Abraham Lincoln proved to be a logical stopping place for my analysis. Lincoln's rhetoric was a benchmark not only because the war served as a demarcation line between what I call the ungenteel style of romantic pragmatism and the genteel version, but also because Lincoln came, to my mind, to represent the highest rhetorical expression of the ungenteel style in our history.

My interest in small-group communication led me to the discovery of a key dynamic in the development of a group subculture. Work by Professor Bales at Harvard plus my own work at the University of Minnesota revealed the power of dramatizing communication to catch up the members of face-to-face interacting groups until they come to participate in the drama. The force of fantasy as a power in creating social reality for small group members became increasingly evident. Mulling over the materials for my book in the history of religious and reform speaking at the same time as I was caught up in these exciting new developments in small group communication resulted in one of those exhilarating moments of illumination when it seemed clear to me that the force of fantasy is just as strong in mass communication as it is in small group interaction. Merging the discoveries in group fantasies with recent developments in rhetorical criticism provided me with my critical method—the fantasy theme analysis of rhetorical visions.

With the help of another sabbatical leave from the University of Minnesota, I was able to complete this book, which provides a critical analysis of the social reality of those who shared in the evolving rhetorical visions of romantic pragmatism from its rise in the rhetorical crisis of the Great Awakening of the mid-1700s to its culmination in the great speeches and state papers of Abraham Lincoln a century later.

This book was written over the last twenty-five years in conjunction with the development of my lectures for a course in religious and reform speaking at the University of Minnesota. Over those years I have received much support and help in developing my ideas and in finding sources from students and colleagues. The manuscript has also profited from careful and helpful readings from Paul Boase, Kathleen Jamieson, Waldo Braden, James Andrews, Robert Cathcart, and Parke Burgess.

The University of Minnesota has supported me with several sabbatical leaves and the Graduate School has provided travel support to visit libraries and manuscript collections. I was particularly aided by a grant for one of my sabbatical leaves from the Minnesota Foundation.

Joan Lund and Ellen Bormann provided valuable assistance in preparing the manuscript for publication. Throughout the preparation and writing Nancy C. Bormann has been fellow traveler, counselor, guide, and encourager as well as consultant, editor, and copyeditor. The editors at the Southern Illinois University Press have been supportive, competent, and efficient.

I wish to thank the Speech Communication Association of America for permission to use sections of my articles "The Rhetorical Theory of William Henry Milburn" (*Speech Monographs*, 36 [1969], 28–37) and "Fetching Good Out of Evil: The Rhetorical Uses of Calamity," (*Quarterly Journal of Speech*, 632 [1977], 130–139) in this book.

THE
Force of Fantasy

❧ 1

The Critical Analysis of Seminal American Fantasies

In October 1854, Abraham Lincoln, a prosperous Illinois lawyer, spoke in Springfield after Senator Stephen A. Douglas had presented the case for the Nebraska bill the preceding day. Lincoln concluded his speech with the following peroration:

> Our republican robe is soiled, and trailed in the dust. Let us repurify it. Let us turn and wash it white, in the spirit, if not the blood, of the Revolution. Let us turn slavery from its claims of "moral right," back upon its existing legal rights, and its arguments of "necessity." Let us return it to the position our fathers gave it; and there let it rest in peace. Let us re-adopt the Declaration of Independence, and with it, the practices, and policy, which harmonize with it. Let north and south—let all Americans—let all lovers of liberty everywhere—join in the great and good work. If we do this, we shall not only have saved the Union; but we shall have so saved it, as to make, and to keep it, forever worthy of the saving. We shall have so saved it, that the succeeding millions of free happy people, the world over, shall rise up, and call us blessed to the latest generation.[1]

Lincoln's vision was analogous in crucial respects to that of the evangelical abolitionists of the 1830s. Like them, he celebrated the founders of the government, and he sought to "repurify it." The drama of repurification began with the Puritan rhetoric in the sixteenth century and by the 1850s had become a rhetorical form of mythic proportions in the oral traditions of America. Lincoln's language suggests the religious sources of the appeal when he speaks of the need to wash the republican robe "white, in the spirit, if not the blood, of the Revolution." Restoring the purity of the founding ideals and readopting the Declaration of Independence was to save the Union and assure the future for posterity. Lincoln's peroration alludes to several of the powerful dramas which evolved and sustained a native rhetorical tradition of great popularity and power. He touches the themes of saving the great experiment of representative democracy and of making the right decision because so much of the future is dependent upon it.

My theme in this book is the move from the sacred to the secular in rhetoric. My research began with the notion that the sacred flowed into and vitalized the secular persuasion for reform in the history of mass communication in the United States. To me the crucial transition point seemed to be the working-out of the antislavery impulse in the rhetoric of the abolitionists in the 1830s. Starting from that focus I began a study which traced the arguments and appeals backward in time toward the beginnings of settlement in North America and forward in the direction of the cataclysmic Civil War. As I pulled the threads which formed the rhetorical patterns of the 1830s, I found them leading me back through the camp meetings of the uneducated lay ministers in Kentucky, of circuit-riding Methodists, Baptist Farmer Preachers, and New Light Presbyterians educated, if at all, in the log colleges of the frontier. I searched back through what I discovered to be a rhetorical crisis in the Great Awakening of 1739–40 and there, finally, and not so surprisingly, found the ur-style of the Puritan sermon itself.

More surprising to me was the discovery that the threads moving forward led me to the rhetorical style of the western wing of the New Republican party of the 1850s. My study finally came to rest firmly upon the speeches and state papers of Abraham Lincoln.

Lincoln's major communication efforts in his Anti-Nebraska speeches from 1854 to 1857, in his debates with Douglas in 1858, and in his major policy speeches and statements as president were directed to a rhetoric of unification: to hold the country together symbolically, and to reconstruct the Union after secession. Lincoln's archetypal fantasy was that of *restoration*. Lincoln's drama of restoration portrayed a nation fallen on evil times, a nation which needed to restore itself, to return to the purity of the time of its founders, to renew the basic values and ideals of the Declaration of Independence, and to restore the Union to the original foundations of the constitution to show that the great experiment in self-government could work and that "the last best hope of mankind" would be lost forever if it failed.

However, Lincoln's use of the restoration drama was actually the continuation of a series of such portrayals that came to be a recurring rhetorical form. The rhetorical fantasy type of purification through rebirth and restoration was central to the Puritan persuasion of the founders of New England, was the key to the rise of the evangelical persuasion of the New Lights of the Great Awakening, was the basis for the restoration movement of the Disciples of Christ, and was the foundation of the vision of the evangelical agents of abolition. The fact that the restoration fantasy type was the central rhetorical form of Ronald Reagan's first inaugural address in 1980 provides further evidence for its longevity and staying power.[2]

The documentation and description of a major rhetorical tradition in which the restoration drama was a central recurring form is an important part of this book but my major purpose is to provide a rhetorical criticism of the communication practices that my historical analysis discovered.[3] My purpose is to illuminate how individuals talk with one another about their here-and-now concerns until they come to share a common consciousness and create a sense of identity and community, how they then use communication to raise the consciousness of inquirers until the latter convert to the new consciousness, and how they use communication to sustain the converted and keep them committed to the established vision.

My effort will be to explain the way members of a rhetorical community, who share the same consciousness and rhetorical vision, discuss their problems, concerns, delights, hopes, fears, and dreams as they go about their daily business, their worship, and their social affairs.

My title, *The Force of Fantasy*, embodies the main discovery of my rhetorical criticism of popular religious and reform discourse in the years prior to the Civil War. I found that the analysis of shared group and community fantasies based on the social scientific communication theory of symbolic convergence provided a critical key to open up the way of communication under study worked to create a shared consciousness.

My viewpoint combines humanistic and social scientific perspectives to reinterpret the historical record in terms of communication. Fantasy theme analysis is a humanistic approach to the rhetorical criticism of human communication.[4] However, fantasy theme analysts use the symbolic convergence theory as part of their basic scholarly perspective when studying communication events. They thus bring to their criticisms all the explanatory power of the general theory. Rhetorical criticism involves more than descriptions of discourse and the background, emergence, growth and decline of public consciousnesses. Once the rhetorical critics document the presence of rhetorical visions, communities, and consciousness, they can make a humanistic evaluation of the quality of the rhetoric and the social realities of the people who share the consciousness. A critic needs to evaluate and to judge the discourse and to provide added insight into how it works.

Fantasy theme analysis views the entire process of communication, practice, criticism, and special theory as the object of analysis. To explain my scholarly viewpoint, then, it is necessary first to delineate the major features of the symbolic convergence theory of communication, which forms an important part of my perspective.

Scholars studying rhetoric and communication have used the term *theory* in several different ways.[5] One way to sort out the differences in definition and to avoid the confusions that often result from them is to distinguish between special and general communication theories. Special theories are artistic formulations that specify the nature of conventional forms and usages and provide practical advice on how to take part in the communication episodes to which they relate. Special theories relate only to the communication practices of a community restricted in time and sharing a common culture. General theories, on the other hand, are more analogous to the theories of the natural sciences that account for broad classes of events.

Special communication theories deal with conventional agreements among the practitioners as to how the communication should be formed and practiced. These conventional agreements include the rules that both constitute and regulate participation. The participants may choose to obey or disobey these rules. General communication theories, on the other hand, deal with tendencies in human communication events that cannot be ignored or rescinded by the participants.

The symbolic convergence communication theory is a general theory that accounts for the creation and use of special theories. The basic communicative dynamic of the theory is the sharing of group fantasies which brings about symbolic convergence for the participants. Investigators in small group communication laboratories discovered the process of sharing fantasies when they investigated dramatizing messages and their effect on the group.[6]

A dramatizing message is one that contains one or more of the following: a pun or other wordplay, a double entendre, a figure of speech, an analogy, an anecdote, allegory, fable, or narrative. The most important element of dramatizing messages for the rhetorical tradition of romantic pragmatism is a narrative or story about real or fictitious people in a dramatic situation or setting other than the here-and-now communication of the group.

If, in the middle of a group discussion, several members come into conflict, the situation would be dramatic, but because the action is unfolding in the immediate experience of the group it would not qualify as a basis for the sharing of a group fantasy. If, however, the group members begin talking about a conflict some of them had in the past or if they envision a future conflict, these comments would be dramatizing messages.

As they studied these messages, small group investigators found that some of them seemed to fall on deaf ears; the group members did not pay much attention to the comments. Some of the dramatizing, however, caused a greater or lesser symbolic explosion in the form of a chain reaction. As the members shared the fantasy, the tempo of the conversation increased. People grew excited, interrupted one another, laughed, showed emotion, and forgot their self-consciousness. The people who shared the fantasy did so with the appropriate responses.

When a fantasy is shared by a larger audience such as the congregation in a Puritan meeting-house or at a Kentucky camp meeting, the members of the audience will indicate nonverbal participation by facial expression, bodily posture, nonverbal evidence of rapt attention, and by laughter, moans, groanings, sobbings, and, if the communication style encourages and sanctions it, by verbal exclamations such as "Hallelujah!" and "Glory be to God!"

Fantasy is a technical term in the symbolic convergence theory and does not mean what it often does in ordinary usage, that is, something imaginary, not grounded in reality. The technical meaning for fantasy is the creative and imaginative interpretation of events that fulfills a psychological or rhetorical need. The scholar working to reconstruct the consciousness embodied in the sharing of rhetorical fantasies of the past must depend heavily upon the traces left in the messages that created those fantasies. Rhetorical fantasies may include fanciful and fictitious scripts of imaginary characters, but they often deal with things that have actually happened to members of the community or that are reported in authenticated works of history, in the news media, or in the oral history and folklore of the group. The content of the dramatizing message that sparks the fantasy chain is called a *fantasy theme*.

Many a reform speaker and preacher of the nineteenth century used the rhetorical device of personification to create scenarios in which abstract entities became characters in the dramatic action. For example, Theodore Weld personified the abstraction of slavery in the following fantasy:

> The spirit of slavery never seeks shelter in the Bible, of its own accord. It grasps the horns of the altar only in desperation—rushing from the terror of the avenger's arm. Like other unclean spirits, it "hateth the light, neither cometh to the light, lest its deed should be reproved." Goaded to phrenzy in its conflicts with conscience and common sense, denied all quarter, and hunted from every covert, it vaults over the sacred enclosure and courses up and down the Bible, "seeking rest, and finding none." THE LAW OF LOVE, glowing on every page

flashes around it an omnipresent anguish and despair. It shrinks from the hated light, and howls under the consuming touch, as demons quailed before the Son of God . . .[7]

Certainly the religious speakers of the period under study often utilized supernatural characters in their sermons. They dramatized god personae, angels, devils, and assorted witches and spirits intervening in human actions. Thus, Jonathan Edwards, in a famous passage, depicted a human being held by God over the hell fires like a spider suspended by a slender thread.

Many fantasy themes were about personal experiences. The Methodist circuit riders, for example, used stories about their adventures on the circuit as well as about their religious experiences as their rhetorical stock in trade. And, of course, many fantasy themes interpreted important local and national events.

The scholar's main task in making a fantasy theme analysis is to find evidence that symbolic convergence has taken place, that groups of people have shared a fantasy. When similar dramatizing material such as wordplay, narratives, figures, and analogies crops up in a variety of messages in different contexts, such repetition is evidence of symbolic convergence.

Other evidence of the sharing of fantasies is furnished by cryptic allusions to symbolic common ground. When a group of people have shared a fantasy theme, they have charged their emotional and memory banks with meanings and emotions that can be set off by a commonly agreed upon cryptic symbolic cue.

The inside-joke phenomenon is an example of such a trigger. Only those who have shared the fantasy theme that the inside-joke refers to will respond in an appropriate fashion. But the symbolic cue does not necessarily have to be an inside-joke. The allusion to a previously shared fantasy may arouse tears or evoke anger, hatred, love, and affection, as well as laughter and humor. The symbolic cue may be a code word, phrase, slogan, or nonverbal sign or gesture. It may refer to a geographical or imaginary place or the name of a persona.

Code terms that have worked as symbolic triggers for rhetorical communities in the history of the United States include *Reagonomics, McCarthyism, Remember Pearl Harbor, Munich, Hoovervilles, Remember the Maine, Remember the Alamo, Bleeding Kansas, the Spirit of the Missouri Question, Slavocracy, the New Birth, New Measures*, and *Davenportism*. Among the best materials available for the scholar searching to find evidence that groups of people have shared fantasies is the presence of symbolic triggers within the discourse. People cannot employ such in-cues without first laying the symbolic groundwork by sharing fantasy themes.

The symbolic cue phenomenon makes possible the development of *fantasy types*. When a number of similar scenarios or outlines of the plot of the fantasies, including particulars of the scenes, characters, and situations have been shared by members of a group or larger community, they form a *fantasy type*. A *fantasy type* is a stock scenario repeated again and again by the same characters or by similar characters. For example, I found repeated testimony by revival speakers as to their call from God to preach that presented them as the protagonist of a drama. The speaker had been a worldly person given to such sins as drunkenness, gambling, and fornication and he had then experienced some dramatic incident such as a moving revival and, as a result, was humbled, had thrown himself on God's mercy, and experienced a shattering emotional conversion. During the conversion, God communicated salvation and called the protagonist to His service. The speaker's life after the "new birth" was dramatically different. These dramas all followed a very similar plot and justified, in my estimation, their being characterized as a fantasy type that I call the *Pauline conversion fantasy* since it repeated, for other protagonists in other scenes and other times, the essential narrative line of Saint Paul's conversion experience.

In the course of my study, I discovered that I could not only construct fantasy types by searching out similarities among narratives but that speakers often use the fantasy type as a rhetorical device in their discourse. Rather than dramatizing a fantasy theme with specific characters in a specific setting, they presented the general story line much as I did above in describing the Pauline conversion type. Generally, the appearance of fantasy types in a body of discourse is an indication of the emergence of a rhetorical vision that is clearly formulated and well understood by both speaker and audience.

Rhetoricians also used an archetypal fantasy as a way to fit the breaking news and the unfolding of experience comfortably into the community's social reality. Thus, if the members of a community share an archetypal fantasy portraying the United State's involvement in the Vietnam war as unsavory and unwarranted, they might refer to new governmental actions in a Latin American country as "Another Vietnam." By portraying the new experience as an instance of an archetypal drama, the rhetoricians explain and evaluate the new events and bring them into line with the overall values and emotions of their rhetorical vision.

When communicators begin to use fantasy types or allusions to types in their messages, it is further evidence that fantasy themes have been shared. People cannot generalize to the more abstract type without having first shared at least several themes of a similar nature.

types, they may integrate them into a coherent rhetorical vision of some aspect of their social reality. A *rhetorical vision* is a unified putting-together of the various scripts which gives the participants a broader view of things.

Rhetorical visions are often integrated by the sharing of a dramatizing message that contains a master analogy. The master analogy pulls the various elements together into a more or less elegant and meaningful whole. Usually, a rhetorical vision is indexed by a key word, a slogan, or a label. Such indexing is a special case of the symbolic cuing phenomenon, but in this instance, the rhetorical community has reached such a high level of symbolic maturity that the cryptic allusion can be not just to details of fantasy themes and types but to a total coherent view of an aspect of their social reality. Recent labels for rhetorical visions in the United States have included *The New Deal, The New Frontier, Black Power, The Cold War, The New Left, The Silent Majority,* and *The Moral Majority.* Labels for rhetorical visions during the period under study in this book included *New Lights, Unitarianism,* and *Free Soil.*

When a rhetorical vision emerges, the participants in the vision (those who have shared the fantasies in an appropriate way) come to form a rhetorical community. Membership is sometimes formalized and can be documented. Some typical formal symbols include induction ceremonies, confirmation and baptism, paying dues, and carrying a card.

Rhetorical visions may be more or less compelling and relate to matters of greater or lesser importance to the individuals who share the fantasies. A given individual may share several rhetorical visions providing social realities for such things as hobbies, politics, intimate relationships, and religion. Some of these visions may be shared by only a few people, and the visions may last only for short periods of time. On the other hand, some rhetorical visions are so all-encompassing and impelling that they permeate an individual's social reality in all aspects of living. I call such all-encompassing symbolic systems *life-style rhetorical visions.* Many of the religious and reform rhetorical visions of the nineteenth century in the United States were life-style rhetorical visions. Once a person crossed the boundaries of the rhetorical community and became a Methodist, or once an individual converted to the vision of the Agitators for Abolition or became a follower of Charles Grandison Finney, the individual's entire life was changed.

Fantasy theme analysis forces the scholar to search for the boundaries of rhetorical communities and reveals the complex and complicated symbolic terrain in a period like the 1830s. Such analysis is a strong antidote to interpretations that select out of such complexity a cluster of ideas and suggest that this cluster represents the essence of a historical period in national life.

Even selecting a half-dozen such clusters would oversimplify the rhetorical diversity in the history of North American communication.

Much of what has commonly been thought of as persuasion can be accounted for on the basis of group and mass fantasies. The fantasizing is accompanied by emotional arousal; the dreams embodied in the fantasies drive participants toward actions and efforts to achieve them; the sharing of fantasies provides a social reality peopled by anthropomorphic forces and imagined and historical personages in dramatic confrontations. My study of religious and reform speaking confirmed Robert Frost's insight that "society can never think things out: it has to see them acted out by actors."[8]

Because people have difficulty thinking things through and need to have them acted out, the public can most easily understand the issues that disturb society when speakers portray them by placing symbolic personae in dramatic action in which they contend with other symbolic personae symbolizing other positions.[9] For the evangelical antislavery agents, the persona of John C. Calhoun of South Carolina came to symbolize the hated proslavery position of the antebellum South. For the pro-Southern sympathizers in the decades prior to the Civil War, William Lloyd Garrison came to symbolize the hated abolitionists.

The power of the symbolic convergence theory stems from the human tendency to try to understand events in terms of people with certain personality traits and motivations, people who make decisions, take actions, and cause things to happen. We can understand a person making plans in order to achieve goals and succeeding or failing to do so, because we often interpret our own behavior in that way in our personal fantasies.

Interpreting events in terms of human action allows us to assign responsibility, to praise or blame, to arouse and propitiate guilt, to hate and to love. When we share a fantasy, we make sense out of what prior to that time may have been a confusing state of affairs and we do so in common with others who share the fantasy with us. Thus, we come to symbolic convergence on the matter and envision that part of our world in similar ways. We have created some symbolic common ground, and we can then talk with one another about that shared interpretation with code words or brief allusions along the lines of the symbolic cue phenomenon.

The unfolding of experience is often chaotic and confusing. Fantasy themes, in contrast with experience, are organized and artistic. When people dramatize an event, they must select certain characters to be the focus of the story and present them in a favorable light while selecting others to be portrayed in a more negative fashion. Without protagonists (heroes) and antagonists (villains) there is little drama. Shared fantasies are coherent accounts of experience in the past or envisioned in the future that simplify and form the social reality of the participants. The community's shared dreams of the future, no matter how apocalyptic or utopian, provide artistic and comprehensible forms for thinking about and experiencing the future. Fantasy themes are always slanted, ordered, and interpreted; they provide a rhetorical means for several communities of people to account for and explain the same experiences or the same events in different ways.

The artistry with which the leading communicators for a community create the rhetorical fantasies that come to shape the social reality of participants may vary greatly. Some communities may share dreams in which cardboard characters enact stereotyped melodramas. Others may live in a social reality of complexity peopled with characters of stature enacting high tragedies. The dramas themselves, however, always interpret, slant, suggest, and persuade. Sometimes two rhetorical communities living side-by-side in the same culture will have mirror-image rhetorical visions; that is, one group of people may share visions in which a number of historic personages are heroes while another group may portray the same people as villains. One group may celebrate certain courses of action as laudable while the other denigrates the same scenarios.

A new religious cult or denomination or a new revolutionary or reform movement begins with a diffuse and unfocused impulse on the part of some people. To become an organized effort, people sharing an impulse must begin to communicate with one another and create a new consciousness. Only after the emergence of a shared consciousness will they begin organizing behaviors and develop their rhetoric of organization, including terms for status and leadership and for formal organizational units such as committees, circuits, and parishes.

Rhetorical innovation, on occasion, may begin when one creative person fantasizes a powerful personal consciousness and does so with such skill that his or her consciousness is shared by converts and becomes the rhetorical vision that forms a community's consciousness. Innovation often results, however, from small group meetings of people drawn together by a similar impulse. During these meetings, members begin to share fantasies and in the process come to symbolic convergence; they create the raw material for the new rhetorical vision. Such was the case of the Holy Band to which Whitefield and the Wesley brothers belonged at Pembroke College, Oxford, and which produced the new consciousness that came to be cued by the term *Methodism*.

Often, the flow of communication in consciousness-creating meetings is not from the speaker to the listeners; instead, the chain is triggered by the first dramatizing message and is then picked up and elaborated by the others. People caught up in a chain of fantasies may experience moments similar to the creative experience of individuals when they daydream about a creative project or an important problem and suddenly get excited about the direction of their thinking. Then, the others feed back ideas and new dramatizations to add to the original comment; messages begin flowing rapidly among the participants until, under the suggestive power of the group fantasy, the constraints that normally hold people back are released; they feel free to experiment with ideas, to play with concepts, wild suggestions, and imaginative notions. Soon a number of people are deeply involved in the discussion, excitedly adding their emotional support and often modifying the ongoing script.

These innovative dramas may be radical departures from most of the rhetorical visions known to the participants or they may be adaptations of historical and contemporary fantasy types. One way for groups of people to develop radical new rhetorical visions is to take a contemporary vision and stand it on its head. This was the way the new consciousness of the radical abolitionists centered in Boston emerged, for example, with rhetoricians like William Lloyd Garrison dramatizing the Fourth of July as a day devoted to hypocrisy and the Constitution as a compact with the devil.[10] Other groups may create a new consciousness by using historical and contemporary fantasy types and making modest changes by using different personae and adapting them to new events. In this way the new political consciousness of the Free-Soil party emerged through adaptation of the fantasy themes and types of the evangelical antislavery vision.

A pressing rhetorical problem for aggregates of individuals moving towards a sense of community is the creation of a common identity. People create a common consciousness by becoming aware that they are involved in an identifiable group and that their group differs in some important respects from other groups. They also become aware that because they are members of the group they are personally somewhat different from others who are not symbolically tied together by the experience of sharing the same fantasies. To come to such awareness, the members need to identify their collective self.

A rhetorical device that members may use to identify their group is to personify it in terms of an individual, an animal, or an elemental force, or simply to treat the group as a persona acting as a human individual. Often, the movement will use some human being, usually associated with the founding of the community as a symbolic persona to stand for the entire movement. The personae of George Whitefield, John and Charles Wesley, William Lloyd Garrison, and Charles Grandison Finney served such unifying functions in the period under study.

Dealing with their identity often gets the group to share fantasies about the boundaries of their movement. Who are the outsiders? Typical personae who can symbolize the outsiders are a useful device for identifying the insiders and drawing boundaries around the community. Fantasies that clearly divide the sympathetic, good people (we) from the unsympathetic or evil people (they) aid the group's self-awareness and are crucial to the emergence of its consciousness. Indeed, an important question for a rhetorical critic relates to the way participants in a new consciousness celebrate themselves and their group. For the values implied by and the motives imbedded in such fantasies are often among the most important aspects in the rhetorical vision.

Once the sharing of fantasies identifies the group and distinguishes between insiders and outsiders, the members have clear rhetorical and symbolic boundaries to serve as guidelines for terminating rituals to force members out and for initiation and acceptance rituals for recruits. For example, the participants in the new consciousness associated with the persona of James Davenport in the Great Awakening began to refer to one another by using the familial designations of *brother* or *sister* and once newcomers were accepted into the community, they received and used the familial appellation as evidence of having crossed the boundaries of the vision.

Symbolic change begins with innovation created by fantasy sharing. If the innovation is interesting and comes to the attention of others, they may be drawn into participation in the basic fantasies. At this point in the development of the consciousness, it becomes important whether or not the members share some version of a proselyting fantasy type.

When people share fantasies celebrating the insiders, they answer the question "Who are we?" In the process of answering this question, they often share fantasies that depict themselves as better than outsiders and their rhetorical innovations as an improvement over current ways of viewing the world.

If their first shared fantasies have aroused high emotions and interest, they are predisposed to go on and share fantasies that portray one or two diametrically opposed futures as desirable. In such cases, they may portray the innovations as valuable and in danger of being diluted or polluted if they become popular; only a few of the elite deserve to become members and share the new higher consciousness. As a result, they tightly restrict their membership. At the other extreme are groups that envision a future in which they, by vigorously seeking converts, promote the new awareness until it is universal or nearly so. They answer the identity question in terms of their being the forerunners of a new consciousness that when widespread or universal will improve humankind. The latter dramatizations about the future are versions of the proselyting fantasy type. All of the rhetorical visions of romantic pragmatism contained powerful proselyting fantasies. Charles Grandison Finney, for example, envisioned a future of perfected humankind as a result of the conversion of the entire country to his persuasion within a few years.

Proselyting groups need to develop communication events that will (1) attract potential converts, (2) shake them loose from any emotional attachment to other rhetorical visions, and (3) get the potential converts to share the fantasies that comprise the group's rhetorical vision. I call such recurring communication events *consciousness-raising* communication episodes.[11] Small group communication is as important to consciousness raising as it is to consciousness creating. Where the tenor of consciousness-creating groups is innovative and open to diversity, the ethos of consciousness-raising groups is persuasive and closed to alternative dramas.

Often, the process of consciousness raising or conversion to a new rhetorical vision was accomplished in nineteenth-century North America by a complex system of powerful exhortative sermons, lectures, and persuasive speeches integrated in intensive group meetings and two-person counseling sessions. A series of revival sermons in a protracted meeting by a speaker such as Charles Grandison Finney would attract the potential converts and begin to shake them loose from their attachment to other rhetorical visions. Inquirers might come forward to the "anxious seat" and be identified so members of Finney's "Holy Band" could work with them in small-group consiousness-raising meetings and in counseling sessions.

The rhetorical task of consciousness raising begins with what the nineteenth-century evangelicals called "breaking up the old foundations." The communication style is designed to get the potential converts to share fantasies that break loose their emotional attachments to the rhetorical visions in which they participate.

The best candidates for conversion are often people who are no longer strongly committed to their rhetorical vision. Perhaps they inherited it and were never tied to it with the commitment of people who participated in the excitement of the first sharing. Even so, they will still have favorite scripts that help to hold their symbolic world together and give them some anchor.

As the first stage of consciousness-raising communication gets underway, the potential converts often feel a combination of revulsion and attraction. They are confused and emotionally disturbed. Among the more important targets for attack are their definitions of self, the fantasies in which they create their own self consciousnesses. Being social creatures people tend to

define themselves in terms of the group consciousness in which they participate, so the attacks on self definition are often attacks on the core fantasies of
the old visions.

When the old foundations have been broken up, the individual feels lost,
disturbed, and upset. The next phase involves what the evangelicals called
"pouring in the truth." This is a phase that essentially gets the neophyte to
share the positive fantasies that form the core of the new consciousness. During
the rhetorical processes of breaking up the old foundations and pouring in the
truth, the individual may be torn between the old and the new. Depending
upon the strength of the commitment of the old core fantasies, the person will
go through a longer or shorter period of struggle.

At some point, and the testimony often portrays this as a sharp and
sudden awareness, the individual will click into the new rhetorical vision.
Suddenly, the person sees the world in a new way. The old fantasies are now
seen clearly in their despicable light. Indeed, the new fantasies will often
evoke hatred for the old ways of thinking, believing, and acting. The person,
suddenly seeing through the lenses of the new rhetorical vision, usually feels
joy, excitement, and peace. The doubts have been resolved; the struggle is at
an end.

The last step of the process is confirmation in the form of action. The new
members often must demonstrate commitment to the new consciousness
publicly. In the case of the nineteenth-century evangelicals, this could have
been through confirmation and baptism. In the case of the antislavery reform
groups, it could have been through demonstrating in the streets, breaking up
church services, or going door-to-door to get signatures for petitions advocating antislavery programs to be sent to the Congress.

Once a rhetorical community emerges with a coherent rhetorical vision
and clear symobolic boundaries to discriminate the insider from the outsider,
the members must face more or less severe rhetorical problems of holding the
group together. Some rhetorical visions are unstable; they suffer from a
continuous threat of spontaneous internal combustion. Such was the vision of
agitators for radical abolition. The group for whom the persona of William
Lloyd Garrison served as a unifying symbol was plagued by internal disputes,
divisions, and breakups. Other rhetorical visions are stable and inflexible and
persevere through long periods of time. Such was the vision of the Puritans of
New England, which sustained a community for several hundred years.

The rhetorical problem of sustaining consciousness is often most pressing during the periods of maturity and decline. Members with a low threshold
of boredom or a short attention span may begin to lose interest. While some
love to hear the old familiar stories told and retold, others seek new symbolic

sustenance. When backsliding and falling away of individuals is followed by disaffection on the part of cliques and factions, the community members feel the need to develop a style of consciousness-sustaining communication.

The rhetorical problem that is common to consciousness-sustaining communication styles is the need to revitalize the individual's commitment to the vision. The typical communication process for such revitalization is severe criticism of the backslider by a speaker or a group of people who put pressure on the individual to conform to group thinking and behavioral norms. Such criticism requires a common rhetorical vision as the basis for evaluation. If the communication style emphasizes small-group techniques, the other committee members typically put the individual "on the carpet" in intensive group sessions in which the person to be criticized is the focal individual. They then bombard the wayward one with messages that compare the ideals of the rhetorical vision with the person's behavior. They accuse the person of having a bad character (that is, one that departs from the models of the good personae in the basic shared fantasies). They also criticize the person for enacting bad scenarios and failing to emulate good scripts.

A successful communication session results in the objects of criticism making a public confession of wrongdoing. Such a confession is often followed by public repentance and testimony from the individual that he or she has a renewed commitment to the vision and will bring future actions into line with the standards of the community.

A typical example of group consciousness-sustaining communication is furnished by the Oneida Community's "Mutual Criticism" sessions. The Oneida Community was a communal group of Christian perfectionists, and an important part of their community governance was based on a standing committee of criticism selected by the members and changed every three months. Whenever a member felt the need for criticism or when the community felt a member needed such criticism, the committee would subject the individual to scathing criticism in front of the entire group. Mutual Criticism was based on rules of procedure and on norms of how to give and receive criticism.[12]

Other communities have used the device of a public speech or sermon delivered by a persona who has the right to criticize the community, the audience, segments of the audience (young people, women, old people, men, etc.), and individuals. The rhetorical tactic of "taking the hide off the audience" in the nineteenth century was useful not only in breaking up the old foundations as a prelude to consciousness raising but also as a way to revitalize the faith.

Some communities have also used the tactic of celebrating the group's saga. Periodically, these communities would have a communication episode in which speakers pronounced encomia on personae such as the founder or founders, the community itself, its geographical location, and outstanding episodes in its history. Recounting these celebration fantasies in detail served to arouse emotional responses of attachment to the community and identification with unifying personae. Many nineteenth-century Fourth-of-July orations functioned in this way.

Some communities have also used the tactic of repetitive detailed argument in support of the rhetorical vision as a way of consciousness sustaining. Speakers prove and prove again the validity of the community's social reality. The Puritans of New England used this tactic in sermons and lectures to perform sophisticated exegesis on the sacred text in the cause of proving the validity of the Puritan rhetorical vision.

A viable rhetoric must also accommodate the community to the changes that accompany its unfolding history. The rhetoric must deal with anxiety aroused by times of trouble, by the evil within the social reality. The rhetoric must deal with changing circumstances, social conflict, success as well as failure. Communication is the means by which the community makes and implements plans and interprets their success and failure. In much of the functioning rhetoric, therefore, problem-solving communication, argument, logic, evidence, proof, and refutation play a prominent part. To be sure, some rhetorical visions celebrate hardheaded, scientific, fact-oriented communication while others put less emphasis on such messages, but for many visions, the question of argument becomes an important one for the rhetorical critic.

When I first began my study, I was of the opinion that shared fantasies were different in kind from argumentative discourse. As I probed deeper into the workings of various historical rhetorical visions, however, I found that reasoned discourse and shared fantasies were not entirely different. I discovered that argument ultimately related to shared fantasies in that the latter were a necessary and prior condition for the former. I concluded that the force of fantasy not only accounts for the irrational and nonrational aspects of persuasion but that it provides the ground for the rational elements as well.

The sharing of fantasies within a community establishes the assumptive system that is the basis for debate and discussion. Discursive argument requires a common set of assumptions about good reasons and the nature of proof. For instance, the Puritan vision gave highest place to evidence not of the senses but to revelations, from God. The assumptive system undergirding the Puritan arguments was a grand fantasy type in which a god persona revealed the ultimate truth by inspiring some humans to write a sacred text. Supplementing this core drama was the fantasy type in which the god persona inspired ministers to speak the truth when preaching and teaching. These fantasy types provided the ultimate legitimization for the Bible as a source of revealed knowledge and for the ministers as the proper teachers of biblical truths. Therefore, discursive parts of Puritan sermons were often arguments based upon the extraction of the revealed truth from biblical quotations. Every rhetorical vision that I examined had some such core fantasies that provided the ultimate legitimization of knowledge, and, thus, of the proper way to provide good reasons and arguments for belief and action.

I also found that when a new communication style is introduced into a culture and begins to attract converts, the result is a controversy relating to such issues as: What are good reasons? How can we prove a point in debate? What is the court of last resort, the final ultimate argument? William Ellery Channing, for example, was a spokesman for a new style of preaching when he delivered his famous sermon "Unitarian Christianity." Channing devoted roughly the first half of his sermon to the question of what was the proper way to use the Bible in theological disputation. Channing's rhetorical tactics involved the portrayal of a new god persona and a new series of dramas in which God assumed a more parental and teaching role and in which the Bible emerged from historical forces as well as from supernatural inspiration. Only after the dramatizations of the origin of the Bible and its claim as knowledge did Channing turn to the concrete details on the way it might be used to argue such questions as the unity or trinity of the Godhead.[13]

My subtitle, *The Restoration of the American Dream*, embodies the second main feature of my analysis. I found that an important strain of reform rhetoric that grew out of the religious speaking traditions of the early years of settlement and the beginning decades of the new nation was in a profound sense conservative. While the successful speakers looked about them and found times of troubles, sinfulness, and societal ills that required reform, they cast their solutions into a mighty panoramic drama of history that essentially portrayed the successful reform effort as requiring first a *restoration* of society to its original foundations. Many American reformers began their journey forward into a better society by moving backwards towards the true foundations, by a restoration of the original dream of the founding fathers.

In the period I am studying, there were a number of large rhetorical communities that did not have the restoration fantasy type as a central drama of their rhetorical vision. Many communities shared fantasies that celebrated the status quo. Daniel Webster, for example, was representative of a host of speakers who portrayed the country as essentially sound and on the steady route to progress. Far from seeing any need to reform and restore, Webster, in one masterful commemorative address after another, envisioned a country that was happy, contented, and free.

Among those seeking change, there were communities that came to share a consciousness that, far from seeking restoration of a grand experiment in self-government, saw the society as built on a rotten foundation and aimed at a complete overthrow of the entire political system.

When a host of publicists, speakers, and campaigners create a rhetorical movement based on a new consciouness that begins with a grand panoramic portrayal of the evils of society, that attributes the evils to the community's falling away from the purity of the original vision upon which the society was founded and then dramatizes a millennial future that will follow upon the rigorous pursuit of the right path, namely, the restoration of society upon its original foundations, the result is a rhetoric which periodically celebrates the common bases of society. By dramatizing again and again the nature of the founders and their vision, the rhetoric of the movements for reform served to revivify the traditional values of the society.

My argument is that there are several major schools of persuasion in pre–Civil War America but that one popular and influential tradition is represented by a family of communication styles, each member of which differs from the others but all of which have a close enough resemblance to one another to justify calling them a rhetorical tradition. The tradition stems from the ur-style of the Puritan sermon and evolves through the successive generations of the envangelical revival style, the ungenteel style of frontier preachers and lawyers, and the evangelical reform style of abolition, to culminate in the Free-Soil vision of Abraham Lincoln.

The tradition was *romantic* in that it subordinated form to content, manners to feeling, and encouraged freedom of invention and delivery. Methodist circuit riders often evaluated a particularly effective sermon as one in which they were able to speak "with freedom." To swing free in a revival sermon and move into an emotional chanting communion with an audience which interrupted with shouts, moans, and cries was an ecstatic experience for the participants in the style. The rhetoric emphasized imagination, emotion, introspection, and intuition as central to the art of communication. The speeches themselves often celebrated nature, the common people, and the freedom of will and spirit. The natural orator, untrained and therefore unspoiled by formal educaton, was the exemplar of the good speaker.

The participants in the tradition were, however, pragmatists as well as romantics. They emphasized everyday practicality. They stressed the usefulness of their messages, and the immediate and visible effect of their speeches was evidence of success or failure. The good speaker was a common man and able to deal with practical problems such as grubbing stumps and quieting an unruly mob. They found little authority in precedents and abstract and ultimate principles and looked instead to the usefulness, workability, and practicality of ideas and proposals for criteria of judgment. For the most part uneducated in a formal sense, the rhetoricians of the tradition were caught up in a crude sort of pragmatism which portrayed bookishness as impractical and their own knowledge as largely gained from experience—either the direct experience of nature or the close reading of human nature. Their practicality was that of the self-reliant frontiersman able to survive the rigors of natural disaster, or the cleverness of the inventor creating gadgets to meet practical necessities.

Charles Grandison Finney, one of the leading rhetorical theorists in the tradition, caught its pragmatic essence in a lecture entitled "A Wise Minister Will Be Successful" when he said that "the amount of a minister's success in winning souls (*other things being equal*) invariably decides the amount of wisdom he has exercised in the discharge of his office."[14]

My argument for the rhetorical tradition of romantic pragmatism is based upon the distinction between special artistic theories of rhetoric and communication and general social scientific theories. Recurring patterns of communication that are conventional rather than lawful constitute a *communication style* and result when a community of people share common artistic ideal models of communication and apply the resulting standards to shape their practice into recurring forms.

By *communication styles* I mean the broad usage of a community of people engaged in significant discourse for which they understand the rules, customs, and conventions. *Style* also has a much narrower definition in the sense of a strikingly different mode of expression unique to an individual. The old aphorism "style is the man" points to the idiosyncratic features of an individual's characteristic mode of expression.

My emphasis is upon the norms of communication that characterize a group of people who share a consciousness based upon a rhetorical vision and that constitute a rhetorical community. Individual style and the style of the community are not unrelated. Individuals practice communication within the assumptions of a given rhetorical community. Joint social ventures such as dances, musical performances, games, and communication episodes have the common characteristic of allowing individual variations of style in performance, but these individual variations must always be according to the rules, norms, customs, and ideal models relating to the joint venture. A person with a striking communication style is practicing within the conventions of a larger community and according to the agreed-upon conventions of the joint enterprise that results in the recurring form and stands out against that background. When Abraham Lincoln spoke as a striking stylist in the ungenteel tradition at Gettysburg Cemetery, he was on the same program with Edward Everett, a striking stylist in the classical Ciceronian style popular among well-educated intellectuals from the Eastern seaboard.

A special theory of communication consists of a number of components all necessary and important to the practice of communication. First, the special rhetorical theory contains shared fantasies and fantasy types that provide a philosophical rationale for the communication practice. These shared fantasies will imply or specify such things as the functions of communication, a justification for the ideal type of communication, and often some application of the ultimate legitimization fantasy type for the way to truth. Second, the special theory includes exemplars of the ideal way to communicate in the form of concrete communication transactions. Sometimes a persona whose practice reveals the ideals will serve as an ideal type and sometimes the ideal will be described in more general terms. Exemplars include the way participants should invent, construct, and exchange verbal and nonverbal messages in the varied contexts that the vision selects and focuses on for communication. Third, the special rhetorical theory contains "rules-of-thumb" that serve to guide practice and anticipate the production of good or effective communication transactions. These rules-of-thumb are used by instructors to coach newcomers to enable them to improve their communication practices.

In a mature rhetorical style, the exemplar communication events imply the sorts of argumentation that the practitioners of normal communication within the constitutive and regulatory rules of the style will use. Not until the style reaches maturity and the rhetorical community has shared the requisite fantasies to provide the symbolic ground of assumptive systems will a critic discover highly developed esoteric argumentation and long patches of reasoned discourse. When the style is mature, participants in an argument can use the inside-cue to allude to the grounds that support the argument.

How does a communication style come into being? Rhetorical practice furnishes the grounds for a style. A new style begins with consciousness-creating groups. If among the newly shared fantasies are some that denigrate the current rhetorical style, the participants will often find some novel group fantasies setting communication precedents. Others may emulate these precedent-setting communication events in subsequent meetings and gradually the members of the group start communicating in ways that are unusual when compared to ways that are currently in vogue.

In the last half of the sixteenth century in England, a number of the ministers of the church began to meet together to discuss their grievances. They shared fantasies that celebrated preaching and placed it as central to the church service. They developed a philosophical rationale and an ideal model of preaching that stressed such things as a plain use of language and vigorous nonverbal gestures. This was quite different from the style practiced by much of the established ministry of the time. Transported to America, the maturing new style resulted in the recurring rhetorical form of the New England Puritan sermon of the seventeenth century.

Communication styles are artful creations of human beings that evolve as people go about their daily affairs talking to one another for many different reasons. They are creations in the sense that they arise out of innovation, novelty, and unpredictability. One is never born a good communicator in a given style but must always be taught to appreciate it. People who participate in a communication style become connoisseurs who appreciate good communication according to the standards of the style.

A new communication style begins with practices that violate the norms, customs, and rules of established styles. Because the new beginnings have no established criteria for evaluation or teaching, they are first propagated by modeling behavior. People drawn to the new practice try to emulate a sample of the communication with which they have come in contact. When sufficient samples of the new style are available, some general rules-of-thumb evolve, which the initiated can use to teach neophytes and to evaluate communication. If a new style becomes popular, partisans of the practice need to instruct more and more newcomers to appreciate and practice the style. They often set up special instructional facilities for that purpose. Where the early Puritans set up prophesying sessions for the training of preachers, the early American Methodists established an apprentice system in which a young exhorter rode the rounds with an established circuit rider and was taught the proper way to exhort and preach.

Gradually, ideal and abstract models of communication emerge from the give-and-take of practice and teaching sessions. The natural specialization within interacting groups results in some members emerging as experts who can critically evaluate communication according to the ideal models and who can coach newcomers to improve practice and encourage appreciation of "good" communication within the rules and customs of the style.

With the rise of a group of communication experts comes a refinement of the concepts and a move to greater abstractness in the formulation of advice on how to communicate well. The experts come together to discuss their common interests in the communication style, and as they share the same assumptions about the general shape of the ideal commuication events, their discussions and arguments are largely focused on solving problems within the confines furnished by the assumptions. In the course of their discussions, the communication specialists develop a *theory*. Because the theory is based upon prior practice and criticism, the discovery of works that present a new communication theory provides evidence of the maturing of a rhetorical style.

My general procedure has been first to trace the break in communication practices and document the rise of the new rhetorical practices, then to discover and outline the mature special rhetorical theory that grew out of the practice and criticism, and finally to describe the rhetorical vision associated with the style. Although I emphasize the stylistic elements of communication, my purpose is to discover the emergence, growth, maturity, and decline of an evolving series of public consciousnesses related to religion and reform. I examine the creation of each new consciousness and provide a critical analysis of the rhetorical function, efficacy, and moral force of the communication style, rhetorical vision, and social reality of each.

Chapter two illustrates my general approach, even though the Puritans brought to the New World a mature consciousness with a well-established rhetorical vision and communication style. In Chapter two, therefore, I do not need to examine the consciousness-creating phase of development. I begin with a summary of Puritan preaching practices, turn next to Cotton Mather's formulation of the special rhetorical theory that undergirded the recurring form of the Puritan sermon in its maturity, and then describe the rhetorical vision and its associated consciousness.

The Puritan rhetorical community forms the background for the development of romantic pragmatism, and since its rhetorical vision continued on unchanged in its main outlines for many decades, the scholarly connoisseurs of the style embroidered and embellished the vision until it achieved a high degree of density and complexity. A detailed study of the intricacies of the Puritan rhetorical vision would require a bookshelf. My chapter presents only a sketch of the main *rhetorical* features of Puritanism as a background to the study of romantic pragmatism. My aim is to describe the rhetorical features of the popular vision and not the complex theological or philosophical views of the intellectuals who were keepers of the vision.

Subsequent chapters document the breaking up of the rhetorical vision of the Puritans and the rhetorical crisis associated with the creation of a new consciousness at the time of the Great Awakening of 1739–1740. In this period of symbolic disarray, a new consciousness emerged which involved the first of the family of romantic and pragmatic rhetorical styles and visions in the form of the new rhetorical community of the revivalists of the Great Awakening. I use the communication of Jonathan Edwards as illustrative of the transition from one style to another and the speaking of George Whitefield as the exemplar of the new style. I piece together the special communication theory associated with the new style from the debate over the proper way to communicate that took place as an aftermath of the revival. My emphasis is upon the special theory implied by Jonathan Edward's defense of the revival. I conclude with a rhetorical critical analysis of the social reality of the new community.

The next rhetorical community in the family of romantic pragmatism is that associated with the ungenteel style. After discussing the communication practices of the new community, I document the emergence of a new consciousness in the communication of the Methodist circuit riders and the Baptist farmer preachers. The special communication theory spelled out by William Henry Milburn provides a coherent and complete account of the basis for the mature style.

The transition from the sacred to the secular comes with the rise of a new consciousness in the form of the communication practices of Charles Grandison Finney and his supporters and the reform efforts of Theodore Dwight Weld and his antislavery agents. I refer to the recurrent forms of the new rhetorical community as the evangelical reform style of communication. Finney provides me with a complete and coherent account of the special communication theory associated with the practices of the evangelical reformers.

Because the evangelical reform rhetoric is the pivot of my argument concerning the relationship between religious and reform communication, I examine all of the persuasion associated with what is commonly known as the abolition movement. When examined from the viewpoint of fantasy theme analysis, utilizing symbolic convergence concepts, the rhetoric of abolition divides into two consciousnesses. The two rhetorical communities use two quite different rhetorical styles, and as time goes by the two communities divide their formal organizational structures along the line of the rhetorical boundaries separating them. In my rhetorical criticism, I juxtapose the rhetorical visions, the communication styles, and the shared consciousnesses of the two communities and compare and contrast their social realities.

The final chapters work out the further secularization of the reform rhetorics and the emergence of a new consciousness with a much heavier emphasis on secular political fantasies than on the religious dramatizations of the earlier rhetorical visions. The new consciousness employs a communication style similar to the ungenteel style of the hot gospel and results in the formation of new political parties such as the Free-Soil and Republican parties. Abraham Lincoln's practice of the ungenteel style and his participation in the new consciousness with its modified rhetorical vision resembling that of the evangelical reformers is documented and critically evaluated.

My study reveals four discernible, new shared consciousnesses evolving through the years from 1740 to 1860. The four new rhetorical communities are those of (1) the revivals of 1739–40, (2) the hot gospel of the postrevolutionary period, (3) the evangelical revival and reform of the 1830s, and (4) the Free-Soil and Republican parties. These shared consciousnesses are different enough from one another to be considered separate, and each has a different communication style. Despite these differences, however, each succeeding community shares a rhetorical vision that is essentially a modification of the previous visions. While the core fantasy types and integrative analogies of the rhetorical visions may differ, they all share heavy romantic and pragmatic qualities. They thus form a family of rhetorical visions that constitute a rhetorical tradition of importance in nineteenth-century American popular culture.

Individuals in rhetorical transactions create subjective worlds of common expectations and meanings. Against the panorama of large events and seemingly unchangeable forces of society at large or of nature, the individual often feels lost and hopeless. One coping mechanism is to dream an individual fantasy that provides a sense of meaning and significance for the individual and helps protect the person from the pressures of natural calamity and social disaster. The sharing of group fantasies serves much the same coping function for those who participate in the rhetorical vision and often has much more force because of the power of group pressure upon the individual and because of the supportive warmth of like-minded companions.

The rhetorical critic can describe the social reality contained in the shared consciousness as represented in the rhetorical vision constructed from a study of the fantasy themes and types, the analogies and figurative language in a body of discourse. The critic can then go on to illuminate how people who share the consciousness associated with the rhetorical vision related to one another, how they arranged themselves into social hierarchies, how they dealt with conflict and changing circumstances, how they acted to achieve the goals embedded in their dreams, how they were aroused by the dramatic action and by the dramatis personae of their rhetoric.

The remainder of the book is devoted to the description and critical analysis of one important family of communication styles that forms a rhetorical tradition in North America. The tradition is Protestant, popular, pragmatic, and romantic. Practitioners of the tradition of romantic pragmatism tended to be reformers whose persuasion was largely cast into religious, recurring rhetorical forms and whose basic vision was a conservative one of the restoration of an essentially good society to its former glory.

❧ 2

The Puritan Rhetorical Style

Forerunner of Romantic Pragmatism

Among the early settlers of the British colonies along the Eastern seaboard of North America in the seventeenth century was a community of religious dissenters who, in their fantasies, had portrayed themselves as the elected saints of God's invisible church. Prior to their migration, they had been part of a major expression of the Protestant Reformation in England. They were known as Puritans because in their shared dramas they saw their role as that of reforming the established church by restoring it to the primitive purity and simplicity of the early Christian church. They dreamed of ridding the Church of England of all remaining popish trappings and of its worldly and sinful morality.

In England, they had evolved new communication practices which dramatized preaching as the central communication transaction for their community; they had developed a complex canon which guided their communication criticism; they had formulated a sophisticated rhetorical theory. In short, they brought with them to America a mature rhetorical style. They were, when they signed the Mayflower Compact off Plymouth Rock, already a tightly knit rhetorical community.

Seldom in the history of white settlements in North America or in the history of the United States has a group of speakers developed which had such a clearly shared and uncontested rhetorical vision with its concomitant rhetorical theory, criticism, and practice. By the latter half of the seventeenth century, the Puritan rhetorical style, shaped by the rhetorical needs of a new community facing the unique circumstances of adapting to the wilderness and by the pressures for conformity within a highly cohesive group, had become detailed and consistent. Perry Miller judged of the Puritans in North America that "they developed, amplified, and standardized a type of sermon for which the rules were as definite as for the ode." He labeled the native American Puritan sermon a "jeremiad" and "noted that it quickly became so precise a formula as to be immediately recognizable to the student of types—as, no doubt, it was to the audiences of the time."[1]

Of first importance to the consideration of the speechmaking of the Puritans was the way they fantasized about the drama of preaching itself and its role in religious observations. Responding to some of what they viewed as lax practices of the established clergy, the founders of the Puritan vision participated in fantasy themes which emphasized the necessity and importance of preaching; the vision raised preaching to the central place in the church service. Viewing the duties of the minister in this fashion provided the participants in the vision with motivation to work hard and long on developing speaking skills and on preparing sermons. In the dramas, which featured a scenario in the meeting-house with the ideal minister as protagonist, the minister was characterized as a man of God, a prophet who declared to his people the "ministry of the gospel." To this job he brought neither a "moral homily" nor a "philosophical disquisition"; rather, he preached with the "authoritative declaration of the will of the Blessed God." Out of the scenarios featuring preaching as the highest duty of the minister, the Puritan preacher came to see his duty as instructing and teaching the members of his congregation and came to see himself as a man striving to deliver the pure word of God.[2]

Any community which participates in and is given cohesion by a rhetorical vision which stresses the importance of speechmaking will impel its adherents to utilize extensive speaking practices. Certainly, the Puritans in colonial New England were no exception to the rule. The ministers delivered sermons on all important occasions, on election day, on holidays, at hangings, at weddings, at funerals, at Thursday meetings, and twice on the sabbath.[3]

The Puritans' general denigration of things of the sense and their reaction against popery resulted in their creating a context for the communication events which was crude, grim, and uncomfortable. The Puritans, in practice, rejected statues, magnicent church buildings, rich vestments, and elaborate liturgy. In the early buildings, the congregation sat on rough benches and the minister spoke from behind a simple desk. In the first generation, the men were segregated from the women and the children were collected together in the gallery. Increase Mather preached a sermon on conversion in which he noted that "there never was any man that did not believe, but he found hard work of it."[4] Certainly the setting in which the minister spoke in the early years of the colony assured that the audience would make "hard work of it." The service contained little pomp and circumstance to appeal to a sense of beauty and ritual. It consisted largely of long prayers, hymns, and long sermons. The meeting-house was often in poor repair and birds and squirrels shared the rafters with cobwebs. Unheated, it was bitter cold in winter; unprotected from the sun, it was often stiflingly hot in summer.

All members of the town were required by law to attend the services whether they were members of the church or not. Leaders of the community, pillars of the church, Negro and Indian slaves, white indentured servants, adventurers, sinners, drunkards as well as the godly—all came to meeting. Indeed, the audience sometimes contained a number of dogs because dogs were a necessity on the frontier and they often accompanied their families to meeting.

Packed into the small meeting-houses, recognizing the possibility of, and, perhaps, expecting some manifestations of the supernatural, the audience was highly suggestible. A skillful speaker could generate a fantasy chain that would move through the congregation and, in turn, stimulate him to greater emotional involvement. When such moments came, the devout would interpret them as evidence of God's spirit moving among them, which added further stimulus to deep emotional and religious experiences. That such moments were not routine and that sometimes the audience grew restless and fell asleep before the reading of the word, indicates that many speeches fell short of the ideal and were often pedestrian, routine, and uninspired by either man or God.

Forced by the merciless recurring deadlines of the weekly meetings, the sabbath services, and the occasional sermon to write thousands of words each week, the Puritan preacher attended as rigourous and practical a school of rhetoric as any contemporary journalist or speaker. In addition, he was conditioned to view his writing as his most important work. It posed a mighty and awesome responsibility. Great preaching was the most praiseworthy accomplishment to which he could aspire. It was the primary means by which he fulfilled his obligation to man, raised his status, and met his duty to God.

Many were in their studies early each morning for five or six days a week. Typically, the minister wrote his sermon and committed it to memory, reconstructed it from notes, or read it from the manuscript. The carefully wrought, workmanlike rhetoric, written into notes or in a small booklet to be placed on the pulpit, while fulfilling Cotton Mather's advice that it be *"well beaten Oil* for the *Lamps* of the *Golden Candlestick,"* often suffered from the fault of what the rhetorical critics of the next century would call "smelling of the lamp."⁵ The manuscripts often became a barrier to communication rather than an aid. While writers of handbooks for preachers often decried the tendency of the minister to "put off" the *"Hearers* with an heavy *Reading* to them," very few suggested that the sermon be delivered extemporaneously.

The Puritan sermon was for the instruction of the audience and the speaker carefully designed it to be memorable. The sermon was first and foremost long—typically one-hour-glass-long, although a popular fantasy theme about Hugh Peters asserts that he told the congregation that he knew they were good fellows and invited them to "take another glass" as he began a second hour.

The Puritan sermon was based upon a text not as a literary device or as a springboard for a moral homily but as the basis for the central truth of the entire speech. The texts were often short, sometimes only one verse, and they were opened up in great repetitive detail. The sermon was divided into two main sections, the first designed to convince the understanding, and the second to engage the heart. First light and then heat. Within the major divisions of the sermons there were a number of subdivisions, and sometimes these were further divided. Each division was forecast by a clear statement of partition and was usually headlined with a device to aid the memory, such as firstly, secondly, thirdly.

The Puritan sermon rose, pyramid-like, from its apex, the narrow compass of a scriptural text, then was expanded by firstlies, secondlies, and sometimes even seventhlies and eighthlies to the inevitable references and quotations from the Bible. The structure was nodular rather than organic. Each cell of the speech was fitted into the structure by a clear transition that often made a rude joint. To some extent, the nodules could be moved from place to place without destroying the overall structure of the speech. The Puritan sermon developed mechanistically. The parts were like discrete building blocks, each retaining its outline and identity like individual blocks in a building.

When the structure of a Puritan sermon unfolded from the pulpit, the effect was like the dropping of stone blocks of the same size upon a single stake. Each subdivision drove the central interpretation of the text deeper and deeper into the audience; over and over, the same basic theme was repeated until the one basic idea and the one basic emotional mood was grated into the auditors.

The practice of Puritan speakers exhibited a plain use of language. They cast convoluted theological points into understandable phrases and paragraphs of basic English. The ornamentation of language was kept to a minimum. The basic illustrative devices consisted of allusions to the Bible or to dramatizing Biblical persons and events or quotations from the Scriptures. The one rhetorical device that they used generously was the comparison or what they called a "similitude." Many spoke as Cotton Mather advised when he wrote: "Accustom yourself to find out *Similitudes*, wherewith you may cloath your Ideas, and make them sensible to the lowest and meanest Capacities, yea, to all *Flesh*."[6]

In addition to the similitudes from the Bible the pastors used comparisons from the universal human condition. The bodily functions furnished comparisons to spiritual matters. Good spiritual things were likened to nourishing food, sound digestion, and healing blood. Common physical ailments of unsavory connotation were associated with objects, sinners, and sins to be castigated—problems of elimination, stomach upsets, physics (in the sense of purgatives), unhealthy conditions in general, dung heaps, festering sores, open wounds, and so forth. Comparisons drawn from the common insect life of the community often served as well—stinging and poisonous insects were particularly useful.

A comparison was doubly effective if bad things could be associated with something that was revolting in everyday affairs as well as in biblical allusion. Snakes served admirably being both poisonous and revolting in the here and now as well as having played a deadly role in the garden of Eden. Locusts, flies, spiders, dragons, frogs, and rats all served as the bases of similitudes. The speaker used the ubiquitous dog as well as goats, cows, swine, and lambs—all animals common to the experience of the audience, some carrying a large freight of biblical symbolism as well.

Generally, the barnyard metaphor was common. In addition to the feeding and elimination of farm animals and the sowing and harvesting of crops (the chaff and the wheat), the tools with which the farmer handled the soil, chopped the trees, and built his houses and barns often appeared in similitudes. The hammer that breaks the rock was like the word that breaks the hardened soul of a sinner. Spiritual matters were illuminated by comparison with homely features of everyday life such as candles, brooms, tables, beds, pillows, and chairs.

For the grander sweep, the minister called upon comparison to things in nature—to pools and woods for more tranquil moods, and to storms, lightning and thunder, winds and gales at sea, for the more turbulent comparisons. The moon, the stars, and the sun were also commonly referred to.

When the need arose to demonstrate that things of the spirit were more valuable than things of this world, these spiritual things were often favorably contrasted with jewels, precious metals, gold and silver.

The mainstay of Puritan rhetoric was the authoritative, unqualified, flat assertion. Deny the authority of the speaker, as the twentieth-century reader of the sermon often does, and the rhetorical machinery comes to a halt. Puritan speeches may seem to us dull, even ridiculous. Unless the listener saw the speaker as a higher being—as a person with both the right and the duty to administer tongue-lashings—he did not feel the requisite guilt to be moved. The member of the audience who rejected the authority of the speaker was more likely to feel anger, disgust, or at least distaste for the sermon. The authority of the Puritan divine, that is, the source of his power to see the truth more clearly than other men, and his right and duty to do the will of God, this authority became a crucial element in his speeches.

The ethos of the Puritan preacher stemmed partly from the fact that he was a learned man, a member of the ruling circle of the town and colony, but the most powerful source of his credibility was his invocation of the highest supernatural power. He spoke not as a man but as the spokesman for God. His most successful moments were those when God used him—those times when the blood of the Savior was sprinkled on his words. He developed his image as God's spokesman first by the use of the personal experience fantasy themes in the first person. The fantasy archetype was that of Saint Paul, a worldly sinful man struck by a shattering moment when he was visited by a miraculous experience of the supernatural. The outward shows of the call of God were as striking and amazing as the difference between day and night. A man's life divided in twain: the first part was rife with worldliness and sin; the second showed forth the beauty of a changed life. In the recounting of the moments of conversion, the basic drama usually contained the same elements. Thomas Shepherd, in his autobiography, for example, told of his years at Cambridge when, as a Sophister, he wrestled with his sin. He seemed to win, but he broke loose again from the Lord. The next year he was moved by a sermon of Dickinson's but fell into "lewd company to lust & pride & gaming & bowling & drinking." Still a third time he felt an incipient call, but again he fell into loose company. He was "fearfully left of god" and began drinking once again, until, "I dranke so much on day that I was dead drunke & that vpon a saturday night & so was carryed from the place I had drinke at & did feast at, vnto a Schollers chamber." The next day, "sick" with his "beastly carriage," he went in "shame & confusion" into the fields where he spent the sabbath lying hidden. It was here when Shepherd had been his "woorst" that God "began to be best vnto" him.[7]

Because of the crucial importance of God's sanction, the most damaging ad hominem argument to destroy the speaker's effectiveness was the charge that he was not in truth a spokesman of God. Mistress Anne Hutchinson, in the early years of the colony, began to hold sessions in her home in which she commented on religion and the sermons and lectures of the ministers, clarifying and teaching in an informal way. At first, the preachers thought her work good and useful but when her followers began to rumor that only two preachers in the colony, John Wheelwright and John Cotton, were sanctified of God's grace and sealed in his spirit and that all the rest, including John Wilson, preacher of the church in Boston, were scribes, wolves in sheep's clothing, and priests of Baal, she struck at the basic source of the ministers' rhetorical power. Wilson complained that Anne Hutchinson and her band were "casting dung on the ministers' faces."[8] Well might he complain, for he found some of his congregation walking out of his services and others remaining behind to ask challenging questions about the assertions in his sermon.

The speaker carefully developed his image as a spokesman of God by attributing the success of his speeches to God's power. Alone he could accomplish nothing. Only with God's help could he effectively reach his auditors. He was not cynical about these appeals to justify his authority. Whenever he had moments of worldly pride and was tempted to think that his own rhetorical power had moved his audience, he would throw himself on his knees and pray for strength to resist temptation.

Finally, God gave the speaker authority because he was elected to sainthood, which assured that he saw the truth more clearly, and because he was prepared to discover the truths revealed in the Bible. Every man and woman could read the Bible for his or her edification, but scholarship was required for an authoritative exegesis of the sacred text. The congregation required a teacher. The speaker thus spoke with the authority of the ultimate source of knowledge, the Bible, to which his scholarship furnished an important key.

The men who came to teach in the New England meeting houses constructed in the wilderness of the New World were a highly trained group of intellectuals. To understand the rhetorical theory which had evolved in England and further developed in America, we must examine the education of the Puritan leaders and understand how their chaining fantasies celebrated some of the dramas of their university contemporaries and rejected others. The typical emigrating minister had spent seven years at a college, acquiring both a bachelor and master's degree.[9] Emmanuel College, Cambridge, was a Puritan stronghold founded in 1584 by Sir Walter Mildmay. At least thirty-five of the emigrants to New England in the early years were from Emmanuel

College. Included among these were such leaders as Thomas Hooker, John Cotton, and John Harvard.

Among the early leaders who came to New England were men who ranked with the best Puritan talent in the old country. Certainly Thomas Hooker and John Cotton were in that category. Charles Chauncey, who became a president of Harvard College, was an outstanding scholar at Cambridge. He served for a time as lecturer in Greek at Trinity College.

The Puritan ministers received a thorough rhetorical training in grammar school and college. Disputations were common exercises in the grammar schools where the boys spent much time on declamations and orations.[10]

When a student moved on to Oxford or Cambridge he received a classical and literary education designed to develop his forensic skills and prepare him for the ministry. He spent much time in forensic exercises and declamations. His standing in the graduate class as well as his chances for success after graduation rested largely on his performance in these exercises. Under these circumstances, Morison judges that "it is no wonder that so much of the student's training was pointed toward forensic skill."[11]

Inertia often characterizes educational practices, and when Harvard College was founded and required its students to prepare declamations, syllogistic disputations, orations, and commonplaces, the practice was similar to British educational traditions; indeed, the rules for syllogistic disputations had changed little from Abelard's days in the Middle Ages. Still, important changes in rhetorical theory had taken place in England in the last quarter of the sixteenth century, and these were reflected in the New World. The influence of the educational theories of the sixteenth-century French scholar Peter Ramus on the teacher of logic and rhetoric in England from 1574 to 1681 has been extensively documented by Wilbur Samuel Howell.[12] The educational philosophy of Ramus was imported into the country and dominated the first century of colonial education.[13]

Since the leading rhetoricians of the Puritan style were learned and scholarly men, it is not surprising that their vision dramatized the importance of training and education. Certainly, the vision needed fantasy themes to explain the role of logic and rhetoric itself in God's scheme of the universe, to legitimatize ways of knowing, and to aid in distinguishing truth from falsehood. Indeed, one of the important fantasy types presented the scenario of the hypocrite who claimed election to sainthood when, in fact, he had experienced no such revelation. Another dramatized the protagonist who had been deceived by the devil and was thus not speaking truth but falsehood. Equally important for scholarly rhetoricians was the need for a vision which provided a satisfactory interpretation of study and learning. The Puritan leaders were in the process of generating a new rhetorical vision at the time that the ideas of Peter Ramus were imported to England. They found his analysis of logic and rhetoric most congenial to their needs.

Ramist dialectic was a reaction against scholasticism. The schoolmen had developed such elaborate games of disputation based upon Aristotle's syllogistic forms that "logic" came to be an intellectual exercise largely divorced from the practical common sense affairs of men. Thus, the Puritans, whose vision, as we shall see, contained a goodly portion of pragmatism, found it congenial to embrace many of Ramus' notions.

Compared to the scholastic tradition, Ramus was less Aristotelian than he was Platonic. (There was much in the Puritan rhetorical vision that resembled the philosophy of Plato. Emmanuel College grew not only Puritans but the Cambridge Neoplatonists as well. Samuel Eliot Morison, in his history of Harvard, regrets that "the tolerant and generous philosophy of these men . . . could not have set the tone of Harvard College." But even as he regrets it, he recognizes that "Harvard must have been puritan, or not have existed. A neo-Platonist could not be a man of action, a pioneer an emigrant, any more than a Hindu. The Kingdom of God was within him, not in Massachusetts Bay.")[14] Even so, the Puritan world view held a large component congenial to Plato and that tendency goes a long way to explain the transcendentalists of the nineteenth century in the United States. It also helps account for the adoption of Ramist thought to the religious and rhetorical needs of the Puritans.

Like Plato, Ramus assumed that a clear and basic order governed the universe and that the material world was but a reflection of the ordered mind of God. Logic simply mapped the way things were, and the Ramist analysis of logic was not merely supposed to be a set of useful categories but a reflection of the eternal structure of the universe. For Ramus, the discovery of such order was, as it was for Plato, an inward illumination of the eternal verities.

The Puritan speaker found Ramus' system compatible with his emerging rhetorical vision. It cleared away much of the syllogistic gamesmanship of scholasticism but it is not what is commonly thought of as the deductive or symbolic logic of today. In fact, Ramist logic did not long survive the competition with other methods of analysis such as the Lockean system. Ramist logic did serve admirably to cloak vehement assertions of eternal truths although it was less well adapted to the traditional tasks of logic—analysis and proof. In this respect, too, Ramus was useful for the New Englanders, for their sermons consisted largely of assertions sanctioned by the supernatural and supported by authoritative Biblical texts.

The core of the Ramist system was the doctrine of "dichotomy" that asserted that all ideas go in pairs. In a balanced symmetrical world, one expects such mirroring. The duty of the speaker is to arrange his ideas into pairs and to take care that he does so at the proper level of abstraction. Once these pairs are discovered, further inspection reveals that they are either in harmony or that they are contraries. Natural reason is so constituted that once the proper pairing is discovered, it can immediately perceive the true alternative. Logical conclusions come from the prompt and clear exercise of natural reason.

To the Ramist assumptions, Puritan rhetoricians added the characteristic theological sanction. All men can reason in this fashion, but when the grace of God infuses an individual, when he becomes elected to sainthood, his natural reason is heightened. He can now see clearly more of the divine pattern and the essential truth of God. Such a man is more likely to make the proper judgment about truth.

Cotton Mather expresses this position when he tells the candidate for the ministry not to spend much time on "that which goes under the Name of LOGIC." He is referring to the syllogisms of Aristotle which will only serve to give the student "a Parcel of *Terms*, which instead of leading the Mind into the *Truth*, enables one rather to carry on *Altercations*, and *Logomachies*, by which the Force of *Truth* may be at Pleasure, and by some little *Trick*, evaded." On the other hand, "the Power and Process of *Reason* is *Natural* to the Soul of Man." He finds much of the "vulgar" logic is like trying to teach the art of eating or drinking or walking. The end all and be all of logic is the syllogism and yet "it is notorious, that . . . all *Syllogizing* is only to confirm you in a *Truth* which you are already the Owner of."[15]

When critics judge, therefore, that Puritan sermons are severely logical, they are using the term in a metaphorical rather than a descriptive way if one is thinking in terms of contemporary symbolic logic or in terms of Aristotelian logic.

Not only was the Ramist dialectic consonant with the Platonic tendencies in Puritan theology, but it also resonated with the basic dramatic scene of the Puritan preacher. The notions of continuum or difference in degree rather than kind were alien to the Puritan theology as were such scenic structures as process, evolution, and organism. The Calvinism of the Puritan vision, transposed into a Ramist key, saw the world clearly divided. Of foremost importance was the division of reality into matters of spirit and of flesh, into worlds of light and of darkness, of the hosts of God and the hosts of the devil, of the elect and the damned, of saints and sinners. John Cotton very aptly expressed the bifurcation of the Puritan social reality, coincidentally illustrating the best Ramist method at the same time, when he said that "All the men in the world are divided into two ranks, Godly or Ungodly, Righteous or

Wicked; of wicked men two sorts, some are notoriously wicked, others are Hypocrites: of Hypocrites two sorts (and you shall find them in the Church of God) some are washed Swine, others are Goats."[16]

When Cotton Mather wrote a treatise giving advice to young men preparing for the ministry and had it published in 1726, he had the practice of almost a century of New England Puritan preaching to serve as the basis for his rhetorical theory.[17] The major theme of Mather's work is that the minister must make every effort to speak with the true words of God. Should the power of God inspire him and his words, then his language would become a weapon for the greater glory of God and for man's salvation. Mather advised the young minister: "About the *Way of Studying* a Sermon, I exhort you, That all be with a Spirit of PIETY, and therefore very *Prayerfully*, carried on."[18] Further, he insisted that "when you are to *Preach*, you should go directly from your Knees in your *Study*, to the *Pulpit*; and when you are thus on your Knees in your *Study*, you should bewayl the *Faulty Defects* in your life." The minister should also "bewayl" the fact that his sermon "is no better fitted for the awful Service that is before you." And then Mather made the ultimate appeal to the proper source of power for rhetoric: "Your Sermons must also be such, that you may hope to have the *Blood* of your SAVIOR sprinkled on it, and His *Good* SPIRIT breathing in it."[19]

Both the sacred and secular training of the Puritan minister combined to form his approach to the discovery, arrangement, and communication of knowledge to his audience. From the scholastic traditions of medieval times reformed by Peter Ramus, he learned a way of study and its implied theory of communication.

Ramus made clear divisions as to the proper subject-matter of each discipline. The Ramist rhetoric, which Cotton Mather spurned as "tropes and schemes," warning a young man against "squandering away your Time, on the RHETORIC, whereof no doubt, you tho't, your *Dugard* gave you enough at School," thus consisted only of what we today would call language and delivery.[20] Rhetoric, in this sense, represents but a small part of the total impact of Ramist thinking on the Puritan preacher. Rather, the Ramist dialectic and rhetoric together furnish the method that reflects the Puritan theory of communication.

Ramist method led to particular habits of investigation, analysis, and development. Intellectual treatises grew, under Ramist analysis, in a shape like an inverted pyramid resting on an apex, consisting of a broad definition of the essence of the study and moving evenly outward and upward with systematic divisions, divided, again and again. Ramus illustrates the technique neatly in his own treatise on dialectic. The text begins with the definition that "dialectic is the art of disputing well." The subject is divided into two parts, invention and arrangement. Invention is divided into explaining arguments and sources of arguments. The first section is further divided into artificial argument and inartificial argument. Artificial arguments are divided into primary and derivative; primary arguments reveal four species with each species having four aspects. With the discussion of the aspects of the argument, Ramus finally reaches his foundation terms. Ramus notes the divisions with mathematical precision, marks the transitions clearly although with little art or elegance, and always places concrete material, illustrations, and support at the end of the discussion of a division.[21]

To arrive at decisions about the proper way to divide up a subject, the scholar used logic. Perry Miller judges that the Puritan rhetoricians were "logicians to a man, and Puritan sermons were severely logical in structure, but all according to the logic of Ramus, which was a relatively simple, clear-cut, and commonsense system."[22]

In the early years, the Puritan rhetorical theory revealed not only a characteristic dichotomous method but also a careful balancing of what at first glance might seem to be contraries rather than harmonious pairs. Indeed, the heirs of the early Puritans found the careful balancing of method impossible and thus moved to emphasize one at the expense of the other. But in the early years, the New England preachers relied upon reason *and* intuition to guide them to religious truths.

Reason prepared by scholarship was one important way to truth. The Puritan intellectuals were interested in the new sciences and avidly kept up with the latest developments in the Royal Society. They read Newton and Locke when these works became available, and they studied natural phenomena with great interest. But once reason had climbed as far as it could, up the ladder of truth, the regenerative power of God was necessary to find the ultimate way. The New England intellectual thus moved in a rather Neoplatonic way from reason to mysticism. He found that to know the truth by reason was different from experiencing truth as it glowed with the power of God.

Neither way alone would suffice. Both were required. Reason alone was barren without the life-giving power of God's grace. But there was also a danger in the neglect of reason. Should one argue, as Anne Hutchinson, for example, did, that the only path to knowledge was the inner power of God, then the way was open for any man or woman to preach and claim the sanction of supernatural authority. Neglect of scholarship implied enthusiasm, schisms, and heresy. So the Puritan rhetoric balanced for many years the claims of reason and scholarship with the intuitions of the inner spirit. The proper sermon, therefore, consisted of first light then heat, first reason and then emotion.

The supernatural moved the rhetoric of the Puritan preacher not only because it sanctioned the authority of the speaker, but also because rhetorical proofs were divided into two kinds: those inspired by God, and those invented by man. The proofs of the first kind were inerrant and absolutely true, while the proofs of the second kind, those that natural man might invent with his wit and training in rhetoric and dialectic, were, at best, an aid to the understanding and illustrating of the first. Exegesis of a text became the central organon for the discovery of knowledge. The typical argument of a Puritan sermon consisted of a conclusion asserted as true, with a demonstration consisting of quotations from or allusions to the Bible. Given the supreme authority of the Bible, the main task of rhetorical analysis was to search out the meanings of the text, to interpret these meanings with the necessary proofs, and then to accommodate them to the understandings of the audience.

The tools of rhetorical proof thus were philological. A knowledge of the languages in which the texts had been delivered from God to man was necessary. Cotton Mather recommended Arabic and Hebrew in addition to Latin and Greek.[23] The speaker studied word meanings and conflicting interpretations of ambiguous passages of the text as well as the etymologies of words in order to discover truth. He then presented the results of such study to his audience with a brief explanation of his conclusions in the sermon itself.

The Puritans made a fetish of the plain style. The Puritan speaker did not trick out his discourse with the flowers of rhetoric or the pretensions of scholarship. He did not want to delight or impress his hearers; he wanted to save their souls. In a telling passage, Cotton Mather presents a fantasy theme about the change in style that accompanied his grandfather's conversion to the Puritan point of view. John Cotton had his reputation "added unto" by a "University Sermon, wherein sinning more to preach *Self* than *Christ*, he used such Florid Strains, as extremely recommended him unto *the most*, who relished the *Wisdom of Words* above the *Words of Wisdom*; Though the pompous Eloquence of that Sermon, afterwards gave such a Distast into his own *Reverend Soul*, that with a Sacred Indignation he threw his Notes into the Fire."[24]

The ideal model was the style of the Bible. Cotton Mather asserted that "there can be nothing so *Beautiful*, or so *Affectuous* as the *Figures*" used in the Scriptures, because "they are *Life*." But more important than the beauty of the Bible is the fact that the words of the Scriptures ". . . are an *Hammer that breaks the Rocks to Pieces*. In them the GOD *of Glory Thunders*, yea, does it very marvellously!"[25] Although the praiseworthy style was plain it was not to be dull or ineffective. It had to prick, cut, goad, sting, and be a hammer.

Cotton Mather's description of the preaching style of his father may not be an accurate picture of Increase in the pulpit, but it reveals, in the things the son praises and the things he despises, a clear set of critical standards. Of his father's style Cotton Mather wrote:

> He much despised what they call *Quaintness*. . . . though he were such a *Scholar*, yet his *Learning* hindred not his Condescension to the Lowest and Meanest Capacity: aiming to shoot not over the *Heads*, but into the *Hearts*, of the Hearers. He was very careful to be *understood*, and *concealed* every other *Art*, that he might Pursue and Practise that one *Art* of *Being Intelligible*. . . . A *Simple Diet*, he counted the most *Wholsom Diet*.[26]

In general the Puritans praised a delivery that had more vehemence and directness than the manner of the Anglicans. If the speaker's audience was to be struck with awe like that produced by the fall of thunderbolts, a dull droning from the desk would not serve, nor would a patterned reading.[27]

In summary, then, the Puritan rhetorical theory emphasized the centrality of preaching in the duty and practice of religion. Speech was useful in the most important work of man—the work of the spirit—saving souls, defending the true religion, and attacking heresy. As a speaker, the preacher's duty was to God and the truth, not to the worldly wishes of his audience. Though many in the meeting house might have been pleased to hear him speak of other and more pleasant things, he was not to bend his message to their desires and wishes. when he moved people, he did so not by winning them with flattery and telling them what they wished to hear; rather, he moved them with the mighty authority of his role as speaker of the inspired truth, with his blistering castigation of their sins, and with the power of his exhortation.

Associated with the Puritan rhetorical style was an awesome panoramic vision which portrayed the creation of the universe, the unfolding of history, the development of the community, and the role of each person within the community. The Puritan rhetorical vision participated in many of the traditional dramas of Christianity and the Protestant Reformation. The whole grand design from the drama of Genesis in which God created heaven and earth and the subsequent unfolding of the scenario was predestined by God for His own purposes. The point of the entire experiment was the culmination of the individual dramas in which each soul met the day of judgment. Yet God had also entered into a covenant with the community, which was a drama analogous to the tendering of covenants to the Old Testament Israelites, and like the Israelites, the Puritans were, so long as they kept to the compact, God's chosen people.

The rhetorical vision accounted for the entire observable chain of being and posited a number of unobservable personae of supernatural significance to round out the explanation. The vision also accounted for the unfolding of history in its abstract manifestations as well as in the most minute details of an individual's daily life. All observable events could be cast into interpretative fantasies which fit neatly into God's grand design. No matter how mysterious that design may have seemed to the limited mind of human beings, it was always there and provided the point and purpose to every living thing and accounted for the facts of natural disaster as well as for the unfolding of social reality.

Although the vision had much in common with the rhetoric of Christian Protestantism in the sixteenth and seventeenth centuries, it had its unique fantasy themes and structure. The rhetoricians who broke away from the established Anglican traditions of sixteenth-century England and began to generate the new vision, chained into dramas provided by the adherents of John Calvin. The fantasies that emerged in their small-group discussions and subsequently in their sermons featured an everyman persona who was a lowly, mean creature, tainted with the guilt of Adam's sin. In all scenarios, man was universally and completely dependent upon God. He had not the ability to determine his own salvation. The God persona was a just, beneficent, stern, and awesome character, who was under no obligation to provide eternal life for any of the unworthy human beings who populated the vision. Yet, in his infinite grace, God selected certain people to be saints and have everlasting life, and these saints composed his true and invisible church. In all the dramas, as one might expect from a Protestant vision, the relationship between the God persona and the human character was direct and required no intermediary. Indeed, the Puritan preacher portrayed the Catholic dramas with their priests and the pope interceding with God for man as among the most villainous aspects of the vision.

Those elected to sainthood became aware of their regeneration in a fantasy type in which a divine revelation was the central dramatic action. For the elect, the practice of true religion was sweet and pleasant. Once elected, the minister was able to see more clearly the basic pattern of God's universe and was better able to appreciate the wisdom of such fantasies as the poignant one in which an unregenerated infant was condemned by a just God to eternal damnation. The elect were chosen for eternity and their covenant would not be withdrawn. The remainder of mankind, who were not elect, were doomed to the most heinous of eternal sufferings.

The central fantasy type from which all other dramas of the Puritan vision radiated was that of election to sainthood. The fantasy put each member of the audience firmly in the role of protagonist. The speakers worried about individual souls—their own first and then those of their congregations. Cotton Mather wrote that "the *Gaining* of one Soul to GOD by your Ministry, will be of more Account with you than any *Gain* of this World; than all the *Wealth* in the World."[28]

Again and again, the minister would outline the scenario of the high drama. The sinful, slothful member of his audience who was secure in health and material goods and felt free to merely observe the unfolding sermon was brought up short. The speaker forced him to assume the role of protagonist. With all his art of assertion, imperatives, and descriptive language, the minister *searched* out all the hiding places and brought each member of his audience center stage to fight for his own salvation. One of the highest words of praise for a sermon was to say that it was "searching" in just this way.

Turn and dodge as the listener might, the skillful minister kept driving him to the recognition of his personal spiritual drama. The odds against success were enormous, the fruits of victory unbelievably sweet, the results of defeat incredibly awesome and terrifying. Thomas Hooker does a superlative job of picturing the mighty drama of individual salvation:

> Imagine thou sawest the Lord Jesus coming in the clouds, and heardest the last trump blow, *Arise ye dead, and come to judgment*: Imagine thou sawest the Judg of all the World sitting upon the Throne, thousands of Angels before him, and ten thousands ministring unto him, the Sheep standing on his right hand, and the Goats at the left: Suppose thou heardest that dreadful Sentence, and final Doom pass from the Lord of Life (whose Word made Heaven and Earth, and will shake both) *Depart from me ye cursed*; How would thy heart shake and sink, and die within thee in the thought thereof, wert thou really perswaded it was thy portion? Know, that by thy dayly continuance in sin, thou dost to the utmost of thy power execute that Sentence upon thy soul: It's thy life, thy labor, the desire of thy heart, and thy dayly practice to depart away from the God of all Grace and Peace, and turn the Tomb-stone of everlasting destruction upon thine own soul.[29]

While the central feature of the Puritan rhetorical vision was the obligatory scene in which each participant came face to face with the God persona and heard the joyous or dreadful words, the preparatory background and the fantasy themes leading to the climactic moment in each individual drama were thickly textured, complex, and intricate.

The Puritans based their attempt to reform the English church on the truth of the Scriptures. In the beginning, they discussed theological questions relating to salvation. Among the fantasy themes which chained and chained again through the communication channels of the new Puritan community were dramas of a covenant—a pact or agreement between a god persona and the community of Puritans. One form of the covenant fantasy portrayed the biblical narrative relating to God's relationship to the People of Israel as analogous to the emerging relationship of God and the Puritans. After a time, the ministers shared fantasies which interpreted the historical biblical dramas as having God tendering two covenants to Israel, a pact based upon works and a pact based upon grace. The emerging Puritan vision did not celebrate a pact based on works, but it did emphasize a covenant of grace centered on the persona of Jesus Christ and based on faith.[30]

Eugene White judged that John Cotton, a leader of the Puritan community in England, who emigrated to the New World, "perhaps tended to reflect more closely the absolute values of the covenant of grace than did the English framers themselves."[31] Cotton dramatized the compact as one in which God requires that His people have faith in Jesus Christ, maintain obedience to that faith, be in a melting frame of spirit in regard to all their sinfulness and moan and weep and wail for their evil ways. The miserable creature which is man will sin and fall away from the law, but God will nonetheless keep the compact if the people who break any law of God are brought to see the error and mend their ways. That a people shall fail in their obedience of faith proves that human beings are poor, empty creatures, and the proper response is to bring their souls lower and lower, and closer to Christ. Indeed, such abasement and prostration before God is proof that a community is, in fact, in everlasting covenant with God. The compact also includes a cursing which applies to those who do not receive it or are apostate from it. God's punishment for those who do not receive the covenant is severe, but more severe still is the curse upon those who receive and transgress against the covenant in full knowledge that they are disobeying God's will.

Cotton portrays the covenant as requiring first that the chosen people must fall down before the Lord, confessing their unworthiness to receive any mercy or grace. Second, the people must confess their inability and want of strength to take any hand in their own salvation. When God made the covenant with Abraham, Cotton reminded his congregation, Abraham fell on his face in a sense of his own unworthiness.

The majority of the Puritan community who emigrated to New England viewed the Church of England as a true but somewhat corrupted church; they wished only to cut away the corruption from within, not to separate from the church (although separatists also came to the New World.) When they failed to purify the church and began, instead, to feel the pressure of harassment from the establishment, they dramatized their time of troubles and persecution in line with their vision of the covenant as evidence that the emigration to the New World was the will of God. Thus were born two archetypal fantasy types which became pervasive and persistent in the rhetoric of Americans both before and after the Revolution. The first scenario was that of God giving His chosen people a time of troubles as a warning for the evil of their ways in turning out of ignorance away from Him. In the scenarios with a happy ending the chosen people used God's time of troubles as a spur to an understanding of their sin. They searched to find God's will in the matter. When they found God's way again, the result was a glorious happy ending, a time of regeneration and rebirth, as indicated by the prospering of the community in this world.

In the bad scenarios, the individual or community failed to heed the evidence of God's displeasure and, now aware of their sinfulness, turned in proud apostasy against the covenant and sank into greater and greater sinfulness. Increase Mather took the occasion of two Harvard students drowning while skating on Fresh Pond to fantasize the events as an omen of willful turning away from the compact. He said in part:

> This fatal blow looks ominously on the poor *Colledge*. Considering some other circumstances; there is cause to fear lest *suddenly* there will be no *Colledge* in *New England*; and this as a sign that ere long there will be no Churches there. I know there is a blessed day to the visible Church not far off; but it is the Judgment of very Learned men, that in the Glorious Times promised to the Church on Earth, *America* will be Hell. And altho there is a number of the Elect of God yet to be born here, I am verily afraid that in process of Time, *New England* will be the wofullest place in all *America*, as some other parts of the World once famous for Religion, are now the dolefullest on the Earth, perfect Emblems and Pictures of Hell. When you see this little *Academy* fallen to the ground (as now it is shaking and most like to fall) then know it is a terrible thing which God is about to bring upon this Land.[32]

Increase Mather than made the application to the audience of students in quite typical persuasive form:

> In the mean time, you the *Students* here, are concerned to bewail the Breach which the Lord has made among you. If you slight and make light of this hand of the Lord, or do not make due improvement of it, you may fear, that God has not done with you, but that he has more arrows to shoot amongst you, that shall suddenly strike some of you ere long. But Oh that the Lord would sanctify what has hapned to awaken you unto serious thoughts about Death and Eternity. Who knows but that God may make these sudden Deaths, an occasion of promoting the Salvation, & Eternal Life of some amongst you.[33]

Thus, the fantasy type of "Fetching Good Out of Evil" gave to an individual's prosperity or the community's success in worldly affairs a meaning of great significance.[34] God assured that nothing happened by chance. Mysterious as it might be, when a saint or a community of the elect fell into a time of troubles, they had offended God. On the other hand, when the elect prospered in this world, their success had great significance for their fate in the spritual realm.

The adherents of the Puritan vision saw the zealous prosecution of the new path revealed by searching God's will, as a way to propitiate the guilt of their sin evidenced by the time of troubles. Insofar as they were cleansed by the experience, insofar as they had suffered enough to balance the magnitude of their sins in the eyes of a just God, their new venture would increase and prosper. When, indeed, they were delivered of a time of troubles, they often enacted a traditional rite of thanksgiving—a time of celebration that they were better because of their having profited from their time of troubles. When they began to fall from God's grace, they would again be visited with hardships. To some extent, therefore, since in their view nothing happened by chance, the prospering of their worldly affairs was evidence of their ability to please God.

When Puritan attempts to purify the Church of England did not prosper, when, instead, they were persecuted by the authorities, the scenario of the time of troubles contained strong motivation to search for God's will and to try to follow the new path. A portion of the leadership began to share fantasy themes that envisioned their destiny as having to emigrate to the New World and achieve the goal of purifying the religion of the old by establishing a model of the true church in the wilderness. They dramatized the emigration along the lines of the classical biblical scenario of the exodus of the Jews from Egypt. Indeed, the analogy of their community as the new Israel served to integrate their rhetorical vision. Thus was created the second fantasy archetype of great importance to successive rhetorical visions in America.

The second fantasy type was that the migration to the New World was not a commercial venture for wealth or an adventure in search of excitement but was, rather, a holy emigration of God's chosen people. John Cotton's sermon delivered when Winthrop's company was leaving for Massachusetts was on the text "Moreover I will appoint a place for my people Israell, and I will plant them, that they may dwell in a place of their own, and move no more."[35] The Puritan vision dramatized the community as conquering new territories for God, saving the souls of the natives, and, most importantly, as setting up in the wilderness a model religious community patterned after the true meaning of the Scriptures to light the way for the reformation still to be accomplished in Old England and in all of Europe.

Two fantasy types of lesser importance but still vital to an understanding of the rhetorical vision of the Puritans were the drama of the pilgrim and the soldier. The pilgrim making his slow, painful, and holy way, beset by many troubles and temptations, was one exemplification of the Puritan self-image. The other was the recurring figure of the Christian soldier fighting God's battles and overcoming all adversaries in order to establish the true church. The first emphasized the abasement, sacrifice, and dedication of the Puritans to things of the other world; the second emphasized their militancy. Theirs was an active and, if need be, violent, bloody vision. When they could not convert the Indians, they fought them and they also fought their fellow Englishmen in the old country for the true faith.

Undergirding the pilgrim and the soldier was the certainty that the entire drama was predestined. God had written the script of the drama and the great pageant would unfold to its foreordained conclusion. Each individual's role was set, predestined for heaven or hell, inevitably elected to sainthood or doomed forever. The excitement came for each participant in the vision because God's ways were not always easy to read and until one played the obligatory scene directly with God and discovered with certainty that one was elected, the suspense was very great.

What was there about the individual psychodynamics and the here-and-now problems of the founders of the new vision that might account for their chaining into the particular configuration of Calvinistic themes with their concomitant motivations to reform the established church?

First, the leaders of the new movement were all educated at a university, which was in itself a rare background. But they were, for the most part, middle-class or lower-class men who had been unusually intelligent children and had, through some happenstance, come to the university. Sometimes they had been tutored in the home of a nobleman with his children. Sometimes a wealthy relative had provided the entrance and the means to education; sometimes they had gone to the university as a serviter (someone who served the wealthy and the nobility and in turn received an education at Oxford or Cambridge). They were, therefore, ambitious, intelligent, young men of poor family background, unlikely under usual circumstances to climb in the world of sixteenth-century England.

The young Puritan leaders found themselves in a rigidly ordered society in which the nobility stood first and the other classes of society ranged downward to the peasantry. The oldest son in the family of a landed peer would receive the estate according to the requirements of entailment. The younger sons would go into government service, the military, or the law. On occasion, the nobleman would buy a living for a son in the form of a parish church and the young man would serve as minister. One of the excesses that the Puritans found offensive was the low state of the clergy, which resulted from the practice of buying livings for dissolute and ineffectual scions of noble families.

Shut off as they were by a rigidly ordered nobility from any chance of rising to the top of society in this world, the young Puritans must have found the fantasies which shifted the scene of the most important part of life, the life ever after, to another world most attractive. In the new setting, they dramatized a society divided not into layered classes with each individual fixed into place but a spiritual world simply divided into two parts—the world of God's true church on the one hand and all the rest on the other. God's purpose wiped out with a single stroke all of the class differences and privileges of this world and left only the elect and the damned. In the new spiritual scene, the Puritans portrayed themselves in their vision as the elect and the sinful nobility and renegade ministers of the state church as part of the damned.

The appeal of the fantasies to an able and ambitious young man trained beyond his station in life is clear. He became a member of the spiritual nobility in the much more important and enduring domain, while those who may have been above him in the transitory world would likely spend eternity in the nether regions.

When the vision, already largely formed, was transported to the New World, it contained motivations which resulted in creating in Massachusetts a situation mirroring the old one—that is, the elect began to rule in this world. Thus, for the adherent of the vision, there was no inconsistency in the sufferers of religious persecution in Old England coming to power in New England and persecuting religious outsiders with a zeal equal to that of their former persecutors.

What can be said, then, by way of rhetorical criticism, of the Puritan style with its vision, theory, and practice? The historical record indicates that it served to sustain a cohesive religious community against great adversity, that it proved relatively immune to counterfantasies and to changing circumstances, and that it exerted an influence on subsequent visions in the years following its dissolution and decay. In many respects, therefore, it was a rhetoric of great toughness and power. The record also indicates, however, that the participants in the Puritan rhetorical vision were impelled to violence, to stiff-necked and proud treatment of opposing visions and to outsiders, to excessive zeal in furthering the goals of their vision. How did the rhetoric work to provide motivation, emotional evocation, and meaning to adherents of the style?

If we view the Puritans as organisms grubbing away in the wilderness to keep alive or to create material wealth or to achieve worldly status, we find the enterprise relatively mean or trivial. If, however, we examine the internal fantasy life of the community as revealed in the sermons of their ministers, we discover the characters of the drama, their emotional value, their actions, and their relationship to an overreaching supernatural power symbolized by a persona of compelling if aweful stature.

A description of the emigration and the daily externals of life for the settlers in New England would be quite grim. So, too, would be a spare description of the communication event as the minister preached from behind his simple desk to the small congregations huddled in unheated, crude, undecorated meeting houses in the wilderness in the early years of the Massachusetts Bay Colony. The daily routine of the people was one of back-breaking drudgery. The niceties of life were almost nonexistent. Music, the arts, decoration of home or clothing, were largely unavailable. But the Puritans of colonial New England led an internal fantasy life of mighty grandeur and complexity.

Examine first the most personal and compelling of the fantasies. Each individual was a protagonist in a personal salvation drama. Imagine what it was like to live within a vision filled with questions such as: Is it in the eternal scheme of God's plan that I shall be elected to heaven or doomed to hell? Will this year, this month, this day, this hour bring me the conversion experience which will assure me that I am saved? What of my spouse? My children? My other loved ones? Are they safe or not? With families large and death common, the deathbed scenes of joy or grief, depending upon the assurance of salvation or lack of it, were moments of high emotion and drama.

The reader who looks on the Puritan sermon manuscripts with a twentieth-century perspective often does not suspend his disbelief enough to imagine that he "sees the Lord Jesus coming in the clouds." If he cannot accept the premises of the drama, the pull upon his emotions is slight. He may not even be able to reconstruct imaginatively the preoccupation with eternal life, the state of individual souls, or the medieval fear of the supernatural, of witches and ghosts, of devils and of God, that pervaded the audiences that sat in the meeting houses of colonial New England.

An audience observing the drama from the outside might find it lacking in suspense, inartistic, because the basic assumption upon which it rested was the *deus ex machina*. God was the only cause of salvation. Man was completely dependent upon God for election to sainthood. The plot was similar to the pattern of the classical Greek plays. Reading the Puritan sermons today, participating in a different rhetorical vision, we may find the action static, the protagonist an insect squirming helplessly in the hands of an all-powerful diety. But for the listener who shared the fantasy and imaginatively took the central role, the suspense might well have become unbearable. Each hour might have brought eternal salvation or eternal death. In his famous revival sermon Jonathan Edwards said: "And it would be no wonder if some persons, that now sit here, in some seats of this meeting house, in health, quiet and secure, should be there [in hell] before tomorrow morning."[36]

The predominant emotion which the Puritan vision evoked was that of awe. The focus is upon an afterlife with such potential for ecstasy or terror that it is almost beyond the power of the minsters to fantasize.

The Puritan rhetorical vision contained powerful pragmatic motivations. The basic salvation drama always contained the possibility not of action but of resignation. In the face of such unbearable tensions, the listener could have resorted to passive acceptance of fate rather than be spurred to vigorous action. Increase Mather recognized the tendency when he spoke in answer to the question raised in "I can't Convert my self, and God does not Convert me."[37]

"Sinners," Mather said, "can do more towards their own Conversion than they do or will do. They should give *diligence* to make sure of their being effectually called. They should *strive* to enter in at the strait gate."[38] That, in fact, the result was action rather than resignation the record amply testifies. Not only that, but the preoccupation with time, the fear of death before God's call to election, put great pressure upon the Puritans to do as much as soon as possible. They felt the necessity of improving every hour. The minutes wasted might be those very minutes when all eternity would hang in the balance.

Moving outward from the drama of personal salvation, the two rhetorical fantasies of the covenanted chosen people served to sustain the Puritan sense of community and history for several hundred years. Modified with the changing years, muted to some extent, attenuated at times, exaggerated at others, they carried on as basic justifications for many reform orators of the nineteenth century, and their faint echoes are still heard from the rostrums, radios, and television sets of the twentieth century.

The rhetorical appeal of the fantasy type of "Fetching Good Out of Evil" is a well-tooled machine to furnish impetus to action for reform. One of the basic values of the American people has been activity. "Do-nothing" was an epithet and people who did things, who kept moving, were praised. Contemplation, inactivity, impracticality, and apathy, were undesirable. Working, striving, acting in a hardheaded way, involvement, were all positive values. A fantasy form that began with the rite of self-abasement loaded the audience with a high charge of guilt. It next turned to a plan of action that was providential—it was the path to salvation furnished by God: if they worked hard and did the right thing, they would be rewarded by God's showering success upon them. By working hard and doing the right thing, they released the charge of guilt, and success became the final evidence that their conscience need no longer be troubled. Should their efforts result in failure, the rhetoric used the failure as evidence that they had not tried hard enough, had not been good enough and must therefore work even harder and be even better to win God's favor. Should they succeed, the rhetorical form used the success as evidence that they were pleasing God and therefore even more effort was indicated. In any case, for those who chained into a particular dramatization of the scenario, the motivation would be intense.

The rhetorical appeal to the drama of God's chosen people gave to every social and political action a sense of importance. God's chosen people were special, and their outward evidences of election had to be more perfect than those of other communities and societies who were not blessed in such a way. The rhetorical fantasy that the people who came to the new land were somehow unique sustained the sense of community and importance of the American people through the eighteenth and nineteenth centuries. When the vision of sacred sanction faded, other visions secularized the fantasy type into a form that suggested that the pull of the new land, the sense of danger and adventure, had selected out people of innate fitness and had brought them to the wilderness where the land itself had worked a magic so that they had established a truer society. The American experiment, whether sanctioned by God, Providence, or a more secular offshoot of the theory of evolution, became the wonder and model of the world in the rhetoric of the religious and reform speakers of nineteenth-century America. Those who emigrated were always chosen in some way, either as in the Puritan time, because they had been selected of God and had read the scriptures right, or, in secular terms, because they had been refined in a melting pot that had boiled out the dross of their inheritance from old and corrupt cultures until they emerged, pristine, in the new world. Lincoln alluded to the archetypal fantasy in his annual message to Congress in 1862 when he said that the people held "the power" and have "the responsibility." He said: "We shall nobly save or meanly lose the last, best hope of earth."[39]

The fact that a rhetorical vision whose dramatic action is predestined can be both a comfort in time of troubles and a spur to work hard to reform the world is evidence that audiences, on those occasions when rhetoric works at the deep levels of the subconscious, are not careful to examine the logical consistencies of their rhetorical visions. Life was cheap in seventeeth-century England, and cheaper still in the wilderness of New England. Infant mortality was high, diseases carried off large numbers of people, accidents and natural calamities many more, and the Indians were a source of danger. Johnson finds "the attitude of the Puritans toward death and suffering . . . hardest to interpret in modern terms." It was a "curiously immobile acceptance of a *fait accompli*."[40] When life is capricious and dangerous and the fates seem cruel and unreasonable, the notion that what will happen will happen, that when a man's number comes up he has no choice but to go, is a source of stoicism and comfort. The cruelest loss of a loved one, the fear of death itself, is to some extent comforted by the certainty that God's will is being done and nothing that any mortal can do will change the course of events.

In terms of the larger battle, the Puritan belief in predestination implied that the hosts of God would win. They were inevitable. Perry Miller wonders "how men could work themselves into this frame of mind, combining trust in God's disposing power with an assurance of victory, going through fire and water in order that what was decreed might be fulfilled."[41] One might well wonder how predestination and inevitability could contain the motivations which led to the Puritan's active, tough-minded, and unrelenting endeavor to reform and perfect the world. Again, the deeper rhetoric is not rational; the history of rhetorical visions in the United States and Europe indicates that there were few more powerful appeals than that contained in the slogan "We shall overcome." The Progressives thought that progress was inevitable and fought to achieve it; the Nazis thought that they were inevitable and struggled for their thousand-year Reich; the Communists thought that socialism was inevitable and fomented revolution to achieve it. The Puritan, too, was active in his battle for the ultimate victory. Knowing that his side would win sustained the man who did not want to spend his life in a losing cause. Even today, politicians seldom predict their own defeats during the campaigns. The corroborated fantasies of sin and evil were too apparent in the Puritan's world. If he had had to rely on the *communiqués* he received from his observations of this world, he might well have grown disillusioned and felt that all his striving and work were for nothing. A man is sustained through a progression of defeats by the beacon of inevitable victory. The certainty of his cause makes him more tenacious and fanatic in his attack on the opposition.

Inevitability thus functions as a mechanism to discount corroborations of failure for a reform rhetoric. By discounting corroboration which goes counter to the scenario as short-term setbacks in a long-term trend towards success, the visions which contain this feature manage to stave off disillusionment and inspire continued strenuous effort. Thus, although there was a hardheaded practical strain to Puritanism, the predestination and inevitability features of the dramatic scene allowed for the immunization of the vision from corroborated counterfantasies.

The early preachers of New England, like good Ramist dialecticians, divided the world into the spirit and the flesh, found them contraries, tested them by the light of natural reason, and found that the truth was of the world of the spirit. Yet, in mood, temper, psychology, they balanced the demands of this world with those of the next. They were able to render unto Caesar as well as unto God. They had a hardheaded practical temper and often called the last half of the sermon the "uses" and applied the text to the specific needs of the audience. There was room in their rhetorical vision for an active striving in this world to clear the wilderness, create a community, and earn the material things of this life.

Perry Miller characterizes the Puritan temperament as being one of incessant and unbending pressure. They lived "upon the heights of intensity."[42] By comparison, the Anglicans created a richer, calmer, more mellow culture. The Puritans tended to be narrow, harsh, and literal-minded. They were not lukewarm, halfhearted, or flabby. In both the world of the flesh and of the spirit, they expected little, for God owed them nothing, and from other men they expected the worst. They maintained a balance of zeal and control, of idealism and cynicism, of rationalism and mysticism.

In both worlds, they expected much of themselves. Their words of praise were *diligence, striving, labor, work, meet,* and *proper.* Good sermons were plain, searching, powerful, and painful (painstaking). When they wished to condemn something, they used words like slothful, lazy, proud, unregenerate. A favorite figure of derision was that of those lovers of material and worldly comfort who would have "pillows sewn under their elbows."

The rhetoric of the Puritan sermon sustained the audiences of colonial New England with alternate doses of praise and denigration. They were God's chosen people; their society was the model for the world. They were the salt of the earth. But they were falling short of the ideal. Few speakers held out more rigid standards or more unattainable goals. Inevitably, the model society of God's chosen people fell short. They had to do better. Each individual soul was the focus of God's concern and the concern of the pastor and the congregation. Indeed, each person was more important than all the wealth of the world, but such was the mean miserable sinful nature of man that each individual was unworthy, each was falling short of the glory of God. Thus, the listener swung from the center of the universe—the protagonist in the most important drama in the world—to the meanest being, comparable only to a reptile, an insect, an animal.

Speaking from within the assumptions of such a vision, sanctioned by powerful appeals to the supernatural, certain of his duty to fight sin and to chastise his flock, determined to battle to make his pilgrimage through this world doing good, fighting to achieve a level of conduct in himself and his congregation commensurate with the impossible standards he had erected for both, feeling the chagrin as well as the guilt of his failure, the speaker often sought to ease his conscience by more effort and with an even greater attack on the sin about him.

He was, therefore, a reformer. He focused on the individual soul, but he could not stand by and watch evil grow in the world. It was his duty to save souls and to drive out Satan. If at times his fanatical reform instinct brought him to such terrible actions as the putting to death of witches, it also made him chastise the more contemporary sins. It was his duty to do good—to first set his own house in order, then to work in his congregation, then his town, and finally, his colony. He could speak out with righteous indignation because he was God's spokesman and because he was *right*. The unshakeable conviction of being absolutely right drove an army of American reform speakers from the Puritans to the abolitionists and gave to their rhetoric a certainty and a moral fervor that made the flat assertion persuasive.

Such were the main rhetorical features of the Puritan sermon. Puritan public address was oracular, assertive, imperative speech, filled with righteous indignation. Its logic was that of Ramus, and its method was exegetical. It discovered no new truths and, indeed, for the first century, its speakers systematically resisted different religious formulations. It was often a rhetoric designed to revivify and sustain the group consciousness. The high standards of community and personal conduct were such that mortal man was unlikely to achieve them, and thus, the Puritans felt the need for continual reform of individual and community behavior. But the standards were static; their speeches did not question the nature of God or the godly life.

Such was the rhetorical heritage that furnished the models for the preachers and speakers of eighteenth-century America, who were to participate in a great religious awakening, in a war with France, in a revolution from the mother country, and in the establishment of two new constitutional governments. For the needs of that turbulent century, the Puritan style proved inadequate and so changes were made, but the Puritan rhetoric furnished much of the tradition upon which these modifications were fashioned.

❦ 3

Jonathan Edwards and a Rhetoric in Transition

For a hundred years the changes in the rhetorical vision, theory, and practices of the Puritan ministers were slow and evolutionary. New England, in the meantime, flourished and grew prosperous and worldly.

Although the Puritan rhetorical vision worked very well in sustaining the founders in their attack on the wilderness and in their struggle to achieve a civilized community and the ideal church in the New World, it was less successful in rededicating the inheritors of the rhetoric to its dramas and values. For those who could not shape their experiences into the fantasy type of election and salvation, the vision was extremely punishing. The children of the saints who did not receive word from God were left in a most precarious mental state. Even those adherents who were sure of their own election suffered at the death of an infant child or a loved one who had not been saved.

As life grew easier, the posterity of the founders participated less and less in the social reality of the rhetorical vision. As a result, the vision gradually lost its hold on subsequent generations; there was no sudden revolt against the entire structure of the vision or a dramatic reform or purging from within as had characterized the emergence of the Puritan vision in Old England. Gradually, the old became tame. The zeal of those who had participated in the forging of the vision, who had chained into some of the original fantasies when they were new, such as the Exodus drama, was not passed on to the new generations. Some of the adherents spoke in the old tones and alluded to the old dramas but the emotional evocation was paler, the motivation less intense. Some of the Puritan posterity became tolerant, worldly, and lukewarm.

Despite its loosening hold, the Puritan vision was remarkably impervious to corroboration. Times changed, situations varied, experiences differed, but the vision remained very much as it had been in the days of the emigration. The basic mechanism which allowed the vision to absorb changing situations and events and account for them without radical change in its basic structure was the assumption that the dramas were predestined. Since the Puritans viewed every happening as predestined and according to God's plan and purpose, they could interpret every event, no matter how contradictory it might at first seem to the Puritan vision, as consonant with it. The duty of the speaker was to search for an interpretive fantasy that would fit the event into God's scheme of things. Until a counterfantasy type began to excite the adherents—one which assumed human agency or free will as an explanation for human action—the Puritan vision remained coherent, consistent, and relatively unchanged.

For a hundred years, therefore, the changes in the rhetorical vision, theory, and practices of the Puritan ministers were slow and evolutionary. By the 1660s, the linguistic conventions of the Puritan sermon began a slight but perceptible change. Babette May Levy judges that the "oratory of the Reverend Leonard Hoare, preacher at Boston and later president of Harvard, is a forerunner of that ornate style which was soon to be the accepted fashion."[1] After Hoare's death, Urian Oakes served as temporary president and later as president of Harvard, and he delivered at commencement times a series of extremely witty and ornate Latin orations. Increase and Cotton Mather introduced more rhetorical flourishes and wordplays into their sermons than the founders had used.

By 1700, the changing circumstances included a growing influx of new ideas from Europe. Scientific advancements were impressing the intellectuals with the power of observation, as opposed to the authority of the Bible, as a source of knowledge. Although the Puritan vision included both light and heat, the emphasis was shifting in certain rhetorical centers so that for some speakers the power of intellect and reason was making headway against mysticism, emotion, and extrasensory perceptions of the supernatural as the way to knowledge. In wordly Boston and scholarly Harvard, the vision's balance between reason and mysticism, between rationalism and intuition, was tipping toward reason. In the long battle between Aristotle and Plato, Aristotle was gaining ascendance on the seaboard. Gradually, the churches were solving, in a more perfunctory and less rigorous way than before, the question of what evidence was suitable as proof of election. Fantasy types emerged that portrayed salvation as a gradual and reasonable process.

As the seaboard drifted toward rationalism, an imposing figure grew in prominence in the Connecticut valley and soon dominated the churches in that area. Solomon Stoddard became so powerful on what was then the frontier that some of his enemies referred to him as "Pope." Stoddard rejected the drift towards rationalism and reasserted the primacy of mysticism, emotion, and intuition. Stoddard emphasized, with language reminiscent of the medieval monk, the side of the vision which saw the corrupt nature of man. Man was "vermin," "dead fish," and "worms." He preached that "his whole soul is like a dead carcass, like a heap of carrion, loathsome and noisom, and God may justly abhor him."[2] More importantly, Stoddard emphasized that "the word is as an hammer and we should use it to break the rocky hearts of men."[3] Stoddard led the way in introducing threats of hell-fire to arouse fear and as a whip and goad to changing men. He experienced "harvests" of converted sinners in 1679, 1683, 1696, 1712, and 1718. He asserted that "fear and dread of hell make men do what they do in religion." He fantasized: "What will you think of it when the devil will lay hold of you to drag you down to hell? How will you cry out when tumbling into the lake that burns with fire and brimstone?"[4]

Meantime, the Mathers found themselves advocating a half-way theocracy in defense of a half-way covenant. In Boston itself, Thomas and William Brattle, formerly tutors at Harvard College, joined with John Leverett in January 1698 to found a church of a more liberal, rational, and catholic temper than the orthodox one represented by the Mathers. Thomas Brattle furnished the land and selected for the church's minister a former student of Leverett's named Benjamin Colman. Leverett had been Colman's tutor at Harvard, but when called to Boston, Colman was in England developing a gloss of tolerance and a taste for pleasantry and worldliness. Although he remained a Calvinist, Colman wrote and spoke with a hint of the Enlightenment and of Deism.

Thus, by 1700, the old rhetorical tradition began to contain at least three discernible emphases within the Puritan rhetorical vision, each emphasis resulting in a discernible change in style. The substance of one was in the tradition of the founders, gradually changing and modifying with the change in circumstances and illustrated by the preaching of Increase and Cotton Mather; another reverted to Stoddard's portrayal of the old dramas of the Calvinists, but with an emphasis on scenes full of hell-fire and brimstone and designed to arouse fear; the third consisted of a more worldly, tolerant, and genteel vision. Gradually, the half-way measures of the Mathers lost influence and the styles of Stoddard and Colman waxed in popularity. Stoddard grew in power until he virtually controlled the theological affairs of a group of churches in the Connecticut valley. Meantime, Harvard College swung to the control of the substantial citizens and scholars of the Brattle street church. Increase Mather, invoking the exodus fantasy type, accused Leverett of leading "the voyaging Israelites back to Egypt." The Brattles, Colman, and Leverett, with their more "catholic" and tolerant attitude toward the Church of England and toward secular learning, also irritated "Pope" Stoddard. Preaching an election sermon in Boston in 1703, he asserted that colleges ought not to be "places of Riot and Pride." He charged that " 'tis not worth the while for persons to be sent to the *Colledge* to learn to Complement men, and Court Women."[5]

By the turn of the eighteenth century, the basic tradition of the Puritan style remained, but a gradual change was taking place in the vision, the rhetorical theory, and the content of the speeches. The widely held assumptions about the nature of the world, of God, and of man, and the common rhetorical theories and standards that developed in the first decades of the new settlement were cracking, and as the tensions increased, one was able to see in the hairline outlines the emerging mosaic of speech practices. In the first decades of the eighteenth century, these were still merely tendencies and not new styles, but events were moving rapidly to bring these incipient rhetorical tensions to a dramatic confrontation.

When Solomon Stoddard controlled the valley and grew in years as well as power, he searched about for a successor. He selected his grandson, Jonathan Edwards, and invited him to serve at Northampton in 1726. A year later, Edwards was ordained; in February 1729, Solomon Stoddard died and Jonathan Edwards inherited one of the most powerful pulpits on the frontier. Jonathan was the son of Timothy Edwards of the Harvard class of 1691. Timothy was ordained pastor in Windsor, Connecticut, in May 1694. Shortly thereafter, he married Esther Stoddard, the second child of Solomon. Born on October 5, 1703, Jonathan was their fifth of eleven children (all the rest daughters). He entered Yale college in 1716, finished his course in 1720, and remained at Yale, studying until 1722 when he accepted an invitation to a Presbyterian church in New York. He returned to Yale and took his M.A. degree. After gaining his advanced degree, he continued on as a tutor at Yale until his call to Northampton.

In the beginning, he followed the way of his grandfather, and his preaching was well received. In 1734 and 1735, he delivered a series of sermons that resulted in an unusual awakening of religious interest. Approximately three hundred people were affected, and the whole town was stirred. The awakening was accompanied by certain emotional excesses, and in 1735, at the height of the fervor, Joseph Hawley committed suicide. Hawley was an uncle, by marriage, to Jonathan Edwards. The excesses of the revival caused a reaction against it so that by the end of 1735 the feeling began to ebb. The Northampton revival was one of the most striking in colonial history up to that time. Interpretative fantasies about it spread up and down the valley and other communities experienced similar outbreaks.

In the meantime, a separate revival had been underway in the middle colonies associated with the preaching of Theodore Frelinghuesen, a Dutch reformed minister. All of these small revivals gave evidence of the temper of the times.

The times seemed propitious for revival, but the rhetorical vision of the Puritan speakers contained within it several serious handicaps preventing a successful revival rhetoric. The lines of argument, when their implications became clear, made it difficult for the speaker to exhort his audience to action and belief. The first of the rhetorical handicaps was contained in the very scenic feature that gave the style its immunity from corroboration—the doctrine of predestination. If God's liberty was complete and man could do nothing to save himself, the rhetoricians could provide few reasons for the audience to change attitudes, beliefs, or actions. Furthermore, if all that man did was predetermined and he was not a free agent, he could not logically be held responsible for his actions. Why should a man feel guilty for actions beyond his control? Yet the evocation of guilt provides the energy for the reorientation of a person's individual fantasies so that they coincide with a rhetorical vision, which is the essence of conversion. The argument that he inherited his guilt or that it was the nature of man to be sinful and that he ought to feel guilt because he was a man was, at best, a makeshift attempt to meet the rhetorical situation posed by a revival.

As the years passed, a large number of people in every congregation were unable to furnish adequate evidence of election. The result was a greater emphasis on consciousness-raising communication. Tracy, evaluating the revival of religion in the time of Edwards and Whitefield from the perspective of one hundred years, asserted that the fact that the congregation always contained a large number of people who were "regarded, both by the church and by themselves, as unrenewed, impenitent men, destitute of faith, and of every Christian grace, and in the broad road to perdition" explained "whatever is really characteristic of the 'New England style of preaching,' of which so much has been said." According to Tracy, the "New England habit of assailing hearers, either with argument or entreaty, as men who are to be brought over from opposition to agreement" was based upon that fact.[6]

The problem became so acute that a compromise was worked out in which certain members who were good and decent folks but who had not received evidence of regeneration assumed a place between the saints and the clearly sinful and unregenerate. The issue was posed on the question of who should be baptized. In 1662, a Synod convened to discuss the question and arrived at an answer known as the "half-way covenant," which asserted that the children and grandchildren of the saints had the right to be baptized even though in the case of the grandchildren the parents were not of the spiritual church. Half-way members were of the worldly church but would not be of the eternal church until they received God's saving grace.[7]

A second factor was pushing the speakers toward greater efforts at persuasion in their new environment. Religious toleration was a practice rare in Europe. The sacred and temporal powers had been associated for generations in the Old World. In every major area of Western Europe, the state had an established church. The church was thus protected and sanctioned by the civil government. The pattern was repeated in the early days of Massachusetts. For all effects and purposes, the Puritan religion was the established church in Massachusetts as Roger Williams and Anne Hutchinson discovered at the cost of banishment and as did several Quakers at a higher price. But the pressures of the New World were weakening the relationship between church and state. King's Chapel, an Anglican church, was built by order of Governor Andros in 1688. By that date, the toleration, however grudging, of a group of Baptists and of some Quakers was already a fact. By 1700, the competition of other religious ideas was under way and the Puritans had not only to fight for the souls of the unregenerate among their own congregations, but they also had to fight for such souls against the competing arguments of other faiths.

Rhetoric had long furnished the Puritans with their major form of worship. The sermon was the essence of their religious observance, and the lecture was the method by which the unregenerate were brought to the proper state for God to exercise his liberty and grace. Now, the Puritan had to fight for his church and his faith against the inroads of other doctrines and other denominations. He fought with all his weapons, with his power and status in the community, with his control of the civil magistrates, and with his ability to control opinion. But the Puritan preacher also turned to speechmaking, to disputations, lectures, and preaching to fight for his ideas and his power and position. The Puritan sermon became a prime consciousness-raising instrument.

By 1740, the need for revitalizing the Puritan faith and for defending and gaining new converts for the true religion was apparent to many. For several generations, since the turn of the century at least, when many ministers moved from the Scriptures to their application to the world about them, they raised the question of the degeneration of the society of the saints. The preachers "raising their eyes from the Bible only to see the sins of their people, were never touched by the awakening idea of progress that was stirring minds in England and America throughout the century."[8] In an invocation of the restoration fantasy type, the time of the founders was dramatized as the golden age, and Cotton Mather could call on the authority of founders still living to support his arguments and controversies. The speakers portrayed society as in a state of decline, worldliness, pride, rife with the sin of apathy and the loss of vital faith. The rhetorician found evidence for his analysis in almost every Indian uprising, every trouble with the mother country, and every natural disaster. The perfect society, which was to serve as a model for the world, was in danger of becoming as sinful as any Popish state.

In 1739, when the English evangelist George Whitefield visited the colonies, the changing circumstances provided a symbolic context congenial to fantasies which once again celebrated the significance of preaching. The zealous preacher needed conversions, first to save immortal souls, and then to augment his congregation by winning the apathetic and the sinful away from competing faiths. But preaching for effect was difficult when one believed that God had already divided the elect from the damned and that his decision was irrevocable. The evangelically inclined preachers of the 1730s thus were under pressure to change their rhetorical style when Whitefield docked at Lewes-Town, Pennsylvania, in early November 1739.

Whitefield found the people of the colonies ready for and responsive to his powerful exhortative discourse. His persona came to symbolize the religious enthusiasm of 1740–1741 which was subsequently called the First Great Awakening.

The Great Awakening brought the tension between the rhetorical theory and practice of the preachers of colonial America into open conflict. Johnathan Edwards provides a benchmark for the diverging traditions. In many respects he raised the traditional Puritan sermon style to its highest artistic expression. Perry Miller, in his biography, argues that, as a student of Locke and Newton, Edwards rejected the old psychology and logic of the first generation and recast Puritan thought into new and contemporary patterns.[9] Be that as it may, Edwards's sermons were in most respects typical of the homiletic traditions of the founders. When Edwards began to prepare a sermon, he brought to the task the old habits learned from his father, his tutors at Yale, and his own attempts to emulate the speakers he heard and admired. Edwards's rhetorical vision was essentially that of the Puritan founders. His speech practices conformed to the critical standards of the Puritan rhetorical style. Not only that, but Edwards was, in my estimation, the most consummate artist to work within the restrictions of the Puritan sermon form in New England. His greatest artistic works deserve to be studied and appreciated as rhetorical artifacts just as *Hamlet* might be studied as the highest expression of Elizabethan drama.

Finally, Edwards exemplifies some of the new emphases of the 1740s. On occasion, he preached "hell-fire and damnation." Some of his sermons were designed to be the means for awakening sinners, and they illustrate important features of the emerging revival rhetoric. A critical analysis of Edwards's sermon "Sinners in the Hands of an Angry God" can compare and contrast the beginnings of the new style with the old Puritan rhetoric.

Edward's most famous sermon, and deservedly so, is the one delivered at Enfield, Massachusetts, in the midst of the revival on July 8, 1741.[10] It is dedicated to the explication of a text from Deuteronomy, the thirty-second chapter and thirty-fifth verse: "Their foot shall slide in due time." The theme of his sermon reflects the Puritan preoccupation with time. When a man's time is due, he will slide. The verse is brief, and the treatment of it exhaustive. Edwards selects a narrow theme for his discourse and brings all of his rhetorical energy to the explanation, proof, and application of that brief passage. Like the founders, Edwards proceeds in typical dichotomous fashion, beginning first with appeals to reason, then adding appeals to the heart.

Edwards's practice conformed to the balancing of light and heat in the manner of the typical Puritan sermon. In "Sinners in the Hands of an Angry God," he divided the discourse into parts and began with his exegetical demonstration of the truths he had discovered by his criticism of the sacred texts. After the light, he turned to the heat, the application of the doctrine to his audience.

The core of the exegetical method of argument is the discovery of meanings in words and concepts. In practice, it often resulted in the imputation of congenial meanings to words and concepts. Edwards's long sermon is designed to demonstrate that "there is nothing that keeps wicked men at any one moment out of hell, but the mere pleasure of God." His explanation consists of four discrete cells, each containing an assertion as a topic sentence with biblical texts as support. The assertions which form the topic sentences of each nodule are meanings that he has packed into such terms as "their foot sliding" and "due time." The speaker then unpacks the meanings one after another in careful sequence. Edwards has, in a sense, packed the words of the text with the basic meanings of his particular rhetorical vision, namely, that men are always exposed to destruction, that they deserve destruction, and that only God's grace keeps them from hell. The key words in the text serve such a rhetorical enterprise like empty bags into which the speaker packs the meanings he wants and than unpacks the meanings one after another before his audience.

The Puritan preachers, up to the time of Edwards, packed their rhetorical luggage with the same basic meanings and proceeded to unfold the same basic tenets over and over again in elaborate and repetitive detail. When an ingenious scholar begins a work of textual criticism knowing what he will discover, he will have little difficulty finding it. Since the Puritans' search of the sacred texts did not result in the uncovering of radical new truths, what was the purpose of the elaborate and repetitive exercises in exegesis that three generations of Puritan preachers performed several times each week in much the same way that Edwards did at Enfield? To some extent, the long sermons served as a ritualistic substitute for the more elaborate liturgy of the services of other churches. Certainly, they served to celebrate the faith of the fathers and lend cohesion to the community. They probably provided an audience of connoisseurs of the rhetorical style with an opportunity to observe the dexterity of the minister in discovering texts and ordering his explanations of them. Perhaps they furnished the speaker with a chance to demonstrate his scholarship and reinforce his position of leadership within the culture. Perhaps they furnished a recreation of sorts to people who had few outlets for recreation by giving them the basis for weekly discussion and debates over doctrine. All of these purposes were probably served to some extent by the Puritan exegesis.

Yet, somehow, all these reasons together seem insufficient to explain the Puritan exegetical exercises. One major function of the incessant proving of the case was to sustain the consciousness and keep the faith. Certainly, the rhetorical vision was harsh and many members of the congregation searched their souls when a loved one died in an unregenerate state. The long sections of doctrinal reasons that provided the light of the sermon served the purpose of reinforcing the agreed-upon religious values of the community. The members of the audience could be reassured that their beliefs were valid, true, reasonable, and just and that they were, indeed, God's chosen people. The proof of the faith of the fathers would sustain their belief that the great effort and sacrifice of the first generations in coming to the wilderness was freighted with meaning and not simply folly.

The reinforcement was grounded on the most scholarly, reasonable, and impressive intellectual grounds available in the community. A learned exegesis, involving the careful and explicit drawing out of meanings from ambiguous terms, provided an impressive demonstration of the reasonableness of what, stripped to its bare bones, might strike one today, or some perhaps even in 1740, as a harsh and improbable explanation of the world, of God, and of man.

In the end, Edwards's exercise in textual criticism of the Scriptures (the logic of his argument) results in an authoritative assertion of the shared assumptions of speaker and audience. The notion that man was always liable to eternal damnation and deserved his fate, the notion that time was crucial to his pilgrimage on this earth, the notion that each man had a predestined, appointed time known only to God, were all common to the vision.

In short, the oft-remarked impression of impeccable logic in Edwards's sermons is gained by the rhetorical practice of vehement restatement of the central theme. Edwards taught nothing new and proved nothing new to his listeners at Enfield. What he did do with his merciless plain restatement was forcibly and clearly to remind his listeners of their common faith. When he moved to the artistic, dramatic, beautiful, and awful application, they had nowhere to turn to escape personal involvement in the drama. With the incessant repetition of the contemporary television commercial message, Edwards drove home to his congregation his central point.

Despite the familiar mechanistic structure of several of its portions, the speech represents some departure from tradition in that it moves dramatically like a well-made play to moments of linguistic and emotional climax. The first act, as it were, consists of the exposition of the four points of explanation and the ten points of proof. The first-act-curtain speech is expressed in plain language of some emotional intensity in the last paragraph before the application proper. In that paragraph, the speaker presents a powerful dramatization involving fantasy themes and in-cues alluding to other shared themes and types. This section contains the basic emotional evocation of the entire sermon.

> So that, thus it is that natural men are held in the hand of God, over the pit of hell; they have deserved the fiery pit, and are already sentenced to it; and God is dreadfully provoked, his anger is as great towards them as to those that are actually suffering the executions of the fierceness of his wrath in hell, and they have done nothing in the least to appease or abate that anger, neither is God in the least bound by any promise to hold them up one moment; the devil is waiting for them, hell is gaping for them, the flames gather and flash about them, and would fain lay hold on them, and swallow them up; the fire pent up in their own hearts is struggling to break out; and they have no interest in any Mediator, there are no means within reach that can be any security to them.

With the second portion, the application of the sermon, Edwards shifts his dramatization from the third to the second person. Before, "they" deserved the fiery pit; the devil was waiting for "them." Now, as he builds the first scene of his second act to its climactic moment, he replays the basic theme, changing the force of his charge from some anonymous third party to "the use of this awful subject may be for awakening unconverted persons in this congregation." To such unconverted Edwards says: "That lake of burning brimstone, is extended abroad under you. There is the dreadful pit of the glowing flames of the wrath of God; there is hell's wide gaping mouth open; and you have nothing to stand upon, nor any thing to take hold of." To those members of his audience who still feel they are not in danger and that the charge does not apply to them directly, Edwards says: "You probably are not sensible of this; you find you are kept out of hell, but do not see the hand of God in it."

The second theme of the sermon is that no man has the power to preserve himself. Edwards uses the same basic metaphor to allude to this theme that he will subsequently use to symbolize the first and major statement of the speech. All of man's prudence and contrivances cannot keep him from it. They can "have no more influence to uphold you and keep you out of hell, than a spider's web would have to stop a fallen rock."

After this, Edwards drops the emphasis on man's helplessness and insinuates his major theme into the discourse again, releasing some of the dramatic tension. The variation of the major theme that he plays now is the one emphasizing God's wrath. With considerable artistry, he piles up a series of images building to the last ultimate unifying metaphor, the figure that has caught the imagination of subsequent generations and has come to symbolize the Puritan sermon. He begins with the figure of the "black clouds of God's wrath now hanging directly over your heads." Edwards then compares God's wrath to a bow which "is bent, and the arrow made ready." Only the restraining hand of God keeps the arrow "from being made drunk with your blood." Finally, he develops the climax of his major theme with the full-blown development of the analogy he has foreshadowed and hinted at before: "The God that holds you over the pit of hell, much as one holds a spider, or some loathesome insect over the fire, abhors you, and is dreadfully provoked: his wrath towards you burns like fire." Then, he recites a fantasy dramatizing the awful fervor of the Puritan vision of God and man— a symbolic cry to evoke terror.

> O sinner! Consider the fearful danger you are in: it is a great furnace of wrath, a wide and bottomless pit, full of the fire of wrath, that you are held over in the hand of that God, whose wrath is provided and incensed as much against you, as against many of the damned in hell. You hang by a slender thread, with the flames of divine wrath flashing about it, and ready every moment to singe it, and burn it asunder; and you have no interest in any Mediator, and nothing to lay

hold of to save yourself, nothing to keep off the flames of wrath, nothing of your own, nothing that you have ever done, nothing that you can do, to induce God to spare you one moment.

No wonder "there was such a breathing of distress and weeping, that the preacher was obliged to speak to the people and desire silence, that he might be heard."[11]

Having reached the first climactic development of his analogy of the spider suspended over the pit of hell, Edwards exhibited a strong sense of rhetorical structure and broke the mood of deep terror. He stepped back in more matter-of-fact language to consider "more particularly," the nature of God's wrath.

1. *Whose* wrath it is.
2. It is the *fierceness* of his wrath that you are exposed to.
3. The *misery* you are exposed to.
4. It is *everlasting* wrath.

As Edwards finishes his argumentative section, he begins to build again to his last great climactic moment of celebrating the inexpressibly miserable nature of sinful man. Edwards whips the auditor into the center of the drama. He cannot escape assuming the role of protagonist in the tragedy.

There is reason to think, that there are many in this congregation now hearing this discourse, that will actually be the subjects of this very misery to all eternity. We know not who they are, or in what seats they sit, or what thoughts they now have. . . . If we knew that there was one person, and but one, in the whole congregation, that was to be the subject of this misery, what an awful thing would it be to think of! If we knew who it was, what an awful sight would it be to see such a person! How might all the rest of the congregation lift up a lamentable and bitter cry over him! But, alas! Instead of one, how many is it likely will remember this discourse in hell?

Then, the preacher makes the final application, direct and personal to each listener: "It would be a wonder, if some that are now present should not be in hell in a very short time, even before this year is out. And it would be no wonder if some persons, that now sit here, in some seats of this meeting-house, in health, quiet and secure, should be there before to-morrow morning."

The sermon is drawing near to its end. The minister has driven his theme of man's miserable sinful nature and his precarious state into his audience with repetitions of figures of speech, with biblical quotations, and with powerful fictitious fantasy themes. Not one of Edwards's dramatizations is based upon observable historical characters. He has dramatized for his listeners in simple and graphic langauge over and over again that those who have not been regenerated stand on the threshhold of eternal torment of such awful nature and magnitude as to exhaust his powers of description (which were considerable). If they were not then weeping and moaning in excesses of fear, it had to be because they did not participate in the Puritan rhetorical vision, because they did not accept the speaker as one who had supernatural sanctions and a clearer vision of the truth than ordinary man, or because they did not have the imagination to participate in the central salvation drama of the unregenerate protagonist suspended like a spider by a slender thread over the fire.

Very briefly, after the long and repetitive attempt to arouse fear and guilt, Edwards turns to hope. The ray of light, the good news, is small, but it comes, nonetheless, at the close of the sermon: "And now you have an extraordinary opportunity, a day wherein Christ has thrown the door of mercy wide open, and stands in calling and crying with a loud voice to poor sinners; a day wherein many are flocking to him, and pressing into the kingdom of God." Those who have been elected "are now in a happy state, with their hearts filled with love to him who has loved them."

Edwards swings from hope after a few brief seconds to reiterate his major theme by comparison: "How awful is it to be left behind on such a day! To see so many others feasting, while you are pining and perishing! To see so many rejoicing and singing for joy of heart, while you have cause to mourn for sorrow of heart, and howl for vexation of spirit!"

Edwards's last appeal is the dramatic one that this is the nick of time: "God seems now to be hastily gathering in his elect in all parts of the land; and probably the greater part of adult persons that ever shall be saved, will be brought in now in a little time." Thus, it is now or never for those who are as yet unregenerate. They ought, therefore, to "awake and fly from the wrath to come."

Clearly, the speaker's heart is not in it at the end. When the time came to speak of hope and outline the plan for salvation, Edwards's artistry stumbled and he could not reach the rhetorical peak that he had scaled minutes before with his searching application of the figure of the spider to "some persons, that now sit here, in some seats of this meeting-house, in health, quiet and secure."

"Sinners in the Hands of an Angry God" exemplifies the Puritan sermon in many important features. Its structure reflects the old colonial rhetorical habits of invention, analysis, and arrangement. Its language is an artistic demonstration of the "plain" style. The similitudes reflect the general practice of the Puritan speakers. Edwards reasons in the exegetical mode and structures his sermon in mechanistic, cellular fashion.

Even at a deeper level, "Sinners in the Hands of an Angry God" illustrates Puritan sermonic fantasy types. Edwards places each member of his audience in the role of protagonist in the drama of personal salvation when he tells him, *you* are the spider suspended over the flames of hell. You, sitting here in this meeting-house today, may be in hell tomorrow morning. Where Hooker painted the large canvas of Jesus Christ coming in the clouds and the trumpet blowing the call for all to come to judgment, with God sitting on his throne and the thousands of angels about him, with each member of the audience center stage hearing the final judgment *"Depart from me ye cursed,"* Edwards accomplishes much the same effect by painting hell rather than heaven. Hooker leaves the eternal torment to the imagination; Edwards makes it sensible and, with his metaphors, dramatizes its torment.

Edwards reflects the Puritan preachers' preoccupation with the dramatic potency of time. When the protagonist is in deadly danger and must be saved by a given time or be lost forever, suspense and tension mount. Such dramatic use of time is a *cliché* of modern suspense drama. The bomb that is set to explode and must be discovered before the crucial moment provides the dramatic situation for frantic search. Camera shots of the moving hands of a clock dramatize the inexorable movement of time and add to the suspense. "Sinners in the Hands of an Angry God" presses forward the time theme: now is the time; God's grace is being showered up and down the valley; those left behind now will probably never be called; even the listener who is healthy and secure in worldly affairs may be called to his eternal judgment this night! The main difference between well-made television plays of the twentieth century and the dramatic structure of "Sinners in the Hands of an Angry God"—and that difference is crucial—is that the protagonist fighting against time in a TV melodrama is master of his fate. His frantic activity, his own cleverness, wins out in the nick of time. In Edwards's drama, the citizen of Enfield was driven to imagine himself like the spider, suspended by a slender thread over the fiery pit of hell. The time had come; he was to be saved or to spend eternity in its torments, but he could only wait. Wiggle or scheme as he might, all was in vain, for he was saved or doomed by the intervention of God.

Henry Ward Beecher saw the artistry of the sermon while, at the same time, deploring it. He said in his Yale lectures that "in some respects Edwards's [sic] terrific sermon, 'Sinners in the Hands of an Angry God,' may be ranked with Dante's *Inferno* or Michael Angelo's painting of the 'General Judgment.' But who can look upon the detestable representations of the painter, or the hideous scenes of the Florentine poet, without a shudder of wonder that they should have ever come from such tender and noble hearts."[12]

The level of artistry reached by Edwards in his highest flights owed something to his attempt to give voice to a deep mystical and religious concentration of experience. His language at the climactic moments at Enfield was not the language of thought, the expression of concepts and judgments, but the exhortative cry of a mystic giving vent to intense feeling.

In one metaphor, he concentrated the New England Neocalvinist and Puritan experience:

> The God that holds you over the pit of hell, much as one holds a spider, or some loathsome insect over the fire, abhors you, and is dreadfully provoked: his wrath towards you burns like fire; he looks upon you as worthy of nothing else, but to be cast into the fire; he is of purer eyes than to bear to have you in his sight; you are ten thousand times more abominable in his eyes, than the most hateful venomous serpent is in ours. You have offended him infinitely more than ever a stubborn rebel did his prince; and yet it is nothing but his hand that holds you from falling into the fire every moment.

The whole concept of man is summed up in the spider and the "loathsome" insect. Echoes of the medieval monks' language that characterized man as a "stynkynge slyme" and a "sake ful of donge" and "mete to wormes" sound in the similitude of the "spider or some loathsome insect" and the "hateful venemous serpent."[13] The omnipotent nature of God is caught neatly in the way he holds man over the pit. His wrathful nature is the fire. Earlier, Edwards had alluded to the ability of the fire to singe a thread and burn it through. God's mercy is apparent in his grace in holding one from the fire of his wrath even though each person has "offended him infinitely." The artistry of the language and the metaphor focuses the feelings of abasement, humiliation, and abject guilt into one concentrated emotional expression. Insofar as the auditor threw himself into the drama, assumed his role of protagonist, and participated in the metaphor, if he felt the flames of God's wrath and experienced his infinite offense to an all-powerful God, thus far was he likely to achieve the wealth and fullness of the religious emotion of guilt and abasement that the rhetorical artist was expressing.

Perhaps the most important departure from the mainstream of Puritan rhetorical practices was the emphasis, in "Sinners in the Hands of an Angry God," on the application section. Despite the superficial organization, which resembles the typical sermon in its dichotomous division and its numeration of subpoints, the structure of the application section is artistic and dramatic, building to emotional climaxes, moving from theme to theme in a symphonic or organic rather than a mechanical way. The balance between reason and emotion, between light and heat, indeed, the basic division between reason and emotion, is erased by the rhetoric of the sermon. The emphasis is upon raising the religious affections of the audience to a high pitch.

The rhetorical practices of Jonathan Edwards represent a crucial moment in the emerging rhetorical crisis of the 1740s in colonial America. Edwards became the leading advocate of the revival practices in the learned debate about rhetorical styles which followed the eruption of religious interest and of pietism at the time of the Great Awakening. His own preaching illustrates the continuing evolution of the changes introduced by his grandfather, Solomon Stoddard, and the impact of the revival. Edwards thus was a transition figure and "Sinners in the Hands of an Angry God" a benchmark in the rising tide of revival rhetoric. Amid the symbolic disarray resulting from the break-ups of the old rhetorical vision, new consciousness-creating communication was at work. The speaking practices which generated the new fantasy themes and created the new rhetorical vision, however, were those of the more effective evangelists such as George Whitefield, the speaker who became the archetype or model of the ideal revival preacher.

When George Whitefield was eighteen, he was accepted as servitor at Pembroke College. At Oxford, he met the Wesley brothers, John and Charles, and joined their Methodist Society. He underwent periods of great soul searching and fasted and sought God until he was unable to continue his studies. His tutor questioned him as to his failure to do his exercises and came to the conclusion that Whitefield was "really mad."[14]

He was ordained a deacon in the Church of England in 1736 and a priest in 1739. He made a trip to America in 1738 at the suggestion of John Wesley, who had preceded Whitefield to Georgia. The twenty-three-year-old newly ordained minister arrived in Savannah in May. He stayed in the New World but a few months and sailed from Charleston to return to England in September, determined to establish an orphanage for the many homeless children in Georgia. From the time he arrived in London in December of 1738 until he embarked again for America on August 14, 1739, Whitefield was in the midst of a "great pouring out of the Spirit."

Word of Whitefield's field preaching and itinerating had reached America and aroused considerable public interest. Whitefield had an aid named William Seward, who served as a publicist. Whitefield's journals and sermons were sent to newspapers and influential people before his arrival. Benjamin Coleman, for example, was carrying on an extensive correspondence with Whitefield before the latter arrived in Boston. Newspapers advertised Whitefield's published sermons and journals and other tracts and books about him.

On November 8, 1739, Benjamin Franklin's *Pennsylvania Gazette* reported that "last week the Rev. Mr. Whitefield landed from London at Lewes-Town in Sussex County, where he preach'd; and arrived in this City on Friday Night; on Sunday, and every Day since he has preach'd in the Church:

And on Monday he designs (God willing) to set out for New-York, and return hither the Week after, and then proceed by Land thro' Maryland, Virginia and Carolina to Georgia."[15]

In the spring and summer of 1740, Whitefield returned to Philadelphia and made circuits into the middle colonies, preaching in New Jersey and New York. On September 14, 1740, he arrived by sloop in Rhode Island. For the next forty-six days, he itinerated through New England. He spoke in Newport three days, moved to the Boston area for ten days, often preaching twice a day. He met and was befriended by the Governor, Jonathan Belcher. Dr. Colman invited Whitefield to use the pulpit of Brattle Street Church for his first sermon in Boston. Saturday, Whitefield preached at the Old South Church and in the afternoon spoke at Boston Common. Sunday, he preached at the First Church and in the afternoon once again upon the Common. Monday morning, he preached the morning service at the Reverend John Webb's meetinghouse and in the afternoon was scheduled to preach at New South.[16]

Towards the end of November 1740, Whitefield wrote to Benjamin Franklin, friend and publisher of his sermons, that, "I think I have been on shore 73 days, and have been enabled to travel upwards of 800 miles, and to preach 170 times, besides very frequent exhortations at private houses. I have collected, in goods and money, upwards of £700 sterling, for the Orphan-house, blessed be God!"[17]

Whitefield's grand revival tour of 1739–1740 was probably as exciting an event as had befallen the Colonies since the Indian wars thirty years earlier. He moved spectacularly from place to place. When he left Philadelphia in December 1739, he was "accompany'd to Chester by about 150 Horse."[18] Itinerating with his great entourage, including carriages, horses, and people afoot, he brought drama and excitement to the countryside. Good yeomen who depended upon Sunday services in the meeting-house or a trip to the tavern for excitement to liven the long drudgery of their routine, often dropped their work in the middle of the week to travel to hear Whitefield. He was aided in collecting a crowd by the practice of announcing the dates and places of sermons in the newspapers—a practice that was highly unusual at the time. For example, Franklin's paper carried a notice on November 13, 1740, to the effect that

> He [Whitefield] designs to preach the same Day at Gloucester in the Morning, and at Greenwich 12 Miles from thence, in the Afternoon. On Tuesday, at two a Clock in the Afternoon, at Piles-Grove. On Wednesday, at two a Clock in the Afternoon, at Cohansie. On Thursday, at two a Clock, at Salem. On Friday, three a Clock in the Afternoon, at Whiteclay-Creek. Saturday, two a Clock in the Afternoon, at Forks Mannor. And, Sunday Morning and Evening at Nottingham.[19]

Nathan Cole, a farmer and carpenter from Connecticut, provided an account of the impact of Whitefield's dramatic itinerating on the colonial yeoman.[20] Cole heard of Whitefield's preaching in Philadelphia and understood that the evangelist was preaching "like one of the old aposels" to many thousands who were flocking to hear him. He felt the spirit of God working on him and was "more & more hoping soon to see him." Word came that Whitefield was in Long Island, in Boston, and then in Northampton. Cole's expectations were rising and his hope to observe the great preacher was at a high pitch when

> one morning all of a Suding about 8 or 9 oClock there came a messenger & said mr. whitefield preached at hartford & weathersfield yesterday & is to preach at middeltown this morning at 10 o clock i was in my field at work i dropt my tool that i had in my hand & run home & run throu my house & bad my wife get ready quick to goo and hear mr. whitfeld preach at middeltown & run to my pasture for my hors with all my might fearing i should be too late to hear him.

The Coles had more than twelve miles to ride double on one horse in a little more than one hour's time. Cole drove his horse as fast as he could and when the horse tired, he jumped off and ran along beside until he was winded. Proceeding in this way, they "improved every moment to get along as if we was fleeing for our lives all this while fearing we should be too late to hear the Sarmon." When they came to within a mile or a bit less of the road from Hartford to Middleton, they saw what Cole thought was a cloud of fog rising over the road. He thought it was coming off the river, but as they came nearer, they heard the roar of the horses' feet and discovered that it was not fog at all but a cloud of dust raised by the long column of poeple going to hear Whitefield. When they came to within twenty rods of the road, they saw men and horses slipping along like shadows and "it was like a stedy streem of horses & their riders scarsely a horse more then his length behind another all of a lather and fome with swetther breath rooling out of their noistrels in the cloud of dust every jump every hors seemed to go with all his might to carry his rider to hear the news from heaven for the saving of their Souls."

Cole slipped his horse into the column and his wife complained that their clothes would be ruined, for they were soon covered with dust until everyone looked the same color and the whole tableau—horses, men, women, coats, hats, and shirts—all assumed one hue. When they arrived at the old meeting-house

> thare was a great multitude it was said to be 3 or 4000 of people asembled together we gat of from our horses & shook off the dust and the ministers was

then coming to the meating house i turned and looked toward the great river & saw the fery boats running swift forward & backward bringing over loads of people the ores roed nimble & quick every thing men horses & boats all seamed to be struglin for life the land & the banks over the river lookt black with people & horses all along the 12 miles i see no man at work in his field but all seamed to be gone.

When Cole recollected his experiences, he did so in an interpretative fantasy that portrayed Whitefield as an angelical and slender youth, who looked out over the crowd with bold assurance. Cole had heard how God was with Whitefield "everywhere as he came along," and the thought that he might now witness God's power "solemnized" his mind and put him into a "trembling fear" before Whitefield began to speak. The evangelist appeared to Cole as if he were "clothed" with authority by "the Great God" and a "sweet solemn solemnity sat upon his brow." Cole was not disappointed, for Whitefield's preaching gave him a "heart wound" and his "old foundation was broken up."

Cole's narrative is an excellent example of a nonfiction personal experience fantasy theme with the narrator adopting a participant voice. Cole must have had conversations with small groups of acquaintances in which fantasies had chained out about Whitefield's dramatic preaching in Philadelphia. Sharing the fantasies had evoked the hope that he might see the great preacher in person and aroused the feeling that the spirit of God was working on him. The narrative interprets the events in highly emotional terms; he was put into a "trembling fear" and found the protagonist "clothed" with the authority of God. The context, the chaining fantasies which had preceded his coming to Middleton, the drama of the actual situation, and finally the preaching itself resulted in Cole's conversion.

Again, a nonparticipant might have described the externals of the ride to Middletown as relatively mundane, dirty, and unexciting. Cole's internal fantasies, however, drove him forward, alternately riding with his wife and running alongside to save the horse's energy. His internal fantasy life was filled with anticipation, excitement, fear, and hope. Cole's dramatizing is an illuminating clue to the fantasies that chained through the populace and that were to create the new rhetorical vision.

Whitefield's sermons were delivered with great power, and his message was clear, simple, and well adapted to the needs of a revival. They were dramatic performances in the theatrical sense of the term. He was a master of rhetorical fantasy. He was good theatre in an era in which traditional theatre was not available to large groups of people in North America.

Whitefield's strength lay in his ability to draw the audience into the vision his powerful fantasizing created. Basic to that strength was his ability at nonverbal communication. Garrick, the actor, is said to have testified that Whitefield could make an audience tremble or weep with his varied utterance of the word *Mesopotamia*. Naturally, one has to allow for a certain amount of overstatement in such legends; yet no commentator stepped forward to set the record straight. The testimony of friend and enemy alike agrees that Whitefield was a polished as well as a powerful orator. David Hume, too, heard Whitefield and judged that his action was "animated, yet natural." An eyewitness writing in the *New York Gazette* asserted that "he [Whitefield] uses much Gesture, but with great Propriety. Every Accent of his Voice, every Motion of his Body *Speaks*, and both are natural and unaffected. If his Delivery is the product of Art, 'tis certainly the Perfection of it, for it is entirely concealed."[21] Perhaps the most widely quoted and most impressive testimony comes from Benjamin Franklin, who resisted being converted. In his *Autobiography*, Franklin recalled that Whitefield "us'd indeed sometimes to pray for my Conversion, but never had the Satisfaction of believing that his Prayers were heard." On one occasion, when Whitefield visited Philadelphia, he was invited to stay at Franklin's home. Whitefield "reply'd, that if I made that kind Offer for Christ's sake, I should not miss of a Reward. And I return'd, *Don't let me be mistaken; it was not for Christ's sake, but for your sake.*"[22] Franklin wrote:

> He had a loud and clear Voice, and articulated his Words and Sentences so perfectly that he might be heard and understood at a great Distance, especially as his Auditories, however numerous, observ'd the most exact Silence. He preach'd one Evening from the Top of the Court House Steps, which are in the Middle of Market Street, and on the West Side of Second Street which crosses it at right angles. Both Streets were fill'd with his Hearers to a considerable Distance. Being among the hindmost in Market Street, I had the Curiosity to learn how far he could be heard, by retiring backwards down the Street towards the River, and I found his Voice distinct till I came near Front-Street, when some Noise in that Street, obscur'd it.[23]

Franklin also observed that of those sermons delivered repeatedly, "his delivery . . . was so improv'd by frequent Repetitions, that every Accent, every Emphasis, every Modulation of Voice, was so perfectly well turn'd and well plac'd, that without being interested in the Subject, one could not help being pleas'd with the Discourse, a Pleasure of much the same kind with that receiv'd from an excellent Piece of Musick."[24]

Whitefield's sermons were characterized by vivid dramatizations of biblical narratives. One eyewitness recalls often hearing Whitefield provide the scenery for a story by his power of verbal imagery. "As though Gethsemene were within sight, he would say, stretching out his hand—'Look yonder!— what is that I see! it is my agonizing Lord!'—And, as though it were no difficult matter to catch the sound of the Savior praying, he would exclaim, "Hark! hark! do not you hear?"[25] On another occasion, Whitefield was preaching to sailors in New York, using a fantasy theme relating to a voyage on a stormy sea when the tempest rages and the sail is gone. Whitefield asked "What next?" and the sailors in the audience, sharing the fantasy, answered, "Take to the long boats."

Whitefield was an Anglican and professed the old-style Calvinism of the eighteenth century. But like so many evangelists who were to follow, he did not stress doctrinal differences or ecclesiastical considerations. A forerunner of modern ecumenicalism, preaching from the court house in Philadelphia, he conducted a dialogue with Father Abraham, taking both parts. "Father Abraham, who have you in Heaven? Any Episcopalians?" "No!" "Any Baptists?" "No!" "Have you any Methodists there?" "No!" "Have you any independents or seceders?" "We don't know those names here."[26] He spoke from the pulpits of Anglicans, Congregationalists, and Presbyterians on his journeys across the Colonies.

He preached some hellfire and damnation, but he emphasized the element of rest and peace which awaited the converted in heaven. He pictured the children of God gathered around the holy throne. He emphasized the importance of the meek and the poor in the eyes of God. The latter portion of his sermons, sometimes as much as one fourth, was often a passionate exhortation for the listener to come to Christ. Where Edwards held out a brief section of hope at the conclusion of the Enfield sermon and bent his rigid Calvinism only slightly to meet the requirements of an audience situation in which decisions were his goal, Whitefield often spoke in such a way that his listeners could easily assume that, by an act of faith on their part, they would be saved. Such phrases as "come poor, lost, undone sinner, come just as you are to Christ. . . . He will receive you with open arms; the dear Redeemer is willing to receive you all" and ". . . a poor soul then throws himself upon this Jesus . . . [and] receives from Jesus the thing Promised" easily suggest that the listener can make a decision and receive the "new birth."[27]

Whitefield's practice thus made many concessions to the needs of the persuasive speaker. Whitefield stressed the joys of salvation, held out much more hope than Edwards, and spoke in his exhortations at the conclusion of his sermons in a way that suggested that, if the auditor willed to come to Christ and had faith, he would receive salvation.

At Enfield, Edwards made but passing references to Christ until he came to his brief appeal at the end of his sermon where he suggested that "Christ has thrown the door of mercy wide open" and that many are "flocking to Christ." Whitefield, on the other hand, often stressed the peace and joy that come from Christ. "My dear friends, I am now talking of heart-religion . . . which you must have, or you shall never sit with Jesus Christ," he said in his sermon on the "Kingdom of God." He continued, "for Christ's sake examine upon what this peace is founded—see if Christ be brought home to your souls. . . . Is God at peace with you? Did Jesus Christ ever say, 'Peace be to you?' "[28]

Whitefield brought a distinctive style of public speaking to the New World: dramatic, extemporaneous, passionate, and powerful. He changed some of the rules, he spoke on weekdays in the open air, and he itinerated from place to place. He emphasized piety, experimental religion, and the mystical and emotional experience of the supernatural. Many emulated Whitefield's manner of speaking so that he became an archetype or exemplar of the new style of evangelical preaching. The new tradition can be compared most clearly with the old by an examination of the speaker who exemplified the new tendencies in an extreme fashion.

In the summer of 1741, James Davenport, grandson of one of the founders of New England, graduate of Yale, minister at Southold, Long Island, began a wild evangelical tour into Connecticut. What Whitefield had done Davenport did, but where Whitefield reflected some of Edwards's balance and Puritan perspective, Davenport carried the Whitefieldian tendencies to an extreme.

The twenty-five-year-old Davenport had graduated nine years earlier as the youngest member of his Yale class. At college, he was part of a group of mystics under the influence of David Ferris, who later became a Quaker and who emphasized the immediate, sudden, and conscious qualities of the "new birth." Another member of Ferris's Holy Club was Jonathan Barber, who took a pastorate at Oyster Pond only a few miles from Southold. When Davenport and Barber got word of Whitefield's dramatic itinerating, they both came under the spell of the emerging consciousness. Davenport felt the power of a supernatural call and preached, on one occasion, to his congregation for close to twenty-four hours before he collapsed. Later, he journeyed to Philadelphia and met Whitefield. Both young men came away from the meeting impressed by their mutual piety. Whitefield noted in his journal that "to add to my comfort, the Lord brought my dear brother Davenport from Long Island, by whose hands the blessed Jesus has of late done great things."[29]

Sometime during this perid, Davenport discovered that God had provided him with supernatural powers. Among these was the ability to distinguish between those who were authentically born again and those who were not. He began to call the saints in his congregation "brother" and "sister" and those who were still in a natural state "neighbor."

At Stonington, Connecticut, Davenport held a spectacular series of meetings and claimed more than a hundred decisions from his first sermon and a hundred more, including twenty Indians, during the next eight days. He moved into Rhode Island and back into Connecticut, applying his power to distinguish the regenerate from the damned to the minsters who met him along the way. At Windham, he condemned the venerable Eliphalet Adams as unregenerate, and at Saybrook, he suggested that William Hart was a wolf in sheep's clothing. Like Whitefield, he preached from pulpits when offered and from fields when necessary. Everywhere he demanded to examine ministers as to their experimental knowledge of the "new birth." Those who agreed to be examined were often denounced and those who did not agree were always characterized as blind guides.

Davenport spent a hectic fall in New Haven; he denounced ministers, aroused the wrath of the powers at his alma mater, and became the center of consciousness-creating communication that resulted in a separation in the churches as his followers founded their own. The power of the chaining new fantasies is evidenced by some of his adherents experiencing transports and visions at New Haven. He returned to Southold for the winter and the next spring started out again. By the end of May, his activities in Stratford had aroused enough opposition so that several citizens came to Hartford where the General Assembly of Connecticut was in session and filed a complaint against Davenport and another itinerating evangelist, Benjamin Pomroy. The citizens, Captain Blacklatch and Samual Adams, charged that the two itinerates and the lay exhorters who soon began to preach with them were assembly-ing people, mostly women and children, and under the pretense of religion were inflaming them with a bad spirit and were disturbing law and order.

A warrant was issued, and Davenport and Pomroy were brought before the Assembly. Tracy reports a graphic vignette that catches the flavor of Davenport's manner, attitude, and use of fantasies based on supernatural sanctions. The trial lasted for several days, but at the end of the first day, the sheriff was conducting Davenport to his lodgings when the evangelist stopped on the front steps of the meeting-house where the Assembly was holding the session and began to preach to the crowd. The sheriff tried to move him along by grabbing hold of him. Davenport shouted, "Lord, thou knowest some-body's got hold of my sleeve. Strike them, Lord, strike them." Pomroy, standing nearby, said, "Take heed how you do that heaven-daring action!" Davenport's supporters then rushed foward and almost overpowered the sheriff.[30]

The Assembly decided that Davenport's ministry was destroying and disturbing "the peace and order of this government." However, they further found that he was "under the influence of enthusiastical impressions and impulses, and therefore disturbed in the rational faculties of his mind."[31] Davenport was then banished from Connecticut and sent home to Southold.

He did not stay long with his home parish but instead set out for Boston. The reaction of the established authorities in Boston was similar to that of the New Haven and Hartford authorities. The association of ministers was in session when Davenport arrived, and they soon made public a "declaration with regard to the Rev. Mr. James Davenport and his conduct." Among other things they asserted that

> We judge also, that the Rev. Mr. Davenport has not acted prudently, but to the disservice of religion, by going with his friends singing through the streets and high ways, to and from the houses of worship on Lord's days and other days; and by encouraging private brethren to pray and exhort in larger or smaller assemblies of people gathered for that purpose; a practice which we fear may be found big with errors, irregularities and mischiefs.[32]

Davenport continued his public exercises nonetheless, representing some of the ministers as unconverted and likening the rest to "Jehosophat in Ahab's army." Reverend Andrew Croswell of Groton, Connecticut, replied to the minister's declaration in defense of Davenport, and the controversy grew warm in the Boston area. The case was brought before civil authorities in a grand jury that took it up in August. Again Davenport was chastised for his behavior, and again it was excused on the grounds that "he was *non compos mentis*."[33]

Davenport continued his itinerating, arousing controversy and also winning a considerable number of strong partisans in eastern Connecticut. His evangelical career came to an end in March 1743 in New London. He had been invited by a group of supporters and immediately received word from God to purify the company. He ordered his followers to bring their clothes, jewelry, and wigs to him and then burned them. Next, he instigated a book-burning ceremony in which works by such famous Puritans as Increase Mather and Sewall, as well as the works of the tolerant Colman and the revivalist Jonathan Parsons, were burned.

After the book burning at New London, Davenport was relatively inactive until the next summer when he published a letter retracting the errors that he had made. He particularly singled out "the awful affair of books and clothes at New London" of which he said that he was "the ringleader in that horrid action." He accounted for his errors by attributing them to his being "under the powerful influence of the false Spirit, almost one whole day together, and part of several days."[34]

Davenport represented such a departure from established speech practices that a reaction against them soon developed. The reaction was not confined to Davenport, but his activities and the behavior of some of the most radical of his followers provided evidence to be used against Whitefield and Edwards. From the Boston-Cambridge complex of reason and intellectualism came Charles Chauncey to dispute the claims and means of the evangelists and to defend the old consciousness. Soon, he was indirectly contending with the intellectual giant of the revivalists, Jonathan Edwards, on the nature of conversion and tactics of the Awakening. The debate became a discussion about the proper rules and tactics for religious rhetoric, a sure sign that the old style of the Puritan sermon was now being challenged by the adherents of the revival with a new style.

The partisans of Davenport, the new consciousness, and the new way of preaching were called the "New Lights" while those who reacted against the revival and what they thought were excesses and heresies were called the "Old Lights." Within the Presbyterian church, the same division was often referred to as the "New Side" versus the "Old Side." In the decades following Davenport's wild and exciting itinerating, a number of colonial churches divided into separate congregations as a result of the controversies over the nature of religion and the proper form of preaching generated by the Great Awakening. A new consciousness and a new communication style had emerged out of the turmoil of the Great Awakening. A great number of Congregational churches divided, with a separate New Light church emerging from the division. The same pattern was repeated by the Baptists. Although the separate congregations declined in the early years of the nineteenth century, many of the rhetorical features of the New Light preaching were carried on as religious freedom and heterodoxy became the predominant ways in the United States.

The speech practices of Whitefield and Davenport gave extreme expression to a strong romantic and pietistic impulse. They were emotional and intuitive. Speaking extemporaneously, these men projected the illusion of spontaneity and naturalness. Whitefield, particularly, provided an exemplar for other speakers to emulate. Soon the practice of the New Light speakers generated critical standards and shortly thereafter rhetorical theories to sustain the emerging rhetorical style. In this chapter, I have described the essential features of the new practices. In the next, I shall delineate the emerging style and criticize its rhetoric.

The bifurcation of the Puritan rhetorical theory and practice that followed upon the heels of the Great Awakening with its concomitant debate on theological and rhetorical matters was to set the pattern for religious and reform speaking in this country until the First World War. Indeed, parallels can still be found in contemporary public address.

❦ 4

The Evangelical Style

Theory and Criticism

The outburst of piety and romanticism in the 1730s and 1740s was not confined to North America. Western Europe experienced similar waves of renewed interest in emotional religion. Whitefield and his early associates, the Wesleys, participated in a general awakening in the British Isles at the same time. My concern is not to explain the unique features of the American experience, nor yet to explain the revival. A number of scholars have applied themselves to that task.[1] My purpose is to examine the *rhetorical* implications of the sometimes violent religious enthusiasms that accompanied the Great Awakening in America. In chapter three, I described the communication practices which emerged from the revival. In this chapter, I examine the special communication theory and rhetorical vision associated with the new style.

As speech events, revival meetings under such preachers as Whitefield, Jonathan Edwards, Gilbert Tennent, James Davenport, or any of the other successful preachers, were highly charged, emotional experiences. As the speaker castigated his audience for their sins, whipped them into feelings of guilt, and impressed upon them their deadly danger throughout eternity, members of the audience began to utter sounds. Some groaned, some wailed unintelligibly, others cried out. The speaker had visible evidence of the power of his words. The revivalists dramatized the results of such preaching in the language of the Christian warrior—echoing the old Puritan fantasy type. They talked of "many being wounded" and of persons who "fell" under the word. They dramatized case histories of people who fell on the floor in a senseless state and could not move. Hardened sinners were not only wounded but were, on occasion, melted. The elect, too, felt the powerful emotional impact of the atmosphere of the revival meeting. When Whitefield preached in Northampton on October 19, 1740, "Mr. Edwards wept during the whole time of exercise."[2]

The Reverend Jonathan Parsons of Lyme, Connecticut, was one of the most powerful of the local revivalists. He reported that during one of his sermons, "many had their *countenances changed*; their tho'ts seemed to *trouble* them, *so that the* Joynts of their *Loyns were loosed, and* their *knees smote one against another*. Great numbers cried out aloud. . . . Several Stout Men fell as tho' a Cannon had been discharg'd, and a Ball had made its Way thro' their Hearts. Some young Women were thrown into Hysterick Fits."[3]

At first, the revival was immensely popular. For a generation, the New England ministers had called for a regeneration of the faith of the fathers. Now God seemed to be shedding an unusual shower of His grace upon them. Many interpreted the Awakening in accordance with the scenario of the fantasy type of a time of troubles followed by a showering of God's grace. They saw the revival as evidence that the chosen people had once again found their way out of Egypt. A host of ministers heard Whitefield, found him inspiring, and began to model their speaking manner after him.

Whatever other influences Whitefield may have had upon colonial society in social, religious, and economic matters, he did serve one important function: he focused attention upon a crisis in rhetorical theory and practice. Whitefield brought a distinctive style of public speaking to the new world— dramatic, extemporaneous, passionate, and powerful. He emphasized piety, the mystical and emotional experience of the supernatural—"experimental" religion, as friends of the Great Awakening described the experience of the "new birth."[4] He graphically demonstrated the power of vigorous gestures, clear enunciation, and expressive vocal inflections. The Puritans had a rhetorical vision which balanced light and heat and which resulted in sermons divided into proof and application. Over the years, the balance proved precarious, tipping now in one direction and then in the other. Whitefield spoke mostly to the heart and evoked mystical feelings of piety, and the balance was never quite the same again in the New World.

Whitefield was one of the first in North America to systematically develop a persuasive climate to surround his preaching. He skillfully employed all the media of communication available to him—newspapers, letters, and word-of-mouth—to publicize his processions through the countryside. The fact that he preached in the open, during weekdays, added an aura of the unusual and dramatic. Because he was exciting, controversial, and newsworthy, he collected the curious as well as the devout. Whitefield's coming was an event of great significance to the humdrum routine of the eighteenth-century American. The decade of the 1740s was a time of relative peace and calm. The Indians were, for the moment, quiet; the French and Indian war was still in the future. In New England, going to the theater was sinful, reading material was still scarce and expensive, and many people were illiterate. The need for spectacle and excitement, for entertainment and recreation, was great, and Whitefield's itinerating provided all of these in generous measure in a form that was not only socially acceptable but often applauded.

In addition, Whitefield fantasized in his published journals and sermons that when he spoke, his listeners often experienced the "new birth," that they were wounded or melted, that decisions were made, and that people were saved. Thus, Whitefield's tour was billed as more than just spectacle and excitement; it was an event of significance in terms of spiritual rebirth. Nathan Cole had heard enough of Whitefield to feel the "Spirit of God drawing me by conviction" until he longed to hear the evangelist. Whitefield created an expectation that at the great open-air meetings, supernatural power would be made manifest. He alluded to a keystone of the Puritan rhetorical vision, which had, since the time of the founders, dramatized the ministers as the spokesmen of God. Whitefield stressed again and again in his publications that it was the power of God that moved his words and melted his audience.

As Whitefield moved across the country, he collected important personages who traveled with him. Leading ministers, and in Massachusetts Governor Belcher himself, added the prestige of worldly authority to the supernatural sanctions that Whitefield claimed. Important leaders from all walks of life added their ethos to the evangelist as they moved from community to community.

Finally, the crowds added to the persuasive climate. Nathan Cole slipped his horse into the long column, interpreting its movement as a silent, almost desperate rush of a great crowd to get to the meeting-house in time for the sermon. When he looked out across the river, he saw hundreds of people coming across. The very crowds testified to the importance and significance of the evangelical event.

Thus, the context in which Whitefield spoke tended to render his listener suggestible to the sermon. When the slender youth looked out boldly over the assembled thousands at Middeltown or in the Boston Common, the listeners could well expect mighty and awesome things to happen. He was an international celebrity, a man who had started a great revival in England and Wales, a controversial figure in the Old World, a man whose activities made published news and were rumored about by word of mouth. He moved with purpose and speed. He seemed driven by the importance of his work. His journals reported that he was frequently ill, that he was weak, but that he was able to gather his strength together to preach. He preached twice a day on many days and then held audience in private homes, exhorting, praying, and counseling disturbed people. His was a great cause to which he was ready to dedicate his health and his life itself if need be. Wherever he went, he gathered a crowd and created an aura of excitement. Those who crowded around the platform with Nathan Cole at Middeltown had just participated in a hurried and hectic dash to hear the sermon. Here, then, was a speaker of great reputation, a dramatic figure, a man with a mission. For many in the audience, Whitefield's coming may well have been the most dramatic and exciting break in routine for several years. They were predisposed to hear a great sermon. Whitefield seldom disappointed them.

Franklin wrote in the Pennsylvania *Gazette* of June 12, 1740, that "the Alteration in the Face of Religion here is altogether surprizing. Never did the People show so great a Willingness to attend Sermons, . . . Religion is become the Subject of most Conversations. No Books are in Request but those of Piety and Devotion."[5]

To what extent Whitefield caused all of these things to happen has been the subject of much scholarly controversy. As with every subsequent evangelist in the history of the United States, the friends of the revival submitted evidence of strong and permanent increase in piety, church attendance, reformed sinners, and so forth. The enemies argued that the effect was unnatural, overrated, and transitory. Certainly, Whitefield's speaking was not the only factor in the revival, for Whitefield returned again and again to the New World, and while he continued to draw large audiences and many were melted, he never again left behind him such a widespread preoccupation with piety and religion as he did on his second visit in 1739–1740.

Whether Whitefield did or did not move the New World with his lone voice is beside the point for many of the contemporary observers chained into fantasy themes in which he did. Franklin, for example, reported that the extensive change was due to "the successful Labours of the Reverend Mr. Whitefield."[6] Thus, the preachers and speakers who observed him and heard of his work in other places had abundant corroboration that his kind of preaching worked. True, his friends may well have attributed many of the apparent effects to God's intervention or to His use of Whitefield's words as a *means* to forward the Awakening, but even so, the evidence of God's support and pleasure with such preaching only gave added weight to its impressiveness.

Whitefield introduced two important innovations in public speaking in the colonies. First, he itinerated and indirectly encouraged others to travel around the colonies or to visit towns other than their own. Second, the itinerating enabled Whitefield to give the same sermon on many different occasions and he could thus deliver it extemporaneously or from memory without notes. The practice of giving the same speech over and over again with variations adapted to the immediate audience is so important to understanding Whitefield and so common to the subsequent history of rhetoric in America that it deserves a brief note of explanation.

An itinerating minister or a lecturer on tour moved from place to place, speaking to new audiences. In the eighteenth and nineteenth centuries, communications were slow and inefficient, and remarks made in one town were seldom fully reported in another. The common practice, therefore, was to deliver essentially the same speech over and over again. During the course of developing such a speech, the more skillful rhetoricians introduced new material and embroidered the old fantasy themes in a continual effort to improve the speech. Some of the new fantasies would chain through the audience, and the speaker would keep those that proved more effective in enticing fantasy sharing in the sermon and drop the material that fell flat. Gradually, the speaker collected a reservoir of supporting material suitable for each of his main points.

A Broadway play is often developed in an analogous way. The play is put into rehearsal with the playwright watching. When scenes or lines seem unsuitable during the course of preparation, the playwright will revise or delete them. Once the play opens in the out-of-town tryouts, the producers will watch the response of the audience very carefully; then, the play is often rewritten once again in light of the way it works with the audience. Thus, the playwright, director, actors, and the *audiences* work out the play among them. In other words, the audience has a partial hand in the development of the final product. The itinerating evangelist often developed his sermon in the same way.

Once the speech was prepared, the itinerating speaker had a general outline of topics in mind, plus a store of suitable illustrations, biblical narratives, biblical quotations, and exhortative appeals that were tried, modified, tested, modified again, and tested again for audience response. He could speak without manuscript or notes because he had thoroughly memorized the main outline. The speaker adapted to the immediate audience by watching them and adding or subtracting material from his original plan, depending upon the way they shared or failed to share the fantasy. He amplified a particular fantasy because the audience was responding well or because they seemed unconvinced or skeptical about the point he was making. He telescoped a section because it was not going well or because the audience had already accepted his basic premise. Amplification consisted largely in supplying more fantasy themes or symbolic code words for previously shared fantasies. In the same way, the speaker cut the length of the speech by omitting certain supporting material. A skillful speaker using the technique of the all-purpose speech gained many advantages over the memorized speech or the speech read from manuscript. He could speak extemporaneously and directly and still express himself with aptness of language. Through repeated rehearsal, he could polish various sections of his speech as to both language and delivery. He could solve such technical problems as the proper timing and emphasis with which to deliver the punch lines of a fantasy, the best way to deliver a line for maximum emotional response, and the way to build a section of the speech to an emotional climax. Whitefield had several dramatic biblical narratives that he had worked up in this manner. One of the most effective of the dramatizations was his rendition of Abraham offering up his son Isaac. Another was the story of the return of the prodigal son.

Repeated delivery of the same sermon allowed Whitefield to polish his vocal expression as well. Oliver counted fourteen successive sentences in one sermon of Whitefield's which began with "Oh."[7] The fact that Whitefield was a master at expressing emotion through the varying vocal inflection of exclamations such as "Oh" might in part account for the difficulty that some subsequent historians have had in accounting for Whitefield's success on the basis of the pedestrian nature of his published sermons.

Whitefield's success caused many preachers in the new world to reevaluate their own speaking. Jonathan Edwards, for example, began to preach more extemporaneously after Whitefield's tour, using first long outlines, and then shorter notes. Hitchcock studied the hundreds of Edwards's sermon manuscripts in the Yale collection and found that before 1746, most were completely written out, but after that date, Edwards used outlines more often. At first, the outlines were almost as complete as the written sermons but later became more sketchy. Some of the last sermons Edwards delivered at Stockbridge were from an outline that was little more than a list of the main heads of the speech.[8] A number of zealots took Whitefield's claims to inspiration and his apparent ability to deliver an extemporaneous sermon without preparation at face value. They began to speak as the spirit moved them, without the careful preparation that had hitherto characterized most of the preaching, particularly in New England. The most radical departure of all was the emergence of lay exhorters who took the sanction of God's inspiration as sufficient justification to deliver God's word.

In short, the rhetorical tradition of the Puritan preacher, which had stressed a balance between the intellect and the emotions, first light and then heat, that had trained its speakers in Ramist logic and rhetoric and forensic disputation, that had required well-prepared sermons for the teaching of the word, was faced with a new departure in rhetoric. The new model stressed exhortations and de-emphasized the rational elements in the speech. Instead, it emphasized extemporaneous or even impromptu speeches, delivered out of a great emotional need (or inspiration) by the speaker.

After a time, the practices of Whitefield and the excesses of Davenport as well as the activities of the itinerating exhorters began to arouse opposition. The result was a debate over the proper style of preaching. Among the more important features of the debate was the revivalists' use of the *ad hominem* argument, or the attack on the ethos of the speaker as a source of truth.

The charge that a minister was a hypocrite and unconverted was, of course, a most damaging argument. For generations, it had been all but outlawed in the theological disputations of New England. The fact that the extremists in the revival party were willing to use the ultimate forensic weapon, denying the other party the right to use the authority of God, indicates the depth of the controversy. No more dramatic charge could be made, given the rhetorical context of the preaching and the debating. Charging that the opponent was unconverted emphasized the importance of the intuitive and mystical element that played a large but equal part in the rhetorical vision of the founders. By relegating reason and learning to a secondary place and focusing on the infusion of Grace, the revivalists prepared the way for lay preaching.

Soon, a number of exhorters were impressed into service by an intuitive experience that was interpreted as a "call" to preach. The exhorters took upon themselves the authority of supernatural sanction by recounting their personal conversion experiences. For some revivalists, the *call* was all the justification required for preaching. The conservatives charged the exhorters with a lack of learning and a tendency to disorder and emotionalism. Enemies of the revival like Charles Brockwell, an Anglican rector of Salem, developed their own negative fantasy type, charging that "it is impossible to relate the convulsions into which the whole Country is thrown by a set of Enthusiasts that strole about harangueing the admiring Vulgar in *extempore* nonsense."[9]

If the minister's speaking was not accompanied by the appropriate effect, adherents of the new vision would judge him dead and not sanctioned to preach the word. When rhetorical standards sanctioned by the supernatural are coupled with a colonial-wide relgious controversy which results in a new consciousness that divides congregations, the need to win souls for Christ in the next world is joined with the need to win converts in this one, and the result is a powerful motivation to strive for effective speaking.

In short, the new vision once again exalted preaching as it had been stressed in the Puritan ur-style of the sixteenth century in England.

Jonathan Edwards, whose mysticism supplied an important link in the development of a romantic, pragmatic, common, and emotional preaching that emerged as the "New Light" style, was both a preeminent scholar and a Calvinist committed to predestination. Edwards remained a transition figure because of his continuing emphasis on learning. His fantasies served as a stimulus to the new consciousness although he never fully shared it.

In an ordination sermon preached for the installation of Reverend Robert Abercrombie at Pelham in 1744, Edwards expressed the traditional balanced rhetorical theory. He took as his text the words "He was a burning and shining light" and discussed the "True Excellency of a Gospel Minister." Using a fantasy theme with John the Baptist as protagonist, Edwards asserted that "the excellency of a minister of the gospel [is] to be both a burning and a shining light." In order to be a shining light, a minister must "be one that is *able to teach*, not one that is raw, ignorant, or unlearned, and but little versed in the things that he is to teach others." He must, in addition, be "one that is well studied in divinity, well acquainted with the written word of God, mighty in the Scriptures, and able to instruct and convince gainsayers." But the good minister must be "both a burning and a shining light." It is not sufficient that the minster be learned: "When there is light in a minister, consisting in human learning, great speculative knowledge and the wisdom of this world, without a spiritual warmth and ardor in his heart, and a holy zeal in his ministrations, his light is like the light of . . . some kinds of putrifying carcasses that shine in the dark, though they are of a stinking savor."[10]

The new vision, however, reveled in fantasies celebrating mystery and pietism. The "new birth," the experimental knowledge of Christ, was an emotional and mystical experience. The more dramatic that experience, the more likely it was to be creditable. The older Puritan vision justified the speaker as the spokesman of God because he had been called by God and this fantasy type was revitalized and emphasized in the new style. The archetypal fantasy of St. Paul and the sudden conversion after a life of sin and false hopes gained new symbolic power. The moment when the speaker came to the certainty of election or salvation was recounted in detail and in ecstatic language in memoir, autobiography, and journal. Always, the experience was cast in the form of the Pauline fantasy type.

The emphasis on piety and mysticism gave the new vision a strong romantic cast, but the way the fantasies of the adherents interpreted the emotional response of the audience added a pragmatic dimension to the romanticism. When the preaching was effective, the evidence was plain for all to see in the overt response of the auditors. The new vision interpreted the drama of a preacher evoking strong visible response from an audience as God placing his seal upon the minister by providing an appropriate response to his efforts. The speaker aimed for practical or pragmatic effects in terms of visible results.

In the Great Awakening, therefore, the written sermon came under attack. Whitefield made much of the inspiration of the supernatural. In the case of Davenport, the sermons became even more impromptu and rambling, and many of the lay exhorters raised the inspiration of the moment to such heights as to justify preaching without scholarship or practice. The Separates felt that the practice of bringing a sermon manuscript into the pulpit and then praying for divine help in giving the speech was hypocrisy. They also felt that the reading of sermons was a falling-away from the practice of the early founders.[11]

Finally, the new rhetorical theory emphasized again the old Puritan rhetorical values that a good sermon was *plain, powerful,* and *searching.* A plain sermon was carefully aimed at the common understanding. A powerful sermon would move the audience. Some would be melted, others wounded. Some might cry out or see visions or be, in other ways, clearly moved by the experience. A searching sermon would "search" out every member of the congregation and force him to face up to his unregenerate state. In the tradition of Edwards, every member of the audience would be driven to place himself in the center of the preacher's condemnatory tongue-lashing until he was convinced of his sinful nature and felt the flood of guilt required to move him to action. The Reverend Thomas Prince, junior pastor of Old South Church in Boston, used the special theory associated with the new vision as the basis for his critical evaluation of Gilbert Tennent. Of Tennent's preaching, Prince remarks that it "was as searching and rousing as ever I heard."

Without regard to pleasing his hearers with polished manner or gesture, Tennent, in Prince's account, aimed "directly at their hearts and consciences, to lay open their ruinous delusions, show them their numerous, secret, hypocritical shifts in religion, and drive them out of every deceitful refuge wherein they made themselves easy." Under the searching words of the evangelist, "many who were pleased in a good conceit of themselves before, now found, to their great distress, they were only self-deceived hypocrites." With that discovery, "some at first raged" but often the "power of God so broke and humbled them" that they wanted to know more and returned to hear Tennent preach again so that "the secret corruptions and delusions of their hearts might be more discovered; and the more searching the sermon, the more acceptable it was to their anxious minds."[12]

To those who were not adherents of the new rhetorical vision and who did not understand the dynamics of consciousness-raising communication, the effectiveness of a blistering attack on the audience seemed difficult to explain. Benjamin Franklin, for example, after fulsome praise of Whitefield's effectiveness with the "Multitudes of all Sects and Denominations that attended his Sermons," went on to note that "it was matter of Speculation to me who was one of the Number, to observe the extraordinary Influence of his Oratory on his Hearers, and how much they admir'd and respected him." All of this, according to Franklin, "notwithstanding his common Abuse of them, by assuring them they were naturally *half Beasts and half Devils*."[13] "The God that holds you over the pit of hell, much as one holds a spider, or some loathsome insect over the fire, abhors you," Edwards told his audience at Enfield. "You are ten thousand times more abominable in his eyes, than the most hateful venomous serpent."[14]

In delivery, the new style of speaking was vehement and active. The evangelist and lay exhorter fought hard to bring about the evidence of audience rapport. They moved, stamped, shook their fists, and were vigorous in their manner and gesture. A kind of excited, rapid, chanting inflection characterized the "New Light" speakers. Trumbull, in an early history of Connecticut, wrote of James Davenport that "with his unnatural and violent agitations of the body" he also adopted "a strange singing tone, which mightily tended to raise the feelings of weak and undiscerning people. . . . This odd, disagreeable tuning of the voice in exercises of devotion, was caught by the zealous exhorters, and became a characteristic of the Separate teachers. The whole sect was distinguished by this sanctimonious tone."[15]

Tracy, writing in 1841, asserts that "the tone and manner of public speaking which Trumbull ascribes to him [Davenport] have been preserved, even to this day."[16] Goen traced what he called the "holy whine" in some detail and judges that the speaking style "was carried wherever the Separates went, to the northern and western frontiers, and to the South by the Separate Baptists."[17]

The rhetorical vision which emerged as the foundation for the evangelical style was, thus, primarily a modification of the older Puritan vision and deserves to be considered along with it as part of a rhetorical tradition. The major features of the vast panorama of the Protestant narrative from Genesis on to the moment of individual salvation or damnation remained the same. However, the specific details relating to the nature of communication between God and man about election to sainthood were rearranged in the new vision. More importantly, the scenic assumption of predestination began to fade as more emphasis was placed upon individual belief and an ever-willing God.

The most important of the new fantasy types for its effect upon subsequent rhetorical developments was that of the "new birth," which shifted the perspective of the participant from a deterministic context in which all that had happened had a purpose and design but in which human agency was relatively unimportant to a scenario in which human actors could make free decisions. Not only that, but with the human protagonist center stage, an individual could start anew, cast off the old personality, the old life, be a better person, and live a more satisfactory existence. The scenario of the "new birth" furnished a psychology of conversion as well as an interpretation of the most dramatic moment in an individual's life.

The revival sermons of the 1740s and 1750s were preached to cause the listener to be born again. Joseph Tracy gathered into a book some of the most important primary source materials dealing with the Great Awakening. In the preface to that collection, Tracy asserts that the key to understanding the first great American revival is the "idea of the 'new birth'."[18]

Tracy summed up the fantasy type of the "new birth" one hundred years after the Great Awakening, by which time the special rhetorical theory of the revivalists had solidified into a commonly accepted pattern. The drama consists first of a protagonist's awareness of not living as the gospel requires. The protagonist is then alarmed by the thought that he is in hourly danger of eternal death. Next, he examines his life and compares it with the Christian standard. The inevitable result of such searching is the appalling and powerful discovery of guilt—the conviction of sin. No person faces such a discovery calmly. Under deep emotion he searches for a remedy. Often he undergoes great spiritual anguish until he is filled with a conviction of salvation. Whereas he was full of guilt and miserable before, he now feels great peace and joy. Although some may take months to move through the steps, many are converted suddenly and with great emotion in a short period of time. None move gradually to sainthood without being aware of such a "new birth." When a person is born again, he is filled with the conviction and the direct experience of religion, with "experimental" religion.

The psychology of conversion dramatized in the fantasy type of the "new birth" became an important part of the rhetorical theory of American revival speakers for the next century. The revival speakers had a specific goal. They spoke for convictions and conversions. The evidence of success was quite clear. They simply counted the numbers of those saved. Counting was not difficult if the saved provided concrete evidence of their conversion by confessing, testifying, coming forward, or signing some document. Thomas Prince, Jr., edited a weekly report called *The Christian History*, which was published for two years, beginning in March of 1743. *The Christian History* was designed to chronicle the success of the revival and contained the reports of ministers who had participated. It is full of case histories of conversions, listing estimates of the total numbers of those converted in their parishes.

Tracy sums up the effect of the speaker's psychological analysis of conversion and his drive to win converts as follows:

> From beginning to end, it [the revival] all looks at practical results; it seeks to produce the phenomena of a revival; it aims to work a change in the sinner's mind, of which he will be sensible, and which others may observe. . . . in the hands of some men of a later day, it was too much biased in favor of whatever scheme promised to work well in bringing sinners under conviction. In other words, its continual regard for practical utility led some to embrace doctrines which they judged to be convenient, instead of doctrines which they had proved to be true;[19]

Edwards, one of the native wellsprings for the revival rhetoric, was not ready to give up his hard theology to accommodate the demands of a speech situation that emphasized effectiveness. He did not "embrace doctrines . . . convenient" to the demands of the speaking situation if they contrasted with his view of the truth. Clearly, Edwards's rhetorical vision was a handicap to effective revival preaching. He could, in good conscience, speak to the first step of the "new birth," namely, the searching of individual consciences to discover hypocrisy and sin. His theology was well suited for fantasies dealing with terror and hellfire, for the omnipotence of God, and for the mean, sinful, and miserable nature of man. But Edwards could not be consistent with his personal vision and still urge his audience to make a decision for Christ, for he taught with unmistakeable clarity that man was powerless to affect his own salvation. He was *completely* dependent upon God's grace for that. Why, then, speak at all?

John Wesley posed the issue with clarity in his debate with George Whitefield over the doctrine of election. Wesley argued that election was inconsistent with evangelical preaching.

> . . . then [if there is election] is all preaching vain: it is needless to them that are elected; for they, whether with preaching or without, will infallibly be saved.

Therefore, the end of preaching to save souls is void, with regard to them. And it is useless to them that are not elected; for they cannot possibly be saved; they, whether with preaching or without, will infallibly be damned. The end of preaching is therefore void, with regard to them likewise.[20]

Edwards had several theological arguments to justify revival preaching from Calvinist assumptions, and Whitefield, in his answering argument, refers to Edwards as a source of his reply. Nevertheless, Wesley's clever argument illustrates the usefulness of the dilemma for the debater contending with an opponent who had a dichotomized rhetorical vision like that of Jonathan Edwards. How could Edwards and Whitefield have avoided the horns of such an argument when their position allowed for no third alternative? Whitefield argued that "preaching of the word" was the means designed by God to bring the elect to salvation. Ministers do not know the elect from the damned and must therefore "preach promiscuously to all." Not only that, he felt, but the word may help even the damned to lead a less sinful and wicked life and thus has its uses even for them.[21]

The justification for revival preaching that grew out of the Puritan vision was primarily that, although regeneration was a free gift, a person had to seek it; one could not wait passively to be elected. In a subtle interpretive fantasy type, the vision suggested that if people earnestly sought salvation, it would not be denied them. If God made a person sensible of his or her sinfulness and the need for grace, it was a "hopeful sign" that God would elect the individual to sainthood because if God had not predestined a person for election, the individual would not find himself or herself seeking salvation.

Since the major function of the sermons was to create a state of mind where listeners would feel the compulsion to seek salvation, the regular hearing of the word and the practice of a virtuous life were the means to achieve a proper state prior to the climactic scene of individual salvation. Since preaching was portrayed as the means required in these preparatory scenes building to the climax of the individual drama, those who shared the fantasy were strongly driven to emphasize preaching.

Once again, the outsider might find the drama relatively unexciting since it is entirely predestined and all of the human protagonists are at the mercy of the arbitrary decisions of God. Yet, for the participant who shared the vision, the drama was filled with suspense and high motivation. For the individual living in the social reality of the Puritan rhetorical vision, the experiences of day-to-day living posed choices fraught with significance. Tempted to adultery, faced with the opportunity for drunkenness, feeling pride, the Puritan viewing the options from a limited human perspective may well have interpreted them as choices that he or she could make to strive to enter heaven. From the all-seeing perspective of God, the choices might be predestined—and Jonathan Edwards's elaborate argument on the freedom of the will attempted to prove that they were—but from the limited vision of the human actor, they might well function dramatically as decisions bearing upon the final salvation drama. Choosing to lead a good life was based not on a fantasy which promised salvation as a result of good works but upon a drama which interpreted such choices as the necessary steps to bring oneself into a proper state to be called should that be God's will.

In terms of the revival, even the elected need to be in a proper state to be harvested. A person needed to be convicted of total worthlessness, be debased, and express the most abject humility before the omnipotence and infinite goodness of God. The revival sermon was the means by which such conviction was attained.

Having confessed all this to God, the individual would then, if it were so predestined, be visited with the evidence of election. The evidence of election tended to fall into the pattern of the fantasy type of the Pauline conversion as modeled by the ministers themselves. Personal experience fantasy themes testifying to the thoughts, feelings, and visions of the converted provided the evidence for the examining committees which decided the validity of the election for such practical purposes as church membership. Over the years, from 1620 to 1730, the accumulated testimony as to the conversion experience became a stereotyped fantasy. The examining committees came to be less rigorous in their standards of evaluating the fantasies. With the revivals of the 1730s, however, the question of the nature of the true religious experience became, once again, an important feature of the rhetorical context of the revival.

As the revival pressed on and the temptation to evaluate communication on the grounds of effectiveness grew, the tacit assumptions of the Puritan vision in regard to predestination and the role of preaching in the salvation process were brought to the conscious attention of the communication specialists. The person who had done his or her best to "awake and fly from the wrath to come" would then, if it were so predestined, be visited with the evidence of his election. Aside from this, he could do nothing, and revival preaching could do nothing to save the sinner. Should he be worked into such a condition during the course of preaching and not receive word of election, the future had to look dim indeed. The only hope then was that he had not been sincere but rather had been deluded by Satan. He could then try to work himself into the proper state once again. No wonder members of the audience who heard the revival preachers of the Great Awakening and were "wounded" often cried out, as did those who heard Jonathan Parsons at Lyme, Connecticut, "Woe is me! What must I do?"[22]

The fact remains that to this basic question, "What must I do?" Edwards could not, consistent with his vision, give much of an answer. Having brought a person to the first stage of conversion by driving home to the individual a deep conviction of sin and guilt, he could not consistently do much more. In fact, he did very little in the way of offering a plan for salvation, and he offered but little hope. What little hope he did hold out was based upon his view of revivals. Edwards believed that God, on occasion, showered grace upon the world, causing a revival. In Edwards's estimation, the revival of 1740–1741 was such a showing of God's favor. Consequently, he told his audience at Enfield that this was "a day wherein Christ has thrown the door of mercy wide open, and stands in calling and crying with loud voice to poor sinners."[23]

But even as rigid, consistent, clear, and honest as Edwards was in refusing to adopt doctrines more suitable to the rhetorical situation faced by the revival speaking, the demands of that situation bent even his language. Little wonder, then, that the followers of the revival tradition in the next century soon shared fantasy themes and then abstracted from the themes more general fantasy types, relating to salvation, in which the scenic assumption of election was replaced by free grace. By 1835, Charles Grandison Finney was saying in his *Lectures on Revivals* that a revival was not a miracle but "a purely philosophical result of the right use of the constituted means."[24] McLoughlin judges one of the differences between Edwards and Finney was that "one believed that revivals were 'prayed down' and the other that they were 'worked up.' "[25]

In what way was Edwards's rhetoric bent by the demands of preaching for conversion? A listener untutored in theological distinctions might assume from the language that he ought to do something to achieve salvation. A careless interpretation of the Enfield sermon might find motives to believe or to do in the drama. After recounting the awful state of those "left behind at such a day," Edwards asked, "How can you rest one moment in such a condition?" A member of the audience, careless about theology, suffering a high pitch of emotional guilt, might be tempted to answer, "I cannot rest. I must be up and doing." His next question then would be, even as at Lyme, "Woe is me! What must I do?" Edwards did not answer his own rhetorical question but instead asked another: Do not the people of Enfield have souls as precious as those who live in Suffield? And he asserted that at Suffield "they are flocking" to Christ. "Flocking" is an active verb. Again, it suggests that the people who are "flocking" to Christ are up and doing something to achieve salvation. The language contains an implied metaphor to birds and gathering together into a flock, and to the unwary listener this could imply that he, too, should take wing.

A bit later, Edwards asked the young people in the congregation if they would "neglect" the opportunity to renounce youthful vanities. They had "an extraordinary" opportunity. In his final plea to the entire audience, he told them to "hearken to the loud calls of God's word." In his conclusion, he urged that "every one that is out of Christ, now awake and fly from the wrath to come."

Edwards could probably have defended every one of these statements in terms of his rhetorical vision. In a sense, each member of the audience could awake to his sin. That he could fly from God's wrath or flock to Christ is an ambiguous question open to different interpretations. Certainly, Edwards provided little of value to the hardheaded, practical member of the audience who demanded concrete directions on how to be saved. Thus, the drive for effective speech aimed at decisions—a rhetoric in which effectiveness was measured in terms of the number of those converted—created a tension between the demands of the speaking situation and the rhetorical vision of the Neocalvinists of the 1740s. The vision essentially implied that man must wait passively for the contract (covenant) to be tendered to him. But if one wanted to preach for decisions, the rhetorical situation tempted the speaker to talk as though the listener could make the decision to be saved, as though the listener could flock, or fly, and be received.

When the revival came under attack from those whose rhetorical vision emphasized the rational side of Puritanism, such as Charles Chauncey, Jonathan Edwards took up a defense of the speechmaking of the evangelicals. Whenever the basic rules of a speaking style are breeched by practitioners, those who continue to speak within the rules often respond with outrage. Thus, as one vision fades and is replaced by another which is essentially a modification or reform rather than a diametrically opposed vision, the result is a debate about rhetorical theory. When a vision arises which is antithetical to the older vision, that is, the two visions have casts of heroes and villains which are mirror images of one another and the values implied by both visions and the motivations embedded in them are diametrically opposed, there is no possibilty of debate. The new vision of the campus radicals and the "new left" of the 1960s was so diametrically opposed to the older academic vision that adherents of the two visions did not debate with one another but rather "confronted" one another. The radicals did not negotiate, that is, discuss and debate their demands with the administrations of colleges and universities; rather, they presented "non-negotiable demands." The new consciousness that emerged from the Great Awakening, however, was not based on a mirror image of the older Puritan vision but rather constituted a substantial modification of it. At the same time, the group consciousness that motivated the reaction to the revival and that was the forerunner of what, over the next hundred years, came to be the vision of Unitarianism and transcendentalism in the time of William Ellery Channing and Ralph Waldo Emerson was also only a substantial modification of the Puritan vision. Although Chauncy and Edwards differed substantially, they, nonetheless, shared enough common symbolic ground from the older vision that they could debate the rules of the newer rhetorics.

The issues raised in a debate such as the one that followed the Great Awakening about the proper rhetorical style for preaching and the way the advocates of the various positions presented their arguments serve to illuminate the essential features of the rhetorical visions undergirding the new styles.

Edwards took up a defense of the revivalists in his *Thoughts on the Revival of Religion in New England 1740*. Noting that "one thing that has been complained of" was the fact that the revivalists spoke "rather to the affections of their hearers, than to their understandings," and that the preachers of the Awakening had tried "to raise their passions to the utmost height, rather by a very affectionate manner of speaking, and a great appearance of earnestness, in voice and gesture, than by clear reasoning and informing their judgment," Edwards affirms that he believes it is profitable to "endeavor clearly and distinctly to explain the doctrines . . . and unravel the difficulties that attend them, and to confirm them with strength of reason and argumentation, and also to observe some easy and clear method and order, in their discourses, for the help of the understanding and memory." The crucial issue, however, according to Edwards, is that "the objection that is made, of affections raised without enlightening the understanding, is in a great measure built on a mistake, and confused notions that some have about the nature and cause of the affections, and the manner in which they depend on the understanding."[26] The problem is a faulty psychology. "All affections are raised either by light *in the understanding*, or by some error and delusion *in the understanding*; for all affections do certainly arise from some apprehension in the understanding."[27]

In short, Edwards argues, the understanding and the affections are not distinct and separate faculties of the mind, but are one. Here, Edwards certainly departs from the Ramist analysis of knowledge and the psychology of his age. In theory, he erases the difference between light and heat. The minister whom he praises as a "burning" and "shining" light will achieve the desired effect with the same beam. Not only that, but he poses the question not whether the affections should be raised, but whether the affections are raised in the apprehension of the truth. If they are, high emotion is desirable. The only other qualification that Edwards would insist upon is that "their affections are not raised beyond a proportion to their importance, or worthiness of affection."

Edwards sums up the new psychology and its application to preaching as follows:

> I know it has long been fashionable to despise a very earnest and pathetical way of preaching: and they only have been valued as preachers, that have shown the greatest extent of learning, and strength of reason, and correctness of method and language: but I humbly conceive it has been for want of understanding, or duly considering human nature, that such preaching has been thought to have the greatest tendency to answer the ends of preaching: and the experience of the present and past ages abundantly confirms the same.[28]

His age, according to Edwards, abounded in correct and scholarly preaching. "Was there ever an age wherein strength and penetration of reason, extent of learning, exactness of distinction, correctness of style, and clearness of expression, did so abound?" With all these fine qualities, the age was also characterized by "little sense of the evil of sin. . . . little love to God . . . and holiness of life." What was required was clear. "Our people do not so much need to have their heads stored, as to have their hearts touched; and they stand in the greatest need of that sort of preaching, that has the greatest tendency to do this."[29]

The emphasis on heart-to-heart preaching was to prove an enduring one in the history of rhetoric in America. As we have seen, it was always part of the Puritan preaching tradition, but now, with the Great Awakening, the balance between reason and emotion was not simply tipped in one direction or another but splintered into a series of emphases. From the splintering, two important and enduring rhetorical traditions emerged. As one of the most sophisticated theoreticians of the preaching with "the greatest tendency" to touch the "hearts" of the audience, Edwards deserves a place in the history of preaching.

The debate over the proper style of preaching indicates that reason, logic, and evidence played a much less important part in the new evangelical vision than they had in the Puritan rhetoric. To be sure, the minister still saw the Scriptures as the inspired revelation of God and quoted passages to prove points in theological debate, but the main avenue to salvation was a high pitch of belief which belied reason. The main rhetorical tool was exhortation. Every salvation drama fit into the same fantasy type. The protagonist had to come to realize his sin not by cold, reasonable analysis but through experimental religion, through sense and feelings. The protagonist then had to throw himself on God's mercy, take Christ as a mediator and believe. When he had done that, he received salvation and an ecstatic glorious feeling of peace.

The most important means to achieve the drama was the powerful exhortative preaching of the word of God. A searching, plain, powerful sermon was the best way to break up the "old foundations," to give the sinner a "heart wound" and bring the reluctant person to conviction of sin. Thus, the first part of a revival sermon had to be a scathing denunciation of the sinful auditor. Only when the sinner had been brought to the point of crying out, "Oh Woe is me. What must I do?" could the speaker present the "good news" about the path to salvation. The drama of salvation was a highly emotional one, and sober and industrious citizens found nothing incongruous in their falling into faints, weeping, moaning, or crying aloud because the scenario of their vision interpreted such behavior as visible evidence of supernatural forces at work.

The new rhetorical vision served to create and sustain a new rhetorical community. The powerful emotions evoked in small group sessions or in the revival meetings created a strong sense of group identity and a clear delineation of the boundaries of the community. To symbolize the uniqueness and importance of membership, the adherents referred to the participants in the vision as "brothers" and "sisters" in Christ and to outsiders by some other appellation. The visible evidence of the time of conversion and the practice of telling one's conversion experience in the form of a dramatic and emotional personal experience (nonfiction fantasy theme using the participant voice) marked the insiders from the outsiders and served to delineate the boundaries of the vision. In addition, the motives within the vision impelled the adherents to adopt a life style consonant with the scenarios of how a newly born Christian lived, and the changing life style was a further means of drawing the boundaries around the community. An individual was, thus, clearly either a participant in the new consciousness or not. One crossed over the boundaries of the vision through enacting the fantasy type of the "new birth," which was a difficult and painful crossing.

All of the features of the rhetoric that celebrated the insiders, that made the identification of members of the community clear, and that made the crossing over into participation difficult, served to provide the participants in the new vision with strong motivations for commitment to the community and to its values.

The new rhetorical vision was not attractive to a number of the learned and influential clergymen in the older settled portions of the colonies. They generally found the emphasis on emotion-evoking fantasies tasteless. They abhorred the denigration of learning. They saw those who shared the new consciousness as crude, unlearned, and repulsive. On the other hand, the evangelical vision was attractive to people living in frontier conditions without the benefit of education and some of the other niceties of manners and culture which were common along the eastern seaboard by the 1740s. The dramatizations of the vision were attractive, too, to those who were not part of the new elite in the East. Many were drawn into sympathetic participation and shared the fantasies. In New England, the Puritan saints were, in a sense, the new nobility. The new style's emphasis on emotion, denigration of learning, and growing acceptance of free grace made it attractive to those who were not a part of the new elite. The evangelical rhetoric had an incipient anti-intellectualism about it. The pragmatic edge of the evangelical vision celebrated the speaker who could deal with practical everyday affairs and the common people and saw the learned clergyman or professor, locked away in his study and devoted to scholarship, as impractical and unable to meet the difficult demands of exhorting ordinary folks. One needed no learning or education to experience the transports of the new piety.

The person living an uncultured life of hardship on the frontier or in a seaboard city could find in the sharing of the new vision a purpose for himself and his life that, ironically, functioned much in the same way as had the Puritan rhetorical vision for the well-educated but poorly born young men in Old England in the sixteenth century. For those who shared the new consciousness, an uneducated, uncultured person could be born again and have everlasting life and be better in God's eyes than the most wealthy and cultured Boston Brahmin learned in knowledge of this world but unfamiliar with experimental religion.

❧ 5

The Ungenteel Style

The bifurcation of the rhetorical styles stabilized after 1740, as did the commitment to the new revival conciousness, and many of the congregations divided over the question of preaching and the nature of conversion. Separate churches sprang up across the colonies. The religious community was divided on the revival question, and for that part committed to "heart" religion and the "new birth," there was a revival in progress somewhere during most of the years between 1740 and 1800. To be sure, the last sixty years of the eighteenth century were filled with turbulent military and political events. Religion had to fight for its place in the public concerns, along with the French and Indian war, the Revolution, the formation of the Articles of Confederation, and, subsequently, the new Federal Constitution. The Revolution was particularly distracting to the ministers. William Warren Sweet judged that "the unanimous testimony of the religious leaders of all the religious bodies following the close of the war was that there was a rising tide of iniquities fast sweeping American youth to the brink of ruin."[1] Sweet argues that there was a general irreligion after the war and that Deism, which began with the upper classes before the Revolution, became a popular position after the conflict.

Regardless of whether or not the decline of religion was actually as precipitous as it was portrayed in the fantasy themes and types of those most committed to its improvement, many ministers did feel the need to advocate greater fervor in the calm period after the adoption of the Federal Constitution. Up to the first Great Awakening, the concentration of piety in the colonies was greatest in the areas under Congregational and Presbyterian influence. In the period following, the "New Lights" moved into the most influential of the southern colonies, Virginia. Religious developments in the Old Dominion from 1740–1780 provided a seedbed for much of the consciousness creating and raising that resulted in the hot gospel that evangelized the southern and western frontier after the Revolutionary War.

In the 1740s, a number of New Light missionaries became active in Virginia. They soon aroused the ire of the authorities and found themselves embroiled with the established church and threatened with civil action. The first wave contained such New Lights as the Reverends Robinson, Roan, and Blair.

The Reverend Patrick Henry, the namesake uncle of the famous Virginia political orator, dramatized the activities of the New Lights from the Anglican rhetorical vision as follows:

[the New Lights] strive with all their might, to raise in their hearers, what they call convictions, which is thus performed. They thunder out in awful words, and new coin'd phrases, what they call the terrors of the law, cursing & scolding, calling the old people, Grey-headed Devils, and all promiscuously, Damn'd double damn'd, whose (souls?) are in hell though they are alive on earth, Lumps of hell-fire, incarnate Devils, 1000 times worse than Devils &c and all the while the Preacher exalts his voice puts himself into a violent agitation, stamping and beating his Desk unmercifully until the weaker sort of his hearers being scar'd, cry out, fall down & work like people in convulsion fits, to the amazement of spectators, and if a few only are thus brought down, the Preacher gets into a violent passion again, Calling out Will no more of you come to Christ? thundering out as before, till he has brought a quantum sufficit of his congregation to this condition, and these things are extoll'd by the Preachers as the mighty power of God's grace in their hearts, and they who thus cry out and fall down are caress'd and commended as the only penitent Souls who come to Christ, whilst they who don't are often condemn'd by the lump as hardened wretches almost beyond the reach of mercy.[2]

Henry was also disturbed by the New Light tendency to call ministers of the established clergy "strangers to the true religion."

After a short period of evangelizing, the first New Lights were harried from the colony, but they were replaced by one of the more judicious and capable dissenting ministers to serve in Virginia. Samuel Davies was ordained in 1748 by the New Light Presbytery at New Castle for the particular purpose of going to Hanover, Virginia, to preach to the people there who had petitioned for a minister. Davies was educated at the log college of the Reverend Samuel Blair at Fagg's Manor in Pennsylvania. Blair had preceded Davies to Hanover in the first wave of New Light agitation. Blair himself had been educated in the famous Neshaminy Log College of William Tennant, Jr., and was an associate of Gilbert Tennant.

While a New Light and a revivalist, Davies was much more like Jonathan Edwards as a preacher than he was in the mold of a James Davenport. Indeed, upon Edwards's death, Samuel Davies accepted the position of President of Princeton. His published sermons resemble Edwards's speeches in their studied eloquence and the balance between heat and light. In a letter to Thomas Gibbons, Davies wrote that only "once in three or four months I preach in some measure as I could wish." On those rare occasions, he preached "as in the sight of God, and as if I were to step from the pulpit to the supreme tribunal." He echoes the typical New Light rhetorical standards when he describes those moments when he is satisfied with his speaking, for then he feels his subject, melts into tears, or shudders with horror as he denounces "the terrors of the Lord." At such moments, Davies writes, "I glow, I soar in sacred extacies."[3]

Davies approached the authorities in Virginia through proper channels and in a more persuasive way than the agitators who had preceded him. He was licensed to preach and thus established a dissenting church with legal sanctions in Hanover and supplied several other congregations in the neighborhood. When he was accused of itinerating, however, he denied the charge, arguing that he was simply meeting the needs of a sparsely settled community. Davies' revival meetings were seldom characterized by emotional frenzies or ecstasies.[4]

While the New Light Presbyterians were establishing a beachhead for their dissenting church under the leadership of Davies, the Baptists in Virginia divided on the revival question into the "Regulars" and the "Separates." The Separate Baptists were zealous, and their meetings were frequently noisy. Physical symptoms of the effects of revival methods were prominent in the Separate meetings: excessive trembling, jerking, falling, barking, crying, and rolling on the ground marked some of their meetings. Daniel Fristoe attended a meeting where he saw "multitudes, some roaring on the ground, some wringing their hands, some in extacies [sic], some praying, some weeping; and others so outrageous cursing and swearing that it was thought that they were really possessed of the devil."[5] The Separate Baptists also practiced the "holy whine" when preaching and were vehement and impassioned in their manner of delivery.

The Separate Baptists made strong attacks on the established church. They attacked the pleasure-loving Anglican ministers as well as infant baptism. The Regular Baptists, on the other hand, were much calmer in their religious observances and applied for licenses to preach under the Toleration Act. As a result, the bulk of the religious persecutions during the colonial period in Virginia centered on the Separate Baptists.

The revival excesses of the Separate Baptists were used by the defenders of the established church as evidence against the New Lights in much the same way that Davenport's example was used against Whitefield and Edwards. The record indicates, however, that at least after Davies appeared in Virginia, the New Lights conducted their revivals in a calmer and less violent manner than the Separate Baptists.

The end of the Revolutionary War found the Presbyterians and Congregationalists the largest and most influential denominations in the new country. Both of these old established religious communities had wealth, learning, able leadership, and tradition on their sides. The Anglicans were discredited by their association with the mother country and the fact that some of the ministers had been Tories during the war. Despite their strength, the Congregationalists were divided and fell to contending among themselves after the war. Hudson reported that although southern New England lost almost 800,000 inhabitants to the West between 1790 and 1830, "much of the Congregational blood in the newer regions was flowing through other denominational veins."[6]

Oddly enough, the Presbyterians and Congregationalists did not prosper as one might expect, given their resources. The religious energy of the country expressed itself in the rapidly growing Baptist and Methodist communities. Many of the New Side Presbyterians and separate churches of the Great Awakening were absorbed by the Baptists. While the Baptists had grown in social acceptability and now counted people of education and wealth among their numbers, their strongest appeal was still to the common people, whom they addressed with their aggressive revivalism. In 1790, there were 688 Baptist churches, 710 ordained ministers, many more licensed preachers, and a membership of 65,000. The success of the Baptists on the frontier is indicated by the fact that by 1810, there were fifteen Baptist associations in Kentucky, consisting of 286 churches and 16,650 members. By the same year, the Baptists had six associations of 102 churches and 11,693 members in Tennessee.

The Methodist societies, nominally a part of the Anglican community, thrived in the postwar religious competition. The Methodists adopted a system of itinerating lay exhorters and ministers and a circuit-riding technique that proved most effective when coupled with a revivalistic rhetoric. While the Anglicans lost members, the Methodists set up a separate establishment with a rigidly structured episcopal organization and prospered so much that, although they only had 5,000 members in 1776 and but 10,000 in 1781, they grew to approximately 57,600 in 1790. By 1820, the Methodists had a strong base in New York and western Pennsylvania, had moved into the Ohio valley and the seaboard areas of the South, had established themselves in Kentucky, and were making beginnings in New England. They were, by 1820, the largest American denomination, even larger than the Baptists.

The third great denomination on the frontier was an indigenous development growing out of the evangelical tradition in the Presbyterians. Known ultimately as "Christians" or "Disciples of Christ," this denomination was formed to achieve unity among Christians who believed in the practice of the primitive church and a strict adherence to New Testament precedents. The emphasis was upon "experienced" Christians. The movement spread in the South and Northeast. It was active in Virginia and Kentucky as well as in Vermont and Pennsylvania. The Christians promulgated their doctrine with the same basic rhetoric as the Baptists and the Methodists. The most important leader of this denomination was Alexander Campbell of Pennsylvania.

In the contest with the hosts of the devil for the future of the new republic, the posterity of Whitefield and Edwards turned to what Winthrop Hudson has called "the tried and proved expedient of revivalistic preaching."[7] Goaded by what they judged to be a general decline of religion and piety, evidenced by the growth of Deism, and the lack of religious instruction for the new immigrants to the frontier, the preachers of the evangelical style continued to preach the "new birth" and tried to be both burning and shining lights. While they had continued success in certain regions in the period from 1745 to 1775, it was only after the successful rebellion against the mother country that their efforts were rewarded with such a widespread increase in interest and commitment as to justify comparison with the awakening of 1740–1743. The Baptists and the Methodists had continued to preach revival sermons with considerable success in the intervening years, but this base increased during the 1790s revivals among the Congregationalists in New England and among the Presbyterian students at Hampden-Sydney and Washington Colleges in Virginia. These student revivals brought a number of young men into the Presbyterian ministry and moved into the Carolinas, Kentucky, and Tennessee, arousing an excitement which culminated, in 1800, in camp-meeting revivals in Logan County, Kentucky. The camp meeting became a revival institution, particularly for the Methodists.

Soon, Kentucky and Tennessee, Carolina, Virginia, and Western Pennsylvania were caught up in a considerable awakening of religious enthusiasm. Central and western New York experienced a revival at about the same time, and in 1802, there was a student revival at Yale. The religious excitement of the early 1800s continued on into the 1820s and found its expression in New York under the leadership of Charles Grandison Finney.

From 1785 until 1835, one of the major rhetorical traditions—romantic pragmatism—which emerged from the Puritan sermon under the impact of Whitefield, Edwards, Davenport, and the itinerating ministers and lay exhorters of the 1740s, was tested in the crucible of religious freedom and rapidly expanding new nation with its mobile and rootless population. The wave of religious revivals and the increase in the influence and membership of the denominations practicing that form of persuasion testified to its effectiveness, and this same effectiveness was often used, as it had been in the first Great Awakening, as its justification.

As the new style evolved, it was characterized by a growing emphasis on the romantic and pragmatic features within the revival rhetoric of the 1740s. The rhetorical tradition of romantic pragmatism was, by 1830, a widespead and influential persuasive style in the religious and cultural life of the United States. It was, in secularized form, to furnish the vision which sustained the great wave of reform rhetoric that began to dominate public opinion in the three decades prior to the Civil War, either as a successful means to conversion or as a spur to a counterrhetoric.

The rhetorical tradition of romantic pragmatism was a broad and general impulse characterizing several large religious communities. The communities shared a strong romantic impulse. They celebrated nature and the *Naturkind*, the common man, and freedom of the spirit. They preferred content to form, feeling to manners, and stressed the importance of imagination, emotion, introspection, and intuition. In addition, the communities were pragmatic in their emphasis upon practicality, usefulness, and the importance of effectiveness in evaluating the success or failure of a speech. The style was Protestant and proselyting. Many of the competing traditions were less zealous, less widespread, less influential, and often tended to appeal more to the wealthy, the educated, and the cultured.

Within the broad stream of romantic pragmatism, several nuances of style evolved so that by 1830, one could discern several wings to the rhetorical tradition. The New Light or left wing of the revival rhetoric became, in the theory and practice of such speakers as the Methodist circuit riders and the Baptist farmer preachers, what I call the ungenteel style. The right wing continued much in the style of the Puritanism of Jonathan Edwards and was illustrated by the practice of the eastern revivalist, Lyman Beecher. The center of the tradition, particularly of the Presbyterian heirs of the New Light rhetoric as illustrated by the theory and practice of Charles Grandison Finney, became the foundation of the reform rhetoric. But since the move from sacred rhetoric to secular in the rise of reform speaking was much influenced by the ungenteel wing and since that wing sustained the largest of the religious communities of the country, my purpose in this chapter is to describe the practice of the left wing. The next chapter will then examine the rhetorical vision that characterized the ungenteel speakers, including its associated theory and criticism.

The population of the late eighteenth and early nineteenth century in the United States was on the move, and the more aggressive of the evangelical communities found the itinerating practice of Whitefield and Davenport useful to meet their needs in the South and West. The Methodists, for example, systematized the itinerating into circuits and soon developed a technique for staffing and supplying a number of Methodist classes with itinerating ministers. Methodist circuit riders gained the reputation of appearing on the frontier shortly after the Indian scouts and often before permanent shelters were erected. Apprentice preachers were assigned to an established circuit rider and gained their speech training by working with and watching the experienced preacher. The apprentice and his mentor talked of the craft, and the student often found himself exhorting or leading prayer meetings under the eye of his instructor. The rigors of the circuit assured that only men who were physically strong, practical, and zealous would survive.

The Baptist equivalent of the Methodist circuit rider was the farmer preacher. Like the circuit rider, the Baptist farmer preacher was often an uneducated layman licensed to preach on the basis of a "call." He usually worked a farm for his personal support and donated his services to the church. On occasion, in the sparsely settled frontier sections, he itinerated from place to place to serve several congregations.

As the rush to the frontier got underway, even the Presbyterians modified their educational requirements for the preparation for preaching. Three major revolts against Calvinism on the frontier stemmed from Presbyterians. One began in Logan and Cumberland county in south central Kentucky, another one two hundred miles north in Bourbon County, Kentucky, and a third in southwestern Pennsylvania, western Virginia, and eastern Ohio. The first erupted under the preaching of James McGready; the second was associated with the speaking of Barton W. Stone; the third originated under the leadership of Thomas Campbell, although his son Alexander ultimately played a more important role. All of the anti-Calvinist impulses were associated with highly emotional preaching and audience effects. Barton W. Stone and James

McGready were frontiersmen without college training. The tendency to sanction the use of lay exhorters that began in the 1740s was, thus, institutionalized by many of the revival groups in the years following the Revolutionary War.

The Baptists of the southern and western frontiers preached in much the same way as the Methodists. Particularly those ministers who moved from the persecutions of the eastern states tended to reject clerical formalities and ignore educational qualifications. One Mississippi Hardshell Baptist group was so aggressively against an educated ministry that it challenged "the learned world to show any divine authority for sending a man to school after God has called him into the ministry." Walter Brownlow Posey, in his study of the Baptist frontier preacher, judged that "an education could actually be a serious handicap and impair rather than add to the ability of a Baptist preacher. In a region where the prevailing illiteracy was unduly high, it is little wonder that many churches did not want an educated minister to use "'high-falutin' words to render them uncomfortable.'"[8] What the early Baptists wanted were preachers "raised up" by the call to preach. The Baptists relied heavily on personal experience fantasy themes rather than book learning for the content of a good sermon. Jeremiah Bell Jeter, recalling his youth in Bedford, Virginia, characterized the preaching of the early nineteenth century as evangelical. He wrote that it was "confused in arrangement, meagre in thought, obscure, ungrammatical and coarse in style, and vociferous and awkward in delivery; but, with few exceptions, it disclosed, with more or less distinctness and force, the atonement of Christ and the necessity of regeneration." Many sermons dramatized the conversions, sorrows, conflicts, and perplexities of a soul as it passed from death to life in the manner of *Pilgrim's Progress*. Jeter remembered little variety in the preaching; the typical sermon "began with the fall of man, touched on the principle doctrines of revelation, gave a Christian's experience, conducted him safely to heaven, and wound up with the resurrection of the dead, the general judgement, the retribution of eternity, and an application of the subject."[9]

Many of the sermons were an hour and a half to three hours in length. The preacher often "spiritualized" his text. Jeter discusses several sermons in which the minister took a plain passage of Scripture and by imaginative exegesis drew forth lessons as quaint as interesting. One preacher took as his text "Wherefore, gird up the loins of your mind," and performing the exegesis on the word *loins*, which he confused with the word *lines*, he then partitioned his discourse around various kinds of lines such as the lines used by carpenters, the division lines of the surveyor, stage coach lines, lines used to guide unruly teams, and so forth.[10]

Finally, Jeter recalled that much of the preaching was "uttered in a monotonous, singing tone." He felt that among "a plain, uncritical people" the singing tone had "a wonderful mastery over the sympathies." Many ministers were adept at intoning sermons. Jeter recounted a personal experience with a parishioner who told him that he was the greatest preacher the man had ever heard. When Jeter pressed him for details, the parishioner responded with, "You have *most the mournfulest voice* of any man I ever did hear."[11]

A closer examination of a practitioner of the ungenteel tradition will provide the details to clarify the practice of the ministers. Baptist representatives would serve my purpose as well, but I shall select a famous Methodist preacher with a legendary reputation in his own time. Many a fantasy theme of the Methodist community related to the heroic adventures of Peter Cartwright. Cartwright came to symbolize the circuit riders with all his adventuresome life and his strength and pugnacity.

Cartwright was born in Virginia in 1785 but soon moved to Kentucky. The wilderness was unsettled and the dangers of the frontier still very present when young Cartwright grew up. Cartwright's autobiography outlines his conversion experience as typical of the Pauline fantasy type. He was, "naturally a wild, wicked boy, and delighted in horse-racing, card-playing, and dancing." Somewhere around 1800 or 1801, so he testified, some Presbyterian ministers held a sacramental meeting in Cane Ridge, Kentucky. The Cane Ridge meeting was one of the most famous of the early camp meetings, a spontaneous combustion of piety that showered sparks on the entire region and became the prototype for subsequent camp meetings. Baptist, Methodist, and Presbyterian ministers cooperated in the meeting. The session lasted for weeks and the emotional excesses, the crying, jumping, jerking, and fainting exercises, surprised many of the sponsors. The meeting continued night and day, stands were erected for the preachers, and sometimes three, four, or more preachers would be speaking at the same time at different places on the camp grounds.

Cartwright attended one of the meetings resulting from the Cane Ridge revival. It was called by Presbyterians, but in the spirit of the frontier, John Page, a Methodist, was invited to participate. When the church was too small to hold the many who came to the meeting, a stand was erected in a grove nearby. People came from long distances in their wagons, bringing food and sleeping on the ground or in the wagons. Many stayed for several days. Cartwright maintained that "the power of God was wonderfully displayed; scores of sinners fell under the preaching, like men slain in mighty battle; Christians shouted aloud for joy." He participated in the protracted meetings, and on Saturday, he accompanied "weeping multitudes" to the front of the stand and bowed in prayer. As he was struggling with his soul, "an impression was made" on his mind as though a voice said, "Thy sins are all forgiven thee." Cartwright saw "divine light" that flashed all around him and "unspeakable joy sprung up in my soul." When he arose to his feet and looked about him he really seemed to be in heaven. Even the "trees, the leaves on them" seemed to be praising God.[12] Cartwright was approximately sixteen at the time, and his education consisted of a short period of time at Beverly Allen's boarding school, but in Cartwright's words, "my teacher was not well-qualified to teach correctly, and I made but small progress. I, however, learned to read, write, and cipher a little, but very imperfectly."[13] Like so many of his colleagues his main justification for the ministry was the dramatic and powerful experience of religion, which divided his life—the first part when he was a wicked gambling, horse-racing, drinking youth, and the second when he was a saved and saintly man.

In May of 1802, Cartwright was given a license to exhort. Such a license, given by the Elders of the Methodist Church, was the first step toward the ministry. Exhorters were allowed to speak to the class and urge them to repent and lead better lives. They were allowed practically all the freedom of a minister except that they could not take a text and expound the gospel. Only a fully licensed minister was given the privilege of teaching. Cartwright began with a large circuit that included parts of Kentucky and Tennessee, and as his career continued, he rode his rounds in Indiana, Ohio, and Illinois. He moved to Illinois in 1824 to avoid the evils of slavery. In 1828 and 1832, he was elected to the Illinois General Assembly, defeating Abraham Lincoln in the latter election. He died in September 1872. By the time of his death, he was a legendary American folk hero, and the fantasy themes of that legend provided a great part of the authority or ethos of the uneducated minister on the frontier, whether he was Baptist, Methodist, or Disciple of Christ.

We have very few sermon manuscripts from Cartwright or any of the other circuit riders because they did not believe in writing out sermons. The itinerating circuit riders had an opportunity, however, like Whitefield, to deliver the same sermon over and over again and thus polish up their supply of illustrations. That they were inveterate users of personal experience fantasy themes is sufficiently illustrated by the spate of autobiographical and biographical sketches that flowed from the presses of the Methodist Book Concern in Cincinnati. These documents are studded with personal-experience, nonfiction fantasy themes in which the narrator is usually a participant in the dramatic action and quite often the hero. The speakers often artfully designed the fantasy themes so that they would point up a moral lesson or a religious position. Clearly, many of the narratives recounted in biographies, memoirs, and sketches were honed and polished by repeated telling at prayer meetings and in sermons. They are, thus, good sources for the fantasies which chained through the rhetorical community, and I have drawn on them in the absence of sermon manuscripts.

A typical example is furnished by Peter Cartwright's autobiography, which is largely composed of statistics relating to the growth of the church, arguments against heresies, and personal experience fantasies. Among the many narratives that Cartwright includes in his autobiography, one relating an incident of sinful young people teasing the old preacher is typical of the rhetorical flavor of many of the circuit riders' autobiographies. Cartwright recalled a day in Springfield, Illinois, when his excellent "racking" pony had the "stiff complaint." He dropped in at a local store and saw two young men and a girl who were strangers to him. They did not speak, and after making his purchases, Cartwright mounted his lame horse and started for home. After several miles, he came upon a light wagon drawn by a good team of horses. The wagon was covered, but since the day was pleasant, the top was rolled up. Cartwright noticed that the three young people from the store were riding in the wagon. As he approached, they began to sing with great vim some Methodist camp-meeting songs. Then, the girl began to shout, "Glory to God! Glory to God!" One of the boys answered "Amen! Glory to God!"

At first, their performance was so good that Cartwright thought they had been across the Sangamon River, where a camp meeting was then in progress, had gotten religion and were happy. When Cartwright came closer, the girl began to sing and shout again. One young man fell down and cried out to God for mercy. The others began shouting at the top of their voices, saying such things as "Glory to God! another sinner's down." They then began to exhort and say to the fallen man, "Pray on, brother; pray on, brother; you will soon get religion." The man who was down then jumped up and shouted "God has blessed my soul. Halleluiah! halleluiah! Glory to God!" Cartwright felt like riding up and joining in the songs and shouts of joy from the happy members of the wagon but when he came still closer he could tell from "some glances of their eyes at each other" that all "was not right." They were carrying on this way to mock him and "sacred things." He reined in his horse and tried to drop behind them but they slowed down and the driver changed places with the "saved" boy and fell to the wagon bed and the whole performance was repeated. Cartwright was now angry and toyed with the idea of riding up and horsewhipping the two young men but decided not to because of the presence of a woman. When Cartwright spurred his horse and tried to get ahead of them, they cracked the whip on their own strong team and kept up with him. Thus they proceeded, continuing the shouting and parody of a Methodist meeting.

While he was being pestered in this fashion, Cartwright remembered a big mudhole some distance up the road: "It was a long one, and dreadful deep mud, and many wagons had stuck in it." He also remembered that there was a small path that wound through the brush to avoid the mudhole. He decided that when they approached the mud he would take the bridle path and put the spurs to his horse since the wagon could not go through the mud very quickly and in this way he would escape. The mudhole was particularly hazardous because to the side of the deep mud in the center was a stump some two feet high. To negotiate the mudhole successfully, a wagon had to approach the stump as closely as possible to avoid the deep hole in the center.

Cartwright followed his plan, entered the bridle path, and spurred his horse. The driver of the wagon, seeing that Cartwright was escaping, cracked his whip and put his horses at high speed. They were going so rapidly that they did not see the stump on the right. The front wheel struck the stump, the wheel mounted the stump, and the wagon tipped over. The two men leaped away from the wagon and landed up to their waists in the mud. The girl, who was dressed in white, landed on "all fours," her arms went into the mud up to her armpits, and her mouth and face were stuck in the mud. As the young men helped her up, Cartwright wheeled and returned to "see the fun." He stood in his stirrups and shouted, "Glory to God! Glory to God! Halleluiah! another sinner's down! Glory to God! Halleluiah! Glory! Halleluiah!"

After Cartwright had his revenge of shouting over them he said, "Now, you poor, dirty, mean sinners, take this as a just judgment of God upon you for your meanness, and repent of your dreadful wickedness; and let this be the last time that you attempt to insult a preacher; for if you repeat your abominable sport and persecutions, the next time God will serve you worse, and the devil will get you."

A bit later in his autobiography Cartwright reports that, "at one of those prosperous camp-meetings . . . I had the great pleasure to see all three of these young people converted to God. I took them into the Methodist Church, and they went back to Ohio happy in God."[14]

Whatever corroboration there may be for the story, as Cartwright developed it in his autobiography with descriptions of the characters, dialogue, and story line, it was a well-tooled fantasy theme designed to lure the listener into sharing the fantasy and to build the ethos of the speaker, hold the audience's interest, and make a number of persuasive points. Cartwright was clearly the hero of the drama. He was minding his own business and buying a few items in the store when he saw the three young people. The first complication of the story was that his usually fine and speedy horse was lame. The old preacher was mocked and teased by the frivolous young people, who had a fine set of horses and a good wagon; the girl was dressed all in white, which suggests a considerable elegance and pretension. In their wickedness, they were out for sport. Still, their mockery, which Cartwright described in detail with appropriate dialogue, was funny. No matter what opinion his listeners might have had of Methodists, they could appreciate the histrionics of the young people. Cartwright tried to overcome his problem by dropping back, but they would not let him. He then tried to run away from them, but the lameness of his horse was an obstacle to that plan. Next, he considered horse-whipping, but the presence of a lady complicated that solution. Finally, he recalled the mudhole. He laid his plan; while they had to slow down to negotiate the mudhole, he would get away despite the lameness of his horse, for the bridle path was too small for the wagon to follow. Then came the climactic moment. Cartwright put his plan into motion. He dashed around the mudhole, but the young people now took action of their own; quite in character with what we know of them from their previous actions, they recklessly decided to catch him. In graphic language, he described their overturning wagon, the flight into the mudhole, and the young lady in her white finery up to her armholes in the mud.

Finally came the dramatic reversal as Cartwright stood in his stirrups and threw back the very words they had used to taunt him: "Another sinner down!" In the end, Cartwright personally saw the three converted at a camp meeting and safe and happy in the Methodist church. Perhaps Cartwright is correct in his facts and the incident happened as he reported it. If Cartwright did not embroider the events in order to increase their drama and impact, nature did, on this occasion, emulate the art of the storyteller, because all of the elements of the well-made short story are present in the tale.

The fantasy theme of the sinful and thoughtless young people is but one of a host of such stories in Cartwright's recollections: Cartwright arguing down the Baptist minister at a camp meeting, Cartwright besting a learned medical doctor in theological dispute, and Cartwright outwitting a rough who challenges him to a fight at the camp meeting. Each fantasy theme has Cartwright as a hero, and there is a sinner of some sort—hypocrite, heretic, drunkard, or agnostic—as antagonist. Many of the anecdotes contain conflict, the suspenseful climax, and Cartwright carrying the day to the successful conclusion of converting the sinner.

Seldom is Cartwright bested. Only once does his autobiography hint that he may have met his match in theological dispute. Early in his career, he was given a circuit near Marietta, Ohio, which was settled by a colony of Yankees. The circuit had a bad reputation for the Methodists. Cartwright heard that the Yankees "could not bear loud and zealous sermons, and they had brought on their learned preachers with them, and they read their sermons, and were always criticizing us poor backwoods preachers." In the first Methodist family he visited, he found a lady who was a thorough Universalist. Cartwright said "she was a thin-faced, Roman-nosed, loquacious Yankee, glib on the tongue, and you may depend on it, I had a hard race to keep up with her, though I found it a good school, for it set me to reading my Bible."[15]

Cartwright was not alone. Another circuit rider, William Henry Milburn, recounted the events leading up to his appointment as chaplain to the Congress when he rode a river boat and discovered a number of drunken, carousing, gambling congressmen on board. He determined to make a public rebuke of their sins when the captain asked him to hold Sunday services. Amazingly, they did not resent his castigation but offered him the post of Chaplain to Congress.[16]

Finley, in his *Sketches of Western Methodism*, recounts as bloody and wild a tale of Indian warfare, hand-to-hand combat, and bloodshed as any contemporary motion picture scenario or television script can afford. To illustrate how the chief, Rhon-Yan-Ness, was like Saul of Tarsus, who changed from an enemy to a courageous fighter for Christianity, Finley recounts the adventures of Adam Poe, a heroic figure, who, with seven other white men, took to the trail of a band of renegade Wyandotts. The leader of the Indian band was an immense chief named Big Foot, and the subsequent encounter was full of wrestling, musket misfiring, tomahawking, and scalping.[17]

The dramatic fantasy theme full of action and simple characters, playing out a plot that often ended in victory for the good Methodists and illustrated a point of theology or morality, served the frontier preacher well, and their chaining fantasies helped create a new consciousness that celebrated the frontier experience. In short, not all of the western myth was a creation of subsequent generations looking back on the era of settlement and adventure from the quiet security of an urban culture and celebrating their ancestors by glorifying the cowboys and river boatmen of the nineteenth century. Some of it was created by those who lived it in their rhetoric as they proceeded about their adventures. For example, Milburn, in his *Ten Years of Preacher Life*, published in 1859, was already contributing to the legend of the keelboat men, including that of Mike Fink, the best shot of them all. He quotes his friend Col. T. B. Thorpe to the effect that when the boatmen who pushed the boats up the Mississippi had a moment of repose in camp, one would usually leap to a bit of high ground like a "game-cock" and roll up his sleeves and challenge the assembly as follows:

> I'm from the Lightning Forks of Roaring River. I'm *all* man, save what is wild cat and extra lightning. I'm as hard to run against as a cypress snag. I never back water. Look at me—a small specimen, harmless as an angle worm—a remote circumstance, a mere yearling. Cock-a-doodle-doo. I did hold down a buffalo bull and tar off his scalp with my teeth; but I can't do it now—I'm too powerful weak, *I am*. . . . I'm the man that, single handed, towed the broad horn over a sand-bar! the identical infant who girdled a hickory by smiling at the bark, and if any one denies it, let him make his will, and pay the expenses of a funeral. I'm the genuine article, tough as bull's hide, keen as a rifle. I can out-swim, out-swar, out-jump, out-drink, and keep soberer than any man at Catfish Bend. I'm painfully ferochus, I'm spiling for some one to whip me—if there's a creeter in this diggin' that wants to be disappointed in trying to do it, let him yell—whoop hurra![18]

The circuit-riding preacher developed the art of storytelling to a high level of effectiveness. Lucius Davis wrote in the preface of a fictionalized treatment, *Life in the Itinerancy*: "Let no one affirm that this is a work of fiction," because "every incident here narrated has its basis in facts which may be abundantly quoted."[19] Davis portrayed a fantasy theme of a controversy between an itinerating minister and some of his disgruntled parishioners. One said to the minister, "I wish you would be a little more practical in your sermons." When the minister asked what he should discuss, the brother responded, "Discuss! I wouldn't have you discuss anything. It ain't discussion we want. It's something to stir us up. We have got light enough, give us a little more heat." The minister reminded him that the sermon on the previous Sunday had been on the necessity of the "new birth." Would not that qualify as a practical subject?

"Well, yes,—not exactly, though. We need exhortation, with startling incidents and anecdotes for illustrations. Why, one of Brother Bacon's anecdotes will accomplish more in a revival than all the rest of his sermon."[20]

The rise of personal-experience fantasy themes to a place of great importance in the speechmaking of the religious and reform speakers in this country is an important factor in their rhetoric. In her study of English preaching from 1640 to 1670, Caroline Richardson found that "compared with the English sermons of preceding centuries, the seventeenth-century pulpit discourse made little use of 'exempla.'" While she found much quotation from classical authorities she found little of the "informal, colloquial 'I knew a man who . . .' or 'There was a woman that . . .'" She discovered that "there are no 'good stories' of timely interest and pleasantly personal as may be read on page after page of sixteenth-century sermons." She accounts for this lack of narrative by referring to the fact that the style of the day emphasized "not narration, but analysis and unexpected figures."[21]

The seventeenth-century New England sermon also contained few anecdotes and personal-experience fantasy themes. But from the time of Whitefield, who did a masterful job of using narrative techniques in dramatizing his message, until the mid-nineteenth century, the personal-experience fantasy grew in prominence as a speech technique.

The personal-experience and the biblical narrative came handy to the uneducated minister of the postrevolutionary times. Without the resources of scholarship, the Peter Cartwrights of the early 1800s turned to the Bible and to their personal experiences for speech material.

The lay exhorter often began his career as a preacher dramatizing his personal conversion experience. The use of fantasy themes and particularly personal-experience narratives was modeled after a religious prototype that gave them a greater sanction than a simple secular dramatization and a larger purpose then merely catching the interest of the audience. Edward Eggleston had, for a time, been a circuit rider, and in his novel *The Circuit Rider*, a young convert with little experience as an exhorter is pressed to preach because the old minister to whom he is apprenticed is waylaid by bullies. Although the preacher batters his two attackers, breaking the ribs of one and the nose of the other, he receives a blow on the jaw that makes it impossible for him to preach. The young apprentice is eager to try his hand at preaching, but he is also very frightened of the great responsibility. The old preacher advises the young man to take his Bible into the woods and pray in preparation for his sermon. When the young exhorter comes back to the cabin, he is appalled at what he finds. "The house, the yard, the fences, were full of people." A chair is placed in the doorway so he can speak both to the crowd within the log house and to those in the yard. Seeing the young man's fright, the circuit rider leans over and tells him, "If you get confused, tell your own experience." Eggleston added that "the early preacher's universal refuge was his own experience. It was a sure key to the sympathies of the audience."[22]

Dramatizing his own conversion experience was an important part of the lay minister's speech training. Recounting the details of his conversion enabled him to draw about him the sanction of the supernatural for his call to preach. Since he was telling of his own deep mystical experience, he was able to clothe his feelings in unstructured but emotional words. It also allowed him to forget himself and his stage fright and speak with "freedom." The connotations of the word "freedom" for the early frontier preacher are somewhat difficult to capture. Clearly, for the speakers of the Methodist rhetorical vision, the term had a highly charged meaning. When a speaker forgot himself and swung free, the audience often began to melt, to shout, to fall on the floor. Speaking became a chanting religious incantation, and as the listeners gave evidence of their emotional sharing of the fantasies, as in the days of 1740, the spirit of God seemed to be among them. Thus, the diaries, journals, and memoirs of the circuit-riding Methodists often refer to a particularly effective sermon as one in which they were able to speak "with freedom."

The artful fantasy theme was also well adapted to the speaker's purposes and to the situation in which he spoke. Fighting for converts in an environment of religious pluralism, driven by a desire to achieve a large church membership (Cartwright always reports the increase in size of the Methodist church at the time of each conference), forced to hold the audience's attention, preaching a gospel of high emotion, the preachers found the story with its potential for arousing pathos and holding interest well adapted to their needs. Not only that, but since they emphasized extemporaneous speaking, eye-to-eye, close to the audience, they could watch the effect of what they said, and since the audience often interrupted the speaker to shout "Halleluiah" or "Amen, Brother," they soon discovered the rhetorical techniques that worked to draw people into fantasy sharing. For a rhetorical community whose vision included a powerful proselyting fantasy type, the power of dramatization for consciousness raising was most important.

For the unlettered and unpolished members of the audience who had little appreciation for the subtle niceties of biblical exegesis and for sophisticated wordplay, the dramatic narrative held considerable charm. The fantasy theme was easy to follow; it contained a hero, and there were villains or the forces of evil to overcome. The conflict between good and evil created suspense. The listeners could empathize with the mother who lost a daughter, with the minister harassed by misguided and mischievous youngsters, or with the white man fighting in mortal hand-to-hand combat with Chief Big Foot.

The colloquial and vigorous practitioners of the ungenteel tradition in the early nineteenth century developed the Puritan practice of the searching sermon to a high level of vituperative perfection and, thus, justly deserve the label *ungenteel*. They aimed to humble their audience, to break up their listeners' foundations, and reveal their mean sinful natures. Where Whitefield called his auditors half men and half beasts, and Edwards compared them to spiders and other loathsome insects, the uneducated preachers of the hot gospel systematically took the "hide off" their enemies and their auditors.

In *The Circuit Rider*, Eggleston describes a camp-meeting scene in which a group of rowdies began to harass the preacher. (The scenario of drunken rowdies having fun with the preacher only to be bested by his violence, his wit, or by the will of God was so common it can be thought of as a fantasy type.) An old circuit rider leaped to his feet and began to exhort in a violently aggressive style. He started with the "true old Homeric epithets of early Methodism." He exploded the epithets like bomb-shells. "You are hair-hung and breeze-shaken over hell," he cried. "You'll go to hell . . . and when you get there your ribs will be nothing but a gridiron to roast your souls in!"[23]

Vice and sin tended to be obvious, loud, and crude. Drunkenness and fornication were high on the list as were blasphemy and profanity. The frontier preacher met sin with righteous invective. Even the smaller foibles of the congregation were treated with the same direct castigation. The fantasy theme of circuit rider James Axley's rebuke of a tobacco chewer crops up several times in the recollections of early Methodists, suggesting that it probably chained through small groups of preachers at quarterly meetings and probably was retold in many sermons. Axley, according to the scenario of the fantasy, sat in church on one occasion while another minister delivered the sermon and then arose, not to exhort but to "administer a rebuke for improper conduct" which he observed during the meeting. After chastizing a number of members of the audience (including a teenage girl for the worldliness of her bonnet), he climaxed his rebuke with the following diatribe:

> Now, I do hope, when any gentleman comes to church who can't keep from using tobacco during the hours of worship, that he will just take his hat and use it for a spit-box. You all know we are Methodists. You all know that our custom is to kneel when we pray. Now, any gentleman may see, in a moment, how exceedingly inconvenient it must be for a well-dressed Methodist lady to be compelled to kneel down in a puddle of tobacco spit.[24]

A similar fantasy theme in which James Craven was the protagonist took place during a sermon in Virginia when he reportedly said:

> Now here are a great many of you professors of religion; you are sleek, fat, good-looking, yet there is something the matter with you—you are not the thing you ought to be. Now you have seen wheat . . . which was very plump, round, and good-looking to the eye; but when you weighed it you found it only came to forty-five or forty-eight pounds to the bushel. There was something the matter. It should be from sixty to sixty-three pounds. Take a grain of that wheat between your thumb and your finger; squeeze it, and out pops a weevil. Now, you good-looking Christian people only weigh, like the wheat, forty-five or forty-eight pounds to the bushel. What is the matter? When you are squeezed between the thumb of the law and the finger of the Gospel, out pops the negro and the whisky bottle.[25]

The speakers of the ungenteel style continued to employ some themes popular in the Great Awakening of 1740. Graphic descriptions of the torments of hell abounded in their ministries. Often the speakers would peer down at the floor before them and describe the action taking place off-stage in the fiery pit. They also dwelt upon the peace and glory of the heavenly reward. Their language was frequently studded with exclamatory "O's" in the tradition of Whitefield. Short exhortatory phrases all beginning with an exclamatory vowel allowed them to express their mystical feelings of religious ecstasy. Frequently, the audience chimed in with exclamations, so speaker and audience stimulated one another as a chaining narrative caught hold of them and rendered them suggestible for emotional chanting or singing in an exhortatory manner.

Abel Stevens, writing from a mid-nineteenth-century vantage point, undertook, in his *Essays on the Preaching Required by the Times*, to sketch the general outlines of the "Old Methodist preaching." Stevens summarized the strengths of the old circuit riders as consisting of "the right *themes*, the right *style*, energetic *aim at direct results*, and popular or *extemporaneous* addresses." The circuit rider aimed directly for effect; thus, his preaching naturally tended to eloquence and to a simple and urgent style. Aiming for effect also resulted in a natural manner of delivery, expressed in just the right vocal inflection and gesture.

While the themes of the old Methodists were not unusual when compared to those of other preachers, the style of their preaching was different. They preached, more than most of the clergy in other denominations, *ad populum*. "They came out from the people, and knew how to address the people." They were generally unlettered and unprepared and could not bring "traits of literary purity" to the task of exalting the character of moral truth. Even so, what they lacked in literary polish was more than made up for by "simple, direct, and often strenuous speech."

The Methodist manner of illustrating the truth consisted largely of similitudes from common life. The staple of their exposition was the thrilling anecdote. Stevens admits that in some cases the preacher almost became an "anecdote-monger." Most particularly, Stevens noted the preachers' general habit of "giving *experimental illustrations* from their own personal religious history." While some might chide the minister who used personal experience, Stevens defends the practice. "How often, when the rest of the discourse has apparently failed . . . have we seen the multitudes melt with emotion when these experimental attestations have been adduced!"[26]

The itinerating habits of the circuit riders contributed to strong stout bodies and strong lungs. The results were loud and vehement discourses. The circuit riders were sons of thunder, who shouted and stamped and pounded the desk. Quite often, they adopted a singing tone with strong vocalizations and grunts between words. So common was the practice that a writer for the *National Magazine* noted that "when the speaker waxes mighty, this eloquent exclamatory gasp gives an impetus to each word, like a puffing locomotive behind, instead of before, the car."[27] One circuit rider cautioning against the overuse of a stylized and rhythmic vocal intonation wrote: "Dear ah! Brother Ah!—When-ah you-ah go-ah to-ah preach-ah take-ah care-ah you-ah don't-ah say-ah ah-ah!"[28]

The practice of the ungenteel speakers reflected its practitioners ambivalent attitude towards education. Even as the preacher ridiculed the rounded and polished periods of the educated orator, he would swing into a serious peroration of his own which was often a windy parody of the very style he ridiculed. It was almost as though he wished to prove that he could do as well as the product of the most erudite seminary. He picked up what Latin and Greek phrases he could to salt his discourse and then turned back to the tactic of ridicule when his supply of long words of Latin derivation was exhausted. His tactic was often to coin new words of pretentious sound and form. One New England circuit rider recalled a poignant moment when the retired circuit riders were eulogized by a preacher who said they were no *"clericus lofus."*[29]

The speaking practices of the uneducated lay ministers, which soon came to be comprised largely of fantasy themes, either biblical narratives or personal experience anecdotes, created a new consciousness, a new rhetorical vision, and a new style of speaking. To be sure, the vision was a modification of the evangelical style that emerged from the Geat Awakening and thus a variation of the Puritan rhetorical style. But, by 1830, the emphasis in the ungenteel rhetoric had shifted to the hot gospel, to the extemporaneous and sometimes impromptu speech, to the search for fantasies that would chain through the group or audience, and to the conventions of audience participation of shouting and singing and crying aloud to stimulate the chaining process by which fantasies created a focused psychological crowd that was highly suggestible. For those caught up in the chaining fantasies, the experience was emotional and exciting. They were taken out of themselves into a deep mystical experience of religion.

In the period following the Revolutionary War with its opening of the western frontier and the scramble for new lands, the ungenteel style proved more effective in gaining converts than the older traditions of the established religious communities such as the Congregationalists and the Anglicans. The simple rhetorical vision which supported and sustained the ungenteel style was thus to mark the cultural, social, and intellectual history of the country for the first century of the new constitution. This vision was optimistic, crude, jingoistic, romantic, and pragmatic.

⚘ 6

Nature and the New Birth

The Ungenteel Vision

If the term *genteel* is taken to mean well-bred, refined, polite, elegant, stylish, affected, pretentious, and delicate, the rhetorical practices discussed in chapter five may well be called the *ungenteel* style. Although the rhetorical theory of the ungenteel style was not codified and taught in a scholarly way, the practitioners of the style discussed it in meetings, wrote about it in religious periodicals, and eventually commented about it in longer works. My purpose here is to piece together an account of the special communication theory largely from the writings of an obscure Methodist minister and circuit rider by the name of William Henry Milburn.

From surveying a number of descriptions of speakers and speeches in journals and autobiographies of frontier preachers to reconstruct the underlying theory, I have concluded that Milburn is representative of the ungenteel style. In addition, Milburn is one of the few who directly considers matters of rhetorical theory. For example, he examines the language of the frontier and provides an explanation for its "rude proverbial forms." What can be discovered by my procedure are such things as the characteristics and traits that built ethos for the speaker, the recommended manner of delivery, the nature of the frontier audiences and an analysis of their psychology, the influence of the context on the speeches, the purpose of frontier rhetoric, and the rationale for practices which other styles of rhetoric might have considered unsound or in bad taste.

Because they were men of action, often speaking several times a week, who had little time and less training for writing learned monographs, the speakers of the ungenteel style seldom left coherent treatises on their special communication theory. William Henry Milburn was one of the few who, because of temperament, physical disability (he was nearly or totally blind for most of his life), and circumstance, had the leisure, literary ability, and intelligence to write a theoretical analysis and justification of the speaking practices. In addition, he was one of the few who still retained a commitment to the rhetorical vision that supported the ungenteel style.

Milburn testifies in his autobiography that, as a youth, he was an omnivorous reader, and he prepared himself well enough to be admitted to Illinois College in Jacksonville. By 1843, after a short period in college, he had so impaired his health that the doctors advised him to leave college and devote himself to physical exercise in the outdoors in order to build up his strength.

Milburn took the advice and began to ride the circuit as an exhorter in the Methodist church. In a short time, he passed his examinations and was licensed to preach. After a year on the circuit, Milburn went to St. Louis in the autumn of 1844 to get treatment for his eye. His doctors offered him a free ticket to attend lectures at the medical school, and a St. Louis lawyer befriended him. The young circuit rider alternated lectures at the medical school with the society of his lawyer friend who introduced him to "the great English essayists, and . . . some of the great English poets, especially Shakespeare."[1]

Although Milburn's ten months in St. Louis afforded him unusual educational opportunities for a circuit rider, they did not improve his eyesight. When he returned to the Methodist conference in Springfield, Illinois, in September 1845, he was nearly blind and severely handicapped in meeting the rigors of the circuit. The conference sent him east as a fund-raising agent for a female seminary to be established in connection with McKendree College in Illinois. During the course of his agency, Milburn was asked to serve as chaplain for the House of Representatives in Washington. He spent a year in the capital, listening to the debates of the House and Senate and reading with what little sight he had left at the Library of Congress. He married in 1846 and took up the agency for the girl's seminary once more. When his health broke and the physicians suggested that he move south, Milburn spent the next few years as a settled pastor in Montgomery, Alabama.

He took the opportunity afforded by the relative leisure of serving as a settled pastor to devote himself to intensive study. Despite his failing eyesight, he spent many hours a day reading theology, literature, and philosophy. He read Carlyle, MaCaulay, Emerson, Wendell Philips, and Theodore Parker. He studied Confucius and Schelling, Zoroaster, Aristotle, Plato, Thomas Aquinas, Duns Scotus, Descartes, Leibnitz, Kant, and Fichte. He adopted Germany as his intellectual fatherland. He read Neander, Strauss, and De Wette. After his two-year immersion in the current intellectual fashions, Milburn testified that "despite the spirit of free inquiry, I was held fast by the feelings of earlier years. Prayers learned when a child—views informed from the heart and vital with its blood, rather than those statuesque idioms of thought chiselled by the pure intellect—had become a part of me."[2]

Milburn emerged from his bout with higher criticism and German scholarship with his rhetorical vision largely intact. As his sight gradually deteriorated, he turned to writing, and thus, in his mature years, as he wrote such books as *Ten Years of Preacher-Life, Preachers and People,* and *The Rifle, Axe, and Saddle-Bags,* he brought a trained intelligence to bear upon the questions of rhetoric. Despite his wide reading, however, he turned to the basic group consciousness and the rhetorical style of his Methodist frontier upbringing.

Milburn was unusual because he was both a literate, educated man and a proponent of the ungenteel rhetoric. Quite often, the commentators on homiletics and rhetoric within the Methodist and Baptist denominations were, by 1850, torn between praising the effectiveness of the "old line" preaching and apologizing for its crudity, emotional excesses, and illiteracy.[3]

Rhetorical theory, as we have seen, grows from and sustains the practice of a given communication style and always contains a large measure of critical standards relating to the qualities of a good speaker or a good speech. Often the standards of excellence which both reflect and shape a style of public address (what the critics praise, the teachers teach, and the students emulate) are personified by nonfiction fantasy themes which cast historical personages with legendary speaking reputations as ideal types. The fantasy themes depicting the ideal speaker imply the standards of good speaking. In Milburn's rhetorical theory, the touchstone of sacred eloquence was the exemplar furnished by the dean of the Illinois circuit riders, Peter Cartwright, and the secular ideal was portrayed by the speaking of the Mississippi lawyer and orator, Sergeant S. Prentiss.

Writing of his youth, Milbrun recalls meeting Cartwright, who was then an elder of the Illinois church.[4] The circuit rider was "a man of medium height, thick-set with enormous bone and muscle." He was grey-haired and wrinkled but "his step was still vigorous and firm." Cartwright had been a preacher in the backwoods for forty years, "ranging the country from the Lakes to the Gulf, and from the Alleghanies to the Mississippi." The frontier preacher was used to every hardship and "looked calmly at peril of every kind." Milburn then provides a catalogue of the typical perils, "the tomahawk of the Indian, the spring of the panther, the hug of the bear, the sweep of the tornado, the rush of the swollen currents, and the fearful chasm of the earthquake." Among the hardships Cartwright had endured were laying "in the canebrake" or upon "the snow of the prairie" or "on the oozy soil of the swamp."

The Cartwright of Milburn's fantasy themes was a sort of rustic renaissance man. "He had preached in the cabin of the slave, and in the mansion of the master; to the Indians, and to the men of the border." Cartwright "had stood on the outskirts of civilization, and welcomed the first comers to the woods and prairies." The hardships and perils were borne for no "hope of fee or reward; not to enrich himself or his posterity, but as a preacher of righteousness in the service of God and his fellowmen."

As to the circuit rider's method of dealing with the world, he had "confronted wickedness' everywhere and "rebuked it." His method had been "irresistible sarcasm and ridicule" coupled with "the fiery look of his indignant invective." Under the fire of his sarcasm, ridicule, and invective, "every form of vice had shrunk abashed."

If the legendary Cartwright had a fault, in Milburn's view it was that he had a "slightly exaggeraged infusion of the frontiersman's traits." His conduct was not marked by the Christian spirit of meekness on all occasions. "Many a son of Anak has been levelled in the dust by his sledgelike fist." The circuit rider's "congenial sphere" was that "of a pastor in the woods." And most importantly, Milburn notices that "learning he had none, but the keenest perceptions and the truest instincts enabled him to read human nature as men read a book."

By mid-century, a group consciousness that celebrated the frontier was already a powerful force for the cohesion of a large community of Americans, and the virtues of the frontier were those Milburn attributed to the itinerating preachers of the years from 1785 to 1835. The Cartwright that emerges from Milburn's romantic fantasies is a man able to wrestle the bear as well as any mythical Daniel Boone. Cartwright has slept on the ground and withstood the challenges of nature. He is also quick to meet the challenges of sinful man. He blisters sin and sinners, applies ridicule and sarcasm to wickedness and cant, and uses invective on every form of vice. In short, the preacher had to develop his right to speak not only on the basis of a call that gave his supernatural sanctions but also as a rough, if need be violent, strong and courageous he-man.

The secular dramas of the ideal speaker related to the career of the Mississippi lawyer and orator Sergeant S. Prentiss.⁵ The speaker who emerges from Milburn's portrayal has many of Cartwright's characteristics. Prentiss was "the master of nearly all manly accomplishments, a fearless rider and bold hunter." Although he had a deformed leg, he lived a vigorous and manly life. Milburn praised the Mississippian's "eloquence of invective" and wrote that "nothing since the days of Demosthenes equal [s] . . . his thunders against Mississippi repudiations." Prentiss was the most effective stump speaker in the country, and yet he had "shone conspicuously in its highest courts." Prentiss was "cogent in argument, copious in imagination. "He was, according to Milburn, "master of all the passions of the human soul, and moved them as the expert musician draws from his instrument a concord of sweet sounds."

Like Cartwright, Prentiss was a frontier Renaissance man; he could "stand before a crowd of repudiating Mississippi voters, hurling at them taunts, ridicule, sarcasm, defiance, until their faces grew pale and their lips livid with rage." He could also devote weeks to nursing the sick when pestilence broke out, and without thinking of his personal danger, nurse strangers with tenderness and patience. Children and Indian warriors both idolized Prentiss; he delivered the greatest speech ever made in the Halls of Congress, in Milburn's judgment, "yet the people of the backwoods grew almost delirious under the spell of his eloquence." In a duel, "before the pistol of an antagonist at ten paces, his mien was calm, his nerves firm as steel; but if introduced to a lady, his knees trembled, and his embarrassment would have been ludicrous had it not been so painful."

Prentiss rode his secular circuit just as Cartwright rode his sacred one, and, according to Milburn, "riding the circuit in Mississippi . . . was no child's play." On the judicial circuit, the lawyer rode over roads knee-deep in mud or forded flooded streams, crossed swamps, and faced the dangers of quicksand. Where Cartwright itinerated saving souls, Prentiss made his way be using his legal skill to defend those who were unjustly accused.

The rough and ready rhetoric that Milburn celebrated was conditioned by the audience and the speaking occasions, and Milburn's rhetorical theory included a thorough analysis of both. The frontier preacher had to develop a new rhetoric because, "the place is different, the hearers are different." The speaker preached "in the vast unwalled church of nature, with the leafy tree-tops for a ceiling, their massy stems for columns; with the endless mysterious cadences of the forest for a choir; with the distant or nearer music and murmur of streams, and the ever-returning voice of birds sounding in their ears." The audience was composed of men "whose ears are trained to catch the faintest foot-fall of the distant deer . . . whose eyes are skilled to discern the trail of savages, who leave scarce a track behind them . . . whose eye and hand are so well practised that they can drive a nail or snuff a candle with the long, heavy western rifle." These men may have been uneducated in a bookish sense, but they had been "educated for years, or even generations, in that hard school of necessity, where every one's hand and woodman's skill must keep his head; where incessant pressing necessities required ever a prompt and sufficient answer in deeds; and where words needed to be but few, and those the plainest and directest, required no delay nor preparation, nor oratorical coquetting, nor elaborate preliminary scribble."[6]

Milburn wrote on the eve of the Civil War, when the conflict over the proper means of preaching was already a century old and the new rhetoric firmly established. When he compares the two styles, the characteristics of the latter are clear. "The spoken eloquence of New England is for the most part from manuscript," he asserts. Milburn accounts for this on the basis of the influence of the Old World upon the New England founders; in his vision, the Old World was essentially a pernicious influence, for "preachers were set at an appalling distance from their congregations. Between the pulpit, perched far up toward the ceiling, and the seats, was an awful abysmal depth." The entire setting of the sermon established a social distance between speaker and audience. Even the manner of delivery served to emphasize the lack of direct audience contact. The speaker's "eye was averted and fastened downward upon his manuscript, and his discourse . . . was delivered in a monotonous, regular cadence." In addition, "it was not this preacher's business to arouse his audience." The theory of worship was different, according to Milburn. The people did not "wish excitement or stimulus, or astonishment, or agitation. They simply desired information; they wished to be instructed." Under the circumstances, "the preacher might safely remain perched up in his far distant unimpassioned eyrie."

Milburn contrasts the old rhetoric of New England with frontier speaking. How would such speaking "be received out in the wild West?" Put the manuscript-reading and learned New England preacher on a stump, he suggested, and surround him with people pressing around him on every side close and direct with no chasm between speaker and audience. The audience with "eyes intently perusing his to see if he be in real earnest—'dead in earnest'— and where, as with a thousand darts, their contemptuous scorn would pierce him through if he were found playing a false game." No studied and artful emotional appeal would work in such circumstances. He would feel their contempt and hear it too if he was "trying to pump up tears by mere acting, or arousing an excitement without feeling it."[7] Milburn then repeats Cartwright's ridicule of a well-educated young eastern minister. Cartwright said that a well-educated young minister who delivered a written sermon made him think of "a gosling that had got the straddles by wading in the dew."[8] The very popularity of that description is illuminating. The barnyard metaphor of the gosling with the straddles was typical of the speaking style. It ridiculed the pretensions of the educated speaker and laughed him off the stump. One of the important fantasy types of the vision consisted of the scenario about the practical and "dead earnest" speaker, who had no book learning but who was a close student of human nature and who bested the pretentious and pompous learned clergyman. Cartwright himself, in his autobiography, claims to have discomfited a learned opponent in a theological debate by responding to a comment studded with Latin with another in frontier German that the learned man took for ancient Hebrew.[9] Milburn quotes a "well-known" fantasy theme about what he asserts was a common practice: pricking a speaker's flights of eloquence with "some stinging joke, probably bearing no particular relation to the speaker's speech, and applicable only because successful."

The story relates to a "windy" gentleman who, in the midst of a gorgeous flight of eloquence, is interrupted by someone calling out from the audience, "Guess he wouldn't talk quite so hifalutenatin' if he knowed how his breeches was torn out behind!" The speaker, deceived by the unexpected comment, "clapped a hand to the part indicated, and was destroyed—overwhelmed in inextinguishable laughter."[10]

What Milburn praises when he describes the contrasting rhetoric is equally instructive. While he admits that "the figures of speech and forms of rhetoric which characterize western eloquence, partake," to some extent of a characteristic "bombastic and unsound" quality, he argues that this was not true "of the best of the western orators." In addition, he argues that "we must not judge of the power exerted upon the people, nor the good done them, merely by estimating the amount of positive information furnished by the speaker, and his grade of intelligence." Rather, one should judge "from the stimulation" which the audience experiences "from his pouring out and rendering up to them the treasures of his own life and soul." The "rude speeches and sermons of the West task and stimulate the intellects of the people, and set their minds in motion. The steam is turned on; and when that is done, the engine must move forward or backward, or else explode."[11]

While praising the emotional, heart-to-heart eloquence of the crude, vituperative, sarcastic, and ridiculing uneducated speaker who had been to "brush College" or the "School of hard knocks" and condemning the cold, instructive reading of the educated New England preacher, Milburn at the same time praises education and book learning. The Methodists were zealous in the establishment of schools. Seldom have so many uneducated men worked so hard to further the cause of education. They seemed, on the one hand, to hate the sin but love the sinner, and, on the other, to hate the educated man but love education.

Thus, Milburn in his praise of Cartwright, after commending his ability to read the book of human nature although he was uneducated, goes on to praise Cartwright for having "sold more books than probably any man ever did in a new country." Cartwright traveled everywhere with his saddle-bags crammed with books, for "the Methodist economy enjoined it as a duty on the preacher to diffuse a sound literature." Because of Cartwright's work, "many a youth, who, but for him, might have slumbered on without intelligence or education" owed the circuit rider a debt of gratitude.[12]

Milburn argued that the rough people, born and bred in the wilderness had, "after the universal human fashion, expressed a characteristic and interesting representation of its traits and tendencies in its language." He suggested that there was a "western Anglo-American language" and that this language was "thickly studded with rude proverbial forms, all redundant with wild untrained metaphors, some of which . . . we will call cant and slang."[13] Milburn found a strong vein of humor running through western speech and a tendency to coin "singular words and phrases." These coinages, he maintains, are due to the fact that the frontier language was too "dry and meagre" to express the feelings of the populace and they thus turned to making up words or using them in analogous ways that gave to their speech an often unintended wit and quaintness.[14]

Milburn suggested that when the frontiersman needed a new word, he either took an old one and modified it to fit his needs or made one "out of whole cloth"; in the latter case, the result was often a "ridiculous exemplification" of "*onomatopoeia*." The process of modification resulted in words like "spontanaceous" for spontaneous; "obfusticate" for obfuscate; "cantankerous" for cankerous; "rampagious" or "rampunctious" for rampant; "hifalutinatin" for high-flying; "tetotaciously" for totally. The "whole cloth" process produced expressions like "sock-dolager" for a powerful blow; "explatterate" for smash; "explunctify" for crush; and "honey-fuggle," for flatter. The speaker used the vernacular and vulgar speech of his hearers and prided himself upon his ability to talk their language.[15]

Piety and their environment led the frontier preachers to the worship of nature and the natural man. They thus participated in that general intellectual, literary, and rhetorical tendency often characterized by the term *romantic-*

ism. Their rhetorical theory turned its back on *elocuation* or scholarly training and, instead, glorified natural eloquence, native rhetorical genius, the untrained speaker, the upwelling of genuine, sincere, and honest words, no matter how ungrammatical, unpolished, or unstructured they might have been. Like the Puritans, they urged the speaker to approach the service with a feeling of piety and to pray for the help of God's power. Like the New Lights of 1740, the emphasized the strength of their "call" and utilized the same Pauline fantasy type to legitimatize their ethos; but unlike the Puritans, they did not urge the speaker to leave his knees in his *study* for the pulpit. Rather, they urged him to go out into nature.

Finley reveals the rhetorical vision of the ungenteel tradition in his encomium on the natural orator.

> Nature is the fountain from whence the orator must draw his inspiration, and the field whereon he must develop his powers. As the eagle, who soars away from the homes and the haunts of man, to bathe his undazzled eye in the sunbeam, and pillow his breast upon the storm, so the child of genius must become familiar with Nature in all her aspects. One of the most eloquent divines, of the same school of theology to which Bascom belonged, discourses thus on this subject: "The orator must be much at home, that is, he must study himself; his own nature, and powers, and states of mind; and he must be much abroad, that is, he must go out and study Nature in all her moods." . . . As all the lines of Nature are lines of beauty, so are all her movements, and he who would be truly effective and graceful as an orator, must follow no other copy. Bascom [the early Methodist preacher whose life Finley is sketching] has been heard to say, in reference to the composition of his sermons, that a room was so contracted it had an influence upon his thoughts, and he could only think freely and grandly when out in the midst of nature, beneath her boundless skies and extended landscapes. It is said that an Indian mound, in Kentucky, is pointed out to the traveler as the spot whereon he composed some of his greatest sermons. [16]

In the same sketch of Bascom, Finley expounds the rhetorical theory that the orator is born rather than trained and that the natural genius of a born orator is a gift of God as mighty and awesome as the Niagara Falls.

> The graces of oratory, which others gain, like Demosthenes, by a severe and tedious process, with him were gifts of nature, and not the product of education. . . . he was born an orator, and to have cast his genius in any model would have destroyed his power. God makes but few such men. Towering up like Himalaya, or sublimely grand like Niagara, they stand out apart from their species to excite our wonder. . . . Had his genius been cramped by the laws of the schools, which are often about as useful in making an orator as a note-book

would be to a nightingale, or as the laws of motion and sound would be to the dash and roar of Niagara, the thunder of whose anthem is the voice of nature, we might have had, and doubtless would have had, a Bascom polished with all the arts of elocution; but, like the nicely-adjusted and exquisitely-wrought automaton, there would have been a stiffness in his movements; and although the precision which should mark them would indicate the wonderful power of art, still we should have had nothing but the mimic artificial man. [17]

In tune with the romantic temper, the heirs of Whitefield glorified feeling at the expense of form. Though they were crude and ungrammatical, they felt the emotion and moved the audience. Finley said of John Collins that when "the tear would start form his eye like the rain-drop which falls from the heat of the cloud, then you might know that the Spirit of the Lord was upon him, and might expect with certainty to witness displays of Divine power." [18]

In delivery, the rhetorical theory glorified a deep feeling and a shouting, loud, and emotional manner. When the critic applied this rhetorical theory to the preaching of a minister and found the speaker praiseworthy, one of the commonly applied terms of praise was "thunder" or "thundered." A foreword prepared for Cartwright's autobiography by W. P. Strickland praised the speaker in the following way: "There, from a central platform, this Son of Thunder deals out the awful truths of revelation, and preaches at the top of his voice 'of righteousness, temperance, and judgment to come.' Sinners of every stamp are smitten by these appeals; they 'drop right and left,' like beasts of slaughter; the wail of repentance is followed by the prayer of faith, and many are 'powerfully converted.'" [19]

Milburn wrote in appreciation of one of the early camp meetings, where eight or ten ministers from different denominations were "holding forth in their loudest tone—and that was a very loud tone, for the lungs of the backwoods preachers were of the strongest. They roared like lions—their tones were absolutely like peals of thunder." [20]

The general expectation of the audience and speaker of the hot gospel was that the inspired minister must speak extemporaneously. Only in that way could the speaker express the inspiration of the supernatural. If the minister prepared his remarks ahead of time, he was hypocritical because, until the magic moment when audience and speaker confronted one another and began their communion, there was no assurance that the words of the minister would be inspired. When that moment came and God spoke through the preacher, the inspiration of the moment was vital and prepared words useless.

Cartwright expressed the typical sentiment in his autobiography when he recounted his experience with young college-trained preachers from the East. The young men came with "a tolerable education . . . tolerably well furnished with old manuscript sermons." The sermons, Cartwright charged, had been preached or written a hundred years before. For the most part, they read the sermons to the audience. The manner of reading a sermon "was out of fashion altogether in this Western world, and of course they produced no good effect among the people." What people of the West wanted, according to Cartwright, was "a preacher that could mount a stump, a block, or old log, or stand in the bed of a wagon, and, without note or manuscript, quote, expound, and apply the word of God to the hearts and consciences of the people."[21]

Cartwright reiterated his position in an anecdote about a Presbyterian preacher from the East. Cartwright asserted that he told the man that he must quit reading his old sermons and learn to speak extemporaneously. He told the Presbyterian that "the Western people were born and reared in hard times, and were an out-spoken and off-hand people; that if he did not adopt this manner of preaching, the Methodists would set the whole Western world on fire before he would light his match." The Easterner tried for a time but grew discouraged and "left for parts unknown."[22]

The vision's typical attitude toward careful sermon preparation is reflected in a fictionalized fantasy theme of *Brother Mason, the Circuit Rider: or, Ten Years a Methodist Preacher*, published in 1856. The first time around his circuit, the preacher, Brother Mason, stops to see Brother D. The circuit rider comments that he needed time for rest and study. "'As to the study,' said Bro. D., 'I don't believe in it any way. It's no use; just get up, and look to God, and fire away. That's the way our old preachers used to do; and I am sure they had a fine work wherever they went. Sinners were converted in crowds, and people were much more zealous than they are now.'"[23]

A bit later, Brother Mason was trying to go over his notes for the sermon when he was visited by three other brethren. He went down to meet them with his notes in his hand and one of them said, "What, do you read your sermons? Because if you do, we don't want you—no 'Piscopalians here—nor Pruspatarans nother." Mason assured them that he did not read his sermons and that the papers simply contained an outline of the main ideas of his speech. The brother said, "That war' not the way the preachers did in old times; they jist went into the stand, and opened the Bible any whar', and tuck the fust text they found, and jist banged away. Then we had sich good old fashioned times."[24]

The tendency to sanction the use of lay exhorters that began in the 1740s was institutionalized by many of the revival groups in the years following the Revolutionary War. Through the rhetorical theory that sustained and modified the speakers of the ungenteel style in the new century ran a strong ambivalence on the entire question of education. The rhetorical vision of the revivalists in the late eighteenth and early nineteenth century celebrated a cluster of values associated with common practical people and with the new lands of the West and South.

In the dramas of the rhetorical vision, the frontiersman was uneducated in a bookish way, but it did not follow that he was a lesser person for all of that because he was educated in the ways of survival in the woods and prairies. He could read a trail, hunt a deer, and triumph against natural disaster. He was crude and uncultured to be sure, but crudity and lack of culture were virtues in the setting of the new lands. The unpolished listener was sincere and honest. The people in the new lands expressed real feelings and did not hide behind a veneer of manners and cultural polish.

Paradoxically, even while the vision celebrated the emotional, heart-to-heart eloquence of the crude, vituperative, and ridiculing uneducated minister, the rhetorical theorists often praised education and book learning, as we saw in Milburn's treatment of Cartwright. The rhetoric reflected an ambivalence towards scholarly training in the arts of speech. The ambivalence was, to some extent, a reflection of a feeling of inferiority. On the one hand, adherents of the style fantasized themes that celebrated the unschooled speaker and his auditors. On the other hand, however, even as they participated in such fantasies to furnish suitable values to live by and to provide a sense of community and worth, they often praised education, promised it for their posterity, and argued that their heroes, while not formally educated, had read widely and were as erudite as college graduates even though "self-educated." For many years, the rhetoric of the revivalists would reflect this ambivalence towards education. They argued against educated men even as they spoke in praise of education. Ironically, they employed the trappings of educated disputation even as they argued against intellectuals. They proved with the forms of scholarly argumentation, for example, that the work of the higher critics was not sound and the Bible remained the repository of revealed truth.

For the speakers and theorists of the ungenteel style, the claims of scholarship and social distance, the use of dignity and apartness, to establish the authority of the preacher, which had characterized the power structure of colonial New England, was no longer persuasive. For such claims of speaker credibility, the new rhetoric substituted effectiveness, the ability to talk the language of the common man, unstudied natural eloquence, crudity, and ungrammatical expressions. The techniques became so common that students of twentieth-century speaking sometimes refer to them as "just plain folks" devices for identifying the speaker with the audience. Primarily, the speech needed to be dramatic, interesting, and effective. Effect was the basic seal of success that indicated that God was speaking through the preacher. Learning needed to be useful, practical, and conducive to increased efficiency in the common-sense, everyday affairs of men if it were to serve as part of the speaker's authority. What was not wanted was nonsense, foolishness, airs, pedantry, erudition, dead languages, classical allusions, or studied elocutions. What was wanted was a natural man, deeply feeling the emotion he was trying to communicate to his audience.

The vision's grand panoramic account of the creation, pattern, and purpose of the universe and of mankind was Protestant and Christian, as was that of the Puritan vision. The ungenteel vision began with the creation of the world and of man and woman in the Garden of Eden. Adam and Eve fell from grace, and the long battle between the forces of good and evil ensued. The vision accepted the biblical prophecy that the battle between the hosts of God and the hosts of the devil was to intensify and come to a climax in a final day of judgment. There were two essential variations of the grand scenario on the frontier. One vision saw the crisis deepening, wickedness rising, and godliness in general decreasing until the terrible final battles and the Second Coming of Christ would bring Judgement Day. After the Second Advent, there was to be a thousand-year reign of Christ on earth, a period of perfection. The other vision saw the world hastening to get better, more and more souls being saved for the true religion, less sinfulness, less suffering, greater opportunity, greater progress in all departments of life, the formation of a grand new system of government which would encourage freedom and liberty and the steady march of progress until the world was perfect enough; this state would last a millennium, after which Christ would come for the second time. The more popular of the two visions was the latter one or the vision of postmillennialism. The ungenteel rhetorical vision participated in the millenial dream, which was optimistic and perfectionistic. The world was getting better and better, signs of progress were all about, and the joyous duty of a born-again Christian was to hasten the day by saving as many souls as possible as soon as possible.

The postmillennial vision dramatized and emphasized all the signs of improvement and tended to overlook events which could be interpreted as indicating worsening conditions in the world. The notion of cycles or tides of good and evil was not part of its interpretative frame.

The grand scope of the vision was generally in the background of the rhetoric, taken for granted, providing the common assumptions for theological disputations and for logical proof in the sermons. The immediate dramatic setting was a much more important feature of the vision. The great heartland of North America provided the scene for most of the shared fantasies of the group consciousness of the ungenteel tradition. The Old World had been the site of the first coming of Christ. The New World had been saved for the

Second Advent. God had kept back the New World, and only when the time was ready did he allow its discovery and encourage its settlement. The adherents of the ungenteel style dramatized the subsequent developments such as the Revolutionary War, the drafting and adoption of the Constitution, and the opening of the valley of the Ohio river for settlement as further evidence that man and society were to be perfected in the New World. The ground was sacred; it was glorious in its natural wonders and beauty, and people who came to it from the effete eastern regions or from the Old World were changed for the better as a result of their moving onto sacred ground. The Old World was corrupted and would not be suitable as the setting of the millennium but the new pristine lands of the West were ideal for the Second Coming. The new lands were vital battlegrounds between the hosts of the devil and the hosts of God. The great valley of the Ohio had to be saved for God because if it was not, the glorious opportunity of the new country would be lost. The salvation of souls was of great importance for each individual, but it was of equally great importance for all political, economic, and social developments.

Since the West was rapidly filling up with settlers, the time was short and the crisis was upon the adherents of the ungenteel vision. They measured every success or failure in terms of its reverberations forward into time rather than backward into history. The drama of posterity freighted every victory with meaning and clouded every defeat with ominous significance. What was at stake was not just the present of those living at that time but the future of their posterity. Their children and their children's children would feel the impact of what they did with the virgin lands and the impact of how successful they were in saving souls on the frontier. Since all was fresh and new, each important development, social, political, or religious, was precedent-setting and needed to be treated with the care and attention such significant acts deserve.

God had chosen for the new land a group of inspired founders of a constitution which included individual liberty and religious freedom. The merits of the various religious communities were tested in the open market of religious competition and would wax or wane, depending on whether they won converts and emerged from the test of popular acceptance as good, useful, and true. The United States, and particularly the participants in the ungenteel rhetoric, were given the opportunity to be a model for all the world, to provide the new chance for mankind, and to supply the energy to create a perfect society and usher in the millennium.

The combined scenarios of the vision resembled the adventures of the legendary King Arthur and the Knights of the Round Table, only with the heroes transformed into nature's noblemen. Little bands of honest and honorable people huddled in settlements like islands of law and order in a lawless countryside. Adventure was the order of the day. As a person traveled about the countryside, he was beset by dangers: swollen rivers, wild animals, savage Indians, bullies, outlaws, and rowdies lay in wait for him. But not all of the adventures were dangerous; some were humorous. When a man fell off his horse or found himself in a bed full of bedbugs, or when he was taken by a slick operator, it furnished grist for a fantasy theme, for a tall tale useful in whiling away the hours around the fire some winter evening.

The frontier was furnished with a group of heroes, rough-hewn and dressed in less flamboyant colors than the knights of old. To some extent, the whole myth of chivalry was turned upside down in the rhetorical vision to glorify the leveling effect of a mobile culture and to ridicule and denigrate all pretensions of aristocracy and class structure. Even so, the essential elements of a code of chivalry were present, including the defense of personal honor, the rise of dueling, and the glorification of women. The western knight made no untoward advances to a nice girl. In the presence of women, the strong man was tongue-tied and bashful. Dandies, fops, smooth-talking Philadelphia lawyers were all highly suspect as being insincere and double-dealing types.

The vision's glorification of nature made up for much of the culture and learning that the hot gospeler lacked. In the broad panorama of the vision, nature furnished the participant with cathedrals, with paintings, and with sculpture. Mountains, waterfalls, rivers, woods, and fields provided him with aesthetic pleasures and with an opportunity to commune with God. The rhetoric paints the celebration of nature in rosy and romantic hues. The speakers drew their pictures of the glories of the community in warmer and friendlier colors than did the celebrators of the Puritan community.

What were the fantasy types that celebrated the values of the new vision? The hot gospelers took the basic rhetorical vision established by the Puritans and refurbished it with different values, virtues, and their own evaluation of sinfulness. The Puritan vision had glorified the community as the race of the new Israel on an exodus into the wilderness, as God's chosen people with the true religion, and then had swung its auditors to the merciless examination of their mean and unregenerate nature, to their sins of wordly pride, and their preoccupation with the here and now. The preachers of the hot gospel glorified the West and the frontier. The new lands, they argued, were the controlling factor in developing the essence of America. They celebrated their community by praising crude, unlettered people who were at home with nature, who could hunt the deer, and fight the bear. The community was composed of natural men, stripped of the sophisticated veneer of civilization, left with the eternal verities. They were honest, sincere, real people. They exhibited their sense of humor in meeting the problems of living on the frontier with the tall story and by laughing about the bedbugs, the dirt, the squalor, and the uncomfortableness of the frontier. Every heroic protagonist made his way by what he was, not by what he had inherited. There were no social classes, and those who took upon themselves social airs or pretended to be better than other people were ridiculed and laughed out of countenance.

The rhetorical theory and practice of the ungenteel style already indicate the beginnings of the vision that Frederick Jackson Turner framed in scholarly terms in a famous paper on *The Frontier in American History* at the close of the nineteenth century.[25] Here, too, was one of the sources of the stock scenarios subsequently replayed in dime novels, pulp westerns, motion pictures, radio and television shows of the Virginian who goes west and becomes a straight-shooting, straight-talking, no-nonsense he-man, fighting the evils of a lawless land.

Another important feature of the new vision was the fact that it contained a radically changed characterization of man, when compared with the Puritan rhetoric. The new style dramatized man as perfectible in this world, because one of the products of the "new birth" was a saintly life. The speakers no longer portrayed man as a mean miserable creature and a burden on creation; instead, they now presented him as nature's nobleman, requiring only the infusion of grace to achieve perfection. The new protagonist was not a spider squirming over the pit of hell in a drama completely determined by God but a person deserving of salvation, which a kindly God, through the mediation of Jesus Christ, offered freely to all who came, believed, and asked for it. All the bars were down and every soul was equally worthy. The meanest and most miserable sinner, the least educated and most uncultured backwoodsman, the poorest mechanic, whose ancestors had come as indentured slaves, all of these, even the "least of them," were welcome in the ranks of the elect, according to the shared fantasies of the ungenteel tradition.

The ungenteel rhetorical vision was permeated with dramas of the "new birth" at three levels. First, each individual was a potential protagonist in a spiritual "new birth," which would mean a perfection of this life and life everlasting. Second, each individual was a potential protagonist in a secular "new birth" in the sacred region of the frontier. The "new birth" of the frontier was one in which all of the past traditions, classes, and burdens of the settled regions of the East and of Europe were shuffled off, and each individual could start anew, equal with every other person; all that counted was personal worth, talent, ability, and drive. Third, the human race was a potential protagonist in a grand drama in which the old and corrupted societies of Europe were given a chance at a "new birth" in the new country. A whole series of events, including the settlement of the frontier, the creation of the new country by the Revolutionary War, the founding of the new government based upon the Constitution, were dramatized as a "new birth" for society. Abraham Lincoln, who was, as we shall see, a preeminent practitioner of the ungenteel style, reflected the fantasy type of the "new birth" in his comments at Gettysburg Cemetery when he suggested that the original salvation experience of the country at the time of the founders had been corrupted by slavery and that the Civil War was a time of troubles from which, hopefully, "this nation, under God, shall have a new birth of freedom—and that government of the people, by the people, for the people shall not perish from the earth."[26]

The motives embedded in the vision impelled the adherents to adopt the life style of the heroes of the good dramas. After the "new birth," the drunkard gave up drink, the gambler gave up cards, and the philanderer gave up women. The participants in the vision adopted the rhetorical style praised by the theory and exemplified by the practice of the devotees. They began to refer to other members of the community as brothers and sisters and to express their religious experiences in the appropriate manner at the appropriate time. Most importantly, however, the motives in the rhetorical vision placed great pressure on its adherents to test the means of persuasion against the criterion of success in saving souls. The vision contained strong motivation for charting the growth of church membership, as Peter Cartwright regularly did in his autobiography. At every quarterly Methodist meeting, the number of new converts and the current size of the membership were an overriding concern. In addition, every born-again Christian had a duty to try to save sinners. In this powerful version of the proselyting fantasy type, the burden of hastening the perfection of the world was not left to the minister alone. The vision thus carried with it a strong missionary zeal—in a sense, if a person failed to try to convert a sinner, he would come to participate in the guilt of the sinner. The adherents of the romantic pragmatic tradition were their brothers' keepers. A member of the ungenteel rhetorical style could not sit passively by but, as a part of the laudable scenario, had to take active steps to root out sin, because by not taking action, he came to participate in the sin. Neutrality was impossible, or as the same attitude was expressed in more contemporary times, "if you are not part of the solution you are part of the problem."

The vision contained strong motives to "go public" and to gain converts. The adherents became adept at the conversion process and developed recurring forms of consciousness-raising communication that worked to achieve the easily quantifiable results which the rhetoric celebrated. The persuaders of the ungenteel tradition made masterful use of group pressures for conformity and of the power of chaining fantasy themes in small, consciousness-raising discussion groups. The Methodist circuit rider moved into a new community, talked to people, held prayer meetings, exhorted, preached, and gathered a handful of converts, whom he then formed into a "class." The class continued to meet regularly under a lay class leader while the circuit rider made his rounds. The class meetings provided the cohesion necessary to hold the community together until the circuit rider returned. In the meantime, members were engaged in inviting potential converts to class meetings and using informal conversations to persuade outsiders to participate in the Methodist version of the ungenteel vision. The class meetings consisted of songs, prayers, Bible readings, and the telling of religious experiences. Simple but rousing group hymn singing and impassioned prayer created a climate of suggestibility for dramatizing personal experiences in the ungenteel style. As the fantasies chained through the group, they ignited strong emotional responses which were fed by group members expressing their involvement in the fantasy by nonverbal communications such as moaning, weeping, or rythmic moving and by verbal feedback such as "Halleluiah," "Glory to God," "Amen." The prayer meetings, class meetings, and love feasts of early Methodism utilized the same techniques of group persuasion to arouse feelings of religious ecstasy that were employed in the 1960s by the adherents of rhetorical visions of revolution and reform.[27]

The consciousness-raising sessions of such groups as women's and gay liberation and some radical revolutionaries in the 1960s and 1970s used group techniques to break up the old foundations, to create feelings of guilt, and to reorient individual fantasies to the community's fantasies; these techniques were in the direct tradition of the conversion practices of the ungenteel style.

The rhetorical vision of the ungenteel tradition included a persuasive theory of the psychology of conversion which proved most effective when judged by the crude critical standard of quantification of numbers converted. In chapter four, I outlined the theory as developed by Tracy. The persuader begins by impressing upon the convert that he is not living as he should. In the case of the ungenteel vision, the person was alarmed by the threat of eternal death and hell fires. The individual then examines his life and comes to the appalling and powerful discovery of guilt—the conviction of sin. Under deep emotion, which the persuader's fantasies interpret for the potential convert as hatred, fear, or remorse, the latter searches for a remedy. He undergoes great anguish and then experiences the glorious peace and joy of salvation. Secular persuaders have used the evangelical process of conversion with considerable success in the nineteenth and twentieth centuries in the United States. The abolitionists and Populists of the nineteenth century and the civil rights movement and the social and political revolutionaries of the twentieth century often used the same conversion process.

The general pattern employed in consciousness-raising persuasion is for the propagandist to first impress upon the potential converts the unsatisfactory nature of the life they are living. The rhetoricians impress upon the individual the alarming inadequacies of his or her behavior, based upon the standards of the vision. (In the case of the ungenteel tradition, the Christian standards of conduct and belief as presented in the vision and in the case of women's liberation the standards of equality and self-fulfillment embodied in the shared fantasies of the vision furnish the criteria for self-searching analysis of one's life.) The individual now is filled with the appalling and powerful feeling which both sacred and secular rhetorical visions interpret as *guilt*. The meaning of *guilt* in a conversion rhetoric is interpreted by a stock scenario in which the individual is the protagonist and in which some act of the individual or some belief results in a deplorable effect for which the protagonist is held morally responsible. Since the protagonist, in reality or symbolically, did the terrible things or was an accessory to doing them or by not acting allowed the appalling things to happen, he must now feel badly about it and take steps to assuage or remove the guilt. In the ungenteel style, the guilt was personal, but in many of the later secular visions, the guilt was social or political, and the protagonist shared the guilt of a "racist society" or of the "atrocities in Vietnam" with an entire community. Fantasy themes designed to arouse guilt tend to depict evil things for which the protagonist is to feel responsible in graphic and violent scenes. The abolitionists, as we shall see, portrayed the evils of slavery in bloody and violent terms; the anti-war rhetoric of the 1960s dramatized the atrocities of the war in similar tones.

The feeling of guilt (the conviction of sin or the raising of the consciousness) reveals how repressed and trivial a person's life has been in terms of the individual's terrible moral responsibility. Guilt also points up the individual's need for action to change things and atone for the guilt. People do not take such an interpretation of themselves and their lives lightly. Under deep emotion, the individual searches for a remedy and discovers it in the wholesale reorientation of his or her interior fantasy life to bring it into line with the shared consciousness of the rhetorical community. Once the convert emotionally participates in the dramas of the rhetorical vision, he or she experiences a feeling of peace and a certainty of belief which is comforting. The convert who has gone through the conversion process has shared the salient fantasy types, themes, metaphors, and analogies of the vision in small group sessions, in two-person conversations, and in larger meetings under the sway of public speakers able to dramatize the vision's fantasies with rhetorical artistry, according to the critical standards of the style.

The converts are usually zealous. They have recreated, through their own sharing of the fantasies, the basic values, emotions, meanings, and motives of the vision. They have empathized, sympathized, and identified with the heroes of the scenarios; they have hated and feared the enemies; they have pitied the victims; they have felt suspense and excitement as the battle between the heroes and the forces of evil swayed in the balance; and they have felt sorrow and anguish at the defeat of the heroes or joy and gladness at their victory. The motivations of the vision impel the converts to action, and they adopt the life style of the heroes of the vision and the goals and values implied by the fantasies.

Those who are born into the social reality of the shared consciousness, on the other hand, also hear the fantasies in small group meetings, conversations, and public assemblies, but they do not necessarily go through a conversion process. The may never search their convictions (break up the old foundations), discover their sin and feel their guilt. After all, they are already within the social reality of the rhetorical vision and do not have to cross its psychological boundaries. The inheriters may be much less zealous and committed than those who are converted. The shared consciousness is familiar to those who have been living in its social reality since birth and who have heard its rhetoric from early childhood. They have no other vision to give up and do not experience the emotional trauma of those who give up one vision and take on another.

The fact that the secularization of the "new birth" techniques of conversion has succeeded for numerous persuaders from abolitionists and social reformers to political revolutionaries, reactionaries, and dropouts from society may indicate that the psychology of conversion is an invariable dynamic, amenable to scientific investigation. If so, communication researchers could eventually hope to develop a general theory describing the invariable relations associated with the process. An alternative explanation of the generality of the conversion process would be the notion that the impact of the rhetoric of romantic pragmatism has been so strong in the United States that the recurring forms of its communication style will work for secular visions with no manifest religious content.

The historical record relating to romantic pragmatism does indicate that the process by which a person comes to give up one rhetorical vision and embrace another can be an emotional, exciting, and traumatic one. It also indicates that the trauma of conversion is a function of the relative strength of the vision's romanticism. The greater the extent of powerful emotions evoked by the sharing of the dramas of the vision, and the more powerful the celebration of mystical and pietistic experiences, the greater the likelihood of emotional trauma in the conversion and the greater the energy generated by the motives embedded in the vision. In short, the foregoing analysis of the conversion rhetoric of romantic pragmatism provides an explanation for the correlation between romanticism and fanaticism. The celebration of mystic insight and the denigration of an objective reality, as indicated in chapter one, results in a vision which is insensitive to corroboration. Fanaticism requires a sense of certainty, righteous indignation, the strong evocation of hatred, and ecstasies of love. Corroboration keeps a susceptible vision in a constant state of flux. The visions sensitive to corroboration create a social reality with few fixed points to anchor a fanatical sense of right and wrong, of truth and falsity. When high levels of romanticism are welded to righteous indignation and the certainty of truth, the result is zeal. Zeal need not, of course, be directed to things of this world. The fanaticism of a highly romantic rhetorical vision may be directed to inner contemplation, but in the case of the romantic pragmatists, the romaticism and righteousness were channeled towards the world by a strong admixture of practical fantasy types which interpreted success in terms of saving souls, perfecting society, and progress. American reformers have been, for the most part, in the romantic pragmatic tradition and have been, for the most part, zealots.

Certainly, the motivations embedded in the ungenteel vision were highly charged with energy. The circuit rider worked hard, rode hard, persevered against the problems of frontier travel to make his rounds. The pragmatic bent of the vision urged action in the world which could be judged against clearly quantified results such as an increase in church membership. The vision was competitive and pitted each religious community that participated in it against all the others. Because the rhetorical vision valued the counting of converts, the boundaries of the participating religious communities had to be clear-cut. Minor doctrinal points served to define the various communities that participated in the ungenteel style and to focus the issues of many religious debates among members of the various sects and denominations. The rhetorical vision of the Baptist communities shared the large panorama and the basic rhetorical style with the Methodist and Christian churches and with smaller evangelical sects. The adherents of the ungenteel style shared common assumptions about argument, evidence, and proof, including the literal interpretation of the Bible as the supernaturally sanctioned avenue to knowledge. The proofs of logical cases in debates and sermons consisted, as they had in the archetype of the Puritan sermon, of quotations of Scripture.

The boundaries of religious subdivisions were defined not by the boundaries of the rhetorical vision but by doctrinal differences such as the question of whether or not infants should be baptized and whether baptism should consist of total immersion or sprinkling. Since the boundaries of the subgroups needed to be clear for the competition to take place, minor doctrinal matters were often magnified into major differences. Once the boundaries were clearly understood by all participants, the crossing over of a member from one denomination to another or the conversion of a sinner could easily be counted. One of the vision's most important values, therefore, was to interpret growth in size as something good. Growth was not simply success in terms of this world, although the rate of conversion was evidence of the perfecting of society, but growth was evidence of the success of the enterprise to bring the millennium to this world and to prepare for the glorious Second Advent. Growth came to symbolize progress in the larger design to create the ideal society.

The emotional evocations of the vision included humor, which stemmed from fantasy themes in the form of the tall tale, the practical joke (often uncomfortable and sometimes cruel for those who became the butt of it), and the gulling of pretensions. Anger and indignation were evoked by sinners, rowdies, minions of evil. Fear was evoked by threats of hell. Ecstasy was evoked by religious fervor and dramas of happiness and peace in heaven.

The ungenteel rhetorical style was very successful in attracting new converts. As a consciousness-raising rhetoric it far outdistanced the styles of the older established religions as represented by the Congregationalists and Anglicans. The persuasive appeal of the ungenteel tradition was centered in the drama of the "new birth." For individuals who faced here-and-now problems that made their lives miserable, the drama of the "new birth" was most attractive. Those who were unhappy with themselves and their condition in this world were offered a new start. The appeal of a new start has been a strong and continuing one in the United States. One of the impelling dramas of America has been the old mythic scenario of a quest—whether the specific goal has been the holy grail, the fountain of youth, gold, or fame and fortune. The drama contains excitement, adventure, and opportunity. The dream is appealing because it suggests that a person can leave cares behind and move to a new region, take up a new job, and meet new people. The population of the United States has tended to be restless and mobile. The persuasive mechanism which assured each potential convert that he was valuable and that his soul was equal to that of the most wealthy and well-positioned individual in the community worked persuasively on many people in the years after the Revolutionary War.

At the same time, the secularized dramas of the "new birth" in the frontier region served to celebrate a sense of place and community. The back country, or the frontier region, was an important *place* in the social reality of the adherents. Even though they may have been moving westward from one farm to another, they symbolically remained on "the frontier." The frontier as a place, a territory to identify with and to settle in, even though it moved geographically, substituted for the older concept of a specific home place or geographical territory which had been characteristic of the Old World. The frontier, while ever-moving geographically, remained a rhetorical region which held the promise of a new secular birth. One could, therefore, become a born-again Christian and start anew on a farm or in a business with a fresh chance of becoming a woman or a man of substance in the here-and-now of the frontier.

In addition to fulfilling an individual's personal need for a better life and for a better explanation of the purpose of life, the ungenteel style provided an account and celebration of the community and a meaning for existence. The vision built the individual self-image by providing the supernatural sanction of the "new birth." If a person was unhappy with the circumstances of his or her first physical birth, he or she could, by means of the "new birth" emerge in a better position in relation to others in terms of all eternity. The born-again Christian was, in the evangelical style, the new nobility of heaven. The adherent to the ungenteel style was also an important person, because he or she was part of an important and significant effort in the New World to prepare the way for the millenium.

The rhetorical vision celebrated the community with dramas that valued features of the here-and-now existence, which observers sharing another consciousness often found squalid, mean, and degrading. Visitors from Europe often came to the new country to study its evolving society and culture and some wrote back reports for readers in Europe. Harriet Martineau, Frances Trollope, and Captain Marryat, for instance, observed frontier life and the rhetorical practices of the ungenteel tradition in religious services and revivals and found the experience distasteful if not disgusting.[28] The worldly European observers were often impressed by the filth of the frontier, the lack of conveniences, the lack of niceties of life, the poor quality of literature, of the arts, and of education. The ungenteel vision, however, took the very features of the unfolding experience that the observers denigrated and elevated them to virtues.

The vision created a highly cohesive community of people zealously dedicated to its values, motives, and emotional evocations. The trauma of conversion created commitment. The more difficult and painful it is to gain admission to a group, the more drawn to the group are its converts. The vision also created a competitive framework in which each religious sect and denomination could judge its worth in terms of the number of converts and members. Competition encourages cohesiveness.[29]

The vision had considerable holding power in rededicating the inheritors of the style to its basic vision and to its rhetorical theory and practice. Still, it proved to be not as hardy a vision as that of the original Puritan founders. By the 1840s, dissident groups within both Methodist and Baptist denominations were raising issues relating to the proper mode of preaching. The dissidents argued that the old rhetoric had worked but that its day was past, that the need was for higher standards of reasoning, less emotionalism but more dignity in the pulpit and an educated clergy.[30] In a sense, the vision contained within it several motives which, when they worked themselves out in practice, resulted in a changing set of conditions undermining the vision itself.

The new secular birth on the frontier provided new opportunities for wealth and social position. The newly rich and the new community leaders soon searched for earmarks of status, which were modeled after the fashion of the settled communities in the East. The heirs of the ungenteel style who continued on in the tradition of romantic pragmatism after the Civil War often spoke in a genteel rhetoric which cast a rosy and sugary glow over all its dramatizations and whose adherents never publicly shared fantasies involving a crude sexual allusion, a withering depiction of squalor or poverty, or a harsh and wrathful God.

The rhetorical vision of the ungenteel tradition had elements of a reform rhetoric in it. The main focus in reforming society, however, was upon the conversion of individuals. When an individual was born again, he began to lead a new life and gave up his gambling, drinking, fornicating ways. The prostitute gave up her profession; the slaveholder freed his slaves. The way to reform society was to perfect the individual. Thus, the Methodist, Baptist, and Christian communities furnished little energy for the great benevolent reforms, including that of the abolition of slavery in the years from 1830 to 1860. Just as the Unitarians, the inheritors of the rhetorical tradition promulgated by Charles Chauncey at the time of the Great Awakening, provided few active abolition agents (Samuel May being one leading exception), so the Methodists furnished few agents (Orange Scott, the New England circuit rider being an exception). The direct connection between religious and reform rhetoric and the major motivations for abolition were to come not from the right or left wings of the tradition of romantic pragmatism but from its center, from the New Light Presbyterians exemplified by their leading rhetorical theoretician and practitioner Charles Grandison Finney.

7

The Style of Evangelical Reform

Practice and Theory

The decade of the 1830s in the United States was a period of rhetorical crisis and creativity in which old rhetorical visions relating to religion were coming apart and in which new dramas relating to slavery were breaking through all attempts to paper over the conflict. Across the country, groups and communities were sharing secular fantasies relating to slavery, state sovereignty, and the restoration of the government of the United States to the dream of the founders by means of the destruction of the national bank. In western New York, the evangelist Charles Grandison Finney was the center of a revival with a burgeoning new rhetorical vision catching up masses of people with an intensity and zeal reminiscent of Whitefield and the Great Awakening a century before. Little wonder that in the consciousness-creating process of combining novel fantasies with the fragments of old visions, some of the emerging rhetoric fused sacred and secular forms into a new shared consciousness of reform, centering on the abolition of slavery.

In the beginning, the new evangelical reform style was drawn primarily from the religious rhetoric associated with the revival and only secondarily aroused by the sharing of the graphic melodramas of *The Liberator*, a newspaper published in Boston by William Lloyd Garrison. Conceivably, in this period of consciousness creating, had the Garrisonians come to share in the fantasies of the evangelicals and had the Finneyites come to participate in the agitators' dramatizations of the corrupt nature of secular and sacred institutions, the abolition effort might have become a unified movement sustained by a common rhetorical vision. As it was, as the evangelicals created a new consciousness, they came to place a primary emphasis on the secular reform of antislavery, but in the process they revitalized and shared many of the eccentric fantasies of their religious vision. The Garrisonians rejected the religious fantasies of the evangelicals and the evangelicals, in turn, rejected the agitators' depiction of the corrupt nature of the church and the government. As the new communication practices hardened into mature communication styles, the impulse to free the slaves divided into two main rhetorical camps. Participants in one of the new styles consisted of those who practiced the rhetoric of conversion to antislavery, using as their exemplar the model of the charismatic abolition agent Theodore Dwight Weld. Participants in the other communication style consisted of those who practiced the rhetoric of agitation and revolution after the model of William Lloyd Garrison. Evidence that the abolition impulse had divided into two coherent rhetorical communities came not only from the incompatible content of the central dramas which sustained their visions, but also from the division of the original American Anti-Slavery Society along the boundaries of the rhetorical visions. By 1840, the agitators had succeeded in gaining control of the Society and the evangelicals withdrew.

This chapter is divided into two major sections. In the first, I examine the communication practices which resulted in the emergence of another romantic pragmatic communication style. In sketching the nature of the new communication, I emphasize the career of Theodore Weld, who served as the exemplar of a host of antislavery agents who practiced the style in its maturity, much as Whitefield had served as the exemplar for the evangelists of the latter half of the eighteenth century. In the second part of this chapter, I describe the communication theory associated with the evangelical reform style and use the formulations of Charles Grandison Finney as the basis for my analysis.

The maturation of the ungenteel style was but one of a large number of mushrooming communication practices in the first third of the nineteenth century. In the social reality of Milburn's rhetorical vision, evangelical preaching was a new, different, and unique contribution of the American frontier. The eastern theological progeny of Jonathan Edwards, however, were also active and thriving during the same period.

While the circuit riders chanted at the camp meetings to the shouts and groans of their listeners, Lyman Beecher, a blacksmith's son converted during a revival at Yale College, became one of the leading evangelical preachers of the country. First at East Hampton, then at Litchfield, and finally at Hanover Street Church in Boston itself, Beecher preached in an evangelical style that emphasized zeal but still clung to Jonathan Edwards's belief that to be a shining light, a minister had to be able to teach.

So even while the Unitarians and Episcopalians were publishing sermons and the deists and free thinkers were causing controversies, the eastern evangelical wing of romantic pragmatism was successfully preaching in urban settled communities. The broad evangelical style of preaching was not solely a frontier phenomenon. The same style that moved people in Ohio moved them in New York, Philadelphia, and even in Boston.

While Beecher was gaining a national reputation as a revivalist in the East, the wave of piety radiating from the Kentucky camp meetings was moving northward. The two wings of the revival movement came together, as it were, in western New York, in the rhetoric of the evangelist Charles Grandison Finney.

Finney was clearly in the camp of the heart-to-heart preachers but he did not condone the emotional excesses of the more radical wing of the frontier revivalists. He was not formally trained for the ministry but did not disdain thinking and scholarship. He did not approve of loose emotional rhapsodies in the pulpit but rather stressed strong argumentation to answer objections. He retained some of the trappings of Calvinistic theology with its emphasis on abasement and atonement, but he moved even more in the direction of free will and free grace than did Lyman Beecher. William McLoughlin saw Finney as a creature of his time and as a man of Jacksonian philosophical and social principles. Finney's preaching, according to McLoughlin, consisted, "However inconsistently" of a blend of "reason and faith, science and revelation, self-reliance and divine guidance, pragmatism and intuition, head and heart, moral self-denial and spiritual freedom, social reform and rugged individualism, humanitarianism and piety."[1]

The revival was intense in that area of western New York along the Erie canal. The region came to be known as the "'Burnt' or 'Burned-over' District" by those "adopting the prevailing western analogy between the fires of the forest and those of the spirit."[2] The people of the "Burned-over District" were given to unusual religious enthusiasms and susceptible to sharing fantasies relating to the perfection of human beings and the attainment of the millennium. Around the powerful vortex of the emerging new consciousness of the Finneyites swirled a host of lesser whirlpools and eddies. A small community of devout, who would come to be known as Mormons, were participating in shared fantasies that created a new consciousness relating to a new dispensation from God and a new book of revelations delivered on tablets of gold to Joseph Smith. John Humphrey Noyes was converted in the revival and by the end of the decade, he was the persona who came to symbolize a rhetorical vision of perfectionism. Harried from Putney, Vermont, because their rhetorical vision included dramas celebrating community marriages for the perfected saints, Noyes and his group moved to Oneida in the "Burned-over District" and formed a commune which practiced Christian communism and began to act out their shared fantasies of plural marriages.

Among the secular dramas which large communities of Americans shared were those relating to sectional loyalties, state sovereignty, the tariff, the institution of slavery, and the sacred ground of the territories. In 1830, Daniel Webster and Robert Y. Haynes debated in the Senate of the United States the major political issues which divided the country. For much of the public, the debate was a dramatic acting out of the sectional conflict and the basis for shared fantasies in which the Webster persona symbolized the Northeast and the Hayne persona stood for the south. Hayne included a series of dramas which apologized for and defended the institution of slavery and which, at least, implied a continuation of the practice. In 1833, Webster and Calhoun debated the Force Bill of President Jackson, which was designed to bring South Carolina into adherence with the Tariff Act. Again, the two persona dramatically portrayed the nature of the sectional conflict for the American public.[3]

In the 1820s, elected officials had attempted to deal with the conflict over slavery through the formal channels of communication by a rhetoric of compromise and when that failed, they cut off formal consideration of the issue by means of gag rules. The official attempts to suppress communication about slavery failed, however, when an informal and unofficial rhetoric began to ignite an explosive sharing of fantasies which brought the practice of slaveholding vividly to the public consciousness. William Lloyd Garrison and his newspapaer, *The Liberator*, became, in the 1830s, the basis for a host of interpretative fantasies. Popular dramas portrayed the Garrison persona on a continuum from a heroic, almost godlike figure on one extreme to a villainous archdemon from hell on the other. But no matter how the fantasies interpreted the role of Garrison and the abolitionist which he symbolized, the fantasies relating to the immediate emancipation of the slaves on the soil where they lived were so new, graphic, and exciting, and the symbolic ground so fallow that they could not be suppressed. Some eagerly shared them; many were repulsed by them, but almost all were interested in them.

Many Americans had written about and spoken about slavery before Garrison's vivid dramatizations began attracting or repelling segments of the general public. One important flurry of antislavery rhetoric prior to 1830 came at the time of the Revolutionary War. James Otis and Thomas Paine denounced the institution of slavery in pamphlets during the revolutionary period. Among the founders of the Articles of Confederation and the Federal Constitution, antislavery sentiment was strong. Congress excluded slavery from the Northwest Territory in 1787. By 1804, every Northern state had either abolished slavery or passed laws for the gradual emancipation of the slaves. In 1808, the international slave trade was outlawed, and the Missouri Compromise of 1820 prohibited slavery in the territory north of 36' 30° in the Louisiana Purchase.

Antislavery societies were organized as early as 1775 when the Pennsylvania Abolition Society was formed. They soon spread throughout the new country, both North and South. The various societies sent delegates to a national meeting of the American Convention of Delegates from Abolition Societies. The national body, however, was a weak coalition of organizations with little agreement on methods to be used to achieve emancipation.

A stronger force in the antislavery field was the American Society for Colonizing the Free People of Colour of the United States. The Colonizing Society was organized in 1816 and represented the culmination of efforts that began back in the times of the Revolutionary War. By 1833, when the American Anti-Slavery Society was organized, there were 97 local colonization societies in the North and 146 in the South—yet in the years from 1820 to 1833, the colonization efforts had resulted in placing fewer than three thousand blacks in Africa.

The abolition movement was, in some respects, a continuation of the antislavery sentiment of the earlier times. The antislavery rhetoric of the abolitionists, however, blazed forth with shared fantasies which aroused such zeal and intensity that in a few years, it established one of the great reform movements of American history. To fully understand the new reform rhetoric, one needs to appreciate the religious persuasion of Charles Grandison Finney.

Finney was born in 1792 in Warren, Connecticut. When he was two years old, his family moved to Oneida County, New York. He attended the common schools of the area and Hamilton Oneida Academy. When he was in his teens, he taught school near Henderson, New York, and in 1812, he returned to Warren, Connecticut, to attend high school and prepare for Yale College. By 1814, he had decided against going to Yale and taught for several years in New Jersey. He returned to New York in 1816 and several years later entered the law office of Benjamin Wright of Adams, New York. In 1820, Finney was admitted to the bar and the following year experienced an intense conversion experience, which he cast into the form of the Pauline fantasy type.

Finney dropped the law and began to study with his pastor, the Reverend George Gale; in 1823, he was licensed to preach by the Presbytery of St. Lawrence. He was ordained as an evangelist by the Oneida Presbytery in 1824.

For the next two years, the young evangelist conducted remarkably successful revivals in small towns of western New York. In 1826–1827, he continued his triumphant preaching in Utica and Troy. At Utica, during the height of the excitement, he converted Theodore Weld.

After 1827, Finney went from success to success. He turned eastward to the larger metropolitan areas and conducted revivals in Wilmington, Philadelphia, Lancaster, and Reading. In 1829, he conducted his first revival in New York, and the next year, in Rochester, he experienced his greatest triumph. Subsequently, he carried his revival to Providence and Boston and in 1832 accepted the pastorate of the Chatham Street Chapel in New York. The Chatham Street Chapel was the Second Free Presbyterian Church. Finney's work was sponsored by Arthur and Lewis Tappan, successful merchants and evangelical leaders of the benevolent movement. The next year, in Finney's church, the New York Anti-Slavery Society was formed.

Finney was a product of the combined Presbyterian and Congregational "Plant of Union" churches. Like most evangelicals, he was ecumenical in his approach and as he itinerated through the country, holding "protracted meetings" during which he preached several times on Sunday and regularly during the week, he converted thousands of people in one of the most impressive evangelical tours since the time of Whitefield.

When Finney moved to New York at the behest of Arthur and Lewis Tappan, he became connected with the Eastern branch of an extensive benevolent organization. The Tappan brothers were exemplars of the radical reformers who dedicated their property and their lives to the cause of reforming mankind. They were wealthy merchants, who supported with time and money the causes of temperance, Sunday schools, tract and Bible distribution, Sabbath observance, and education. They were part of an interconnected power structure that controlled a huge empire of benevolent societies. Many of the societies were relatively new when Finney came to New York, the product of the years from 1820 to 1830, but they had by the end of that decade already grown into immense institutions spreading over the entire country and testifying to the attractiveness of the rhetorical vision and style associated with them. The eight largest societies were dedicated to promoting home and foreign missions, distributing Bibles and religious tracts, promoting Sunday schools, propagating temperance, and saving the sinful sailors. In addition to the eight largest, many smaller associations were dedicated to such causes as saving prostitutes, outlawing the wearing of corsets, and promoting manual labor education.

Although the benevolent empire was nondenominational, it was dominated by "New School" Presbyterians of the persuasion of the Great Revival.

The leaders of the societies were relatively few and included, in addition to the Tappans, such people as Thomas Smith Grimké, Gerrit Smith, Anson Phelps Stokes, and William Jay.

Finney's rhetorical vision participated in the general optimism and the belief in the perfectibility of mankind associated with romantic pragmatism. He was interested in reforms including abolition, temperance, dietary regulation, and education. He castigated such sins as drunkenness, the use of tobacco, theater going, card playing, and dancing. Finney's approach to the problem of reform, however, was strongly grounded in his belief that the way to reform society was to regenerate individuals by converting them. The millennium would come when enough revival ministers trained in his rhetorical vision could convert the entire country.

The revival and reform met when Theodore Weld's aunt tricked him into hearing the famous Charles Gradison Finney during the Utica revival. As Finney exemplified the fusion of the western and eastern wings of the heirs of Edwards and Whitefield, so did Weld personify, in his speaking, the fusion of evangelical preaching and the impulse for reform. Weld provides an ideal symbol of the transition from sacred rhetoric to secular speaking.

Theodore Dwight Weld was born in Hampton, Connecticut, in 1803. He came from a long line of Puritans. He numbered among his ancestors Dwights, Edwardses, and Hutchinsons. Both of his grandfathers were ministers and his father, Ludovicus Weld, was a graduate of Harvard and a pastor of the Congregational Church. Young Weld grew up in a Puritan environment that stressed the importance of duty, the clear distinction between right and wrong, and the necessity of stamping out sin, less one become a party to it. When Theodore was still a child, his father accepted a Congregational pulpit at Pompey in western New York. Weld's heredity furnished him with an abundance of what, in his time, was called "animal spirits." He bubbled with enthusiasm, excitement, playfulness and a sense of adventure. He was congenitally incapable of rest. He threw himself into every enterprise and venture with an abandon and singleness of purpose that often broke even his rugged physical equipment.

When, in the soul-searching, introspective rhetorical style of the evangelical reformers, he wrote long accounts of his shortcomings to his future wife, he told of his fatal flaw of playfulness. "It is in my very bones and blood and all the breakings, bruisings, burnings, drownings, exhaustions, toils, cares, conflicts and agonies that have racked me and swept over me and thro' me . . . cannot drive it out." He fully expected to continue "to *cut all sorts of boyish capers* with a perfect *zest*." He would get out of sight and hearing of people who would be *"appalled"* by such behavior and "jump and hop and scream like a loon and run on all fours and wrestle and throw stones."[4]

When Weld was a young teenager, he managed a hundred-acre farm and collected enought money to go to Phillips Academy, where he studied so hard that he developed a severe inflammation of the eyes. The doctors thought he might regain his eyesight if he rested regularly in a dark room for seven years. Weld was full of animal spirits and restless. He would not follow the doctor's advice and cast about for something to do. He always had a poor memory. While at Phillips Academy, he had attended a series of lectures on the art of improving the memory, and he continued to read on the subject. He decided to take to the road as an itinerating lecturer on mnemonics.

The seventeen-year-old Weld proved to be an able lecturer and toured the country for the next three years. With his eyes much improved, Weld, at twenty, was living at Hamilton College in New York in time to be caught up in the Great Revival when it swept through the region. Weld joined Finney's Holy Band and worked with such zeal at the revival that his health failed again and he had to spend the winter of 1827 on a whaling vessel bound for Labrador.

The sea restored his health, and Weld enrolled at the Oneida Institute, a manual labor school permeated with evangelical religion, perfectionism, and reform. Too much was going on, however; too many opportunities beckoned for a man of Weld's ability, temperament, and training, for him to continue long as a student. President Gale of Oneida knew of Weld's persuasive skills and soon had him traveling the country to raise money for the school.

When Finney accepted the Tappans' invitation to take a church in New York, he promised to try to turn some of their contributions toward the Oneida Institute. (Finney had studied with President Gale before he gave up the study of law and prepared for his career as an evangelist.) Lewis Tappan enrolled his two sons in the school and become converted to the manual labor plan. The Tappans, with characteristic zeal, organized a society for Promoting Manual Labor in Literary Institutions. By now, too, the Tappans had their eyes on Weld, and when they offered to make him the agent of their new manual labor society, he accepted.

During his manual labor agency, Weld also lectured on temperance and discussed the evils of slavery. Toward the end of his year, he visited Western Reserve College in Ohio. In a series of intense consciousness-creating sessions, he discussed the problem of the antislavery reform with Professors Elizur Wright and Beriah Green. When Weld returned to New York, he was a convert to the doctrine of immediate abolition.

One of Weld's duties as agent for the manual labor reform was to select a site for a manual labor seminary to train ministers for evangelical religion. Weld selected Lane Seminary in Cincinnati, Ohio. The understanding was that whatever school Weld selected would be given substantial financial support by the Tappans. To Lane, Weld brought a number of his friends, one might almost say disciples, from Oneida—New York men from the "Burned-over District," stamped with the mark of the Great Revival. In addition, he recruited several acquaintances from his itinerating in the South, including Marius Robinson and William Allan.

The Tappans secured Lyman Beecher, the foremost eastern revivalist, for the presidency of Lane and, with the help of Weld, hoped to make the school not only a force for evangelical religion but also the center for antislavery and manual labor reform in the West.

Although asked to join the Lane faculty as professor of rhetoric, Weld decided to return as a student. He was, however, no ordinary student, and even though Beecher was one of the most famous religious leaders in the country, he was not the leader of Lane Seminary in the eyes of Weld's followers. Beecher himself wrote of Weld that he "took the lead of the whole institution. The young men had, many of them, been under his care, and they thought he was a god."[5]

Weld set to work to abolitionize the student body. The result of the efforts of Weld and the Oneida men was a classical case of consciousness raising. He started first with the southern students and converted William T. Allan of Alabama. Most of the antislavery sentiment at Lane, as in the country at large, was channeled into the Colonization Society. When Weld had enough students on his side, he challenged the colonization partisans to a public debate. The debate was held despite faculty opposition. The result was one of the great forensic events in the history of reform speaking. The debates lasted for eighteen evenings, with eighteen speakers delivering major addresses. The first nine evenings considered the question of whether or not the slave states had the duty to abolish slavery immediately. For the first two evenings, William Allan argued for the affirmative, for immediate emancipation. Weld was the closing affirmative speaker. On the ninth evening, a unanimous vote was given for the affirmative. The last nine nights considered the usefulness of the American Colonization Society.[6]

As a result of the debates, the bulk of the students shared a new consciousness dedicated to immediate abolition and formed a society to propagate the new doctrine. Their subsequent agitation for the new gospel aroused the ire of the surrounding community, for Cincinnati was, in many respects, a slave city on free territory. Meantime, the American Anti-Slavery

Society had been organized in Philadelphia and wanted "a number of faithful mighty agents, in whose persons the Society shall live and breathe and wax strong before the public." Elizur Wright wrote that the society had so far fixed upon Garrison and Phelps of Boston and Samuel May of Connecticut. The fourth man was Theodore Weld. Garrison was unwilling to leave the *Liberator* and May and Phelps were unlikely to sign up for an extended agency. Wright trusted that Weld "will consider this a call of Providence to take the field" (p. 121). In hopes that Weld would accept, Wright enclosed an agent's commission. In the particular instruction accompanying the commission, the society stated the basic persuasive line that the agents were to promulgate.

> You will inculcate every where the great fundamental principle of IMMEDI-ATE ABOLITION, as the duty of all masters, on the ground that slavery is both unjust and unprofitable. Insist principally on the SIN OF SLAVERY, because our main hope is in the consciences of men, and it requires little logic to prove that it is always safe to do right. To question this, is to impeach the superin-tending Providence of God (p. 125).

Weld did not accept the commission because he was busy with his good works and the aftermath of the debates at Lane. An aroused community had put pressure on the trustees to stop the antislavery activity. President Beecher was in the East, and since the summer break was soon upon them, the trustees decided to temporize. During the summer, Weld and the others went about their program of sending antislavery propaganda and making abolitionist speeches. When school resumed, the pressure became intense and Beecher was finally forced to take a stand. In the end, he chastized the students, accused Weld and Allan as ringleaders, and threatened them with expulsion. Weld walked out of Lane and took some fifty students with him. Nine or ten enrolled in other schools; four recanted and requested reentrance to Lane. The remainder set up their own school in Cumminsville and began to teach each other and to continue their work with benevolent enterprises in the Negro community in Cincinnati.

The officials at Lane, under the prodding of Beecher, finally agreed to compromise their stand somewhat and to remove the threat of expulsion for Weld, but he decided that his usefulness at Lane was at an end. In October 1834, Theodore Weld became a full-time agent for the American Anti-Slavery Society.[7]

In Theodore Weld's day, the role of professional rhetoricians was played by agents. Where today a contemporary organization facing a persuasive problem will hire a public relations counsel or an advertising agency, in the nineteenth century an organization would procure an agent. A wide variety of organizations, institutions, and societies employed people whose duty it was to forward the goals or the group, to raise money in its behalf, and to gain supporters. The agents were paid enough money to assure that they would be free to devote their entire time to promotion. The primary technique of the agent was oral persuasion. Agents lectured, lobbied at legislatures, and tried to persuade people in conversations to support their causes. Their oral persuasion was directed to converting the auditors and to raising funds.

Weld proved to be a superb agent for the Anti-slavery Society. Reporting to Wright from Putnam, Ohio, in March of 1835, Weld wrote that he had lectured five times at Concord, seven times at Oldtown, nine times at Bloomingburg, and fourteen times at Circleville. He had a public debate with a physician and a Baptist deacon at Oldtown, and at Circleville, he had debates three evenings with a lawyer. Indeed, Weld reported that he handled the debaters so handily that his opponents accused the abolitionists of setting them up as foils.

At Circleville, Weld faced the kind of fierce opposition that he often had to handle. The Presbyterian minister accused him of instigating the trouble at Lane Seminary. He claimed the faculty had warned the public against Weld. Unable to speak in the Presbyterian church, Weld finally gained permission to lecture in the vestry room of the Episcopal church. During the second lecture, a mob gathered and threw stones and eggs through the windows. One of the stones struck the antislavery agent on the head and stunned him. His supporters hung cloaks up to the windows to protect the audience from the missiles. The threats of the mob were so loud that the trustees of the church would not allow him to lecture in the vestry room again. He then found a large room fitted for a store that would hold about one hundred people. Again the crowd threw stones and clubs against the shuttered windows. When Weld came out of the building, a large crowd was waiting for him. "Lamp black, nails, divers pockets full of stones and eggs had been provided for the occasion, and many had disguised their persons, smeared their faces." Weld was uninjured that night and faced an even larger and more violent demonstration for the next several nights. After he had lectured seven times, however, the commotion quieted and for the latter part of the course he had "a smooth sea." Not only that, but "God owned his truth—confounded those who rose up against him—filled gainsayers with confusions, and *now* Circleville may be set down as a strong abolition center" (p. 207).

Through the year 1835, Weld pursued his agency, repeating the story of Circleville over and over again, meeting the mobs and the local debaters, besting them during the course of a protracted meeting, sending his converts out like members of Finney's Holy Band to encourage the wavering, and calling at the close for those converted to immediate abolition to stand. Thus, he made his way in the tradition of the itinerating evangelists. Theodore Weld was an event; he broke the monotony of the frontier routine. Excitement followed in his wake. He caused controversies and mobs. In the shared fantasies of his followers, he was a doer of mighty deeds, and God was at his elbow and inspired his words. As he moved through Ohio, he left behind, in most of the villages and towns, an active antislavery society.

Weld's success so impressed the national committee of the Anti-slavery Society that they decided to increase the number of agents and applied to Weld for aid in their selection. Weld turned back to Ohio and headed for Oberlin. The Lane rebels were pleased to see him. Weld immediately began his series of antislavery lectures. In the middle of his stay, he wrote Lewis Tappan that he had been in Oberlin ten days and had lectured every day. On the Sabbath, he had given the beginning of his Bible argument and would continue it on the next Sunday. Weld lectured in one of the new buildings that was unfinished to an audience seated on rough boards placed on blocks. Five or six hundred people attended night after night, "shivering on the rough boards without fire these cold nights, without any thing to lean back against, and this too until nine o'clock."

Weld was spending an hour or two with the "five brethren who are going out to lecture on Abolition" and "indoctrinating them in the principles, facts, arguments, etc., of the whole subject" (p. 244). Among the recruits were William Allan, James Thome, John Alvord, Huntington Lyman, and Sereno Streeter. Henry B. Stanton was already an antislavery agent in Rhode Island. The new agents went with Weld from Oberlin to Cleveland, where he continued their education into the intricacies of the practice of the profession of antislavery agent. He provided them with facts, fantasy themes, and techniques to handle the difficulties of gaining a hearing and persuading hostile audiences.

Weld and the new antislavery agents had a great harvest in the Western Reserve of Ohio. His followers were cast in the same mold and proved to be the same type of hardy and adventuresome fellows as their leader. John Alvord met James A. Thome in Middlebury, Ohio, and after five meetings, including a Sabbath lecture on the Bible argument, Alvord reported that "last evening Midd[l]ebury puked. Her stomach had evidently become overloaded by the amount of undiluted Pikery [?] she had taken at the two preceding discussions. The system would not endure it. Spasmodic heavings and retchings were manifest during the whole day." Then came the typical threats of violence, the lack of courage on the part of the committee of arrangements, the agents going through with the scheduled meeting, and the collecting of an audience. Thome began to lecture but about eight o'clock, a "broadside of Eggs, Glass, Egg shells, whites and yolks flew on every side. Br. Thom[e]s Fact Book received an egg just in its bowels. . . . I have been trying to clean off this morning, but cant get off the stink. Thome dodged like a stoned gander." Thome appended a postscript to the letter in which he accused Alvord of being "mean" in his description, for Thome was "brave as a warrior; but I did really think the stove was exploding with a tremendous force" (pp. 260–261).

While Thome and Alvord were watching the ropy strings of broken rotten eggs fly about their heads in Middlebury, Weld had moved into Utica, New York. The year before, abolitionists had been routed from Utica by force, but this time Weld carried all before him once again. He toured New York and his success carried his fame throughout the country. He even caught the attention of the Boston Female Anti-slavery Society.

Weld's triumphant tour, his phenomenal agency, continued until he came to Troy, New York. Here Weld met defeat. He was repeatedly mobbed and maintained that the mayor and other officials were unable to keep law and order and had, indeed, emboldened the mob. He charged that one of the city officers was a leader of the mob and reported that several times groups rushed up the aisles to pull him from the pulpit while he was speaking. As he moved from the auditorium to his lodgings, he was again mobbed and missiles were thrown at him.

Weld seemed to sense the fury of the mob at Troy and to realize that all his other challenges had been less than this one. But he would not turn back. "Let every abolitionist debate the matter once for all, and settle it with himself whether he is an abolitionist from *impulse* or principle," he wrote from Troy in the midst of his battle, "whether he can lie upon the rack—and clasp the faggot—and tread with steady step the scaffold." He felt that revelations of character had been made already by that question but that they were *"but the shadow of those to come"* (p. 310).

Despite his best efforts, Weld was unable to tame the mobs at Troy and get a hearing. He kept up his agency for a short time longer with some of his old success but he had, once again, thrown himself into his work with such abandon, had shouted down so many crowds, and put out such a mighty effort at Troy that his voice was gone. He was to speak in public again years later but never with such concentrated energy and such great effect. For all intents and purposes, the premier practitioner of the arts of the benevolent agent of the early nineteenth century was to give up his profession after 1836.

Weld and his men had done a thorough job in Ohio. The evangelical agents were so effective that the American Anti-slavery Society decided to change its tactics. It poured almost all of its resources into increasing the numbers of its paid agents to seventy, the same number as the biblical apostles, and, at Weld's insistence, they agreed to send them into the rural areas. Weld took on the task of recruiting and preparing the new agents. Again, the core of Oneida men who had been Lane rebels and had moved to Oberlin helped him. They weighed the names and even voted on various possible recruits. Finally, a large number of agents congregated in New York in November. For twenty days, eight hours a day, the indoctrination continued. For four days, Weld developed his Bible argument against slavery. The famous band of seventy were, for the most part, speakers in the style of Charles Grandison Finney and Thedore Weld.

At the height of his antislavery agency, Weld's rhetorical vision celebrated the frontier as powerfully as did the ungenteel rhetoric. When Finney took the pastorate in New York, Weld worried that the big city would corrupt the young evangelist. Later, he wrote to Finney, urging him to come to Cincinnati because "you never can move this vast valley by working the lever in Boston, New York or Philadelphia." At any rate, in Weld's opinion, even if westerners came to New York to visit, "their heads and hearts are stuffed with everything but religion. They are whirling in all the hustle and bustle and chaffering and purchasing, confused and perplexed with the details and statistics of filthy lucre" (pp. 66–67). But in the final analysis, the argument was always the same: "Here is to be the battle field of the world. Here Satans [sic] seat is. A mighty effort must be made to dislodge him *soon*, or the West is undone" (pp 67–68).

The rural areas controlled the destiny of the nation. Convert the back country and the cities must fall. Thus, Weld wrote to Lewis Tappan. "let the great cities *alone*: they must be burned down by *back fires*. The springs to touch in order to move them *lie in the country.*" If the money spent in Boston had been applied to the countryside around Boston, much more would have been done. Weld found in Ohio that when it was "utterly impossible to find rest for the sole of my foot in the capitol of the county," he could spend some time in the surrounding countryside "among the yeomanry and instead of being thrust out, I would be invited and importuned to go to the county seat" (p. 287).

Weld systematically developed his ethos as a rough, crude, unlettered man fit for the rough and tumble speaking of the frontier but useless in the polite circles of urban culture. When Weld turned down the invitations to speak (and often even to attend) the conventions and meetings of the antislavery societies, he continually excused himself on the grounds that "the stateliness and Pomp and Circumstance of an anniversary I loathe in my inmost soul. It seems so like ostentatious display, a mere make believe and mouthing, a sham and show off. It is an element I was never made to move in. My heart was never *in* that way of doing things" (p. 286). Typically, Weld would apply his masterly skill at vituperation and ridicule to the ritual and rhetoric of social conventions. "I fear much lest our anti slavery agents get too much in the habit of *gadding*, attending anniversaries, sailing round in Cleopatras barge." What was wanted and what Weld was ready to provide was *"work, work*, boneing down to it" (p. 287). At any rate, he maintained he would be out of place at a convention in the East because, "I am a Backwoodsman—can grub up stumps and roll logs and burn brush heaps and break green sward. Let me keep about my *own* business and stay in my *own* place" (p. 286).

When word came back to Boston of Weld's conquest of Utica, New York, the women of the Boston Female Anti-Slavery Society decided to offer Weld a three-month agency in Boston and eastern Massachusetts. Anne Warren Weston wrote Weld that the women felt "a lecturer, experienced, courageous, and eloquent was needed, and we know of no one to whom we can apply, who combines all these requisites so well as do yourself" (p. 268). One may conjecture at Weld's response to the request of the women from the citadel and symbol of urbanity. His reply, however, was characteristic. After explaining that he was the only agent in New York and that his "personal acquaintance in this state" gave him an advantage which he would not have in Boston, he closed as follows:

> I am a *Backwoodsman untamed*—my bearish proportions have never been licked into *city shape*—and are quite too uncombed and shaggy for "Boston notions"— an [sic] my tastes and habitutes of mind unfit me to act upon the formalities, statliness, courtliness and *artificialities* of *city life*—a *stump* is my throne my parish my home—my element the everydayisms of plain common life—a bear in a millinary or a rhinocros [sic] among flow [er] beds *might by possibility* serve to illustrate the doctrine of *Adaptation*—but enough—[8]

Although Weld's vision was zealous and filled with moral fervor it was also dedicated to argument. When conducting a long dispute with the Grimké sisters about nonviolence and women's rights, Weld noted:

> Every letter almost every line I have received from you on this subject has impressed me deeply with the great *unprofitableness* of discussion on a subject demanding *preeminently* ANALYSIS at the outset, *explicit* statement, *accurate* definition, perfect explanation of terms, and nice adjustment of positions, UNLESS the discussion is conducted under such circumstances that the parties can come to close quarters (p. 452).

On the question of nonviolence, the peace argument, Weld set out his criteria for sound argument. "I conjure you by love of Christ," he wrote, "to *prove*, PROVE all things." He had yet to see anything in the shape of an argument on the question. He admitted that, in his opinion, the quality of thinking in general was "so utterly loose and rambling, prone to jump at conclusions . . . that I know scarcely a single mind in whose results of reasoning I have any confidence" (p. 514).

Although Weld was tough-minded and had high standards of proof, he was also extremely skillful at dramatizing. A summary of one of Weld's temperance speeches appeared in the *Western Recorder* of March 22, 1831. According to the editor, many knew the statistics relating to drunkenness but few "have seen this army mustered, and marched in regular review. This was done by Mr. W." Weld called upon his audience to imagine with him "the mighty host" as he picked them "from the gutters and sewers, the groceries and grogshops, poor houses, prisons and asylums, and marshalled [them] with their bloated and shocking visages, their staggering gait, their filthy and tattered habiliments, their fettered limbs, and their clanking chains." After the picture of the staggering army of wasted drinkers, Weld described another scene which included the "extended grave of 30,000 drunkards, annual victims." The 30,000 stood on the verge of the great grave and behind them the whole "army of the intemperate, and temperate, rank after rank, was arranged in accurate gradation, on to the merest sippers. At the close of the year, those in front were tumbled into the grave before them; and the next rank behind were marched up to take their places; and each posterior rank compelled to make the like advance."[9]

Joseph Farrand Tuttle heard Weld speak during the height of his powers, in May 1836, in the Methodist Church in St. Albans, Licking County, Ohio. Tuttle later became president of Wabash College. He recalled Weld as follows:

> I was never more excited by a public speech than then, and never have I seen an audience more excited. . . . The speaker was a very manly, noble looking man. . . . He used no notes, but spoke with the utmost precision and fluency. . . . His imagination was brilliant, his humor, at times, overpowering, and his invective in all respects the most terrible I ever heard. His voice was wonderful in its compass and power. . . . Indeed, those two hours and a half that night . . . were the most soul-stirring of my life (p. 298, n. 3).

Weld did not write out his speeches before delivery. In addition, he resisted every attempt to publish his speeches and letters in the newspapers. As a result, I have been unable to find any authentic verbatim account of a speech by Weld during his months as an antislavery agent. Weld's most famous effort, however, was his Bible argument against slavery. When he trained his agents, he gave them his Bible argument. Seminary students wrote and asked him to deliver his lectures on it. Wright, when he became secretary of the national committee, continually urged Weld to take out some weeks and write it down. With his voice gone, Weld was attached to the national committee in New York, and when he finally wrote out his lectures, the society published them anonymously under the title *The Bible Against Slavery: An Inquiry into the Patriarchal and Mosaic Systems on the Subject of Human Rights*. Weld, bereft of his ability to lecture, soon learned to be a pamphleteer, and one of the first things he learned was that the oral style was too prolix for written propaganda. He ruthlessly cut the language in his tracts. Even so, his style remained essentially oral and direct. If one assumes that the style of *The Bible Against Slavery* gave the flavor of Weld as he appeared yelling down his hecklers and holding his Ohio audiences spellbound, it can be used as evidence for his ability at invective.

Weld lashed the "spirit of slavery" with all the old Calvinistic fury of his ancestor from Northhampton. Slavery never takes refuge in the Bible of its own accord. "The horns of the altar" are its last resort. Then, collecting the resources of old Testament allusion and quotation, Weld wrote the following fantasy theme in which slavery personified becomes the villainous main character:

> Like other unclean spirits it "hateth the light, neither cometh to the light, lest its deeds should be reproved." Goaded to phrenzy in its conflicts with conscience and common sense, denied all quarter, and hunted from every covert, it vaults over the sacred inclosure and courses up and down the Bible, "seeking rest, and finding none." THE LAW OF LOVE, glowing on every page, flashes around it an omnipresent anguish and despair. It shrinks from the hated light, and howls under the consuming touch, as demons quailed before the Son of God, and shrieked, "Torment us not." At last, is slinks away under the types of the Mosaic system, and seeks to burrow out of sight among their shadows. Vain hope! Its asylum is its sepulchre; its city of refuge, the city of destruction. It flies from light into the sun; from heat, into devouring fire; and from the voice of God into the thickest of His thunders. [10]

In the rolling periods of the great antislavery agent of the West, the rhetoric of the evangelical style of pre-Civil War America culminated in the great moral crusade of the time.

By the time of Weld's agency for abolition in 1835, the practice of the new evangelical style had matured to the point where a consistent set of critical canons and a coherent rhetorical theory had emerged. In late 1834 and early 1835, Charles Grandison Finney gave a series of lectures on revivals of religion in which he presented the rehetorical theory of the center of romantic pragmatism in a clear, consistent, and systematic way. Where I had to piece together the theory of the ungenteel wing from a diversity of commentary and writings, particularly the works of Milburn, the special theory associated with the speaking of the Finneyites is fortunately clearly laid out.

Finney's rhetorical theory is the most important yet considered for the task of tracing the movement from sacred conversion to secular reform since it provides a clear transition between the style of preaching that emerged from the Great Awakening and the speech practices of the famous band of antislavery agents that, under the leadership of Theodore Weld, converted to abolition a great portion of Ohio and other western regions. I shall outline the basic theory as Finney presented it and note its romantic and pragmatic characteristics.[11] I shall also compare and contrast it with the ungenteel theory and the Puritan theory as represented by Jonathan Edwards.

In many respects, Finney's rhetorical style was an amalgamation of that of Jonathan Edwards and the frontier Methodists, Baptists, and Disciples of Christ. He remarked, for example, that "it is evident that we must have more exciting preaching, to meet the character and wants of the age." The old measures of preaching were no longer appropriate. One must look to the Methodists, Finney said. The Methodist ministers were "unlearned, in the common sense of the term, many of them taken right from the shop or the farm." Yet the success of the unlettered Methodist circuit riders was apparent for all to see. They had pushed their way and won souls in all regions. Their "plain, pointed and simple, but warm and animated mode of preaching has always gathered congregations." By contrast, few Presbyterians had managed to do so well. Some urged a continuance of the same "old, formal mode of doing things," but Finney argued that "as well might the North River be rolled back, as the world converted under such preaching." Those who adopted a different method of preaching similar to the Methodists "will run away from us." Finney argued that the public mind simply would not be held by the old-style Presbyterian speaking. What was needed was "exciting, powerful preaching, or the devil will have the people, except what the Methodists can save" (p. 273).

Finney's rhetorical theory rested upon one basic axiom and its psychological corollary. The evangelical pragmatic tradition, which we saw as part of the vitalization of preaching for the Puritans in England and which gained new impetus during the Great Awakening, evolved in the years after the Revolutionary War until, for Finney, in the 1830s, the basic criterion with which to judge preaching was *effect*.

In regard to the necessity to judge a speech on the basis of effect, Finney stood solidly with Milburn. Finney told the Presbyterians to emulate the Methodists because the circuit riders were gathering congregations and winning souls. Finney gave advice on all aspects of the speaking situation from the cleanliness, ventilation, and heating of the meeting place to the preparation of the sermon. But all of his suggestions were tested against the one touchstone of audience effect. The basic question was whether it worked.

The psychological corollary of the criterion that the proper rhetorical theory was one that worked was the assumption that the conversion experience was sudden, deep, and brief. Half-hearted, protracted, evolutionary effects were not the basis for evaluating the success of a speaker. Since the conversion was sudden and deep, one could make an immediate evaluation of the excellence of a sermon. "Protracted seasons of conviction are generally owing to defective instruction. Wherever clear and faithful instructions are given to sinners, there you will generally find that convictions are *deep and pungent*, but *short*" (p. 378). Finney further asserted that "so far as I have had opportunity to observe, those conversions which are most sudden have commonly turned out to be the best Christians. I know the reverse of this has often been held and maintained. But I am satisfied there is no reason for it. . . ." (p. 379).

The first and foremost characterization of a good sermon, therefore, was that it be practical. A "prime object" of the speakers should be to "make *present obligation* felt." Finney was disturbed because "the impression is not commonly made by ministers in their preaching that sinners are expected to repent NOW" (p. 206). The sinner ought also to be made to feel his guilt and should not be left with the impression that he is unfortunate but must be convicted of his personal guilt. The preacher must impress upon his hearers that "religion is something to *do*, not something to *wait for*. And they must do it now, or they are in danger of eternal death" (p. 207).

The proper method to achieve practical effects was the old searching sermon technique of the Puritan founders. The speaker could not rest until he had "ANNIHILATED every excuse of sinners." He had to "tear away the last LIE which he grasps in his hand, and make him feel that he is absolutely condemned before God" (p. 207). The minister was to pour the truth in upon the listeners and search out all the corners where they might hide and excuse themselves or rationalize away the charge. They had to be made to feel so guilty that they would be persuaded to act.

The strong emphasis upon effect, workability, doing something, and on activity in the theory of Milburn and Finney is what leads me to characterize their rhetorical styles as pragmatic. If a speech technique did not work to achieve a clear and immediate effect, if it did not deal with the everyday world and meet the nature of the man in the street, they spurned it for the practices which did succeed.

Finney spent considerable time in his lectures on revivals to discuss the proper education of the speaker. Here, he exhibited some of the same ambivalence toward the college-educated speaker as did the ungenteel theory reflected by William Henry Milburn. Nonetheless, I place Finney in a more middle-of-the-road position because he seriously considered attending college after his conversion when he decided to study for the ministry, and many of his followers did go on, first to Lane Theological Seminary and then to Oberlin College. For Finney, the decision to go directly into the field as an evangelist was a matter of not having time to spend when souls were waiting for conversion. Even so, many of the speech practices of the seminarians bothered Finney as much as they bothered Milburn.

Education was of little value, according to Finney, unless it resulted in an increase in the speaker's ability to convert sinners. Finney dedicated one lecture to the text "He that winneth souls is wise," Proverbs 11:30, and entitled it "A Wise Minister will be Successful" (p. 174). the burden of his discourse was to demonstrate, using the exegetical method, that wisdom, defined as the ability to win souls, was not related to formal education. Finney stated his central proposition in axiomatic form: "The amount of a minister's success in winning souls (*other things being equal*) invariably decides the amount of wisdom he has exercised in the discharge of his office" (p. 183). So that there could be no doubt about the ultimate criterion for wisdom, Finney explained that the amount of wisdom was decided by "the *number* of cases in which he is successful in converting sinners" (p. 183). Finney argued for success as the ultimate test because success was outward evidence that a man "understands the gospel . . . understands human nature . . . knows how to adapt means to his end . . . has common sense . . . has that kind of tact, that practical discernment, to know how to get at people" (p. 184). The words of praise exemplify the center position of the romantic pragmatists of the nineteenth-century rhetoric: a good speaker understood human nature, could adapt means to ends, had common sense and practical discernment.

Finney applied the lesson in a concluding section of his lecture which he called "Remarks." Here, he made the crucial points that a minister "may be *very learned and not wise*" and, conversely, that a minister may be very wise and not learned (pp. 185–186). After making the usual disclaimer—"Do not understand me to disparage learning" (p. 186)—Finney made the typical attack upon formally educated speakers, much as William Henry Milburn and the frontier preachers had done.

Finney discussed the great defect of a theological education. Young men who went through such training ended as less effective preachers than they were before they began their education. The *"want of common sense"* (p. 188) often defeated the ends of preaching. Students were too often kept at their books and segregated from the common people and had little opportunity to study human nature or the great mass of humanity. Their professors, too, should rather have mingled with the church and taken an active part in the world. The men in the field on the firing line were really the only ones who understood the problems of the ministry. Finney found it a "shame and a sin" that theological professors who seldom preached to common audiences were allowed to sit in their studies and write letters and give advice to those who really understood how to preach for effect (p. 192).

Finney met the problem of establishing the ethos of the middle-of-the-road evangelistic speaking in much the same fashion that Milburn met the problem of making the uneducated Methodist circuit rider an authoritative and believable speaker. The Puritan preacher of New England relied upon social status and college education to build his authority in the community. Speakers who subscribed to the Finney and Milburn persuasion had to meet the problem of speaking without scholarly preparation. Finney, like Milburn, said that a minister who knew the common people, who could read human nature and the Bible, and who was out in the world dealing with practical problems was more believable and a better speaker than one trained by books and isolated from the mass of humanity.

Both Finney and Milburn praised sermons if they were *practical*. By *practical* the romantic pragmatists meant that the speech applied directly to the members of the congregation. The speaker, therefore, had to study his audience carefully before and during the delivery of his speech. *"A minister ought to know the religious opinions of every sinner in his congregation. Indeed, a minister in the country is inexcusable if he does not."* The speaker had to know his audience, for "how otherwise can he preach to them? . . . How can he hunt them out unless he knows where they hide themselves?" (p. 199).

Finney raised the doctrine of attention to one of major importance. Here, his emphasis differs from the followers of the ungenteel tradition. Milburn and the frontier preachers stressed the doctrine in their practice but did not emphasize it as clearly and carefully in their rhetorical theory as Finney did. Much of the theorizing about rhetoric and preaching in the nineteenth century implies the importance of attention, but Finney represents one of the most important theorists to emphasize the centrality of catching and holding the audience's attention. Finney justified his "new" measures (changes in his services designed to win converts which were heavily attacked by those of a different persuasion) largely because they succeeded in arresting the audience's attention. He warned specifically against monotony. He compared his measures to convert sinners to the efforts of politicians to get votes. Politicians got up meetings, caused a hullabaloo, sent out handbills, got up parades and floats, all to gain attention and elect their candidate. Politicians knew that unless they aroused excitement and caught attention they would fail. Finney said that "I do not mean to say that their measures are pious, or right, but only that they are wise, in the sense that they are the appropriate application of means to the end" (p. 181).

To the objection of some that his preaching was theatrical, Finney replied that if by theatrical was meant "the strongest possible representation of the sentiments expressed, then the more theatrical a sermon is, the better." Finney dramatized his position with a fantasy theme about the Bishop of London who asked Garrick why actors moved audiences to tears with fiction while ministers could not get a hearing with discourses on solemn reality. "It is because we represent fiction as a reality, and you represent reality as a fiction," was Garrick's reply. Ministers who were unwilling to be theatrical could go on "with their prosing, and reading, and sanctimonious starch," but as they did so, the theatres would be thronged; "the common-sense people *will be* entertained with that manner of speaking, and sinners will go down to hell" (p. 220).

The basic technique for catching attention and arousing excitement was the fantasy theme. Preaching, Finney advised, should be *"parabolical."* Using the precept of Jesus, Finney asserted that Christ constantly used stories to illustrate his instruction. Yet few ministers use stories because they fear someone may reproach them. Finney answered such reproaches as follows: "'Oh,' says somebody, 'he tells stories.' Tells stories! Why, that is the way Jesus Christ preached. And it is the only way to preach. Facts, real or supposed, should be used to show the truth . . . let fools reproach them as story-telling ministers. They have Jesus Christ and common sense on their side."

The fantasy themes should be drawn *"from common life,* and the common business of society" (p. 209). Finney told a story of the minister who illustrated a point in his sermon with a scenario of the way merchants transact business. Another minister heard the sermon and reproached the first because such common materials let down the dignity of the pulpit. But Finney said: "Dignity indeed! Just the language of the devil. He rejoices in it. Why, the object of an illustration is, to make people *see the truth,* not to bolster up pulpit dignity" (p. 210).

In his emphasis on stories, Finney followed the lead and practice of frontier preachers and speakers who discovered the effectiveness of narrative material for their purposes. One of the common characteristics of the rhetorical school of romantic pragmatists and one that was equally emphasized by Milburn, Finney, and subsequently by Henry Ward Beecher in his lectures on preaching was the use of narrative material for support.

Another common characteristic that binds all the wings of the romantic pragmatic rhetoric together was their vigorous defense of the extemporaneous method of speaking. The question of whether a sermon should be written in manuscript or delivered extemporaneously was a major point at issue between the pragmatic rhetoricians and their opponents. As often happens in the history of American public address, an important change of emphasis and its concomitant style of speaking, were, in this instance, revealed by controversies that, from a longer perspective, might seem trivial. Thus, the arguments over the use of stories as support in sermons and over delivering the speech extemporaneously rather than from manuscript are keys to a much more important shift in rhetorical theory. Extemporaneous speech was glorified because it opened the way for the inspiration of God and because it was more natural and less learned and impractical than the written discourse.

The unlearned minister preaching because of a call from God could speak extemporaneously with much greater ease than he could write a sermon. In an important sense, the stress on narrative material and extemporaneous speaking elevated inspiration and downgraded scholarship as virtues for the speaker. Interestingly enough, as the Methodists, for example, became more self-conscious about their lack of education, a controversy broke out within that denomination when some of the members urged more careful preparation and the writing of sermons. The movement towards the writing of sermons within the Methodist group came at approximately the same time that the proponents of extemporaneous preaching were gaining influence in the Presbyterian denomination.

Finney participated fully in the romantic pragmatic emphasis on extemporaneous speaking. He urged that preaching be repetitious and for that reason suggested that writing speeches and using notes be abandoned. If the preacher kept his eyes on the people he could tell if they understood him, and if they did not, he could stop and illustrate the point several times.

Finney suggested that one of the problems with the speech education of the colleges of his time was that they stressed manuscript speaking, declamations, and orations, rather than extemporaneous speaking. He argued that training in extemporaneous speaking was a better method to train thinking than was writing. Finney would give a student a subject "and let him first *think*, and then *speak* his thoughts." He found the mechanical labor of writing a hindrance to "close and rapid thought" (p. 216). Clearly, the controversy over written versus extemporaneous speech was important to Finney; he notes that "I have heard much of this objection to extempore preaching ever since I entered the ministry" (p. 217). For Finney, the differences between oral and written communications were real and important. The language of "good style of writing" was not likely to "leave a deep impression on the mind, or to communicate thought in a clear and impressive manner." More importantly, it was not "the language of nature." A speaker found it impossible to fit his manner and gestures to the language of a written speech. When a speaker tried to gesture while reading an essay, his delivery was a "burlesque upon all public speaking." He concluded that "we can never have the *full meaning* of the gospel, till we throw away our notes" (p. 218).

Finney's emphasis on the "language of nature" was joined with his recommendation of a natural manner in delivery. While Finney's rhetoric puts less emphasis upon nature than Milburn's, both men's theories deserve to be characterized as romantic rhetorics because they do share a common bias in favor of natural speech and deeply felt emotion and against studied preparation and affected manner. Finney was a vigorous advocate of the natural method of delivering a speech. He reiterated again and again the importance of the nonverbal cues that the speaker furnished his audience. "Gestures are of more importance than is generally supposed. . . . The *manner* of saying it is almost every thing." He told of a comment about an uneducated but successful young preacher: "The manner in which he comes in, and sits in the pulpit, and rises to speak, is a sermon of itself. It shows that he has something to say that is important and solemn." He told an anecdote about "one of the most distinguished professors of elocution in the United States" who said, "I have been fourteen years employed in teaching elocution to ministers, and I know they don't believe the Christian religion" (p. 212). The reason the elocutionist made the assertion was that he could not get ministers to talk on religion with the force and conviction they used when speaking on other subjects. The perfection of the art of elocution was to teach speakers to talk naturally on a subject. He could not make ministers speak naturally and eloquently about religion, so he inferred that they did not believe what they were saying (p. 213).

Finney advised that a speaker always "feel deeply his subject"; if he does that, he "will suit the action to the word and the word to the action, so as to make the full impression which the truth is calculated to make" (p. 211). He maintained that "if a man *feels* his subject fully, he will *naturally* do it. He will naturally do the very thing that elocution laboriously teaches" (p. 212).

As to the style of language and delivery, Finney recommended that they both be conversational. The style of language should be colloquial and the words of common usage. The speaker should not use language "half Latin and half Greek" because he was afraid of appearing unlearned. Further, Finney said, that "a minister must preach just as he would talk, if he wishes to be fully understood." The often employed style was "mouthing, formal, lofty," and did no good (p. 208).

The main difference between the rhetoric of Finney and that of Milburn lies in the fact that Finney retained the Edwardian balance between heat and light. The good minister was both a burning and a shining light, and the followers of Finney emphasized not only zeal but also analysis, clear descriptions of facts, and proof. Theodore Weld, perhaps the greatest practitioner of the rhetoric of Finney, wrote to the evangelist from Cincinnati, judging that "The best presbyterian Revival Preachers here preach nothing but the loose disconnected rhapsodies of Methodists in the main. Their preaching is exhortation and appeal, dwelling upon the love of Christ, etc., and all addressed to mere sympathy. They reason little and investigate less."[12]

The matter of dignity in the pulpit reflected the change in rhetorical vision as well as in measures. More was involved in Finney's new measures than persuasive techniques to cause conversions. The Puritan fathers established their authority by keeping a social distance from their congregations. They were set apart by social station and learning. They spoke as authoritative figures who knew more and were more saintly and more dignified because of their social and ecclesiastical position. The new rhetoric achieved identification of the speaker with the audience through the use of "common ground" techniques which broke down the distance between speaker and audience and which stressed that the speaker was one of the audience. Since the minister came from the shops, he could talk the language of the people, he understood them, he was of them and no better than his auditors in any worldly way relating to class or status. In a sense, Jonathan Edwards's God, like Edwards himself, stood apart in awful splendor, and such an abyss yawned between God and man that man could only stand reverent before Him.

Charles Grandison Finney's God, on the other hand, was a much kinder God of love, and one could treat him less deferentially. Indeed, some critics charged that Finney spoke too familiarly with God when he prayed. Man moved into a much more positive relationship with God and with his environment. Man was no longer a mean miserable creature: instead, he was full of potential for development and *perfection*. Since man was perfectible, the drive to make him better than he was made good *common sense*.

The reformers were optimistic. They read the Bible in such a way that their exegesis supported their sense of destiny, adventure, and optimism. The promised thousand years when Satan would be bound and Christ would reign on earth seemed very near.

For the evangelical preacher and reformer of the early nineteenth century, the millenium was so near that the world had to be perfected right then and there. Finney was in a hurry. Members of the audience had to be converted immediately. Now was the time. No better time would ever be at hand. Jonathan Edwards, a century before, had used the predestination argument that God's season was there and that it was the nick of time for many. Finney argued that if a man did not seize the present opportunity, his obstinate refusal would "grieve" the Lord away. The unpardonable sin for many nineteenth-century revivalists was that of resisting the Spirit of God so often that he was grieved away, never to return again. As Finney said in his lectures on revivals: "Sinners are expected to repent *NOW*." The preacher had to impress upon his listeners that "religion is something to *do*." The audience was not to think that they could wait but "they must do it now, or they are in danger of eternal death." The high optimism and the drive for a speedy conversion of the entire country is reflected in a letter that Finney wrote to Theodore Weld when they were debating the wisdom of Weld's single-minded dedication to the abolition of slavery. Finney argued that first the nation should be converted. "We can now," he argued, "with you and my theological class, bring enough laborers into the field to, under God, move the whole land in 2 years."[13]

The speakers using the Finney style were merciless in their attack on sin and corruption. They could not wait for gentle methods. One of their metaphors was that they had to probe to the core of the boil and let out all the pus so the good flesh beneath could heal quickly. Their rhetoric was searching in the old Puritan tradition. Their letters contained merciless and frank appraisals of one another's faults, shortcomings, and sins, always prefaced with the disclaimer that only their "love" of the other person prompted the criticism. Besides, they felt, as did their Puritan forebears, that they were their brother's keeper. If they allowed sin to continue without raising their hand and voice against it, they participated in that sin. Lewis Tappan exemplified the reformers' rhetorical vision when he wrote a reply to his freethinking brother Ben, who had complained that Lewis ought to keep his religion to himself. Lewis wrote that he had to try to convert his brother "because I see you are in danger of eternal damnation. . . . As I love you . . . I urge upon you the obligation of faith in the Son of God. Were I not to do so your blood would be found on my skirts at the Judgment Day."[14]

Although the agitators, particularly Garrison and Wendell Phillips, were more famous, the evangelicals had the greater influence. In the heyday of the antislavery agents, in the early 1830s, the band trained by Theodore Weld took the lectures of the Lane Rebels and Weld's Bible argument and his tactics across the land and converted much of the West and North to abolition. So successful were they in establishing antislavery societies that after 1836, the propaganda effort of the antislavery forces turned more and more to furnishing the membership of the many local organizations with tracts and treatises. At the same time, the split between the agitators and the evangelicals was important in the gradual withering away and loss of influence of the national society, which came to be dominated by the Garrisonians. The next important propaganda move was the uniting of the local forces in a monstrous campaign aimed at sending petitions to Congress. The shift from oral propaganda to petitions was partially a result of the drawing-together of local organizations by Weld and his agents in 1835 and 1836. They had built, according to Gilbert Barnes, "the greatest non-political instrument for propaganda that had ever been achieved in the nation."[15] To that enterprise, the rhetorical tradition of romantic pragmatism had made the major contribution.

✣ 8

The Styles of Antislavery Rhetoric

Revolutionary Agitation Versus Reform Persuasion

This chapter examines the entire rhetoric of abolition, distinguishes the evangelical conversion style from the style of agitation, and critically evaluates both by comparing and contrasting one with the other. My focus remains on the evangelical style, on the evolving tradition of romantic pragmatism, but its essential vision, theory and practice can be illuminated by comparing it with that of the agitators. Examining the relationship between the rhetoric of agitation and the rhetoric of conversion gives insight into the way radical and reform speaking both conflicted and coordinated, hampered and hindered one another in mobilizing public opinion into political action in the decades prior to the Civil War.

Every reform movement in American history has faced several similar rhetorical problems and each can be evaluated critically in terms of how well its persuasive style has met these common problems. First, a reform movement must mobilize popular support in behalf of its program. The movement needs effective consciousness-raising communication to gain converts who become active workers as well as a large group of people, less dedicated, but nonetheless sharing the group consciousness and willing to provide public support for the activities of the committed. Gaining converts poses important subsidiary problems. The effective reform rhetoric must have a rhetorical vision which portrays the things that are wrong and dreams of a better world. The discussion of the vision's "social reality" is usually indexed for the listener or reader by expressions such as "the facts show" or "the truth is." In addition to portraying the evils of the world, a reform rhetoric's vision must indicate the historical meaning of the effort. Where does the movement stand in the history of the general culture? Is it part of a culminating ongoing progression towards an even better society? Is it part of a purging process to cleanse and restore the society to an earlier better time? Is it outside the culture, alien and pure, while the culture is rotten? Every effective reform rhetorical vision provides a complete and plausible answer to such questions.

The second major task of a reform rhetoric is to indoctrinate the converts and weld the true believers into a highly committed and cohesive group. A sense of *esprit de corps* requires a rhetorical vison which furnishes each participant with a sense of fulfillment and with meaning for his or her life. In the face of the inevitable failures and difficulties, the loyal followers must be sustained and encouraged by suitable consciousness-sustaining communication.

The two major styles of persuasion dedicated to abolition met the problems of a reform movement with speeches, tracts, and newspapers that reflected rhetorical visions and practices which were similar in some ways and strikingly different in others.

The agitators associated with William Lloyd Garrison met the first problem of mobilizing popular support with a rhetoric that failed miserably. While their vision contained much the same description of the reality of the institution of slavery in the 1830s and 1840s, their analysis of the nature of their movement and its place in the evolving history of America was much different from that provided by the evangelical vision. The tactic of the agitators was to goad, sting, insult, and attack the favored values implied in the fantasies and rhetorical visions of the neutral and hostile auditors. Garrison and Phillips attacked the Sabbath, the churches, and, finally, the Constitution of the Union. At the beginning of his career, Garrison was already rehearsing the rhetoric of agitation when he delivered a Fourth-of-July address in Park Street Church in Boston. He said in part:

> What has Christianity done, by direct effort for our slave population? Compara-
> tively nothing. She has explored the isles of the ocean for objects of commisera-
> tion; but, amazing stupidity! she can gaze without emotion on a multitude of
> miserable beings at home, large enough to constitute a nation of freemen,
> whom tyranny has heathenized by law. . . . The blood of souls is upon her
> garments, yet she heeds not the stain. The clankings of the prisoner's chains
> strike upon her ear, but they cannot penetrate her heart.

Shortly after attacking the hallowed institution of the church, Garrison turned on the nation itself.

Every Fourth of July, our Declaration of Independence is produced, with a sublime indignation, to set forth the tyranny of the mother country, and to challenge the admiration of the world. But what a pitiful detail of grievances does this document present, in comparison with the wrongs which our slaves endure! In the one case, it is hardly the plucking of a hair from the head; in the other, it is the crushing of a live body on the wheel—the stings of the wasp contrasted with the tortures of the Inquisition. Before God I must say that such a glaring contradiction as exists between our creeed and practice the annals of six thousand years cannot parallel. In view of it, I am ashamed of my country. I am sick of our unmeaning declamation in praise of liberty and equality; of our hypocritical cant about the inaliencable rights of man. I could not for my right hand, stand up before a European assembly, and exult that I am an American citizen, and denounce the the usurpations of a kingly government as wicked and unjust; or, should I make the attempt, the recollection of my country's barbarity and despotism would blister my lips, and cover my cheeks with burning blushes of shame.[1]

Garrison's fantasy theme in which he visualizes himself before a European assembly faced with the decision of whether or not to exult as an American citizen and hold out his country and its government as a model implies an inversion of many of the values of the romantic pragmatists and of other widely popular rhetorical visions in the United States at the time. From within the shared consciousness of the Garrisonians, the other rhetorics sound like hypocrisy and cant. America is not better than the rest of the world; it is, indeed, much worse; one has to search the annals of six thousand years of recorded history to find the equal of American hypocrisy. If Garrison could bring himself to mouth such hypocrisy as was typical of the Fourth of July, his lips would blister and his cheeks be covered with shame. One could not participate in the Garrisonian fantasies without first giving up the old familiar patriotic fantasy types. For the most part, Garrison's contemporaries responded to his dramas with outrage and anger at him and his rhetorical vision rather than being drawn into participation.

As Garrison's agitation continued, the themes of his early Fourth-of-July address were developed with greater richness, greater powers of invective, and more melodramatic fantasies. The basic vision was coming clear in the 1830s, and by the spring of 1842, his attack on the Union was direct and unbending. In January 1843, the agitators gained control of the annual meeting of the Massachusetts Anti-Slavery Society, and the following resolution—"wrapped up," according to Edmund Quincy, who was in attendance, "by Garrison in some of his favorite Old Testament Hebraisms"—was passed: "That the compact which exists between the North and the South is a convenant with death and an agreement with hell—involving both parties in atrocious criminality—and should be immediately annulled."[2]

On July 4, 1854, after the passage of the Kansas-Nebraska Act, which he viewed as the repeal of the Missouri Compromise, Garrison burned several documents including a copy of the Fugitive Slave Law and then, holding up the Constitution, he burned it and said, "So perish all compromises with tyranny! And let all people say, Amen."[3]

Not only did the style of the agitators alienate the uncommitted, but when divisions appeared within the antislavery forces over questions of policy and other elements of the vision or when Garrison's leadership was challenged, the agitators turned the very same style of righteous overstatement against one another. Since a basic fantasy type of the agitator's vision saw every dramatic action which involved compromise as evil and corrupting and since the vision clearly spelled out its basic goals and program, those who failed to agree with all of the vision were dismissed as heretics. The participants would not bend their vision to accomodate grievances and differences because such bending was essentially wrong. The vision provided a clear dramatization of the right, and every failure to stand by that depiction of right was interpreted as immoral.

A vision which contains motives to stand firm for what is right, which impels its adherents to make no compromises, and which arouses high charges of zeal tends to split into contending visions. The inevitable struggle for status and leadership within the movement causes differences among the original membership as to policy and tactics. Cliques develop and coalesce around natural leaders. Since the members of cliques participate in the overall vision, they see their ideas as to policy and tactics as imbued with the same rectitude as do the others. Each subgroup develops a shared consciousness which sees its position as the one "right way" and the others as having fallen away from the truth. The bitterness of the conflict among factions within such a vision is often very great, and visions which denigrate compromise and accomodation tend to splinter and splinter again. Such was the fate of the adherents of the rhetoric of agitation. The agitators split first with the evangelicals and then divided among themselves. The rhetoric of agitation served, therefore, as a divisive force within the antislavery effort as well as a repelling vision for many of those who might have joined the effort.

Gilbert Barnes, who wrote a brilliant study of *The Antislavery Impulse, 1830–1844*, concluded that Garison's intemperate attacks on the churches, which did supply the main support for the antislavery impulse, made him "an enemy of the antislavery impulse itself."[4] Barnes argues that "another handicap to the new society was the unfortunate repute of William Lloyd Garrison.

. . . Over the entire agitation his name cast 'a vague and indefinite odium' which hampered its growth from the beginning."[5]

The rhetorical vision of the speakers and writers practicing the rhetoric of conversion was in some respects similar to that of the agitators, but in its essential features it was different, and so was the pactice of the two styles. When Henry B. Stanton argued for petitions against slavery before the Committee of the House of Representatives of Massachusetts, he exemplified the more persuasive tactic of the rhetoric of conversion. Stanton spoke for three days, giving a summary of Weld's famous course of lectures. He began the second day of his testimony as follows:

> I am aware, Mr. Chairman, that it is customary on occasions like this, to commence by descanting upon the *importance* of the subject under discussion. This is common place. I dislike to stoop to it on the present occasion, lest my reason for so doing should be regarded as trivial. Yet, I will run the hazard. In courts of justice, the advocate often trembles, as he rises to address the jury, when the pecuniary interests of his client are at stake; then what should be my feelings, when I rise to address you, not in behalf of the percuniary interests of one client, but in behalf of the liberties and the lives, the interests, temporal and eternal, of thousands? Ay more—the questions here discussed are not confined in their bearings to the slaves in the District of Columbia; nor in this nation. The cause of freedom throughout the world; the honor of God's law, will be deeply affected by your deliberations. The interests here involved are co-extensive with human hopes and human happiness; wide as the universe, lasting as eternity, high as Heaven. Then, sir, the slave, the master, this Common-wealth, the nation, the world, Jehovah himself, demand that we deliberate patiently, cautiously, impartially. And, gentlemen, your constituents will pardon you for so doing. No subject is more discussed by them, than that now before you; and the intensity of their feelings, not less than their immediate concernment, requires this deliberation at your hands. . . .
>
> And I ask the indulgent attention of the committee, because I believe, that as you shall decide, so the Legislature will act. Your number is unusually large; you justly have the confidence of the House, and to you they look to mature this subject for their action. Upon you, therefore, rests the responsibility of a decision. Hear me then for my cause, and bear with me, because I plead not only for the suffering, but the dumb.[6]

When one contrasts Stanton's handling of the problem of introducing his thesis to a suspicious if not hostile audience with the manner of the agitator, the differences between the style of conversion and of agitation become clearer. Stanton carefully builds the importance of his case and the issue but does not do so with any attack upon the Federal Government, the Constitution, the State Government, or upon the legislators themselves.

Indeed, he assures them of their importance and states that their decision will probably carry the day. Stanton wishes to persuade them to act on the memorials, or petitions, before the committee. He does not outrage them by lashing out at them or baiting them or calling them slaves of the slave power. Rather, he asks for patient, cautious, and impartial deliberations.

When Stanton comes to discuss the program of the abolitionists, he is at pains to indicate that it is not a radical or dangerous scheme.

> And now, Mr. Chairman, what do the petitioners ask you to request Congress to do? I answer;—merely to repeal these odious statutes immediately, and to enact others, if necessary, in their stead. By immediate abolition, they do not intend that the Slaves of the District should be "turned loose:"—nor, that they should be, as a *sine qua non* to abolition, immediately invested with all political rights, such as the elective franchise. But, simply, that Congress should immediately restore to every Slave, the ownership of his own body, mind, and soul. That they should no longer permit them to be "deemed, held, and sold, as chattels personal, to all intents, constructions and purposes whatsoever;" but should give the slaves a fee simple in their own blood, bones, and brains.[7]

The agitators and evangelists both had to describe the things that were wrong and that needed to be changed if they wished to mobilize popular support for the cause. They both utilized a largely similar approach to create a social reality which became part of their rhetorical vision of the institution of slavery, of the South, and of the entire country's reaction to slavery. They created dramatic personae out of archetypal Southern slaveholders who became the archenemy and the motive force behind the evil institution. If they wished to flesh out the character of the enemy in terms of historical personages, they used people like Judge Lynch or John C. Calhoun as symbols. They peopled their letters, speeches, and antislavery tracts with beautiful black and mulatto women forced to submit to the lust of white planters. They dramatized the slave breaker with his whip and wheel. They played variations on the scenario of the slave market and the family divided because of the sale of the father or the mother.

Fantasy themes of cruelty were told again and again by the antislavery speakers and recounted in antislavery newspapers and tracts. The violence of the system was dramatized with the same sensationalism that characterizes much of contemporary television fare. Simon Legree was a favorite stock character of antislavery lectures long before Harriet Beecher Stowe gave him a name and put him in a novel. Indeed, the ultimate vision of the abolitionists was embodied in the work of fiction which Stowe entitled *Uncle Tom's Cabin*.[8] Mrs. Stowe included in her book the character of Simon Legree, wielding his whip, chasing the fugitive slaves with his bloodhounds; she included Topsy, Little Eva, and Uncle Tom. Legree was vicious and contemptible. Uncle Tom was noble and commendable. Little Eva was noble and vulnerable. The dramatic action aroused compassion and tears. But long before the publication of *Uncle Tom's Cabin*, the antislavery rhetoricians were dramatizing similar themes.

Stephen Symonds Foster, in a letter about the clergy entitled "The Brotherhood of Thieves," for example, repeated his charge originally made in speeches that,

> the American church and clergy, as a body, were thieves, adulterers, man-stealers, pirates, and murderers; that the Methodist Episcopal church was more corrupt and profligate than any house of ill-fame in the city of New York; that the Southern ministers of that body were desirous of perpetuating slavery for the purpose of supplying themselves with concubines from among its hapless victims; and that many of our clergymen were guilty of enormities that would disgrace an Algerine pirate!![9]

Frederick Douglass often portrayed the fantasy theme of how Covey, the "slavebreaker," locked up a young woman with a hired male to breed and how joyful Covey's wife was when the woman gave birth to twins.

Henry Wadsworth Longfellow reflected the antislavery vision with circumspection and innuendo, but the drama is nonetheless clear in his poem "The Quadroon Girl." The opening stanzas set the scene with a slave ship waiting in the lagoon and the planter talking to the captain.

> Before them, with her face upraised,
>   In timid attitude,
> Like one half curious, half amazed,
>   A Quadroon maiden stood.
>
> Her eyes were, like falcon's, gray;
>   Her arms and neck were bare;
> No garment she wore save a kirtle gay,
>   And her own long, raven hair.

The planter thinks of his old farm with its barren soil and looks upon the gold the slaver is offering him and then looks at the girl.

> His heart within him at strife
>   With such accursed gains;
> For he knew whose passions gave her life
>   Whose blood ran in her veins.

> But the voice of nature was too weak;
>   He took the glittering gold!
> Then pale as death grew the maiden's cheek,
>   Her hands as icy cold.
>
> The Slaver led her from the door;
>   He led her by the hand,
> To be his slave and paramour
>   In a strange and distant land![10]

Theodore Weld and his wife, with the help of her sister, Sara Grimké, searched thousands of Southern newspaper ads regarding runaway slaves, noted scars and other evidence of physical mutilation and brutality, and requested all friends of the cause who had personal knowledge of nonfiction fantasy themes dramatizing the horrors of slavery to write them their testimony. In his letter of request, Weld asked for

> A multitude of facts never yet published, facts that would thrill the land with horror. . . . Shall such facts lie hushed any longer, when from one end of heaven to the other, myriad voices are crying, "O Earth, Earth, cover not their blood." The old falsehood that the slave is *kindly treated*, shallow and stupid as it is, has lullabied to sleep four-fifths of the free North and West; but with God's blessing this sleep shall not be unto death. Give facts a voice, and cries of blood shall ring till deaf ears tingle.[11]

The result of the research done by the Welds and Sarah Grimké was one of the great antislavery tracts of all time, *American Slavery As It Is: Testimony of a Thousand Witnesses*.[12] The vision of the South which emerged from the tract was one in which the slaves were ill-treated, ill-housed, ill-clothed, and ill-fed. They were beaten, mutilated, and humiliated. Harriet Beecher Stowe, who as a girl in Cincinnati had heard the Lane debates, claimed that she had *Slavery As It Is* in her sewing basket all the while she was writing the fictionalized account of the antislavery vision she called *Uncle Tom's Cabin*.

The panoramic vision of the South included more than scenarios of specific events. The rhetorical visions of both the agitators and the evangelicals interpreted the dramas in terms of their ultimate meaning. Did slavery represent evils of this world to be reformed as evils are reformed by the institutions of the culture, or did they represent sins in the eyes of God? If slavery was a sin, then it was a matter not just of temporal importance but of vital concern to each human being, for one's immortal soul might well be in danger throughout eternity. (Certainly the question of the sinfulness of slavery was something for the devout slaveholder to ponder.) All of the abolitionists participated in a vision which interpreted slavery as a sin, but it was the evangelical rhetoric that wrung the last bit of persuasive power from the portrayal of slavery as a sin and applied the powerful techniques of the searching sermon to its propagation.

As Gilbert Barnes discovered in his historical study of the antislavery agents in the West

> . . . These young men preached the antislavery cause as a revival in benevolence. . . . they carried over into the antislavery cause the zeal of the Great Revival itself. . . . They preached immediate emancipation; but in their hands it was more than the jesuitical "gradualism in a British cloak" of the New York philanthropists; it was an immediatism of repentance from sin. By making the sin of slavery "the standard to which the abolitionist is to rally," these agents made the antislavery cause "identical with religion; and men and women are exhorted by all they esteem holy, by all the high and exciting obligations of duty to man and God . . . to join in the pious work of purging the sin of slavery from the land."[13]

Under the goad of the speaking of the agitators and the evangelicals, the rhetoricians of the South were moved to action. Although there had been a sort of drifting sentiment that slavery would eventually die out in the entire country and even though the Colonization Society had been active in the South as well as in the North, the call for immediate abolition and its aggressive promotion by a coherent and zealous group of rhetoricians forced the thinking Southerners to reexamine their position. Under the attack of the abolitionists, a new shared consciousness that defended the institution of slavery developed in the South. The vision evolved from Southern speakers who fantasized dramas of an agrarian paradise of large houses, gracious landed gentry, and a well-mannered and polite society. Witty and dashing young men swirled gracious and charming Southern belles in waltzes on the veranda or succumbed to glamorous vices like gambling and horse-racing. They created dramatic personages out of the flower of Southern womanhood and filled their speeches with flattering passages dedicated to the archetypal Southern girl. The black servants were beloved and happy. Negro mammies gave the master's children loving care and were dearly beloved in return. Cared for in sickness and in health and given security in their old age, the Southern black servant was, in the rhetorical vision of the defenders of the system, happier and better off than the white wage slaves of the Northern industrial system.

The enemy in the Southern vision was a crude materialistic and fanatic Yankee, Puritan, blue-nosed, unable to sweet-talk a girl, and afraid of having fun. The Yankee reformers had never been South and had never seen conditions firsthand and therefore did not really know what they were talking about. Perhaps the equivalent of *Uncle Tom's Cabin* for the Southern rhetoric was the opening of a novel by Margaret Mitchell, written a century after Mrs. Stowe's book, called *Gone With the Wind*.[14] Although Mrs. Mitchell's book deals with the passing of the antebellum South, her novel, in its opening chapters, dramatizes the essential rhetorical vision of the defenders of the slave system.

When the evangelical antislavery agents made the sin of slavery their main argument, they posed a basic question relating to the ultimate legitimatization of their vision as well as that of their opponents. Was slavery legitimatized by God as part of the eternal order of things or did God see it as an abomination and a sin? Inevitably, the question of supernatural sanction for the visions threw the whole argument into the tangle of biblical exegesis. The Southern rhetoricians searched the Scriptures and discovered that slavery was of divine origin and sanctioned by the Bible itself.

Theodore Weld's most important series of lectures was devoted to the Bible argument. He taught his Bible argument to the antislavery agents who followed him into the field and subsequently wrote it up and published it as a tract.[15]

The evangelical abolitionists evolved a rhetorical vison which valued corroboration. Weld, as we have seen, held out high standards in regard to factual evidence and rhetorical proof. That a romantic and pragmatic rhetorical tradition should begin to take on an empirical flavor is not surprising. Pragmatism and empiricism are, after all, rhetorically very close. The pragmatic emphasis on common sense and what worked in everyday practical affairs led to a celebration of truthful testimony about facts. The despised seminarians and their professors were preoccupied with their esoteric exegesis of ancient texts and their study of dead languages while the useful and effective speaker got his education from experience—from the careful observation of man and nature. The instructions accompanying an agent's commission for the American Anti-Slavery Society read in part: "You will make yourself familiar with FACTS, for they chiefly influence reflecting minds. Be careful to use only facts that are well authenticated, and always state them with the precision of a witness under oath. You cannot do our cause a greater injury than by overstating facts."[16]

In the case of the antebellum attack on and defense of slavery, there was ample corroboration for the anti- and the proslavery visions. There was corroboration for the nonfiction fantasy themes about vicious slave drivers similar to Mrs. Stowe's fictitious Simon Legree. The advertisements for runaway slaves culled from Southern papers by Angelina and Theodore Weld and Sarah Grimké corroborated the missing ears, the scares, the other mutilizations of the slaves. Likewise, there were big houses and dashing young men, beautiful ladies, and beloved house servants. That the incredibly confusing, contradictory, and complex personal relationships, institutional patterns, and economic arrangements of the South contained adequate corroboration for the abolitionist and the apologist for slavery is not surprising. A rhetorical vision must, of necessity, include only selected corroborated fantasies. The vision's discursive descriptions of facts as contained in statistical statements are likewise selective. A rhetorical vision always presents a coherent and *artistic* description of the world. When a rhetorician shapes events into dramatic structures, he changes the contradictory and chaotic qualities of sense experience and observation.

The agitators stressed the sin of slavery much less than the evangelicals. They often used the term *moral* to express the ultimate legitimatization of their vision. If a thing was immoral, it was bad and to be shunned and eliminated. As Wendell Phillips put it: "Those who cling to moral effort are the true champions in the fight."[17] The Agitators argued on moral grounds that slavery was a great wrong. The Garrisonian vision, which saw the churches as corrupt and which impelled its adherents to attack the church, separated its efforts from those of the organized religion of the day, while the evangelicals continued their strong connection with the churches. In the Garrisonian vision, too, the dramas of sin and eternal damnation which filled the evangelical rhetoric were largely missing.

Accounting for, explaining the existence of such a great evil as slavery, was another important feature of the visions of both agitator and evangelical. The evangelicals tended to account for slavery as part of man's sinful nature, and some, like Charles Grandison Finney, argued that the first step in emancipation was to convert the slaveholder to true Christianity. When the Lane Rebels enrolled at Oberlin and were wrestling with their consciences as to the advisability of becoming agents of abolition, Finney argued that they ought to become evangelists instead and convert the country, and that that would accomplish abolition and all other reforms as well.[18]

Both the agitators and the evangelicals, however, agreed that whether or not man's inherent sinfulness was at the bottom of the problem, there was an undemocratic movement afoot, conspiring to sustain and increase the slave power. The slavocracy influenced the Northern institutions because of its political power within the Congress of the United States, because of its influence with organized religion, and because of its economic leverage with Northern business interests.

When Stanton argued his case for freeing the slaves in the District of Columbia, he asked how slavery could exist. His answer was: only because it was sustained by law and because the laws supporting it came from the power of the slave conspiracy. Beriah Green dramatized the power of the slaveholders in his sermon "Things for Northern Men to Do" as follows:

> American slavery makes the creatures who support it, more and more eager, insolent, and outrageous in their claims on all around them for homage and subserviency. These petty tyrants are by no means satisfied with domineering over the helpless slave. Their despotic spirit overleaps the limits of their plantations. It lifts its head among the freemen of the North, threatening to strangle in its snaky folds every one who may dare to resist its claims or oppose its progress. Can we stand by in safety and see it crush and swallow our enslaved brethren? Surely not. The fangs which are now dripping in their blood, must ere long be fastened in our shrinking flesh. Have not slaveholders at the South clearly betrayed a disposition to invade the rights and trample on the interests of the freemen of the North? Have they not insulted us and threatened us? Have they not swung their fists in our faces, and brandished their daggers above our heads? Have they not goaded on their miserable creatures among us to acts of lawless violence;—acts, in which our persons have been rudely attacked, our reputations spitefully assailed—all our privileges as American citizens vilely set to nought? . . . And can we mistake their spirit and designs? Why, they already treat us, as if we had sold our birth-right; as if we had been reduced to brute beasts; as if like goods and chattels we were good for nothing but to gratify the passions and subserve the interests of a bloated aristocracy![19]

One major feature of the rhetorical visions of both wings of the abolition effort relates to both the tasks of mobilizing public opinion and to building dedication for the effort among the recruits. The question of the identity of the movement—who are we and what are we about?—requires an answer in a viable rhetorical vision for reform.

As to developing the group's self-image, the rhetorical vision of the agitators differed markedly from that of the evangelicals. The rhetorical vision of the agitators dramatized their movement as a revolutionary effort standing against and outside the cultural stream of the American experience. Garrison and Phillips burned and cursed the Constitution and denied that the tradition of the founders was a worthy one.

The rhetorical vision of the evangelicals, on the other hand, dramatized its efforts as a continuation of the best of the American experience. Henry Stanton, in his testimony before the Massachusetts legislature, argued from a historical precedent relating to the power of the national government to abolish slavery in the District of Columbia and he defended the Constitution. He fixed the responsibility for the sustaining of slavery not on the Constitution and the foundations of the government but upon laws passed by Congress which Congress had the right and duty to appeal and, thus, eliminate slavery in the District: "Were there time, I would detail a long catalogue of facts, showing, that if there was any compact between North and South, besides the *written* compact, it was not a *pro-slavery*, but an ANTI-SLAVERY compact."[20]

But with regard to more than the outward forms of the government as represented by the Constitution, the evangelical rhetorical vision participated in some of the great sustaining dramas that celebrated the American experience and gave it meaning. One of the most important differences between the rhetorical vision of the agitators and the evangelicals is revealed by comparing Garrison's charge of hypocrisy in his Fourth-of-July oration at Park Street Church in Boston with Stanton's portrayal of the same theme before the committee of the Massachusetts legislature.

> It is expedient that slavery at the Capitol should be abolished, because its toleration brings into contempt our nation's boasted love of equal rights, justly exposes us to the charge of hypocrisy, paralyzes the power of our free principles, and cripples our moral efforts for the overthrow of oppression throughout the world.
>
> The citizens of this nation have deep responsibilities, as republicans, as Christians, as citizens of the world. Our character and reputation are moral capital, loaned us by God, to be invested for the political and moral renovation of the human race. The Reformers of South America and Europe, have anxiously looked to us as the pioneer nation in the cause of human liberty, and hoped that our experiment would demonstrate even to tyrants, that man is capable of self-government. But, by cherishing in the heart of the republic such a system of cold-blooded oppression, as the sun has rarely seen, we have rolled back the tide of reform in other nations, and cut the sinews of struggling humanity.[21]

The Garrisonians repudiated the archetypal fantasy of the "new birth" of an entire nation and, instead, saw the government as rotten from its beginnings, founded on a document based on compromise with slavery. For the agitators, the vaunted promise of freedom and equality was but hypocritical cant which served to apologize for one of the worst tyrannies in history.

Like the rhetorical vision of the ungenteel style, that of the evangelicals was essentially optimistic; they wanted to save America for God and the world in order to better the human condition everywhere. Their view was westward; the great valley of the Ohio had to be saved for evangelical religion and free soil. Theodore Weld, writing from the West, reflected the evangelical vision with these words: "Here is to be the battle field of the world. Here Satans [sic] seat is. A mighty effort must be made to dislodge him *soon*, or the West is undone."[22]

The evidence is clear that the rhetoric of conversion was much more successful at mobilizing popular support for abolition than was the style of agitation. In the year of Weld's great agency, he, along with a handful of Lane Rebels, converted hosts of people to the crusade and established many new local antislavery organizations. In May 1835, before Weld's agency, there were 200 local antislavery organizations—47 were in Massachusetts, 40 in New York, and 38 in Ohio. By May 1836, there were 257 local societies, with 133 in Ohio and 103 in New York, the states where Weld and his men itinerated. There were only 87 in Massachusetts, the home territory of the agitators.[23]

The second major rhetorical problem that both the agitators and evangelists of abolition had to face related to the building of a sense of community and commitment among the members who joined the movement. Both camps of the antislavery forces used appeals designed to make the movement the most important force in an individual's life to build *esprit de corps*.

Both the agitators' and the evangelicals' visions contained powerful dramas for creating high levels of commitment and celebrated the cause of abolition as the greatest of all causes in recorded history. Again and again, the insiders told one another that their cause was the most important in the world. When Garrison left the *Journal of the Times* in 1829 to edit *The Genius of Universal Emancipation*, he wrote:

> Hereafter, the editorial charge of this paper will devolve on another person. I am invited to occupy a broader field, and to engage in a higher enterprise; that field embraces the whole country—that enterprise is in behalf of the slave population. . . . To my apprehension, the subject of slavery involves interests of greater moment to our welfare as a republic, and demands a more prudent and minute investigation than any other which has come before the American people since the Revolutionary struggle—than all others which now occupy their attention.[24]

Both the agitators' and the evangelicals' visions celebrated fantasy themes in which insiders suffered social ostracism, physical abuse, and even death. A reform vision can have few more powerful or ultimate fantasy types than that of martyrdom. When a vision contains a celebration of the adherents dying gladly to further the cause, the participant is likely to make great efforts and great self-sacrifice for the movement. One way in which adherents could demonstrate their solidarity with the movement was to testify to their willingness to die a martyr's death for the cause.

Theodore Weld, writing from the scene of his major defeat as an agent at Troy, New York, when he thought the mobs might indeed kill him, expressed the fantasy type of martyrdom as follows: "Poor outside whitewash! the tempest will batter it off the first stroke; and masks and veils, and sheep cloathing gone, gone at the first blast of fire. God gird us all to do valiantly for the helpless and innocent. Blessed are they who die in the harness and are buried on the field or bleach there."[25]

Writing from jail in Baltimore, where he had been imprisoned for writing an attack on a slave trader, Garrison put it this way:

> Is it supposed by Judge Brice that his frowns can intimidate me, or his sentence stifle my voice on the subject of African oppression? He does not know me. So long as a good Providence gives me strength and intellect, I will not cease to declare that the existence of slavery in this country is a foul reproach to the American name; nor will I hesitate to proclaim the guilt of kidnappers, slave abettors, or slaveowners, wheresoever they may reside, or however high they may be exalted. . . . It is my shame that I have done so little for the people of color; yea, before God, I feel humbled that my feelings are so cold, and my language so weak. A few white victims must be sacrificed to open the yes of this nation, and to show the tyranny of our laws. I expect and am willing to be persecuted, imprisoned, and bound for advocating African rights; and I should deserve to be a slave myself if I shrunk from that duty or danger.[26]

Finally, the rhetorical visions of both agitator and evangelical celebrated their respective movement as having supernatural sanction. The evangelicals made the appeal to God's support basic to their rhetoric, and the agitators, too, built commitment to their movement by using appeals to supernatural sanction.

The appeals to God's support were strongest for the evangelicals and made their style most attractive to the devout Christian. Since slavery was a sin and the evangelicals were battling on the side of God, they had more than human and temporal reasons for committing themselves to the movement. They were God's chosen people and his instrumentality, which meant that they were inevitable and that they had to win. As we have seen in the criticism of the Puritan vision, one is more tightly drawn to a mighty cause so right, so sanctioned by God himself, that it will win and establish a better world.

For the evangelicals in the movement, battling the sin of slavery was an opportunity to avoid the guilt of doing nothing, for by doing nothing a person participated in the sin. By acting, individuals could avoid having the sinners' blood on the shirts on Judgment Day. When, at the end of his manual labor agency, Weld experienced his second secular conversion, he wrote to Elizur Wright that his "soul" had been "in travail upon that subject." He now knew that "firstly and mostly: Abolition *immediate universal* is my desire and prayer to God; and as long as I am a moral agent I am fully prepared to *act out* my belief in that thus saith the Lord—'*Faith without* WORKS *is dead*.'"[27] Weld caught the essence of the emerging evangelical reform vision in that one credo—faith without works is dead! To claim conversion and not take up the cudgels in the fight was, in fact, to be unsaved. Like their Puritan forebears, the evangelical abolitionists were their brothers' keepers.

The rhetorical visions of both the agitators and the abolitionists were extremely successful at creating a sense of commitment to their cause and impelling their adherents to dedicated effort in its behalf. Many risked economic losses and social ostracism and worked long hard hours. Some, indeed, acted out the drama of martyrdom to its ultimate conclusion and died for their participation in the antislavery cause.

The essence of any organization is that it must have a common purpose. When the leaders state the goals of a reform movement, they make a rhetorical move that adds direction and focus to the members' activities and that, depending on their rhetorical tactics and skill, provides a force for greater or lesser cohesion. When the rhetoricians adopt the tactic of clearly spelling out the goals and of describing their program in unequivocal detail, they create the strongest pull for commitment on the membership. Publicists for contemporary political parties tend not to use the attractiveness of clearly specified goals for building party loyalty. The rhetoric of the platforms of major parties today usually is so general and vague that almost anyone can take shelter under those platforms and work for the party. Quite often, party leaders make victory in the election a clear and unequivocal goal that, in fact, becomes the major unifying force, and the platform gets lost in the fantasizing of the campaign. The rhetoricians of a reform movement like abolition often use the opposite rhetorical tactic. Spokesmen take an extreme stand, express the group's goal in unequivocal language, and make their doctrine clear by frequent reiteration. The persuaders increase the level of commitment to the movement by using such tactics even though they may pay the price of restricting the appeal of the reform program to a relatively small group of highly dedicated people.

The antislavery movement divided several times, partly because of the rhetorical handling of the goals of the effort. The evangelicals divided from the agitators on the question of goals, and both wings suffered some loss of support from the general public because of the way their objectives were formulated and debated. Strategically, the rhetoric of the goals of abolition was related to two questions: What precisely did the stated goal of *immediate abolition* mean? Should the movement incorporate as goals other reforms such as temperance, peace, women's rights, the sabbath question, socialism, and dietary reform, as well as abolition?

The difference between abolition in 1833, as opposed to the prior antislavery efforts, was largely a question of time. The first object of the attack of the abolitionists was the Colonization Society with its goal of gradualism in freeing the slaves. From the time of the Puritan rhetorical vision, as we have seen, the rhetoric of romantic pragmatism always exerted great time pressure upon the seeker of salvation. *Involvement, activity, immediacy* have been god-words for the persuaders of many religious groups and reform movements. Weld exuberantly predicted success for his new gospel shortly after he was converted to immediate emancipation. "Mark my word," he wrote, "*two years* will make an overturning from the bottom."[28]

The rhetorical appeal of immediacy has continued on to contemporary times as a permanent legacy from the Puritan style and the tradition of romantic pragmatism. In the civil rights movement of the 1950s and 1960s, for example, one important slogan was "Freedom Now!" Martin Luther King, Jr., told the thousands assembled to hear him during the march on Washington D.C. in 1963: "We have also come to this hallowed spot to remind America of the fierce urgency of now."[29] As a result, many Americans have participated in rhetorical visions which impel them to impatience. They want results fast. They hope for success "immediately if not sooner."

The vision of the agitators was absolutely clear and unequivocal about the meaning of immediate abolition. For them, it signified, literally, freedom *now*. As much as any other factor of their rhetoric, the original interpretation of the goal reveals the difference between the rhetorical visions of the two groups most clearly. The evangelical vision saw practical difficulties in immediately freeing the slaves and tried to develop its goals in a way which accommodated the problems. Recall Stanton's explanation of abolition as not turning the slaves loose nor investing them with all political rights including the vote but simply as restoring to the black man the ownership of his own body. The evangelicals adopted the slogan "Immediate emancipation, gradually accomplished." One is reminded of the Supreme Court's concept of school integration in the 1950s, which was to be accomplished with "all deliberate speed."

Garrison was a young man of twenty-four working with Benjamin Lundy on the *Genius of Universal Emancipation* when the English parliamentary debates over slavery were published in the United States. The more radical of the English abolitionists thought well of Lundy and sent him their papers and pamphlets. Garrison studied the abstract absolutes of the British antislavery rhetoric at the climax of the movement in Great Britain and chained into the dramas of immediate freedom. He saw literal immediate abolition not as a policy to be set by political institutions to meet specific situations but as an eternal principle and therefore bound to succeed any time or any place. Garrison continued to advocate the literal immediatism of emancipation throughout his career. As he put it: "Duty is ours and events are God's. . . . All you have to do is set your slaves at liberty!"[30]

The evangelicals had considerable difficulty trying to explain that by immediate emancipation they did not mean what Garrison meant. Their notion that immediate emancipation simply meant that the freeing of the slaves should start immediately, even if the process would take a matter of time, caused confusion within the ranks as well as among the potential converts.

Subsequently, the evangelicals came to Garrison's position when James Thome and Horace Kimball went to the West Indies to study how immediate abolition was working in practice. They brought back a wealth of information which Weld hammered into another effective rhetorical tract called *Emancipation in the West Indies*.[31] The result of the West Indies precedent caused the New York headquarters to revise the goal of "immediate emancipation, gradually accomplished" to a clear and unequivocal call for immediate freedom. Whatever the practical shortcomings of Garrison's call for literal immediacy as a plan for social action, it was, rhetorically, the more powerful and understandable appeal.

The second question of strategy relating to goals was as important as the nature of the meaning of the term *immediate*. Should the movement have many goals or should it concentrate on the one objective of freeing the slave? Theodore Weld was adamant that only one goal shape and focus the reform movement. As time went by, the agitators embraced more and more reforms and involved themselves in more and more controversies (Garrison arguing the Sabbath question with Lyman Beecher, arguing for women's rights, peace, temperance, and a number of other reforms). Weld, all the while, urged that the main reform effort must be dedicated to one, and only one, goal. He argued that presenting a number of goals confused the followers and the general public, brought converts with a different set of priorities to the movement, and dissipated the energy available for the antislavery reform.[32]

On balance, Garrison's great rhetorical stroke was to discover the power of the concept of immediate abolition, absolute, simplistic, and unwavering. The evangelicals, on the other hand, had the clearer eye when it came to the strategy of staying with one goal rather than chasing after many.

The issue of which was the better style, that of agitation or that of conversion, was sometimes debated by the proponents of both sides.[33] The agitators were adamant that they would not bend their principles one iota to please the corrupt, the apathetic, and the evil. They would go down to defeat and even death before they would compromise or sugar their message to make it sweeter for their audiences. They justified their agitation on the grounds that hot words melted the ice of apathy and that the lubberly public would continue for another two hundred years, living contentedly with slavery unless stinging words were used to goad them to search their sleeping consciences. They argued that people who would never have heard about or considered abolition were forced to do so simply because their harsh and abrasive style caused a furor, made headlines, caused violent counterefforts, forced the racist institutions to take repressive measures. By thus confronting the power structure of the time, their tactics worked to achieve the abolition of slavery. One is reminded of the style of agitation used by student revolutionaries in the 1960s; their style was based on a rhetorical vision which saw confrontation and agitation as the means of goading a repressive and corrupt establishment into showing its true nature. When the regime used police and militia in violent countermeasures, the result, according to the rhetorical theory, would be a radicalizing of the uncommitted and apathetic students.

The argument of the agitators had some merit in light of the historical record. Garrison, Phillips, Foster, and the rest were widely talked about. They became famous or infamous, depending upon the rhetorical vision of the audience. In sum, however, their entire rhetoric was much less successful than that of the evangelicals. The agitators did not gain support from outsiders and managed only limited conversions. The evangelicals, on the other hand, converted enough people to sustain a large petition drive on Congress and subsequently to help form and support a broad-scale political effort. Finally, the agitators did not manage to build a sense of community and dedication to a common cause among the true believers within the movement. Factions continually arose among them. Among the Garrisonians, cliques developed, and leaders fell out and attacked one another bitterly. Typical was the falling-out between Frederick Douglass and Garrison, which degenerated into a bitter quarrel even involving charges about the personal life of Douglass. Symbolically, after the Civil War and the Emancipation Proclamation, after the two old agitators had both basked in the glory of the achievement, even Wendell Phillips and William Lloyd Garrison fought and would not talk to one another for a time.

A critical comparison of the style of agitation with the evangelical conversion style reveals some general conclusions about reform rhetoric. The agitators' rhetorical vision was clear-cut and had implications for a person's entire life. The agitators' persuasion involved those who shared its fantasies in a rhetorical vision so encompassing that it influenced their life style. The vision contained a reversal of many of the popular and familiar dramas which provided a patriotic and panoramic view of the United States and its historic meaning.

Thomas Kuhn, in a historical study of shifts in scientific style and perspective analogous in many respects to this study of rhetorical style and vision, discusses how scientific paradigm shifts come about. Kuhn notes that

> the proponents of competing paradigms practice their trades in different worlds. . . . Practicing in different worlds, the two groups of scientists see different things when they look from the same point in the same direction. . . . before they can hope to communicate fully, one group or the other must experience the conversion that we have been calling a paradigm shift. Just because it is a transition between incommensurables, the transition between competing paradigms cannot be made a step at a time, forced by logic and neutral experience. Like the gestalt switch, it must occur all at once (though not necessarily in an instant) or not at all. [34]

Seeing the world through a scientific paradigm, according to Kuhn, is analogous to what I refer to as a life-style rhetorical vision. To shift to another scientific paradigm would cause a person to see a dramatic shift in the gestalt of the world much like the shift in the popular optical illusion where the outline of a rabbit suddenly becomes that of a duck.

In a sense, the persons who adopted the agitators' vision crossed the boundaries of incommensurable rhetorics. They found themselves in a social reality which was essentially a mirror vision of the reality that sustained the typical patriotic Fourth-of-July address which a Daniel Webster would deliver in the 1830s to celebrate the Union. Many Americans in the 1830s, apparently, were still strongly participative in the patriotic fantasies and failed to cross the boundaries of the Garrisonian rhetorical vision.

The convert to the evangelical vision, on the other hand, could adopt his or her view of slavery and still retain many elements of other familiar and sustaining visions. For example, the born-again Christian could incorporate the evangelical reform vision into the general life philosophy and religion of the ungenteel tradition, the New Light Presbyterian vision, or the Congregationalism of Lyman Beecher. All the born-again Christian needed to do to accommodate antislavery was to accept the Weldian interpretation that the Scriptures revealed slavery to be a sin. Accepting the sin of slavery enabled the New Light to integrate evangelical antislavery with its goals and its depiction of the nature of slavery into the old familiar dramas and fantasies concerning the church, the nature of God and man, and the drama of his own salvation throughout eternity.

Likewise, the person whose secular vision of the American experience celebrated the Declaration of Independence and dramatized the founders as inspired men who created a great Constitution dedicated to freedom and human rights could convert to the evangelical vision of antislavery and still retain the familiar framework of secular justification for the meaning of America and the significance of the enterprise of creating a new nation. In short, one could participate in the fantasies and feel the emotions evoked by a typical Fourth-of-July address and shortly thereafter attend a lecture by one of the Lane Rebels and participate in its vision without giving up the cherished fantasies of America as the model for reformers around the world and the experiment to prove that man was capable of self-government.

The evangelical antislavery vision contained a persuasive mechanism which made it easy for the listener to assimilate the antislavery reform vision into his or her patriotic view of America. The listener only had to share the fantasies that depicted the original Declaration and the Constitution as sincere statements of wise and inspired men who saw the institution of slavery as being on the way to extinction both North and South, that depicted the country as having fallen away from the promise of the original founding and as having been corrupted by the forces of slavery and their supporters in the North who did the slavocracy's bidding for economic and political reasons, and that depicted a solution which was first a restoration to the purity of the founding of the government by emancipation of slaves and then a move forward to fulfill the promise of America.

The evangelical solution, cast in the form of a drama of restoration, was attractive because it was a part of many of the popular and salient rhetorical visions in the United States in the 1830s. The indigenous religious movement stemming from the great western revivals in Kentucky and Ohio was called the Christian or Disciples of Christ and was under the leadership of Alexander Campbell. One of the important elements of the rhetorical vision of the Disciples was the fantasy type of the restoration. Indeed, some referred to the Disciples' reform as the restoration movement. Postmillennial in its basic structure, (Alexander Campbell founded a periodical called the *Millennial Harbinger*), the vision saw the rapid perfection of society in the West but only after the purity of the primitive church was restored. The Disciples sought first to turn back from the pluralism of religion in nineteenth-century America to the ecumenical unity of the original church. They dramatized the differences among the various denominations as the result of human error and urged that a simple belief in Christ was the common ground upon which all could unite in an attempt to shuffle off the unchristian elements of numerous sects and denominations and unify and restore the church to its original basis.[35]

In the secular realm, a political rhetoric associated with the followers of Andrew Jackson evolved a vision which contained a similar restoration drama. Jackson, in his attacks on the bank, the growth of centralized government, and industrialism, saw the economic and political developments as a corruption of the purity of the original founding of the country. The Jacksonian rhetoric called for a purging of the body politic of the bank and other errors and a restoration of the country to the principles of the founding fathers.[36]

The restoration drama in various forms was an important part of the shared consciousness of many Americans in the 1830s. The evangelicals, by casting their rhetoric into the familiar, recurring rhetorical form of the restoration of a polluted institution to the original basis of purity and rightness, gave to many a potential convert a familiar rhetorical form to serve as a common ground with the speaker to make it easier to step into the unfamiliar territory of immediate emancipation. The charm of the familiar balancing the excitement of the new gave the individual some security to help make the transition to abolition.

The Garrisonian vision, on the other hand, provided no transition mechanisms to lead a potential convert from common ground to the notion of emancipation; nor did it integrate consistently and smoothly with other sacred and secular rhetorical visions popular in the 1830s and 1840s. The Garrisonians delighted in taking the occasion of the great secular celebration of the American experience, the Fourth of July, to deliver sarcastic parodies on the typical American flag-waving fantasies which celebrated the Declaration of Independence, the Revolutionary War, the founding of the Constitution, and the subsequent development of American institutions. One could not go from a typical Fourth-of-July oration to a Garrisonian speech on that national holiday without violently and emotionally rejecting either the typical oration or the Garrisonian parody.

Garrison's Fourth-of-July address delivered in 1838 at the request of the Board of Managers of the Massachusetts Anti-Slavery Society demonstrates the all-or-nothing character of the agitators' vision. Garrison began as follows:

> Fellow Citizens: What a glorious day is this! What a glorious people are we! This is the time-honored, *wine*-honored, toast-drinking, powder-wasting, tyrant-killing fourth of July—concecrated, for the last sixty years, to bombast, to falsehood, to impudence, to hypocrisy. It is the great carnival of republican despotism, and of christian impiety, famous the world over! Since we held it last year, we have kept securely in their chains, the stock of two millions, three hundred thousand slaves we then had on hand, in spite of every effort of fanaticism to emancipate them; and, through the goodness of God, to whom we are infinitely indebted for the divine institution of negro slavery, have been

graciously enabled to steal some seventy thousand babes, the increase of that stock, and expect to steal a still greater number before another "glorious" anniversary shall come round! . . . As to the Indian tribes, we have done the best we could to expel and exterminate them; and the blood upon our hands, and the gore upon our garments, show that our success has almost equalled our wishes. . . . Hail, Columbia! happy land! Hail, the return of the fourth of July, that we may perjure ourselves afresh, in solemnly invoking heaven and earth to witness, that "we hold these truths to be self-evident—that all men are created equal; that they are endowed by their Creator with certain inalienable rights; that among these are life, LIBERTY, and the pursuit of happiness!" "Sound the trumpet—beat the drum!" Let the bells give their merriest peals to the breeze—unfurl every star-spangled banner—thunder mightily, ye cannon, from every hill-top—and let shouts arise from every plain and valley; for tyrants and their minions shall find no quarter at our hands this day! Disgusting spectacle! The climax of brutality, and the lowest descent of national degradation![37]

Americans, in the first half of the nineteenth century, were not attracted to the Garrisonian vision. Indeed, they were often frightened by the agitators, angered by them, and grew to hate them. Garrison and his followers came to be leading characters in many fantasy themes which chained through the populace and in which the personification of the movement, the *abolitionist*, was a villain.

The American dream of a society in which there would be no hereditary classes, in which "all men were created equal," and in which everyone had an equal opportunity to rise to whatever class structure as a result of the natural aristocracy of talent and effort was so strong and vivid for so many of the newly immigrated as well as the second- and third-generation citizens that a vision which was a total rejection of the whole society found few converts.

The antislavery reform did ultimately result in an emancipation proclamation and the freeing of the slaves. In pragmatic terms, it was one of the great successful reform efforts in the history of the United States. How, then, did the rhetorical styles of agitation and conversion work in harness to further the cause of antislavery?

Insofar as the ground breaking of the agitators prepared the soil for evangelicals, the two pulled in harness to mold public opinion. However, the distinction which I have drawn on rhetorical grounds between the agitators and the evangelicals was seldom, if ever, drawn by the contemporaries of the reform efforts. The American Anti-Slavery Society originally consisted of the Garrisonians and the New York group. Subsequently, the Society split along the boundaries of the rhetorical visions. Despite the split, the general public tended to identify the evangelicals with the agitators. The speakers for the counterrhetorics often used the guilt-by-association technique to link the ill-repute of Garrison and his followers to the evangelicals. The apologists for slavery and the middle-of-the-road political speakers often identified the antislavery speaker or candidate as an *abolitionist*. When a speaker labeled a person an *abolitionist*, the name-calling often triggered a response similar to the fantasy themes in which Garrison or an agitator played the role of villain, whether the victim of the technique was an evangelical or only sympathetic to the antislavery position without accepting the goal of immediate abolition. Thus, insofar as the guilt-by-association with the agitators reduced the credibility of the antislavery speakers and supporters in the evangelical tradition, the two styles worked at cross purposes.

If one views society's regeneration as following on a mass basis the pattern of individual conversion, the agitators' rhetoric was well designed to break up the old foundations and convict the mass mind of the sin of slavery. They subjected the public to a withering and overstated sarcastic and ridiculing attack on slavery reminiscent of the ungenteel style's tactic of "taking the hide off of" the listener. But when the alarmed and worried potential convert was convicted and asked, "Woe is me! What shall I do?" the agitators provided only a vague and general drama of destruction. They were out to destroy the structures of society through "nonresistance," the nonviolent philosophy of the day, but their style was a militant nonresistance. Although the content asserted nonviolence, the form suggested attack and aggression. Their vision did not see beyond the destruction. They did not provide their audiences with dreams of the future which could provide an attractive alternative to the contemporary society.

The evangelical conversion vision, on the other hand, provided an attractive dream of the future. Eliminate slavery! Give the former slave dominion over his body and the right to the results of his labor. As soon as he is ready, give him other rights of citizenship. Gradually educate and train him until he takes up full participation in society. When the former slave takes his place as a free and equal citizen, the vaunted principles upon which the country was founded will be a reality and America's destiny as a chosen people, as the site of the millennium, as a model for reformers throughout the world, will be fulfilled. It was a noble dream which celebrated values that elevated the nature of man. The believer could view man as able to live up the great sentiments of the Declaration of Independence. Man could be self-governing! The mean and miserable creature of the Puritan vision had certainly grown in stature and nobility. The emotional evocation of the evangelical's vision was excitement to be participating in such an important and fulfilling effort; joy at evidences of success, pride to be a perfectible man or woman, working in the most important effort of all human history. The vision provided the individual with a strong self-image, with a sense of the significance of the effort in behalf of the reform, and with a sense of the meaning of the entire American experience.

The style of the evangelical reform was so successful that by the end of the decade of the 1830s, a large body of public opinion was searching for a solution to the slavery question within the formal communication structures furnished by established political institutions. The emerging political rhetoric included shared fantasies which changed the basic scene from the states to the territories and coalesced around dramas relating to keeping the sacred western regions of the frontier pure and untarnished by the sin of slavery. When the vision matured, the participants selected the slogan "Free Soil" as a rallying cry. These new fantasies took the rhetorical forms of the evangelicals to create and sustain first the Liberty party, then the Free-Soil party, and finally, substantial portions of the new Republican party.

By 1854, a new communication style was emerging around the persona of Abraham Lincoln for the western wing of the Republican party. The persuasion of the groups who came to be symbolized by Lincoln's persona was an amalgam of the ungenteel and evangelical styles. The broad and popular style of the western Republicans came to be the culmination of the rhetoric of romantic pragmatism, and the speeches and statements of Lincoln as war president represent the highest artistic expression of that tradition.

❦ 9

The Rhetorical Vision of
Abraham Lincoln

After the evangelical band of agents had established and nurtured a large number of local antislavery societies, the movement turned more and more to written tracts containing detailed arguments filled with factual materials and to the columns of reform newspapers to propagandize their efforts. In the second phase of the effort, volunteers recruited by the reform speakers, self-taught in the rhetorical visions of the evangelicals or the agitators by studying the facts and fantasy themes in the tracts and newspapers, began to build a larger following by word of mouth. The influence of local leaders was brought to bear in a door-to-door campaign to get signatures in behalf of their ideas on petitions to state and federal legislatures. When an individual called on an acquaintance to sign a petition, he or she brought into play personal influence at a local level. The petition effort was an extremely successful part of the entire persuasive campaign.

As the number of local volunteers grew, the regional and national antislavery societies began to wither away. By the end of the year 1838, the bulk of the state antislavery societies had become defunct, and the American Anti-Slavery Society itself was losing strength and effectiveness. In 1839, John Quincy Adams emerged as the leader of the petition forces in Congress, and the squabbling and disorganization within the ranks of the national society caused him to write a public indictment of the American Anti-Slavery

Society that was a final and near-fatal blow to the organization, which was already starving for lack of financial support.

William Lloyd Garrison and his followers captured the national society by 1840, and it ceased to be more than a minor organization of the more radical abolitionists. The power of the antislavery movement shifted to the struggle for petitions, and its center moved from Boston and New York to Washington, D.C.

In the House of Representatives, the elderly former president John Quincy Adams conducted a unique speaking campaign for the rights of petition and for a moderate and practical mode of emancipating the slaves. Theodore Weld, who had withdrawn from active participation in the effort because of his disgust with the leadership struggle within the antislavery societies, hurried out of retirement to sift the materials in the Library of Congress and develop the briefs for Adams and others among the antislavery representatives such as Joshua Giddings of Ohio, William Slade of Vermont, and Seth M. Gates of western New York.

The debate in Congress reached a climax when Joshua Giddings introduced a series of antislavery resolutions based upon the case of an American vessel called the *Creole* which had been seized by some slaves who sailed the ship to the British port of Nassau. The *Creole* case raised the issue of the status of slaves on an American vessel on the high seas. The Whig colleagues of Giddings censored him for breaking the gag rule against raising the issue of slavery in the National Congress. Giddings resigned his seat and returned to Ohio to run for reelection. When Gidding's constituency returned him with a large majority, the Whig party could no longer maintain party discipline in regard to antislavery statements in Congress, and from that time until the Civil War, the insurgent antislavery bloc in Congress became the center for a new political movement on the national scene.

With the rise of the Congressional antislavery speakers and the emphasis on political action, the abolitionist rhetoric worked its way into the Whig party, eventually divided that party, furnished the basic elements of the rhetorical vision of the new Free-Soil and Republican parties, contributed to Lincoln's election to the presidency, and, ultimately, to the crowning achievements of the evangelical rhetoric of reform, the Emancipation Proclamation, and the Thirteenth, Fourteenth, and Fifteenth Amendments to the Constitution.[1]

When appeals to conscience and petitions to legislative bodies failed to emancipate the slaves, the evangelical abolitionists whose vision celebrated the American system of government had, like so many reform movements in American history, to face up to the tactical question of whether or not to utilize the political institutions of representative democracy to achieve their goals.

The abolitionists, like the subsequent partisans for the temperance reform, the Populist movement of the 1890s and the women's suffrage movement, were reluctant to enter into party politics. Those who shared the agitators' vision, of course, shunned acting within the political system, and they actively fought those who tried to do so. But even the evangelicals whose vision accepted the traditions of the country were reluctant to become politicians. Partly, their reluctance stemmed from the paradoxical dramas of their vision which, on the one hand, celebrated the noble experiment in freedom and self-government while, on the other hand, portraying practicing politicians as compromising hypocrites out for the main chance. Could the reformers remain pure if they plunged into the sinful and corrupt arena of practical politics? Would the reform speakers lose credibility with the American public once they became involved in partisan politics? The rhetorical tacticians debated and divided over these difficult questions before, finally, the evangelicals decided to move into the political arena.

In the spring of 1840, a group of evangelicals assembled in convention in Arcade, New York. They voted to make independent nominations for the upcoming presidential election rather than work as a pressure group to assure antislavery candidates within the two major parties. The convention nominated James B. Birney, a former slaveholder and associate of Weld, for president, and Thomas Earle for vice-president. Gerrit Smith, one of the leaders in the move to political action for the antislavery forces, suggested that the new group call itself the "Liberty" party.

In 1840, the Liberty party was clearly a protest group with no hope for victory. Its candidate spent the period from May to November in England. The party had no local organization and did little campaigning.

Birney, in his first attempt to lead the new political effort, was opposed almost more vigorously by his antislavery colleagues than by the traditional political parties. The "no-human-government" Garrisonians declined to vote since such action would show acceptance of the political system; many of the evangelicals felt that the move from Christian morality and fighting against slavery as a sin to the political efforts to gain office was a degrading one. In addition, the bulk of the antislavery voters who believed in political action were members of the Whig party and many did not want to "throw away" their votes on a candidate who could not win and thus allow a Democrat to win the presidency. As a result, Birney received only slightly more than 7,000 votes in 1840.

In the spring of 1841, the new party held another national convention in New York in conjunction with the meetings of the old American Anti-Slavery Society, now under the control of the agitators, and the new American and Foreign Anti-Slavery Society, formed by the remnants of those of the evangelical vision still interested in a national association. The Liberty party again nominated James G. Birney for president and selected Thomas Morris of Ohio for vice-president. In 1844, Birney campaigned actively and the party had an infrastructure capable of supporting a vigorous campaign. The rhetoricians of the party selected the cedar of Lebanon as the party symbol and developed slogans like "The righteous shall grow like a Cedar in Lebanon." Elizur Wright wrote an "Ode to Birney," which was put to music and became a popular campaign song. The first verse of the lyric was the following:

We hail thee, Birney, just and true,
    The calm and fearless, staunch and tried,
The bravest of the valiant few,
    Our Country's hope, our country's pride!
    In Freedom's battle take the van;
    We hail thee as an honest man.

Many of the evangelical antislavery gatherings had always started with a prayer and the singing of rousing hymns which developed a psychological climate as persuasive as a religious revival meeting. Now, the evangelicals-turned-politicians developed a persuasive atmosphere for their meetings by using the old familiar pattern except that the rousing hymns were replaced by equally rousing campaign songs. In addition to Wright's "Ode," songs like "We're for Freedom through the land" appeared in special songbooks published for the campaign. The latter song contained the following martial words:

We are coming, we are coming!
Freedom's battle is begun!
No hand shall furl her banner ere her victory be won!
Our shields are locked for liberty, and mercy goes before;
Tyrants tremble in your citadel! Oppression shall be o'er.
    We will vote for Birney! We will vote for Birney!
    We're for liberty and Birney and for freedom through
        the land.[2]

Again, Garrison issued rhetorical broadsides, cast into the typical style of the agitator, at Birney and at the political effort of the antislavery forces in the pages of the *Liberator*, but the most vicious campaigning took place between the Whigs and the Liberty forces, for the bulk of the abolition sentiment was to be found in the Whig party. The Whig candidate was Henry Clay and the "Great Compromiser's" chances to win the election were good if he could hold most of the antislavery sentiment within his party. Birney received a popular vote of about 62,300; Clay had a bit over 1,299,000; and Polk received slightly more than 1,337,200.

The increase in power for the new party from four years before was impressive; it had polled enough votes to hold the balance of power in the close election. In New York alone, if Clay had received only one-third of Birney's votes he would have carried the state and the election. Although some critics charged that the antislavery forces, by channeling their energy into a political effort, had succeeded only in electing Polk, a prominent villain in the antislavery fantasy themes, the antislavery forces had also demonstrated that the groundswell of popular support in the North was large and growing and they had delivered a near-fatal blow to the Whig party.

The evangelical rhetorical vision attracted converts at a rapid rate. As it spread over a larger and larger portion of the populace, it lost some of its harshness and clarity of goal. The shared consciousness no longer contained such powerful motives to action, nor did it evoke such intense emotional response, but it was still a forceful, impelling, emotion-arousing vision when compared to the typical rhetorics of the traditional political parties.

In the aftermath of the election of 1844, the Liberty party rhetoricians once again examined the tactical question of developing a set of goals for their party. Now that the movement had become a force in the political arena, some argued that the vision required a comprehensive party platform to broaden its appeal and make it a mass political party. Again, the leadership divided on the question. The Liberty party retained its "one-idea" policy, as the single-minded and dedicated effort in behalf of freeing the slave was called, but a minority seceded, developed a broader platform, nominated Gerrit Smith for the presidency, and under the name of *Liberty League* ran a separate campaign in the election of 1848. The main strength of the political effort remained with the Liberty party, which began to fuse, in 1848, with the antislavery elements in the Whig and Democratic parties and which was carried into the new Free-Soil party by such leaders as Salmon Chase of Ohio and Henry B. Stanton.

In the eight years from 1848 to 1856, the rhetorical vision of the evangelical antislavery forces proved a powerful symbolic force among the remnants of the splintering and crumbling old established political visions. The rhetorical vision of the evangelicals acted as a catalyst in the dividing, recombining, and changing elements of other rhetorical visions of political factions and groups. The vision worked its way through the small but volatile elements of the Liberty party and the Liberty league until a potent new shared consciousness, containing powerful political motives, emerged, coalescing around the slogan "free soil." The free-soil fantasy was a drama which changed the setting of the slavery problem from the Southern states, where the real here-and-now difficulties facing the American electorate lay, to the symbolic world of the frontier—to the territories.

As a small group faced with a difficult here-and-now problem will often begin to fantasize on an analogous situation set in some other time and some other place with a different set of characters, so, too, the rhetoricians of the free-soil fantasy set a drama in the still largely unsettled territories. If in the pure regions of the frontier the institution of slavery could never gain a foothold, slavery would be doomed. If the frontier could be saved for freedom, the very act of stepping into the frontier would purify the individuals, white or black, migrating westward, and slavery, unable to gain a foothold in the West, would surely die in the East.

The free-soil fantasy themes and types began to chain through large segments of the populace in the North, drawing in disgruntled Whigs and disillusioned Northern Democrats. For the middle-of-the-road Northerner who, in the 1850s, was unable to participate in the vision of either the agitators or the evangelicals for abolition but who, nonetheless, was becoming disturbed by their incessant searching sermonizing on the sin of slavery, the free-soil fantasies were most attractive. The problem of slavery seemed to many to be insurmountable. How could one free the slaves in the South without a civil war? Had not the Constitution itself guaranteed the Southern states that the power over the institution of slavery was reserved to the states? Yet, what if slavery was, indeed, a sin? One had to fight sin or participate in it to the deadly peril of one's immortal soul. But if one loved one's country and celebrated the Declaration of Independence and the Constitution, how could one risk a civil war? Symbolically, the fantasy of saving the territories provided a goal which could release the guilt for the individual who felt slavery was a sin without bringing with it the fear evoked by the grisly fantasies envisioning a civil war. The battle could be fought in the sparsely settled regions of the West and South, and the specter of blood flowing in Pennsylvania and Virginia could be laid to rest.

The fantasies of free soil also articulated with many of the established rhetorical visions of the 1850s, which saw the frontier regions as the hope for the future, the cradle for freedom and self-government, and the site of the millennium. As we have seen, saving the frontier for posterity was a widespread drama in many visions and the free-soil fantasies resonated in key with many of them. The psychological needs of many Northerners combined with the most vexing and difficult here-and-now problem of slavery in the states to make the free-soil fantasy attractive. As a result, the fantasies of free soil were widely shared by many people in the Northeast and West who had previously been members of the established parties.

In 1856, the new consciousness composed of free-soil fantasies powered a new political alignment called the *Republican Party*. With a military figure, John Fremont, an explorer of the frontier territories of California and Oregon who enjoyed a glamorous reputation somewhat akin to a twentieth-century astronaut, as the presidential candidate, and with the slogan, "Free soil, free speech, and Fremont," the Republican party polled over a million votes in 1856. Four years later, in 1860, the Republican candidate, Abraham Lincoln of Illinois, was elected president.

Political parties in the United States which gain sufficient support to elect substantial numbers of candidates to Congress or to the presidency are such loose and amorphous organizations that they always contain rhetoricians practicing several styles of persuasion. The new party drew its strength from the Northeast as well as the West and contained within its ranks rhetoricians such as Charles Sumner, trained at Harvard College and practiced in the neoclassical style. When Lincoln, as president, spoke at Gettysburg in the tradition of the romantic pragmatists, he shared the platform with Edward Everett, one-time professor of Greek at Harvard College, who spoke in quite another style.[3] Romantic pragmatism, was, on balance, however, one of the most popular styles used by the Republican stump speakers.

When still a young politician embroiled in local campaigns, and later as a budding Whig on the national scene, Lincoln was adept at "taking the hide off" his political opponents with sarcasm, invective, and ridicule. Often, his invective was harsh and his style clumsy and crude. Indeed, in one anonymous letter printed in the local Illinois paper the *Sangamon Journal*, Lincoln ridiculed James Shields, the state auditor, until the latter was goaded to challenge Lincoln to a duel.

Lincoln's letter was signed "Rebecca" and purported to be from "Lost Townships." The letter consisted of a humorous sketch recounting a dialogue between Rebecca and a neighbor named Jeff. Rebecca was a Whig and Jeff was a Democrat. Jeff was disturbed by a proclamation he was reading in a paper signed by Shields in his official capacity as auditor. The proclamation was to the effect that state officials and school officers could not accept state paper in payment of taxes. The farmer thus found himself in the position of using "sound" money to pay off his debts. Jeff got very worked up and said of the proclamation: "I say its a lie, and not a well told one at that. It grins out like a copper dollar. Shields is a fool as well as a liar. With him truth is out of the question, and as for getting a good bright passable lie out of him, you might as well try to strike fire from a cake of tallow."

Certainly the name-calling in the letter is strong enough to stimulate a man to issue a challenge, but as the sketch continued, Jeff became even more vociferous and finally worked Shields over in the characteristic style of the ungenteel tradition. Peter Cartwright, had he read the Rebecca letter, would have appreciated it as a masterful job of "skinning" a victim. About Shields, Jeff continued:

> I seed him when I was down in Springfield last winter. They had a sort of a gatherin there one night, among the grandees, they called a fair. All the galls about town was there, and all the handsome widows, and married women, finickin about, trying to look like galls, tied as tight in the middle, and puffed out at both ends like bundles of fodder that hadn't been stacked yet, but wanted stackin pretty bad. And then they had tables all around the house kivered over with baby caps, and pin-cushions, and ten thousand such little nick-nacks, tryin to sell 'em to the fellows that were bowin and scrapin, and kungeerin about 'em. They wouldn't let no democrats in, for fear they'd disgust the ladies, or scare the little galls, or dirty the floor. I looked in at the window, and there was this same fellow Shields floatin about on the air, without heft or earthly substance, just like a lock of cat-fur where cats had been fightin.
>
> He was paying his money to this one and that one, and tother one, and sufferin great loss because it wasn't silver instead of State paper; and the sweet distress he seemed to be in,—his very features, in the exstatic agony of his soul, spoke audibly and distinctly—"Dear girls, *it is distressing*, but I cannot marry you all. Too well I know how much you suffer; but do, *do* remember, it is not my fault that I am *so* handsome and *so* interesting." . . . O, my good fellow, says I to myself, if that was one of our democratic galls in the Lost Township, the way you'd get a brass pin let into you, would be about up to the head.[4]

One can well understand Shields's desire for a retraction or satisfaction of honor. The affair progressed to the point where Lincoln specified the weapons—"Cavalry broad swords of the largest size"—and other details of the encounter. Eventually, the matter was arbitrated without a fight.[5]

In July 1848, Lincoln was in the United States House of Representatives and participated in a political debate, defending General Taylor, the Whig candidate for the presidency, against charges of lack of principle. The speech reveals Lincoln as a practitioner of the ungenteel style.[6] Lincoln refers to a speech by a representative from Georgia, Alfred Iverson, and in the typical manner of the frontier preacher and lawyer deprecates the difference in formal education between himself and the Georgian. Lincoln said that Iverson was "an eloquent man, and a man of learning, so far as I could judge, not being learned, myself." Iverson "came down upon us astonishingly," Lincoln continued, referring to the fact that the Baltimore *American* characterized the language of the Georgian's speech as consisting of a "scathing and withering style." Lincoln maintained, however, that "at the end of his second severe flash, I was struck blind, and found myself feeling with my fingers for an assurance of my continued physical existence. A little of the bone was left, and I gradually revived."

As Lincoln refuted portions of the Iverson speech, he noted that "the gentleman from Georgia further says we have deserted all our principles, and taken shelter under Gen: Taylor's military coat-tail; and he seems to think this is exceedingly degrading. Well, as his faith is, so be it unto him." The Democrats ought to be careful about accusing the Whigs of running under a military coat tail, Lincoln reminded Iverson, adding that his party had run the last five presidential campaigns under the "ample military coat tail of Gen: Jackson." Then, warming to the task, Lincoln asserted:

> Like a horde of hungry ticks you have stuck to the tail of the Hermitage lion to the end of his life; and you are still sticking to it, and drawing a loathsome sustenance from it, after he is dead. A fellow once advertised that he had made a discovery by which he could make a new man out of an old one, and have enough of the stuff left to make a little yellow dog. Just such a discovery has Gen: Jackson's popularity been to you. You not only twice made President of him out of it, but you have had enough of the stuff left, to make Presidents of several comparatively small men since; and it is your chief reliance now to make still another.

> Mr. Speaker, old horses, and military coat-tails, or tails of any sort, are not figures of speech, such as I would be the first to introduce into discussions here; but as the gentlemen from Georgia has thought fit to introduce them, he, and you, are welcome to all you have made, or can make, by them. If you have any more old horses, trot them out; any more tails, just cock them, and come at us.

Lincoln next turned to what he called "the military tail you democrats are now engaged in dovetailing onto the great Michigander." He was referring to Lewis Cass of Michigan, the Democratic presidential nominee. Lincoln employed a personal experience fantasy theme to dramatize his ridiculing of the military pretensions of candidate Cass.

> Yes sir, all his biographers (and they are legion) have him in hand, tying him to a military tail, like so many mischievous boys tying a dog to a bladder of beans. True, the material they have is very limited; but they drive at it, might and main. He *in*vaded Canada without resistance, and he *out*vaded it without pursuit. As he did both under orders, I suppose there was, to him, neither credit or discredit in them; but they [are made to] constitute a large part of the tail. He

was not at Hull's surrender, but he was close by; he was volunteer aid to Gen: Harrison on the day of the battle of the Thames; and, as you said, in 1840, Harrison was picking huckleberries two miles off while the battle was fought, I suppose it is a just conclusion with you, to say Cass was aiding Harrison to pick huckleberries. . . . This is about all, except the mooted question of the broken sword. Some authors say he broke it, some say he threw it away, and some others, who ought to know, say nothing about it. Perhaps, it would be a fair historical compromise to say, if he did not break it, he didn't do any thing else with it.

Then, Lincoln good-humoredly fantasized a drama which cast himself as a bit of a military blunderer to make his point about General Cass.

By the way, Mr. Speaker, did you know I am a military hero? Yes sir; in the days of the Black Hawk war, I fought, bled, and came away. Speaking of Gen: Cass' career, reminds me of my own. I was not at Stillman's defeat, but I was about as near it, as Cass was to Hull's surrender; and, like him, I saw the place very soon afterwards. It is quite certain I did not break my sword, for I had none to break; but I bent a musket pretty badly on one occasion. If Cass broke his sword, the idea is, he broke it in de[s]peration; I bent the musket by accident. If Gen: Cass went in advance of me in picking huckleberries, I guess I surpassed him in charges upon the wild onions. If he saw any live, fighting indians, it was more than I did; but I had a good many bloody struggles with the musquetoes; and, although I never fainted from loss of blood, I can truly say I was often very hungry. Mr. Speaker, if I should ever conclude to doff whatever our democratic friends may suppose there is of black cockade federalism about me, and thereupon, they shall take me up as their candidate for the Presidency, I protest they shall not make fun of me, as they have of Gen: Cass, by attempting to write me into a military hero.

Clearly, the letter from "Lost Townships" and the response to Congressman Iverson reveal Lincoln, the frontier lawyer and stump speaker, as adept at the simple, clear, plain, and direct rhetoric of the ungenteel style of the early nineteenth century. In colloquial language, he could use the barnyard metaphor and the fictitious and personal-experience fantasy themes to ridicule the pretensions of the city, the wealthy, the educated, and the cultivated.

Lincoln, in the 1840s, also practiced the same windy eloquence and bombast that was typical of the ungenteel style. In January 1838, he delivered an address before the Young Men's Lyceum of Springfield, Illinois. The Young Men's Lyceum was organized in 1833 but became most active in the fall of 1836. For the next several years, the Lyceum was a leading institution in the cultural life of Springfield. Lincoln could find few better audiences for his oratorical skill, and he put on display what was probably his best effort at the flights of eloquence required of every good speaker in the ungenteel style to prove his ability to match the best efforts of classically educated Easterners. Lincoln chose as his topic "The Perpetuation of Our Political Institutions." He began with rolling periodic sentences as follows:

> In the great journal of things happening under the sun, we, the American People, find our account running, under date of the nineteenth century of the Christian era. We find ourselves in the peaceful possession, of the fairest portion of the earth, as regards extent of territory, fertility of soil, and salubrity of climate. We find ourselves under the government of a system of political institutions, conducing more essentially to the ends of civil and religious liberty, than any of which the history of former times tells us. We, when mounting the stage of existence, found ourselves the legal inheritors of these fundamental blessings. We toiled not in the acquirement or establishment of them—they are a legacy bequeathed us, by a *once* hardy, brave, and patriotic, but *now* lamented and departed race of ancestors. Theirs was the task (and nobly they performed it) to possess themselves, and through themselves, us, of this goodly land; and to uprear upon its hills and its valleys, a political edifice of liberty and equal rights; 'tis ours only, to transmit these, the former, unprofaned by the foot of an invader; the latter, undecayed by the lapse of time, and untorn by usurpation—to the latest generation that fate shall permit the world to know. The task of gratitude to our fathers, justice to ourselves, duty to posterity, and love for our species in general, all imperatively require us faithfully to perform.[7]

The entire speech at the Lyceum is couched in much the same windy bombast as the introduction. Later, as president, at the Gettysburg battlefield, Lincoln placed the event into historical and chronological context by the brief reference to "four score and seven years ago"; but at the Lyceum, he referred to "the great journal of things happening under the sun," and to "under date of the nineteenth century of the Christian era." The sentiments are much the same in the brief comments at Gettysburg as they were at the Lyceum, but Lincoln's style in the 1860s had little of the labored circumlocution of the 1838 speech. At the Lyceum, and at Gettysburg, Lincoln turned to the new nation and its conception. However, at Springfield he said:

> That our government should have been maintained in its original form from its establishment until now, is not much to be wondered at. . . . Through that period, it was felt by all, to be an undecided experiment; now, it is understood to be a successful one. Then, all that sought celebrity and fame, and distinction, expected to find them in the success of that experiment. Their *all* was staked upon it:—their destiny was *inseparably* linked with it. Their ambition aspired to display before an admiring world, a practical demonstration of the truth of a

proposition, which had hitherto been considered, at best no better, than problematical; namely, *the capability of a people to govern themselves*. If they succeeded, they were to be immortalized; their names were to be transferred to counties and cities, and rivers and mountains; and to be revered and sung, and toasted through all time. If they failed, they were to be called knaves and fools, and fanatics for a fleeting hour; then to sink and be forgotten.[8]

Contrast the above with the brief statement at Gettysburg: ". . . our fathers brought forth on this continent a new nation, conceived in liberty, and dedicated to the proposition that all men are created equal . . . that this nation, under God, shall have a new birth of freedom; and that government of the people, by the people, for the people, shall not perish from the earth." Despite the excesses of the style, the 1838 speech contains the seeds of the fantasy of the purity of the founders and the need for restoration which is expressed explicitly and clearly in the speech at Gettysburg. As we saw in the analysis of the evangelical rhetoric, the restoration fantasy was a powerful rhetorical appeal in the nineteenth century, and Lincoln was one of those who began early in his speaking career to practice variations on the theme. When he came to the presidency, he had already had at least two decades of practice in celebrating the founders, the noble experiment, and the need for restoration to the founding basis of the government.

Lincoln's brief career as a national politician during his term in Congress proved unsuccessful. He returned to private life and the practice of law in Springfield. The Kansas-Nebraska Act of 1854 aroused him, and he began to speak against the bill, which he interpreted as a repeal of the Missouri Compromise. He said of himself in this period of his career that "his speeches at once attracted a more marked attention than they had ever before done."[9]

The Lincoln scholar Angle judged that "the crowds who attended these meetings heard a new Lincoln. In earlier years he had brought roars of laughter with raillery and personal jibes and had grappled for any small argumentative advantage. Now he spoke from deep conviction that the nation was in danger—spoke without humor but with an eloquence that he had never before achieved."[10]

The texts of Lincoln's writings and speeches after 1854, however, reveal no such sharp break as Angle's term "new Lincoln" might suggest. The change was more evolutionary then revolutionary. Lincoln continued to use humor, continued, particularly in his campaign against Stephen A. Douglas for the Senate in 1858, to grapple for any small argumentative advantage, and he continued to use personal jibes; but he was growing more eloquent and his eloquence was now sustained by a rhetorical vision which dramatized his effort as a dedication to a greater cause than his personal political advancement.

Lincoln's vision portrayed the issue as one of great historical importance, of the survival of the Union and, with that, the survival of the great experiment in human self-government.

In October 1854, Lincoln spoke at Springfield after Senator Douglas had presented the case for the Nebraska bill the preceding day. He concluded the speech with the following peroration:

> Our republican robe is soiled, and trailed in the dust. Let us repurify it. Let us turn and wash it white, in the spirit, if not the blood, of the Revolution. . . . Let us re-adopt the Declaration of Independence, and with it, the practices, and policy, which harmonize with it. Let north and south—let all Americans—let all lovers of liberty everywhere—join in the great and good work. If we do this, we shall not only have saved the Union; but we shall have so saved it, as to make, and to keep it, forever worthy of the saving. We shall have so saved it, that the succeeding millions of free happy people, the world over, shall rise up, and call us blessed, to the latest generations.[11]

Few more eloquent statements of the restoration theme are to be found in the rhetoric of the 1850s.

By refurbishing the restoration drama and hitching it to the fantasies of free soil, Lincoln not only met the psychological needs of the audience member who was disturbed by the defense of slavery and the fears that it might be sinful and thus a danger to his eternal salvation, but he did so in a way which conserved the fantasies that gave meaning to the community and to the individual. Lincoln's vision was predominantly conservative. He portrayed his effort as a response to dangerous changes in the basic foundations of the government. Proslavery forces had placed it on a new footing with the doctrine of "popular sovereignty" (let the people of the territory decide if they wish to be free or slave territories) and with acts enabling Kansas and Nebraska to become states. Lincoln saw himself as emerging from retirement to restore the government to its original bases, to repurify the republic, and to assure that the union would continue. The conservative strain was present in the rhetoric of the evangelical abolitionists as well. They, too, wished to reform rather than destroy the Union, but as Lincoln searched for a rhetoric to meet the here-and-now problems of 1854, he developed a vision which emphasized the conservation of basic values and institutions grown corrupt until that conservatism became the basic theme of his speaking.

In 1854, Lincoln very nearly was elected to the Senate from Illinois by a coalition of Anti-Nebraska Democrats and Anti-Nebraska Whigs. Although Lyman Trumbull ultimately received the position, Lincoln emerged from the election as the leading Anti-Nebraska figure in Illinois and clearly as the most likely candidate to oppose Stephen A. Douglas in the senatorial campaign of 1858.

The years from 1854 to 1858 were packed with political turmoil and uncertainty. The old sustaining rhetorical visions which motivated political action were breaking up, and rapidly shifting political allegiances were the result. The old political parties were disintegrating, the Whig party much more rapidly than the Democratic party. The unstable condition of the political visions is evidenced by the way the Know-Nothing party sprang up like a mushroom, billowed into national prominence, and disintegrated within a couple of years. The political situation in the Kansas territory, where the fantasy of popular sovereignty was given a staging, was deteriorating. The new political party for those who did not want to accept the label *Abolitionist* or *Know-Nothing* emerged around 1856 and took the name *Republican*.

Also in 1856, Charles Sumner, in a style analogous to that of Wendell Phillips, delivered a speech on the "Crime Against Kansas," which flailed both Senator Douglas from Illinois and Senator Andrew P. Butler of South Carolina. Butler's nephew, Preston Brooks of the United States House of Representatives, accosted Sumner two days later in the well of the Senate and during the course of the ensuing argument began to beat the senator about the head with a gutta-percha cane. Sumner was seriously injured, and the event became the basis for rapidly chaining fantasy themes across the country. Adherents to proslavery visions celebrated Brooks as a hero and sent him canes to show their approval. The antislavery and Free-Soil partisans dramatized the encounter as symbolizing the brutal nature of slavery and the extent to which it would go to repress efforts at free speech.

Lincoln joined the Republican party in 1856 and campaigned for Fremont. In 1858, the Republicans met in convention in Springfield, Illinois, and resolved that "Abraham Lincoln is the first and only choice of the Republicans of Illinois for the United States Senate, as the successor of Stephen A. Douglas."[12] The campaign of 1858 pitted two able stump speakers who both practiced the ungenteel style against one another. Douglas had immigrated as a young man to Illinois from Vermont. His education, like Lincoln's, was largely from experience and his speech training was largely from observing the models of effective speaking in frontier Illinois. To be sure, in 1858, Douglas was one of the leading political figures in the country and a strong contender for the presidential nomination of the Democratic party. In addition, Douglas' speaking style had been polished in the school of senatorial debate for eleven years. He had been to a good school in this sense, for the faculty had included, in his first term as senator, such speakers as Daniel Webster, John C. Calhoun, and Henry Clay.

Douglas began the campaign of 1858 in a flowing Websterian style. For example, he began an early campaign speech in Chicago on July 9, 1858 as follows: "I can find no language which can adequately express my profound gratitude for the magnificent welcome which you have extended to me on this occasion. This vast sea of human faces indicates how deep an interest is felt by our people in the great questions which agitate the public mind, and which underlie the foundations of our free institutions."[13]

By midsummer, Douglas had agreed to appear in a series of seven debates across the state with Lincoln. During the course of the debates, Douglas reverted to the direct vernacular of the ungenteel style. In late August, during the debate at Freeport, Douglas dropped the circumlocutions and proceeded to "take the hide off" Lincoln and his supporters in the audience in typical ungenteel style.

> Well, Trumbull having cheated Lincoln, his friends made a fuss, and in order to keep them and Lincoln quiet, the party were obliged to come forward, in advance, at the last state election, and make a pledge that they would go for Lincoln and nobody else. Lincoln could not be silenced in any other way. Now, there are a great many Black Republicans of you who do not know this thing was done. ("White, white," and great clamor.) I wish to remind you that while Mr. Lincoln was speaking there was not a Democrat vulgar and black-guard enough to interrupt him. (Great applause and cries of "hurrah for Douglas.") But I know that the shoe is pinching you. I am clinching Lincoln now and you are scared to death for the result. (Cheers.) I have seen this thing before. I have seen men make appointments for joint discussions, and the moment their man has been heard, try to interrupt and prevent a fair hearing of the other side. I have seen your mobs before, and defy your wrath.[14]

The two antagonists, in 1858, illustrated in many particulars the basic earmarks of the tradition I have been tracing from the time of Whitefield. Both spoke extemporaneously for the most part, although Lincoln wrote out portions of his earlier remarks. Both used fantasy themes in the form of anecdotes extensively. Both were vicious and direct in personal attacks. Both presented themselves as personae of courage, manliness, and willingness to suffer for their principles. The basic criteria for good, trustworthy, and believable speakers, which both used in their attacks on the other's image, and their defense of their own credibility, were drawn from the ungenteel style. In the opening debate, Douglas praised Lincoln in the following terms:

> He was then just as good at telling an anecdote as now. ("No doubt.") He could beat any of the boys wrestling, or running a foot race, in pitching quoits or tossing a copper, could ruin more liquor than all the boys of the town together,

(uproarious laughter,) and the dignity and impartiality with which he presided at a horse race or fist fight, excited the admiration and won the praise of everybody that was present and participated. (Renewed laughter.)[15]

Lincoln responded in a similar vein: "The Judge is woefully at fault about his early friend Lincoln being a 'grocery keeper.' (Laughter.) I don't know as it would be a great sin, if I had been, but he is mistaken. Lincoln never kept a grocery anywhere in the world. (Laughter.) It is true that Lincoln did work the latter part of one winter in a small still house, up at the head of a hollow. (Roars of laughter.)"[16]

At Chicago, before the debates started, Lincoln made the typical disclaimer about education: "I am not master of language; I have not a fine education; I am not capable of entering into a disquisition upon dialectics, as I believe you call it; but I do not believe the language I employed bears any such construction as Judge Douglas put upon it."[17]

The pleasant raillery of the first debate dropped away as the contest grew more intense. As they traded charge and countercharge, they grappled in a no-holds-barred contest reminiscent of the wrestling matches attributed to Lincoln. One interchange will suffice to indicate the way Lincoln and Douglas cut away at one another.

At the Jonesboro debate, Lincoln quoted a speech that Douglas had made at Joliet after the Freeport Debate and that had been reported in the *Missouri Republican*. Douglas was quoted as having said:

> The very notice that I was going to take him down to Egypt [southern Illinois] made him tremble in the knees so that he had to be carried from the platform. He laid up seven days, and in the meantime held a consultation with his political physicians, they had Lovejoy and Farnsworth and all the leaders of the Abolition party, they consulted it all over, and at last Lincoln came to the conclusion that he would answer, so he came up to Freeport last Friday.

Lincoln commented that the statement "furnishes a subject for philosophical contemplation." Then, Lincoln went on to say that he had "come to the conclusion that I can explain it in no other way than by believing the Judge is crazy. If he was in his right mind, I cannot conceive how he would have risked disgusting the four or five thousand of his own friends who stood there, and knew, as to my having been carried from the platform, that there was not a word of truth in it." Senator Douglas interrupted from his seat on the platform: "Didn't they carry you off?" Lincoln's response:

> There; that question illustrates the character of this man Douglas, exactly. He smiles now and says, "Didn't they carry you off?" But he says then, *"He had to be*

carried off;" and he said it to convince the country that he had so completely broken me down by his speech that I had to be carried away. Now he seeks to dodge it, and asks, "Didn't they carry you off?" Yes, they did. *But, Judge Douglas, why didn't you tell the truth?*

Lincoln went on to point out that he had made a number of speeches in the period between the two debates and concluded that Douglas could only have put out the statement as a "serious document" because he was not "in his sober senses" and that "there is no charitable way to look at that statement, except to conclude that he is actually crazy." Lincoln referred to Douglas's inference that "I would not come to Egypt unless he forced me—that I could not be got here, unless he, giant-like, had hauled me down here." The inference that Lincoln had to be forced to debate in the South indicated that the Senator was "wholly out of his sober senses, or else he would have known that when he got me down here—that promise—that windy promise—of his powers to annihilate me, wouldn't amount to anything." Lincoln asked the audience if he appeared to be trembling and then said: "Let the Judge go on, and after he is done with his half hour, I want you all, if I can't go home myself, to let me stay and rot here; and if anything happens to the Judge, if I cannot carry him to the hotel and put him to bed, let me stay here and rot."[18]

While both Lincoln and Douglas were fantasizing about events that were not part of the here-and-now for their immediate audiences, the debates themselves furnished a dramatic encounter that provided the populace across the country with the raw material for fantasizing at a second level. The "Little Giant" of national prominence pitted against a relatively unknown local politician who seemed to be holding his own was an event that could easily be cast into dramatic form. The "Little Giant" was short and round and the challenger was extremely tall and rawboned. Fantasy themes interpreting the debates chained across the country and gave Lincoln that invaluable political commodity—name identification in the mass mind. Not only that, but the fantasies, whether they cast Lincoln or Douglas as hero or villain, came to characterize Lincoln as the personification and symbol of free-soil and Anti-Kansas and Anti-Nebraska sentiment, and Douglas as the symbol of "popular sovereignty" and compromise with the proslavery forces of the South.

The rise of the mass media of communications facilitated fantasizing at a level removed from the rhetorical event. By 1858, the invention of the telegraph and the development of newspapaers to the point of mass circulation of information assured that the rhetorical events in Illinois in the summer and fall would be available across the country. Contemporary events exhibit the two-step level of fantasizing to a much greater degree than the Lincoln-

Douglas debates, since the electronic media make possible instantaneous dramatizations of a rhetorical event in the form of the television or radio melodrama. The media professionals dramatize the news conference, the interview of a public figure, the convention and rally speech for the mass audience in the United States; their selective and artistic dramatizations usually cause fantasies to be shared by portions of the general public and are, thus, much more important in creating rhetorical visions which shape public opinion than are the actual speeches, conversations, and news conferences themselves. Indeed, the sophisticated rhetorician in a culture saturated by the electronic media plans the tactics of a given speech or press conference with an eye to what the media professionals will dramatize.[19]

Lincoln continued throughout the debates to use the short fantasy theme with an application to reinforce a point in the typical style of the Methodist circuit rider. When Douglas charged that Lincoln and the Buchanan Democrats were in a conspiracy to defeat him, Lincoln told of the woman who came out of her cabin to discover her husband wrestling a bear and who, with fine impartiality, yelled, "Go it, husband!—Go it, bear!"[20]

After Lincoln had pinned Douglas to an explicit explanation of his stand on the apparently contradictory implications of Popular Sovereignty and the Dred Scott decision, Lincoln said: "He has at last invented this sort of *do nothing sovereignty*—that the people may exclude slavery by a sort of 'sovereignty' that is exercised by doing nothing at all. Is not that running his popular sovereignty down awfully? Has it not got down as thin as the homoeopathic soup that was made by boiling the shadow of a pigeon that had starved to death?"[21]

When Douglas charged Lincoln with conspiring with Lyman Trumbull to give Trumbull the senatorial seat in 1854 in return for Lincoln's receiving the seat of Douglas in 1858, Lincoln answered:

> The fraud having been apparently successful upon the occasion, both Harris and Douglas have more than once since then been attempting to put it to new uses. As the fisherman's wife, whose drowned husband was brought home with his body full of eels, said when she was asked, "What was to be done with him?" "*Take the eels out and set him again*," so Harris and Douglas have shown a disposition to take the eels out of that stale fraud by which they gained Harris' election, and set the fraud again more than once.[22]

In 1858, Lincoln still indulged, on occasion, in the excessive bombast that represented eloquence to the romantic pragmatist. In the first debate at Ottawa, he closed with the following peroration:

Henry Clay, my beau ideal of a statesman, the man for whom I fought all my humble life—Henry Clay once said of a class of men who would repress all tendencies to liberty and ultimate emancipation, that they must, if they would do this, go back to the era of our independence, and muzzle the cannon which thunders its annual joyous return; they must blow out the moral lights around us; they must penetrate the human soul, and eradicate there the love of liberty; and then and not till then, could they perpetuate slavery in this country! To my thinking, Judge Douglas is, by his example and vast influence, doing that very thing in this community, when he says that the negro has nothing in the Declaration of Independence. Henry Clay plainly understood the contrary. Judge Douglas is going back to the era of our Revolution, and to the extent of his ability, muzzling the cannon which thunders its annual joyous return. When he invites any people willing to have slavery, to establish it, he is blowing out the moral lights around us. When he says he "cares not whether slavery is voted down or voted up,"—that it is sacred right of self-government—he is in my judgment penetrating the human soul and eradicating the light of reason and the love of liberty in this American people.[23]

But as the debates continued, Lincoln indulged less and less in the excesses of self-conscious stylistic airs, and as he imbued his language with his commitment and conviction, as his fantasy themes became fantasy types, and a coherent and consistent rhetorical vision in regard to slavery emerged to support his style, Lincoln came more and more to give classic expression to the rhetorical tradition of romantic pragmatism. In the final debate at Alton, Lincoln drew the basic issue between himself and Douglas as a moral one. In the direct plain style of the Puritan sermon, shorn of much of the excessive overstatement of the circuit rider, in language resonant with the echoes of the vernacular, Lincoln continued:

That is the issue that will continue in this country when these poor tongues of Judge Douglas and myself shall be silent. It is the eternal struggle between these two principles—right and wrong—throughout the world. They are the two principles that have stood face to face from the beginning of time; and will ever continue to struggle. The one is the common right of humanity and the other the divine right of kings. It is the same principle in whatever shape it develops itself. It is the same spirit that says, "You work and toil and earn bread, and I'll eat it." No matter in what shape it comes, whether from the mouth of a king who seeks to bestride the people of his own nation and live by the fruit of their labor, or from one race of men as an apology for enslaving another race, it is the same tyrannical principal [sic].[24]

Abraham Lincoln, in 1858, was in the midst of building a political party. He was faced with the typical problems of consciousness-creating communication. His rhetorical problems were analogous to those of the abolitionists. He, too, had to attract converts to the movement. He, too, had to dramatize what was wrong in the present and to dream of the better world that would result if the programs he advocated and the goals he sought were but achieved. He, too, had to provide an account of the historical meaning of the effort. Like the antislavery forces, Lincoln had to develop a rhetoric which would create a sense of cohesion and commitment on the part of the newly converted. Although he worked very hard and with great rhetorical skill to disassociate himself from the label *abolitionist*, in many respects Lincoln's rhetorical vision resembled that of the evangelical wing of the abolition movement.

The major respect in which Lincoln's rhetorical practice differed from that of Weld and the evangelical agents was that Lincoln spent much less time on fantasy themes depicting the evils of the institution of slavery than they did. He asserted that slavery was wrong and that every man had the right to eat the bread that he had earned with the sweat of his own brow, but Lincoln did not dramatize in extended fantasy themes the atrocities associated with the institution. Lincoln asserted that the problem was not that slavery was an evil, which he believed, but that recent political events had upset the basis of the original agreement among the founders of the government, which held that the institution was on the way to gradual extinction. The abolitionists, on the other hand, portrayed the problem as the existence of the institution itself so long after the founding of the country. By the early 1830s, the evangelicals were arguing that the efforts of the Colonization Society were too slow and ineffectual, that the whole process of freeing the slave in the states must be speeded up. Lincoln, by contrast, using much the same shape of argument but changing its content, viewed the problem as dating from the Kansas-Nebraska Act of 1854 and dramatized that event as an attempt by Stephen Douglas and the proslavery Democrats to overthrow the Missouri Compromise and allow the spread of slavery into the sacred territories of the Northern frontier to assure the perpetuation of slavery.

Lincoln's vision contained the same basic form as the portrait of the evil painted by the evangelicals, but the colors were muted, the fantasies were set in Washington and in the territories. The followers of Weld saw the drama as essentially taking place in the South and their goal was immediate emancipation there. Lincoln staged the problem in the territories and his goal was the restoration of conditions to the terms of the Missouri Compromise of 1820, which had guaranteed that Northern territories would be free soil.

Lincoln's panoramic view of the South and of slavery in the states was less dramatic and less able to evoke powerful emotions than that of the abolitionists. Lincoln's rhetoric was milder, his fantasies about the South were more tolerant, his celebration of compromise more pronounced, and the result was a watered-down vision, less vivid, less zealous, and, importantly, less frightening to the moderate and uncommitted auditor upset about slavery but not yet ready to become an abolitionist. Adherents of Lincoln's vision were less zealous in their commitment to the cause and more willing to accept a moderate solution to the crisis. Although Lincoln's rhetorical vision paid some price in a reduction of zealous commitment to the cause, he gained in terms of a persuasion attractive to the broad center of Northern sentiment. Whigs and Democrats drawn by the magnetism of Weld's flaming vision but not yet ready to become abolitionists and to be associated with the likes of William Lloyd Garrison and Wendell Phillips could more easily become Republicans and fight for freedom in the territories and for saving the Union.

Lincoln's rhetoric accounted for the country's crisis by means of a conspiracy fantasy theme in which various elements of the Democratic party including the president, Senator Douglas, Chief Justice Roger Taney, and others, were changing the policy of the Federal Government towards slavery. In Lincoln's conspiracy fantasy a series of governmental acts were artistically assembled in a drama in which each act fit into place as part of a design to fasten slavery not only on the territories but on the free states as well. He took such events as the Kansas-Nebraska Act sponsored by Douglas and the Dred Scott decision authored by Chief Justice Taney, along with several other less important actions of the principle characters in the conspiracy, and argued that they formed a design that demonstrated that they were acting in concert. All that was needed to complete the sell-out of the free states was a Dred Scott decision which would apply to the states and then slavery would be spread throughout the Union.

The Dred Scott incident was the result of antislavery forces acting out the drama of the free-soil fantasy. It is not unusual for a rhetorical vision to shape the action of its adherents in such a way that fictitious fantasies set in the future subsequently become scenarios for action. The oft-noted phenomenon of the self-fulfilling prophecy illustrates the dynamics by which a rhetorical vision can influence unfolding action. Dred Scott was a slave who had been taken by his master to Fort Snelling at the juncture of the Minnesota and Mississippi rivers in Minnesota Territory. He had, therefore, stepped upon the sacred free soil of the Northern territories. On that basis, some antislavery partisans took his case to court and asked for his freedom. They fought the case to the Supreme Court where that body declared that it had no jurisdiction, but Chief Justice Taney in an *obiter dicta* added that the free-soil dream of the antislavery forces was unconstitutional.

The antislavery forces found the Dred Scott decision a difficult event to incorporate into their vision. Lincoln could not accept the Taney conclusions and still keep the central fantasy of his vision—the dream of the purifying effects of free soil. But he could not reject the decision without rejecting as well the form of government which sustained the Union. In the debates, Douglas kept prodding Lincoln as to his behavior in Congress should he disagree with further decisions of the Supreme Court.

However, the decision was, if anything, more difficult for Douglas's vision to accommodate. Douglas's central fantasy in regard to the territories was that the people in the territory should vote slavery up or down and that it was up to those settlers to decide. Douglas's fantasy was attractive because it allowed the citizens who lived in the state to postpone making a difficult decision. By moving the drama away from the Congress and forcing the settlers in the territories to make the decision, the adherent of "popular sovereignty" could, in a sense, wash his hands of the matter. But Douglas's dream, too, was subsequently acted out in the Kansas Territory and the results were very different from those originally portrayed in his vision. The proslavery and antislavery forces pumped immigrants into the territory and tried to stuff the ballot boxes to assure either a pro- or antislavery basis for the new state. Fighting erupted and people were killed.

Against the background of conflict in Kansas, Lincoln pressed Douglas hard on the Dred Scott decision. How could Douglas accept the decision that slavery could not be barred constitutionally from a territory when he believed that the people of the territory had the right to bar it according to the fantasy of "popular sovereignty"? Douglas's response was a fictitious fantasy in which he portrayed the demise of slavery in a territory if the people did not take positive steps by means of laws and social mores to support it. At that point, Lincoln charged Douglas with having changed his position to a kind of "do-nothing sovereignty" which was as thin as soup made from boiling the shadow of a starved pigeon.

Lincoln, like the abolitionists, saw slavery as a moral issue and, in his second inaugural address, as a sin. According to Lincoln, Douglas would never say that he thought slavery was wrong but would only assert that he did not care whether the people of a territory voted slavery up or down. Although Lincoln did not stress the sin of slavery in the debates of 1858, he ultimately took the moral ground that the basic and most important issue dividing himself from Douglas was the morality or immorality of slavery.

The resemblance of Lincoln's vision to that of the evangelical abolitionists shows most strongly in the way he handled the question of the place of the Republican party in the historical and cultural context of the country. Lincoln saw his efforts as a continuation of the best of the American experience. He returned again and again to the Declaration of Independence and asserted that the Negro was covered by the phrase "All men are created equal." Lincoln continually dramatized the founding fathers as drafting and interpreting the Constitution as an antislavery document. Indeed, he was so troubled by Douglas's fantasies in regard to the founders that he turned to the record of the votes of the members of the Constitutional Convention on the question of slavery in the territories under the old Articles of Confederation as he prepared his speech for Cooper's Union in New York after the debates.

Lincoln, like the evangelicals, saw the Declaration of Independence and the Constitution as the basis of a great experiment in self-government with implications for all the world and for all history. As he said in the debates: "It is the eternal struggle between these two principles—right and wrong—throughout the world."[25]

Lincoln's vision differed from the evangelical abolitionists in a subtle shift of priorities and purposes which served to make his rhetoric more attractive to a broader range of his fellow citizens. Lincoln viewed the Republican party's importance not so much as a movement to assure free soil, nor as the way to emancipate the slaves, but rather as the means of salvation for the nation itself. Lincoln came out of retirement to work first against the doctrine of "popular sovereignty" and then for the Republican party because he saw the Union endangered. He selected, with a sure rhetorical instict, the biblical injunction that a "house divided against itself cannot stand" to serve as the theme of his campaign.

Douglas, a sensitive rhetorician in his own right, saw the symbolic power of the phrase and made it the basis for one of his major counterattacks in the debates. Why could not the country survive half free and half slave? Was not the country half free and half slave from the beginning of its history? Lincoln's answer was that so long as the institution of slavery was *viewed* as a temporary *evil* and as gradually being eliminated, the country could survive, but when slavery was viewed as a permanent good, then the basis of the original compact had been changed.

Lincoln made an astute move to the level of rhetorical criticism and argued on the basis of essentially a rhetorical analysis. What Douglas and the other conspirators were doing, according to Lincoln, was changing the nature of the fantasies which governed the social reality of the American people. From outside the visions of the antagonists, from the perspective of a subsequent time, a rhetorically naive person might judge that the debate over slavery in the territories was a question-begging exercise since the here-and-now problem facing Lincoln and Douglas was slavery in the states. Lincoln, however, argued astutely that if slavery were portrayed as evil in the territories, then the motive to eliminate it was implied. If, on the other hand, the drama of slavery in the territories was portrayed as a positive good, then the extension of it throughout the country into the states as well as the territories was also implied. If we are to translate Lincoln's analysis into the technical terms of fantasy theme analysis, Lincoln was in effect arguing that if the fantasy of slavery in the territories that came to form the social reality of the American people dramatized that institution as evil, then that fantasy would contain the motive to ultimately eliminate it in the states. If, however, that fantasy portrayed slavery as a positive good, it would contain the motive to spread slavery into the states as well as the territories. In terms of fantasy theme analysis, therefore, the debate over slavery in the territories was tremendously important and deserved all of the rhetorical attention and effort that it received in the 1850s.

By making the salvation of the Union the top priority and subordinating the slavery issue, Lincoln's rhetoric emphasized that feature of the evangelical vision which made it most attractive to the American experience, in the drama of the exodus of a chosen people to become a model for the world, and in the self-sustaining fantasy of America as the exemplar of self-government. Lincoln's genius as a rhetorician lay in his ability to modify the essential vision of the abolitionists so that it incorporated wide common ground with many of the powerful and motivating dramas of other visions, sacred and secular; thus he was able to establish a viable political party. Of course Lincoln was not alone in developing the rhetoric around which the new political movement coalesced, but the debates with Douglas in 1858 were inherently so dramatic that they caused fantasies interpreting them to chain throughout much of the populace. The Lincoln *persona* became a powerful character in these dramatizations, and his words and the rhetorical vision they implied became part of the mass persuasion of the 1850s as the nation rushed headlong into an ever-deepening crisis.

In attempting to build internal cohesion among the followers of the new party, Lincoln argued, with less zeal but essentially the same form as the evangelicals, that the cause of the union and of free soil was greater than he was and that long after "these poor tongues of Judge Douglas and myself shall be silent" the issue would continue to be of importance because it was central to the eternal struggle between freedom and tyranny that had been waged throughout all time and throughout the entire world and would continue to be waged in the future.

At Lewistown in August of 1858, Lincoln delivered an encomium on the Declaration of Independence which was widely quoted and which catches the essence of Lincoln's internal unifying rhetoric. The newspapaer account alleges that Lincoln said:

> Now, my countrymen (Mr. Lincoln continued with great earnestness,) if you have been taught doctrines conflicting with the great landmarks of the Declaration of Independence; if you have listened to suggestions which would take away from its grandeur, and mutilate the fair symmetry of its proportions; if you have been inclined to believe that all men are *not* created equal in those inalienable rights enumerated by our chart of liberty, let me entreat you to come back. Return to the fountain whose waters spring close by the blood of the Revolution. Think nothing of me—take no thought for the political fate of any man whomsoever—but come back to the truths that are in the Declaration of Independence. You may do anything with me you choose, if you will but heed these sacred principles. You may not only defeat me for the Senate, but you may take me and put me to death. While pretending no indifference to earthly honors, I *do claim* to be actuated in this contest by something higher than an anxiety for office. I charge you to drop every paltry and insignificant thought for any man's success. It is nothing; I am nothing; Judge Douglas is nothing. *But do not destroy that immortal emblem of humanity—the Declaration of American Independence.*[26]

While Lincoln's vision did not present the cause of the Republican party as sanctioned by the ultimate legitimatization of God, as did the evangelical abolitionists, he did build the self-image of his group by declaring that the party was fighting for eternal, universal, and unchanging principles. The Declaration of Independence was a "majestic interpretation of the economy of the Universe." The framers of the document were "lofty, and wise, and noble" and understood "the justice of the Creator to His creatures." The men who drafted the Declaration of Independence had "erected a beacon to guide their children and their children's children, and the countless myriads who should inhabit the earth in other ages."[27]

Lincoln raised the Constitution and the Declaration of Independence into sacred rhetorical symbols. They came, in his vision, to hold a position similar to that of the Bible for the evangelical abolitionists. With an exegetical analysis as careful as any Bible student might use, Lincoln, the lawyer, searched the language of the Constitution to find the meaning of the founders. The fact that the Constitution referred to the black people of the country as *persons* rather than *servants* or *slaves* meant to Lincoln that the drafters of the document thought the institution was on its way to extinction and they wanted no trace of it in the language of that document which they wished to serve for all posterity as a model for all those fighting for human freedom and against tyranny.

Lincoln's rhetorical vision contained goals for the new party in relation to slavery, but these goals were less ambitious and the time-table for their achievement was less specific and more flexible than that imbedded in the evangelical call for "immediate abolition." Lincoln never called for immediate emancipation; instead, his vision furnished the adherents with a clear and realizable immediate goal, the assurance that slavery would not be extended and protected in the territories. The compact of the Constitution required that the new party not meddle with slavery in the states, but the Federal Government did have jurisdiction over the extension of slavery into the territories and could take legal steps to assure that the institution never defiled the frontier.

Although Lincoln never called for immediate abolition of slavery, his vision resembled that of the evangelicals of the 1830s when he dramatized his stand on the morality of slavery. Henry Stanton, testifying before the committee of the Massachusetts legislature, had explained the goal of the new abolition movement simply as having Congress restore to every slave "the ownership of his own body, mind and soul." Stanton said that immediate abolition did not mean that the slaves should immediately receive all political rights. Lincoln, in the dabates with Douglas, reiterated the goals of his vision again and again. Douglas kept fantasizing that Lincoln was secretly an abolitionist at heart and wanted social equality for the blacks and intermarriage with them. Lincoln used a counterfantasy that made the point that there was a distinction between not wanting a person to be a slave on the one hand and wanting her for a wife on the other.

At Ottawa, in the first debate, Lincoln presented a fantasy type in which a personalized character of "the negro" played a part to portray his stand on the race question.

> . . . anything that argues me into his idea of perfect social and political equality with the negro, is but a specious and fantastic arrangement of words, by which a man can prove a horse chestnut to be a chestnut horse. . . . but I hold that notwithstanding all this, there is no reason in the world why the negro is not entitled to all the natural rights enumerated in the Declaration of Independence, the right to life, liberty and the pursuit of happiness. I hold that he is as much entitled to these as the white man. I agree with Judge Douglas he is not my equal in many respects—certainly not in color, perhaps not in moral or intellectual endowment. But in the right to eat the bread, without leave of anybody else, which his own hand earns, *he is my equal and the equal of Judge Douglas, and the equal of every living man.*[28]

Finally, at the Alton debate, in Lincoln's last speech of the joint appearance, he spelled out the goal of his vision in clear terms.

> The real issue in this controversy—the one pressing upon every mind—is the sentiment on the part of one class that looks upon the institution of slavery *as a wrong*, and of another class that *does not* look upon it as a wrong. The sentiment that contemplates the institution of slavery in this country as a wrong is the sentiment of the Republican party. It is the sentiment around which all their actions—all their arguments circle—from which all their propositions radiate. They look upon it as being a moral, social and political wrong; and while they contemplate it as such, they nevertheless have due regard for its actual existence among us, and the difficulties of getting rid of it in any satisfactory way and to all the constitutional obligations thrown about it. Yet having a due regard for these, they desire a policy in regard to it that looks to its not creating any more danger. They insist that it should as far as may be, *be treated* as a wrong, and one of the methods of treating it as a wrong is to *make provision that it shall grow no larger*.[29]

Abraham Lincoln deserves to be considered as the great spokesman for the antislavery impulse because his rhetorical modification of the basic vision of the abolitionists couched in the style of the frontier preachers and lawyers swept up large numbers of moderates on the slavery question and built a cohesive party that won the election of 1860.

For Lincoln the rhetorician, however, the persuasive campaign from 1854 and 1860 was but a prelude to the trials and problems of governing the country during the Civil War. The issues of war and peace forced Lincoln to meet rhetorical problems of great magnitude. The presidential rhetoric, coupled with his assassination, resulted in the sharing of many of the familiar fantasy types of romantic pragmatism by large portions of the Northern pro-Union populace. With the victory in the war came the nation's search for a meaning of the experience and the need for a rhetoric to unify the entire country. That need was met by the Lincolnian version of romantic pragmatism assuming mythic proportions in terms of its wide acceptance and its saliency in the states which stayed in the Union.

A complete understanding of the national dreams and fantasies of the United States from 1860 to 1960 requires an account of the romantic pragmatic rhetorical tradition and its evolution and modification, not only in the words of Lincoln himself but also in the fantasies of those adherents of the rhetoric who eulogized his death as martyrdom and who continued to build his persona into a legend within the mythology of America.

10

The Culmination of Romantic Pragmatism

When Lincoln was elected to the presidency, he was faced with the impending secession of the Southern states. By the time he was inaugurated, a number of states had already seceded. Within a very short time, Lincoln became the head of a nation at war encumbered with all the rhetorical problems that such a leader must face.

Lincoln's first rhetorical decision was forced upon him by the necessity to deliver an inaugural address. Some saw Lincoln as the leader of a sectional party. If he had, indeed, been a sectional leader, he could have spoken for the North and hurled defiance at the South, whipping up fervor for the battle ahead and trying to mobilize Northern opinion for a unified war effort. What Lincoln in fact did was to speak for the Union in a conciliatory tone to try to unify the country once again. Lincoln decided to speak for the Union in his first inaugural and he never swerved from that decision. The motive to select the goal of the Union was strongly imbedded in Lincoln's rhetorical vision as we have seen it in Chapter nine. In Lincoln's vision, the Union was the most important thing and its peril was his self-justification for coming out of retirement to return to politics.

From the time of the first inaugural until his death, Lincoln's rhetorical vision transcended the battles and the war. Again and again he translated his vision into tactics of unity and cohesion for all of the states, Southern as well as

Northern. His emphasis was on the symbolic forces that bound the Union together. As he closed his first inaugural, Lincoln said. "The mystic chords of memory, stretching from every battle-field and patriot grave . . . will yet swell the chorus of the Union."[1]

For the remainder of his time in the presidency, Lincoln carefully and with great artistry developed the rhetoric of unity. That he might better accomplish the unification of a community torn by civil war, Lincoln took a rhetorical stance high above the conflict. Every war-time president in the United States has faced the question of how to handle the persona of the *enemy*. A war-time president may choose not to fantasize about the enemy, or he may include the enemy in many of his rhetorical dramas, balancing the villainous characters symbolizing the foe with heroic characters representing the community and its friends, or he may emphasize fantasy themes which depict the evil nature of the enemy. In mobilizing opinion for World War I, Woodrow Wilson selected a tactic which created essentially two personifications of the German people, one villainous and one good. Wilson separated the German people from the German leaders and made Kaiser Wilhelm the symbol for a small group of willful men conspiring against the wishes of the common group.[2] Wilson's rhetorical vision was shaped by his domestic rhetoric, which was progressive in its fantasies and saw the troubles of America as emerging from the exploitation of the common people by a small group of conspiring economic plutocrats. Wilson's vision implied the motive to accept an armistice once the evil leadership of the Kaiser and his group was deposed and also made it easier for the German people to accept an armistice and reject the guilt for the war. Franklin Roosevelt, on the other hand, made the character of the enemy as the personification of evil a salient feature of his rhetoric. In Roosevelt's vision, Hitler became the personification of the evil that resided in the German people and that had twice caused them to ignite worldwide conflagrations by their aggression against weaker countries. Roosevelt's vision contained the motive which impelled the Americans to call for unconditional surrender and the total defeat of the Axis Powers in World War II.

Lincoln, faced with the rhetorical problem of mobilizing public opinion, took a position high above the conflict and spoke in an objective way about both sides in the war. Lincoln never castigated the enemy or fantasized dramas in which hateful Southerners acted out despicable atrocities. Lincoln never made of any Southerner an archvillain such as Roosevelt made of Hitler.

As a participant in the ungenteel style of the tradition of romantic pragmatism, Lincoln had the necessary speech skills to "take the hide off" the Southerners. He could have unlimbered all the vituperation and biblical rhetoric of the abolitionists to castigate the sinfulness, evil, and atrocities of the South. Indeed, many of the radical Republicans who participated in an abolitionist rhetorical vision were unhappy that he did not do so. At the risk of losing the radicals, Lincoln spoke from an Olympian height as one sorrowfully watching the terrible tragedy of the war. He argued that the nation could not be separated, was not separated, but only threatened. He argued that, geographically, the nation was meant by Providence to be one. There was no line that could divide the North from the South in geographical terms, for the two sections would still have to share a common continent regardless of the outcomes of the war. In Lincoln's vision, the Union was an association of people older than the compact of the Constitution. The people were mystically tied to each other and, even in the rebelling sections, many of them were still for the Union. For Lincoln, the major goal was the salvation of the Union and, as the war continued, all else paled by comparison, including the emancipation of the slaves.

Lincoln seldom distinguished between the Northern soldier and the Southern soldier, seldom spoke as a partisan leader for his section in the conflict. In his first inaugural, he said. "We are not enemies, but friends. We must not be enemies."[3] In his speech at the dedication of the cemetery at Gettysburg he referred to "the brave men, living and dead, who struggled here" without inferring that he spoke only for the men of the North.[4]

Lincoln presented the war as relating to an issue that transcended slavery. In his special message to Congress on July 4, 1861, Lincoln said:

> And this issue embraces more than the fate of the United States. It presents to the whole family of man the question whether a constitutional republic or democracy—a government of the people by the same people—can or cannot maintain its territorial integrity against its own domestic foes. It presents the question whether discontented individuals, too few in numbers to control administration according to organic law in any case, can always, upon the pretenses made in this case, or on any pretenses, or arbitrarily without any pretense, break up their government, and thus practically put an end to free government upon the earth. It forces us to ask: "Is there, in all republics, this inherent and fatal weakness?" "Must a government, of necessity, be too strong for the liberties of its own people, or too weak to maintain its own existence?"[5]

At the peak of his rhetorical powers, speaking as the president of the entire country, meeting the issues of war and peace, Lincoln dropped from his speeches the anecdote, the homey barnyard simile, and the ridiculing, the vituperation, and the castigating elements of the speaking style of the ungenteel tradition. For mobilizing public opinion behind the war effort and for unifying the entire country, he harnessed the yet-powerful rhetorical fantasies, now of mythic proportion, which stemmed from the puritan sermonic style. In the second inaugural address, Lincoln rose to the greatest artistic heights in the tradition in a speech that stands as the culmination of romantic pragmatism. The rhetorical tradition had been maturing for two centuries; it found in Lincoln a man who personified its ethos and a man who had the ability and training to develop a thorough craftsmanship in the style. The times and the issues met with a proper spokesman when the momentous issues of the survival of the Union and the emancipation of the slaves found Lincoln in the presidency.

Lincoln's second inaugural is a reflection of his presidential rhetorical vision. In an era of long speeches, Lincoln, who had often spoken for several hours at political rallies, spoke briefly and carefully. There was, he said, "less occasion for an extended address" than when he gave his first inaugural. In a brief introduction, he mentioned the war but said only that "with high hope for the future, no prediction in regard to it is ventured." In a few short words, Lincoln recalled the occasion of his first inauguration and the progress of the war. Then, he surveyed the expectations of the rhetoric of both sides with a studied impartiality.

> Neither party expected for the war the magnitude or the duration which it has already attained. Neither anticipated that the cause of the conflict might cease with, or even before, the conflict itself should cease. Each looked for an easier triumph, and a result less fundamental and astounding. Both read the same Bible, and pray to the same God; and each invokes his aid against the other. It may seem strange that any men should dare to ask a just God's assistance in wringing their bread from the sweat of other men's faces; but let us judge not, that we be not judged. The prayers of both could not be answered—that of neither has been answered fully.[6]

The style of the speech is plain, dispassionate, and objective. The speaker's vision surveys the conflict as though with the perspective of time outside the conflict, even the slight hint of a partisan fantasy theme reflected in the allusion to men asking a just God for help with "wringing bread from the sweat of other men's faces" is quickly balanced by the biblical injunction to "judge not." The first movement of the speech is but the prelude to the central fantasy of Lincoln's appeal. The theme of the speech is foreshadowed in the speaker's reference to both sides reading the same Bible and praying to the same God. The speech, indeed, is a return from the secular rhetoric of the frontier lawyer to the older forms of sacred rhetoric. Wartime rhetoric often attempts to use a god persona as the ultimate legitimizer for the cause. Men participating in a rhetorical vision which dramatizes a god persona as sanctioning their efforts fight with great zeal. But, Lincoln said with compassion and understanding rather than in a chiding tone, "the prayers of both could not be answered—." Even so, Lincoln does create a god persona and uses the characterization for his own purpose as an ultimate legitimization of his vision of saving the Union.

The bulk of the second inaugural picked up the theme of the god persona's relationship to the Civil War. Lincoln began with the assertion that "the Almighty has his own purposes." What are the Almighty's purposes in visiting the terrible time of troubles upon the people of the country? To answer this question, Lincoln redramatized a basic fantasy type imprinted in the collective religious memory of many Americans by generations of sermons. Lincoln returned to the "Fetching Good Out of Evil" fantasy type, as old as covenant theology.

The New England Puritan preachers' "jeremiad" was widely used to mobilize the colonists for their fight with the British in the Revolution. The basic fantasy type which Perry Miller found in hundreds of sermons from all parts of the colonies during the time of the Revolution was that

> We have sinned, therefore we are afflicted by the tyranny of a corrupt Britain; we must repent and reform, in order to win the irresistible aid of Providence; once we have wholeheartedly performed this act, we shall be able to exert our freedom by expelling the violators of the compact; when we succeed we shall enter upon a prosperity and temporal happiness beyond anything the world has hitherto seen.[7]

For the colonial preachers using the fantasy type of "Fetching Good Out of Evil," the evil of war became a purging and cleansing experience out of which the chosen people emerged once again free, happy, and right with their God. The speakers portrayed the evil as an affliction given by God to a sinful people. By accepting the portrayal and participating in the drama, the listeners shared a deeply meaningful explanation of the presence and purpose of evil, of their own place in God's scheme of things, and the place of their community as a people in a unique covenant with God. To such a purpose and for such a people, an individual caught up in the fantasy was willing to dedicate strenuous effort and, perhaps, even life.

The scenes of the scenario are relatively straightforward: the first scene depicts the evil itself; the logic of the scenario next requires a searching of the community for the sin which accounts for the troubles a just God afflicts upon the people. Finally, the speakers discover the way that leads from the evil, the good which the community is to fetch from the evil of the war, and the people then repent, suffer, and atone for their sins.

In the case of the preachers whose sermons urged repentance and the expulsion of the British from the colonies, the scenario also contained a horde of villains, including a tyrannical king and ministers who were oppressing the colonists. When the crisis was at its height and the troubles were most severe, the fantasy type aroused heavy charges of guilt and shame and of hatred for the villains. When victory came, the fantasy evoked feelings of joy, peace, and thanksgiving and provided a way to lift the burden of guilt.

The fantasy type provides a complete and plausible explanation of evil. Evil always has a purpose since God does not afflict his chosen people with troubles unless they are failing to live up to the covenant he has with them. The community members and their spokesman must, therefore, search the evil and discover the good that is within it. The participants do not wring their hands in the face of evil and say, "How meaningless!" or "Why us? Why does this happen to us?" Rather, the participants in the "Fetching Good Out of Evil" fantasy type ask, "How have we sinned? What must we do to be saved?"

On March 30, 1863, Lincoln drafted a proclamation for a National Fast Day which spelled out the basic fantasy with considerably less artistry but much more explicitly than the second inaugural. The proclamation read in part:

> . . . may we not justly fear that the awful calamity of civil war which now desolates the land may be but a punishment inflicted upon us for our presumptuous sins, to the needful end of our national reformation as a whole people? We have been the recipients of the choicest bounties of Heaven. We have been preserved, these many years, in peace and prosperity. We have grown in numbers, wealth, and power as no other nation has ever grown; but we have forgotten God. . . . we have vainly imagined, in the deceitfulness of our hearts, that all these blessings were produced by some superior wisdom and virtue of our own. . . . It behooves us, then, to humble ourselves before the offended Power, to confess our national sins, and to pray for clemency and forgiveness. . . . All this being done in sincerity and truth, let us then rest humbly in the hope authorized by the divine teachings, that the united cry of the nation will be heard on high, and answered with blessings no less than the pardon of our national sins, and the restoration of our now divided and suffering country to its former happy condition of unity and peace.[8]

In the second inaugural, Lincoln develops the fantasy with economy. In language rich with connotations and inferences, he alludes to but does not detail the basic rhetorical form. Like a poem, the rhetoric of the great speech resonates and echoes with the meanings created in substantial portions of the American people by generations of audiences sharing fantasies portrayed from pulpits and platforms over the preceding century.[9]

Lincoln begins his development of the abasement-atonement rhetoric by quoting a biblical text. "Woe unto the world because of offenses! for it must needs be that offenses come; but woe to that man by whom the offense cometh." Lincoln then applies the lesson. American slavery was an offense which God saw fit to visit upon the people of the country because of their sinfulness. The time of troubles in the form of the great war was evidence of God's displeasure. "He gives to both North and South this terrible war, as the woe due to those by whom the offense came." Lincoln asks, "Shall we discern therein any departure from those divine attributes which the believers in a living God always ascribe to him?" He then prays that the "mighty scourge of war" would "speedily pass away." But he concludes his thematic development with resignation and the recognition of the price that a just God will demand for the propitiation of the nation's mighty sin. "Yet, if God wills that it continue until all the wealth piled by the bondman's two hundred and fifty years of unrequited toil shall be sunk, and until every drop of blood drawn with the lash shall be paid by another drawn with the sword, as was said three thousand years ago, so still it must be said, 'The judgments of the Lord are true and righteous altogether.'"

Lincoln's formulation of the fantasy type contains several powerful motives for the unification of the nation. First, Lincoln's panoramic vision of God's relationship to both North and South emphasizes the unity of the American people regardless of geographical region. God stands in the same relationship to both North and South in Lincoln's drama. God is not a partisan even though men may pray to him for a sectional victory. He has given both North and South this "terrible war," for they have both participated in the offenses against God; both North and South share in the sins that have aroused God's terrible wrath.

Much of the power of the unifying appeal comes from the drama of God visiting the war upon both North and South as part of a union, a nation, a chosen people. Lincoln never spells out the basic assumption that God would not bother to discipline a nation unless they were a chosen people like the Jews of biblical times or as the settlers of the New World, establishing a new Jerusalem in the wilderness. But he need not do so because the fantasy type is so closely intertwined with the "Fetching Good Out of Evil" fantasy type in the collective memory of many who have shared in the portrayal of various communities of Americans as chosen people. Indeed, by not spelling it out but rather arousing the connotations by allusion, he gains a poetic compression and richness of emotional evocation that is lost in the more detailed amplification of the relationship in the Fast Day proclamation.

Finally, the long hard war was the way to salvation. The nation was to purge itself of its sins, including the sin of slavery, by expending its treasure until all of the wealth "piled by the bondman's two hundred and fifty years of unrequited toil shall be sunk" and it was to sacrifice its young men until "every drop of blood drawn with the lash shall be paid by another drawn with the sword."

With the poetic invocation of the old fantasy type of abasement and atonement, the bulk of Lincoln's second inaugural message came to an end. Lincoln, in his rhetorical efforts to unify the country, used a fantasy type imbedded in the rhetorical visions of the entire country, North as well as South. Reminiscent of the Puritan style in its nuances, pessimistic, abundant with inferences of determinism, it was also a dramatization of the deepest tribal feeling that the nation, the entire nation, had gone into the wildenress because they were God's chosen people. The eyes of the world were upon them, to be sure, but much more importantly the eyes of God were upon them. They would, as Lincoln put it at the close of his annual message to the Congress on December 1, 1862, "nobly save or meanly lose the last, best hope of earth."[10]

God did stand in a unique relationship to the American nation, but one did not see that uniqueness from the niggardly vision of a partisan in a civil war praying to God for a sectional victory. One saw God's purposes only when one viewed the entire nation blessed by His providence and grace but fallen from favor by sinfulness and neglect until visited with the terrible scourge of civil war. As that war was coming to a successful close for the North, Lincoln, in his second inaugural address, asserted that, with the termination of the war, the sin of slavery would be propitiated and the nation could then go forward, cleansed, to fulfill its destiny.

Still speaking from a lofty perspective of unity, Lincoln ended the address. "With malice toward none; with charity for all; with firmness in the right as God gives us to see the right, let us strive to finish the work we are in." The style of the close was the epitome of Lincoln's eloquence for unity, the evocation of a deeper union than any forged by political compacts. The work that remained to be done included "to bind up the nation's wounds; to care for him who shall have borne a battle, and for his widow, and his orphan—to do all which may achieve and cherish a just and lasting peace among ourselves, and with all nations."[11] The neutral pronoun "him" referred impartially to a persona who had fought and suffered and died whether he had worn a uniform of blue or of grey.

As he closed his first inaugural, Lincoln used the figure of the chords that stretched from the past to swell the chorus of the Union, and as he closed the second, he alluded to the binding up of the nation's wounds. The nation had never been separated in Lincoln's rhetorical vision and his interpretation of the events of the war. The mystical union sanctioned by God was but visited with a terrible time of troubles because of its recent falling-away from the founding principles and the resulting sinfulness. The old fountains of the republic were still sound and what was required, terrible as that might be, was a propitiation of the sin, a purging of the evil, and a restoration to God's favor; from that, a healthy Union would emerge once again.

The impact of the masterful second inaugural was only beginning to be felt when Lincoln was assassinated. Death is an ultimate event for which people need words—a rhetoric—to create a suitable meaning for life as well as mortality. Words that provide an interpretive fantasy of death, a rhetoric of death, provide a family, a community, or a nation an opportunity to develop a sense of cohesion, a culture, a self-image, and a feeling for its own destiny. John Wilkes Booth killed Lincoln at a moment in history when the nation desperately needed to take stock and find a meaning for the great fraternal convulsion. What did the war mean? Why had so many men died? Had they died in vain?

Booth assassinated Lincoln in Ford's theatre in most dramatic fashion. The reports of the event seldom provided sufficient corroboration for the public's appetite for information. The lack of corroboration provided a communication climate in which fantasies chained off in all directions, many taking the form of rumors. The authorities traced the assassin to a barn and killed him but fantasies had him fleeing to Oklahoma and Mexico where he supposedly continued to live as a fugitive. Years later Finis Bates, who was once Attorney General of Tennessee, preserved the corpse of a house painter who claimed he was John Wilkes Booth and rented it to carnivals. Other fantasies, in rumor form, dramatized Lincoln as foreseeing his assassination. Lincoln had dreamed he saw a catafalque in the East Room of the White House. He had seen a double image of himself in a mirror. He had told his cabinet of a dream in which he saw a ship moving swiftly towards a dark shore.[12]

The chaining of the superstitious and uncorroborated fantasies of the more extreme sort testify to the rhetorical potential in the dramatic asassination as well to the psychological need of large segments of the population for an accounting of their recent here-and-now difficulties in a satisfactory fashion. Lincoln's martyrdom, coming only five days after Lee's surrender and only a few weeks after the delivery of the second inaugural, resulted in a great outpouring of fantasies which were shared by substantial portions of the public. Newspapers which had been critical of the president did an abrupt turnabout and began casting him in a heroic role. The eulogistic rhetoric which flowed from pulpit and platform raised his *persona* to legendary proportions.

Lincoln's body was borne across the country from Washington to Philadelphia to New York City. Westward then the black train moved slowly along towards Cleveland, Columbus, Chicago, and finally back to Springfield, Illinois, for burial. Huge crowds lined the way; millions saw the coffin or the funeral train, and over a million viewed the corpse. The relics of the nation's grief testify to the swiftness and power of the fantasies which sprung up around Lincoln's death. Entrepreneurs quickly printed the second inaugural in gold letter with a black border. They also made mementos of Lincoln's farewell speech at Springfield upon assuming the presidency and of his Gettysburg Address, along with the Emancipation Proclamation. Other relics included handkerchiefs with "Lincoln ever Faithful" and watches with Lincoln's portrait on the dial.

From the great flood of eulogizing rhetoric there rapidly emerged salient fantasy themes, then fantasy types, until, finally, the Civil War came to be symbolized in the *persona* of the martyred president. Of all the devices that explain or provide meaning for complex and chaotic events, few are more powerful and effective with the masses than the creation of a *persona* who comes to symbolize a cluster of meanings. The rhetoric of Western civilizations is filled with such *personae*. One thinks of the personae of Socrates, Jesus, Caesar, Attila, Luther, Shakespeare, Da Vinci, Joan of Arc, and Napoleon as examples of the mythification of historical personages. America had heroic *personae* before the assassination of Abraham Lincoln. George Washington, Benjamin Franklin, Thomas Jefferson, and Andrew Jackson had been cast as protagonists in fantasies until their *personae* assumed legendary proportions and began to function rhetorically as symbols for complex political and social events and issues. Often, when a historical personage is cast in a heroic roles in widely chaining fantasies, the legendary persona that emerges from the mythification process is of greater importance to the development of cohesion within the community or nation than the actual deeds of the individual. Lincoln's assassination, coming as it did near the close of the war when the entire country needed a rhetoric of summation to explain the experience, ignited a rapid and gigantic blaze of fantasizing which created a legendary Lincoln persona symbolizing the meaning of the war and of the American experience.

Speakers and writers who celebrate a martyr's life and sacrifice and the cause for which he died need pertinent quotations from his speeches and writings for effective eulogies. If the quotations prove to be eloquent and apt, the effectiveness of the rhetoric of legend building is increased. In Lincoln's case, as we have seen, the speeches were superb repositories of aphorisms, eloquent statements providing a meaning for the American experience, and, in several instances, the speeches were brief enough to be memorized easily and recited or to be included in the anthologies of eloquence. The Gettysburg Address with its pithy restatement of an oft-quoted sentiment—"government of the people, by the people, for the people, shall not perish from the earth"—was a short and eloquent statement of the essence of an important American dream and the cause for which the war was fought. Student orators found the speech easy to memorize and compilers of anthologies often included it in their works. Dramatists could incorporate the Gettysburg Address into pageants and plays without stopping the dramatic action for very long.

Because it was Lincoln who came to be president at the time of the Civil War rather than an eastern leader of the Republican party who would have spoken in a different style, because the eulogies at the time of his death quoted from his speeches so often and paraphrased his rhetorical vision so frequently, because Lincoln was martyred at a crucial time in the nation's history, and because he was an unusual practitioner of the ungenteel style—a natural rhetorical talent thoroughly trained by a long apprenticeship in political stump speaking and in forensic debate—the tradition of romantic pragmatism caught up masses of the American people in the century from 1860 to 1960.

At no time, of course, during the century after the Civil War was a single rhetorical style predominant in the United States in a way analogous to the manner in which the Puritan style dominated New England during the century from 1640 to 1740. Still many of the elements of romantic pragmatism as represented in the rhetoric of Lincoln came to characterize much of American persuasion in the century following the war.

The ethos of the Lincoln persona, which played the leading roles in the stock scenarios of the legend, was a romanticized and softened limning of the ideal frontier orator. What were the qualities that made the Lincoln persona a credible speaker? The Lincoln persona was ill-dressed, unpolished, sincere, and honest. Unschooled, the legendary Lincoln was learned in the study of human nature and wiser than the graduates of Harvard College. Worldly people derided Lincoln and ridiculed his manners and appearances. When he began to speak, however, his sincerity captured the crowd and they forgot his appearance, his lack of education, his back country pronunciation, and were enchanted by his arguments and his good common sense. The legend glorified Lincoln's skill at telling stories, his ability to wrestle, to stand up to frontier bullies, and to meet the common people on common ground. He was one of the people of the frontier of Illinois. Honest Abe, the rail splitter, was sincere, guileless, and devoid of any "city-slicker" polish of dress or manner. He was the clever country lawyer, shrewder than the city lawyers, more honest, more real, more sincere.

Lincoln had roamed the Illinois back country, taking a flatboat down the river for adventure. He had traveled the frontier legal circuit, met the trials of frontier life, and proved himself a practical man who could ford a swollen stream, beat off a gang of villains trying to loot his flatboat, and wrestle all the local champions. No circuit-riding Methodist, not even Peter Cartwright, who itinerated Illinois in the years when Lincoln rose to political fame in the state, created a more attractive or credible image in the tradition of romantic pragmatism than Abraham Lincoln.

Lincoln had freed the slaves, won the war that preserved the great experiment in self-government, and reaffirmed a basic American fantasy in the dream that "all men are created equal." Lincoln was a man who sprang up from nature on the frontier, who was raised in the wilderness in a lean-to and then a log cabin. He personified another potent American dream in rising from his humble beginnings to the highest office in the land. Fortunately, he had on occasion said as much. On August 22, 1864, Lincoln spoke to the 166th Ohio regiment: "I happen, temporarily, to occupy this White House. I am a living witness that any one of your children may look to come here as my father's child has."[13]

Forced by the experiences of the war to search for a meaning for America, Lincoln reaffirmed the basic rhetorical fantasy types of romantic pragmatism. America was unique and covenanted with God to be the "last, best hope of earth." America was "conceived in liberty and dedicated to the proposition that all men were created equal." The war was a trying and testing time to see if human beings could govern themselves or if some form of monarchy, oligarchy, or dictatorship was inevitable in the course of human government.

I have traced a rhetorical tradition which I call romantic pragmatism from the time of its inception in colonial America at the period of the Great Awakening in the eighteenth century through its evolution and growth, until its culmination in the practice and legend of Abraham Lincoln. Although many elements of the rhetorical tradition may seem quaint or distasteful to a contemporary reader, the wide popularity of its essential vision, as portrayed by Lincoln and symbolized by his persona as one of the great popular heroes of America, has left its imprint on the public consciousness of later generations. Many Americans continue to be pragmatic, up-and-doing, impatient, vigorous, anti-intellectual, and romantic people.

I began this investigation with the purpose of discovering the relationship between religious and reform speaking in the three decades prior to the Civil War. In the evolving tradition of the rhetoric of romantic pragmatism, I found a clear, direct, and powerful move from sacred to secular rhetoric. Although other connections between religious speaking and secular persuasion undoubtedly exist and can be documented, to my mind, the relationships revealed by the romantic and pragmatic tradition are the most important because they are so pervasive and because the tradition itself has been so attractive to such a large segment of the American public.

When one examines the evangelical style of Charles Grandison Finney in conjunction with the style of Weld and the agents of evangelical abolition, clearly the influence of religious rhetoric was direct and widespread. The rhetoric of the evangelical abolitionists celebrated the basic political and religious institutions of the country, moved into the political arena, and eventually influenced the persuasion of the Free-Soil and Republican parties. Lincoln's vision represents a rhetorical style heavily influenced by religious persuasion. In Lincoln's vision, however, the supernatural sanction of a higher power is provided by a God persona which treats the entire community, North as well as South, in a just way but does so with particular care since Americans are chosen people. Lincoln adds to the sanction of a superintending Providence the legitimatization of the founding documents of the country.

Lincoln raises the Declaration of Independence and the Constitution of the United States to a level approaching that of the sacred Scriptures themselves. As Weld and his followers often searched the Bible for evidence for the sinfulness of certain courses of action so did rhetoricians in the years after Lincoln's martyrdom search the Constitution for evidence of the rightness of wrongness of a policy. To charge that a policy or action was unconstitutional, was almost equivalent to charging that it was against the Bible.

Whatever truth there is to the aphorism that after the Civil War the "religion of America was America," it owes much of its validity to the tradition of romantic pragmatism as it spread over the country after Lincoln's martyrdom.

Lincoln's vision was successful in providing a sense of meaning for the participant in terms of "what it is to be an American." Americans were the most fortunate people on earth because they had been given the opportunity to take part in the high adventure of settling the land blessed by Providence for the site of the millennium. In Lincoln's rhetoric, the millennium was no longer portrayed with the entire cast of sacred characters which comprised its religious panorama, with its biblical drama of the Second Advent of Christ, but rather it was presented as the culmination of the great experiment in self-government.

America was an attempt to achieve a land of freedom and opportunity with no ceiling on what a person of talent and drive could do, up to reaching the highest office of the land. Every child had a chance to be president. America was the site of the experiment to see if a society could be achieved which would provide each citizen with an equal opportunity to achieve success on the basis of individual merit, unencumbered by the "dead hand of the past" or by discriminating institutions and practices. Lincoln's formulation of the American dream was a vision in which progress was rapidly achieving an open society, "a land of equal opportunity," in which all repression, all tyrannizing by institutions and other human beings would be eliminated and all Americans would indeed be "created equal" and given the opportunity to go as far as they wished, given their natural talent and ability.

The tradition of romantic pragmatism in the vision of Lincoln created a powerful dream which remained attractive at least until the 1950s when Martin Luther King, Jr., in one of his most famous speeches to thousands assembled in Washington, D.C., for a demonstration for civil rights, said that he had a dream which was "deeply rooted in the American dream that one day this nation will rise up and live out the true meaning of its creed—we hold these truths to be self evident, that all men are created equal."[14]

Lincoln's vision also created a strong group self-image for its participants. America's mission was worldwide. A successful achievement of the American dream would be proof to the world that democracy worked and that kings and tyrants around the world would be deposed once the experiment proved successful. The fantasy of America as the model and leader of the world was as old as the settlement of Massachusetts Bay. Its continued saliency through the years testifies to this power as an archetypal fantasy type to sustain the community's sense of worth. The fantasy of America as a model and leader of the world gave to each national cause and crisis a universal significance far beyond its parochial application and gave to the vision essentially a forward- rather than a backward-looking bias. America's significance lay in the future, not in the past. One judged each crisis, each policy, each community action against its potential consequences on posterity and on progress towards the perfect society. The community's importance was shared by the individual. To be an American was to be special, important, and a model, as an individual and as part of a community. For participants in the vision, America's standing in world opinion was important. As late as the presidential campaign of 1960, one of the vital issues was that of America's declining prestige around the world.[15] Individual Americans, too, were impelled to be "ambassadors" and to act in a way which did no discredit to America's image when they were traveling abroad.

Despite the unifying virtues of the vision and its promotion of a good self-image for the community, it contained within it the potential for motives of jingoism and superpatriotism which surfaced, periodically, in the nineteenth century. When activated into motives, these tendencies impelled large segments of the American society to grow discontented with the passive role of model for the world and caused them to strive actively to remake the world in America's image. At the turn of the century, superpatriots like Albert Beveredge, a senator from Indiana, who was steeped in Lincolnian rhetoric and who was to write a biography of the martyred president, fantasized that the American flag should march to the islands of the Pacific, that it was the "manifest destiny" that the flag should eventually fly over an empire as great as that of Great Britain.[16] America's destiny and duty was to spread free institutions around the world. Again in the time of the First World War, the motives to go out and remake the world became salient for many adherents, and in both instances, the fervor stemming from the religious roots came to fruition in moral crusades such as the one led by President Woodrow Wilson to make the "world safe for democracy."

From the time of the Puritan sermon to the time of Lincoln, the rhetoricians of the tradition of romantic pragmatism had set impossibly high standards of conduct for the committed. They had dramatized the righteous life style and the commendable behaviors of the community in such clear terms and set such goals of perfection that it made their achievement, despite the zealous efforts of many, impossible to attain. When individuals fell short of perfection and when they looked about and discovered corroboration that the community, too, was imperfect, they tended to feel personal guilt for their own behavior and for the behavior of the community. Charged with guilt, they were susceptible to conversion to other visions. To continue to sustain a sense of community in the post-Civil War years, the rhetorical vision of Lincoln needed some mechanism, some fantasy type to release the feelings of guilt within the framework of the vision itself.

There had always been participants in other shared consciousnesses in America eager to gain new converts from among the guilt-laden and disillusioned. The Garrisonian vision had denied the basic assumptions of government as fantasized in the evangelical vision. It saw the dream as essentially hypocritical and painted a counterfantasy of what it considered to be the reality of America. Subsequent visions often took the same approach by denying that the dream of a society in which all are created equal is the compelling fantasy of Americans and by suggesting that the actual social reality is one of exploitation, discrimination, dog-eat-dog competition, and a shallow scrambling after money and material goods. Adherents of nihilism, anarchism, and Marxism in such forms as socialism and communism were actively proselytizing for converts in the post-Civil War years.

The Lincolnian vision contained a reform scenario which had proven its attractiveness and effectiveness in the three decades prior to the Civil War. It was to prove equally effective for the next century. The countervisions were largely unsuccessful in raising the consciousness of masses of Americans. The fantasy of restoration, of a return to the basis of the foundation of the government, was a powerful drama for releasing the guilt of falling short of perfection. The restoration fantasy contained a mixture of reform and conservatism. It allowed its adherents to eliminate the imperfections of the hear-and-now without having to convert to an entirely new rhetorical vision. The restoration fantasy was conservative in the most fundamental sense of keeping intact the major structural features of the vision, keeping its panoramic depiction of the American experience, its celebration of the basic values of the founders, its power to provide meaning for the American experience.

Weld and his abolition agents attracted converts with the plea to restore the government to its original foundations and return the Constitution to its original standing as an antislavery document by freeing the slaves. Lincoln eloquently called for a return to the basis of the government and a restoring of the original agreement that slavery was a wrong and should be ultimately extinguished and that denying slavery in the territories was the way to achieve the restoration.

Subsequent romantic pragmatic waves of reform in the post-Civil War years, such as the Populist movement, called for a return to the original foundations of democracy. The Populists, who spoke in the ungenteel style, saw society polluted and corrupted by the evil activities of large business "interests" whose managers and capitalistic owners conspired to exploit the great masses of the workers and farmers by manipulating credit, by monopolizing the marketplace, and by corrupting legislatures, executives, and bureaucrats with bribes and favors. The Populists argued for a reform of society by restoring representative democracy to its original basis and "busting" the trusts, regulating the railroads, assuring that corrupt officials be made more answerable to the general public.

Why was the restoration drama so successful in conserving the vision and keeping its essential features intact despite pressures of here-and-now difficulties? A rhetoric of unity and conservatism needs to celebrate the entire community and for that purpose requires a common heritage. Nations usually build a national ethos on a common history. Most Western European nations have a long recollection of folk legends and an authentic record of historical events to provide a sense of cohesion, identity, and the basis for nationhood. Some communities have built cohesion on a common religious vision which serves to identify the insiders and distinguish the boundaries of the community.

The people of the United States began with a zero-history group of settlements in colonial times, which soon evolved into the practice of religious pluralism. For a time, North Americans could participate in the Old World recollections of the past and think of themselves as, for example, Englishmen, Frenchmen, Dutchmen, or Spaniards, but after the Revolutionary War, they needed a new basis for building a separate nation. How could such a community achieve unity and cohesion? How could the rhetoricians create a sustaining saga to give the people, striving to create a common culture and institutions, the necessary sense of unity? The restoration fantasy provided a powerful and successful partial answer to the problems of a rhetoric of unity.

In sacred terms, according to the restoration theme, the primitive church, Jesus and his original disciples, set the basic values and standards for the Christian religion. Subsequent failure of the earthly church to meet these standards was interpreted not as corroboration for counterfantasies rejecting the entire vision of Christianity but as a falling-away from the authentic and true church. What such a restoration theme implied, in the religious visions which employed it, was a search for the original basis of Christianity and a return of the church to that basis. The Puritans fantasized the return as a purification. The Disciples of Christ dramatized the return as a restoration.[17] In both cases, the result was a glorification and celebration of the core of the original vision and essentially a conservation of the Christian creed and values.

In secular terms, according to the restoration theme, the original founders of the new nation, the signers of the Declaration of Independence and the framers of the Constitution, set the basic values and standards of the United States. Subsequent failure of the government and the society to meet these standards was interpreted not as corroboration for counterfantasies which saw the entire society, governmental institutions, economic arrangements, and social mores as hypocritical or bankrupt, but as a falling-away from the authentic and true basis of the new nation. What such a restoration theme implied, in the secular visions which employed it and certainly in the culmination of romantic pragmatism as Lincoln's rhetoric expressed it, was a return of the nation to its original basis. The result was a religification of the founding of the government and a glorification of its original basis. The new nation had been founded on a universal and perfect basis adequate for all the demands of the future if the posterity of the founders were but wise enough to restore the country to its original basis whenever new conditions and corruptions from evil human design and error caused problems.

In the religification of a golden age in which a group of founders who were exceptionally heroic (and perhaps inspired by God) laid down a perfect (or most perfect to date) system for religious (or for social or governmental) institutions, all who inherit the system have a common bond—a symbolic connection with the period of the founders and with the founders themselves. When a fantasy type such as the drama of the founders establishing a most perfect system becomes ritualized, the fantasy becomes the secular equivalent of a religious myth.

For many communities in the United States, the Fourth-of-July celebrations and the Fourth-of-July oration became the rituals celebrating the founding of the government. By dramatizing the Revolutionary War, the Declaration of Independence, and the Constitution, the Fourth-of-July orators provided an opportunity for the posterity of the community to share the fantasies and thus to come to participate in the unifying vision. New immigrants from other countries were faced with the choice of continuing to be foreigners, of becoming hyphenated Americans, or of raising their consciousness to become *real* Americans. By sharing the drama of the founding and converting to the salient American vision, the immigrant could cut free from the Old World visions and become an adherent of the unifying drama of the founding of the new nation.

When evil crept into the social, political, and economic life of the country and many found themselves in here-and-now conditions which they felt were unsatisfactory, an impulse toward a reform movement or revolutionary effort evolved. When many suffered economic hardship and fantasized their plight as resulting from exploitation by others, or when many felt guilt because of what they interpreted to be injustices and inequalities visited upon others, or when many felt that nature was being exploited by evil forces and people, then conditions were favorable to counterfantasies which contained motives to destroy the established arrangements of society. Historically, such moments of rhetorical tension have appeared regularly in America. I have traced the rhetorical response of one tradition to such a crisis of faith in the treatment of the slaves and the rhetorical responses of the abolitionists in the period from 1830–1860. When the moments of crises came, the restoration fantasy type allowed a rhetorical vision to evolve which was both a means of reform and a means of revitalizing faith in the basic structures of society.

The rhetoric of restoration requires a redramatization and reinterpretation of the events of the founding. Rhetoricians of restoration need to discover heroic figures from the past and to create new scenarios relating to those times. Converts to the reform movement which contains the restoration theme become more committed to the basic values implied by the unifying vision of the community. The process of conversion, as we have seen, is essentially a matter of chaining into and sharing the fantasy themes of the new vision. In that process, the old values are revitalized for the convert. The Christian who is converted to a reform based on restoration becomes a more zealous and committed Christian. The citizen of the United States who becomes a convert based on the restoration theme to the "fountain whose waters sprang close by the blood of the Revolution" becomes a more zealous and committed citizen.

Although the rhetorical vision of Abraham Lincoln as it spread through the social reality of the masses in the post-Civil War years had its faults in terms of its anti-intellectualism, its tendency to jingoism and superpatriotism, to lawlessness and violence, to exploitation of natural resources, and to zealous intolerance of the faults of others, it was, on balance, and as Lincoln developed it, a noble vision. The speaker who phrased the sentiment "with malice toward none" was not a zealot, intolerant of others; he was not willing to be his brother's keeper. Lincoln's vision was to restore the constitution to a basis on which slavery would be extinguished, but that lawfully and according to the original compact among the states. More importantly, when Lincoln developed the restoration theme, his fantasies once again celebrated values as those implied by assertions such as

> In the right to eat the bread, without leave of anybody else, which his own hand earns, *he (the negro) is my equal and the equal of Judge Douglas, and the equal of every living man.* They are the two principles that have stood face to face from the beginning of time; and will continue to struggle. the One is the common right of humanity and the other the divine right of kings. It is the same principle in whatever shape it develops itself. It is the same spirit that says, "You work and toil and earn bread, and I'll eat it." No matter what shape it comes, whether from the mouth of a king who seeks to bestride the people of his own nation and live by the fruits of their labor or from one race of men as an apology for enslaving another race, it is the same tyrannical principle.

To be sure, the values implied in the vision were so high and the code of conduct implied by it required such perfection that the practices of the community sustained by it were continually falling short of achieving them. Lincoln's vision was an impossible dream and such a vision is always dangerous, for disillusionment can destroy the community that shares it. However, the restoration theme can save the high and noble ideals and discharge the guilt of falling short of their achievement at the same time that it gives to the vision a new vitality.

The rhetorical tradition of romantic pragmatism, particularly as given wide popularity in the persona of the martyred Lincoln, has made a significant and long-lasting contribution to the flexible and adaptive (pragmatic) culture of the United States, which has accomodated rapid and massive change and yet kept the same essential political and social values and the same political framework for several hundreds of years.

Notes ✯

Bibliography ✯

Index ✯

Notes 🖎

1. *The Critical Analysis of Seminal American Fantasies*

1. Roy P. Basler, ed., *The Collected Works of Abraham Lincoln* (New Brunswick, NJ: Rutgers Univ. Pr., 1953), II, p. 276.

2. For an analysis of Reagan's use of the restoration fantasy type see Ernest G. Bormann, "A Fantasy Theme Analysis of the Television Coverage of the Reagan Inaugural and the Hostage Release," *Quarterly Journal of Speech*, 68 (1982), 133–45. See also Kurt W. Ritter, "American Political Rhetoric and the Jeremiad Tradition: Presidential Nomination Acceptance Addresses, 1960–1976," *Central States Speech Journal*, 31 (1980), 153–71.

3. More detailed consideration of the methods of rhetorical criticism can be found in Lester Thonssen, A. Craig Baird, and Waldo Braden, *Speech Criticism: The Development of Standards of Rhetorical Appraisal*, 2nd ed. (New York: Ronald, 1970); Edwin Black, *Rhetorical Criticism: A Study in Method* (Madison: Univ. of Wisconsin Pr., 1978); Bernard L. Brock and Robert L. Scott, *Methods of Rhetorical Criticism: A Twentieth Century Perspective*, 2nd ed. (Detroit: Wayne State Univ. Pr., 1980); Robert Cathcart, *Post Communication: Rhetorical Analysis and Evaluation*, 2nd ed. (Indianapolis: Bobbs-Merrill, 1981); Karlyn Kohrs Campbell and Kathleen Hall Jamieson, eds., *Form and Genre: Shaping Rhetorical Action* (Falls Church, VA: The Speech Communication Association, 1978).

4. For a full development of the method of fantasy theme analysis in rhetorical criticism see Ernest G. Bormann, "Fantasy and Rhetorical Vision: The Rhetorical Criticism of Social Reality," *Quarterly Journal of Speech*, 58 (1972), 396–407; Ernest G. Bormann, "Fantasy and Rhetorical Vision: Ten Years Later," *Quarterly Journal of Speech*, 68 (1982), 288–305; Ernest G. Bormann, "Rhetoric as a Way of Knowing: Ernest Bormann and Fantasy Theme Analysis," *The Rhetoric of Western Thought*, ed. James L. Golden, Goodwin Bergquist, and William E. Coleman, 3rd ed. (Dubuque, IA: Kendall/Hunt, 1983), pp. 431–49.

5. For a full discussion of general and special communication theories see Ernest G. Bormann, *Communication Theory* (New York: Holt, Rinehart, and Winston, 1980).

6. See particularly Robert F. Bales, *Personality and Interpersonal Behavior* (New York: Holt, Rinehart, and Winston, 1970); Ernest G. Bormann, *Discussion and Group Methods: Theory and Practice*, 2nd ed. (New York: Harper and Row, 1975); Graham S. Gibbard, John J. Hartman, and Richard D. Mann, eds., *Analysis of Groups* (San Francisco: Jossey-Bass, 1974).

7. *The Anti-Slavery Examiner*, No. 6, *The Bible Against Slavery: An Inquiry into the Patriarchial and Mosaic Systems on the Subject of Human Rights*, 3rd ed. (New York: The American Anti-Slavery Society, 1838), p. 2.

8. The line is from Frost's poem "A Masque of Reason." A number of scholars have emphasized the importance of drama in creating a social reality for communities. See, for example, Murray Edelman, *The Symbolic Uses of Politics* (Urbana Univ. of Illinois Pr., 1964); Les Cleveland, "Symbols and Politics: Mass Communication and Public Drama," *Politics: Australasian Political Studies Association Journal*, 4 (1969), 186–96; Dan Nimmo and James E. Combs. *Mediated Political Realities* (New York: Longman, 1983); Hugh Dalziel Duncan, "The Search for a Social Theory of Communication in American Sociology," *Human Communication Theory: Original Essays*, ed. Frank E. X. Dance (New York: Holt, Rinehart, and Winston, 1967), pp. 236–63; Howard Kamler, *Communication: Sharing Our Stories of Experience* (Seattle: Psychological Pr., 1983). For a representative collection of such writings see James E. Combs and Michael W. Mansfield, eds., *Drama in Life: The Uses of Communication in Society* (New York: Hastings House, 1976).

9. By *persona* I mean a character in a dramatic work; the public personality or mask portrayed in the shared fantasies of a rhetorical community. The characters in a fantasy theme are thus personae. The commonly used term *image* sometimes refers to persona as I use the term but it is also used in a more general way to refer to such things as the image of an institution or corporation. In addition, the term *image* tends to connote a static picture of an individual. *Persona*, on the other hand, implies a dynamic process of character acting in a given setting and interacting with others who participate in the unfolding action. *Persona* connotes a character in process that evolves because the scenarios in which the persona is portrayed change as they are shared through time.

10. For Garrison's typical fantasy themes about the Fourth of July see his address of July 4, 1838, in Ernest G. Bormann, ed., *Forerunners of Black Power: The Rhetoric of Abolition* (Englewood Cliffs, NJ: Prentice-Hall, 1971), pp. 96–103.

11. For a more detailed analysis of consciousness-raising and sustaining small-group communication see Ernest G. Bormann, "The Symbolic Convergence Theory of Communication and the Creation, Raising, and Sustaining of Public Consciousnesses," *The Jensen Lectures: Contemporary Communication Studies*, ed. John I. Sisco (Tampa : Department of Communication, Univ. of South Florida, 1983), pp. 71–90.

12. For a summary of the special small-group communication theory related to the Oneida Community see *Mutual Criticism* (Syracuse Univ. Pr., 1975).

13. The sermon has been widely reprinted. It can be found in Wayland Maxfield Parrish and Marie Hochmuth, eds., *American Speeches* (New York: Longmann, Green, 1954), pp. 230–63.

14. Charles Grandison Finney, *Lectures on Revivals of Religion*, ed. William G. McLoughlin (Cambridge, MA: Belknap Pr. of Harvard Univ. Pr., 1960). p. 183.

2. *The Puritan Rhetorical Style*

1. Perry Miller, *The New England Mind: From Colony to Province* (Boston: Beacon, 1961), p. 29.

2. The general description of the Puritan attitude toward preaching and the quoted characterizations are from Horton Davies, *The Worship of the English Puritans* (Westminster, London: Dacre Pr., 1948), pp. 183–85.

3. See, for example, Robert Hanson, "Form and Content of the Puritan Funeral Elegy," *American Literature*, 32 (1960), 11–27; Harry P. Kerr, "The Election Sermon: Primer for Revolutionaries," *Speech Monographs*, 29 (1962), 13–22; Harry P. Kerr, "Politics and Religion in Colonial Fast and Thanksgiving Sermons, 1763–1783," *Quarterly Journal of Speech*, 46 (Dec. 1960), 372–82; Wayne C. Minnick, "The New England Execution Sermon, 1639–1800,"

Speech Monographs, 35 (1968), 77–89; Harold D. Mixon, "Boston's Artillery Election Sermons and the American Revolution," *Speech Monographs*, 34 (1967), 43–50.

4. Kenneth B. Murdock, *Increase Mather: The Foremost American Puritan* (Cambridge, MA: Harvard Univ. Pr., 1925), pp 91–92.

5. Cotton Mather, *Manuductio ad Ministerium: Directions for a Candidate of the Ministry* (New York: Facsimile Text Society, Columbia Univ. Pr., 1938), p. 90.

6. Ibid., p. 106.

7. Thomas Shepard, "Autobiography," *The Puritans*, ed. Perry Miller and Thomas H. Johnson (New York: Harper Torchbooks, 1963), II, pp. 471–72.

8. Samuel Eliot Morison, *The Founding of Harvard College* (Cambridge, MA: Harvard Univ. Pr., 1935), p. 174.

9. Babette May Levy, *Preaching in the First Half Century of New England History* (Hartford, CT: American Society of Church History, 1945), pp. 10–11.

10. See Caroline Francis Richardson, *English Preachers and Preaching 1640–1670* (New York: Macmillan, 1928), Chapter 1, "The Training of a Pulpit Speaker." See also, Karl R. Wallace, ed., *History of Speech Education in America* (New York: Appleton-Century-Crofts, 1954), in particular: George V. Bohman, "Rhetorical Practice in Colonial America," pp. 60–79; Warren Guthrie, "Rhetorical Theory in Colonial America," pp. 48–59; Wilbur Samuel Howell, "English Backgrounds of Rhetoric," pp. 3–47. Also, Ota Thomas, "The Teaching of Rhetoric in the United States During the Classical Period of Education," *A History and Criticism of American Public Address*, ed. William Norwood Brigance (New York: Russell and Russell, 1943), I, pp. 193–210; Samuel Eliot Morison, *The Founding of Harvard College* (Cambridge, MA: Harvard Univ. Pr., 1935), Chapter 4, "Cambridge: The Arts Course, 1600–1640."

11. Morison, p. 71.

12. See Wilbur Samuel Howell, "Ramus and English Rhetoric: 1574–1681," *Quarterly Journal of Speech*, 27 (1951), 299–310. See also, Wilbur Samuel Howell, *Logic and Rhetoric in England, 1500–1700* (New York: Russell and Russell, 1961).

13. Perry Miller, *The New England Mind: The Seventeenth Century* (Boston: Beacon, 1961). Chapter 11, "Rhetoric," contains an extensive and detailed analysis of the influence of Ramist thought on Puritan rhetorical theory.

14. Morison, pp. 99–100.

15. Mather, pp. 35–36.

16. Miller and Johnson, I, p. 314.

17. Since Cotton Mather's *Manuductio ad Ministerium* is, perhaps, the most complete treatment of the New England Puritan's rhetorical theory I chose it as illustrative. See, for example, Eugene E. White, "Cotton Mather's *Manuductio ad Ministerium*," *Quarterly Journal of Speech*, 49 (1963), 308–19.

18. Mather, p. 102.

19. Ibid., p. 91.

20. Ibid., p. 34.

21. See Howell, "English Backgrounds of Rhetoric," *History of Speech Education in America*, ed. Karl R. Wallace.

22. Miller and Johnson, I, p.29.

23. Mather, pp. 27–32.

24. Miller and Johnson, I, p. 73.

25. Mather, p. 34.

26. Kenneth B. Murdock, *Increase Mather: The Foremost American Puritan* (Cambridge, MA: Harvard Univ. Pr., 1925), pp. 91–92.

27. Mather, p. 106.

28. Ibid., p. 114.

29. Miller and Johnson, I, p. 298.

30. See Eugene E. White, "Puritan Preaching and the Authority of God," *Preaching in*

American History, ed. DeWitte Holland (Nashville: Abingdon Pr., 1969), pp. 36–73; Irvonwy Morgan, *The Godly Preachers of the Elizabethan Church* (London: The Epworth Pr., 1965).

31. White, "Puritan Preaching and the Authority of God," p. 64. White presents an excellent analysis of the rhetoric of the covenants and how it worked. He deals with John Cotton in detail and my summary of Cotton's fantasy of the covenant draws on White's essay (pp. 64–65) with special reference to *A Sermon Preached by the Reverend John Cotton, Teacher of the First Church of Boston in New-England, Delivered at Salem 1636. To Which is Prefixed, a Retraction of his former Opinion concerning Baptism, utter'd by him immediately Preceeding the Sermon here Emitted.*

32. Increase Mather, "Man Knows Not His Time," Miller and Johnson, I, p. 347.

33. Ibid., pp. 347–48.

34. The phrase itself comes from Cotton Mather's treatise on stammering where he tells the stammerer that "'Tis a very grievous *Humiliation*, under which the glorious GOD has laid you in this infirmity." The stutter himself cannot ". . . but fetch many a *Sigh*, when he feels *GOD* continually binding of him." The thing for the stutterer to do, according to Cotton Mather, is to ". . . *fetch Good out of Evil*: and a *prudent Conduct* under it, should be mightily laboured for." Quoted in Ernest G. Bormann, "Ephphatha, or, Some Advice to Stammerers," *Journal of Speech and Hearing Research*, 12 (1969), p. 457.

35. John Cotton, "God's Promise to His Plantations," in *Old South Leaflets*, III, no. 53. For a more extensive analysis of this fantasy type see Ronald F. Reid, "Apocalypticism and Typology: Rhetorical Dimensions of Symbolic Reality," *Quarterly Journal of Speech*, 69 (1983), 229–48; see also Sacvan Bercovitch, *The American Jeremiad* (Madison: Univ. of Wisconsin Pr., 1978).

36. Wayland Maxfield Parrish and Marie Hochmuth, eds., *American Speeches* (New York: Longmans, Green, 1954), p. 88.

37. Miller and Johnson, I, p. 335.

38. Ibid., p. 337.

39. John H. Clifford and Marion M. Miller, eds., *The Works of Abraham Lincoln* (New York: Newton & Cartwright, 1907), III, Part 2, p. 81.

40. Miller and Johnson, II, p. 391.

41. Ibid., I, p. 283.

42. Ibid., p. 59.

3. *Jonathan Edwards and a Rhetoric in Transition*

1. Babette May Levy, *Preaching in the First Half Century of New England History* (Hartford, CT: American Society of Church History, 1945), p. 155.

2. Robert T. Oliver, *History of Public Speaking in America* (Boston: Allyn and Bacon, 1965), p. 29. See also, Perry Miller, "Solomon Stoddard, 1643–1729," *Harvard Theological Review*, 34 (Oct. 1941), 277–320; and Eugene E. White, "Solomon Stoddard's Theories of Persuasion," *Speech Monographs*, 29 (1962), 235–59.

3. Oliver, p. 31.

4. Ibid., p. 30

5. Samuel Eliot Morison, *Harvard College in the Seventeenth Century* (Cambridge, MA: Harvard Univ. Pr., 1936), p. 547.

6. Joseph Tracy, *The Great Awakening: A History of the Revival of Religion in the Time of Edwards and Whitefield* (Boston: Tappan and Dennet, 1842), pp. 3–4.

7. For a discussion of the half-way covenant see Perry Miller, *The New England Mind: From Colony to Province* (Boston: Beacon, 1953), pp. 93–104.

8. Levy, p. 56.

9. Perry Miller, *Jonathan Edwards* (New York: William Sloan Associates, 1949).

10. The Enfield sermon has been reprinted often. The quotations I use are from the text as found in Wayland Maxfield Parrish and Marie Hochmuth, eds., *American Speeches* (New York: Longmans, Green, 1954), pp. 73–90.

11. Tracy, p. 216.

12. Lionel Crocker, "Henry Ward Beecher," *A History and Criticism of American Public Address*, ed. William Norwood Brigance (New York: McGray-Hill, 1943), I, pp. 268–69.

13. G.R. Owst, *Preaching in Medieval England: An Introduction to Sermon manuscripts of the Period c. 1350–1450* (Cambridge: Univ. Pr., 1926), p. 341.

14. George Whitefield, *George Whitefield's Journals* (London: The Banner of Truth Trust, 1960), p. 54. This collection of Whitefield's journals also includes his brief autobiographical sketch entitled *A Short Account of God's Dealings with the Reverend Mr. George Whitefield, A.B. Late of Pembroke College, Oxford from His Infancy, to the Time of His entering into Holy Orders.*

15. Leonard W. Labaree and Whitefield J. Bell, Jr., eds., *The Papers of Benjamin Franklin* (New Haven: Yale Univ. Pr., 1960), II, p. 241.

16. For a detailed accounting of Whitefield's tour of New England, see Eugene E. White, "The Protasis of the Great Awakening in New England," *Speech Monographs*, 21 (1954), 10-20. See also, C. Harold King, "George Whitefield: Dramatic Evangelist," *Quarterly Journal of Speech*, 19 (1933), 165–75; C. Harold King, "George Whitefield: Commoner Evangelist," *Historical Studies of Rhetoric and Rhetoricians*, ed. Raymond F. Howes (Ithaca, NY: Cornell Univ. Pr., 1961), pp. 253–70; Eugene E. White, "The Great Awakener: George Whitefield," *Southern Speech Journal*, 11 (1945), 6–15; Eugene E. White, "George Whitefield's Preaching in Massachusetts and Georgia: A Case Study in Persuasion," *Southern Speech Journal*, 15 (1950), 249-62; Eugene E. White, "The Preaching of George Whitefield during the Great Awakening in America," *Speech Monographs*, 15 (Research Annual, 1948), 33–43.

17. Labaree and Bell, p. 270.

18. Ibid., p. 244.

19. Ibid., p. 290.

20. A complete copy of Nathan Cole's account in which the grammar, punctuation, and spelling have been edited and modernized is to be found in Whitefield, pp. 561–62. An excerpt without editorial corrections is quoted in Edwin Scott Gaustad, *The Great Awakening in New England* (New York: Harper, 1957), p. 54. I have used both versions in my reconstruction.

21. King, "George Whitefield: Commoner Evangelist," p. 263. King discusses Whitefield's delivery in some detail and has collected a number of eye witness accounts.

22. Leonard W. Labaree, et al., eds., *The Autobiography of Benjamin Franklin* (New Haven, CT: Yale Univ. Pr. 1964), p. 178.

23. Ibid., p. 179.

24. Ibid., p. 180.

25. King, "George Whitefield: Commoner Evangelist," p. 262. See also his "George Whitefield: Dramatic Evangelist"; see also his "George Whitefield: God's Commoner," *Quarterly Journal of Speech*, 29 (1943), 32–36.

26. King, "George Whitefield: Dramatic Evangelist," p. 172.

27. Ibid., p. 169.

28. George Whitefield, "The Kingdom of God," in S. E. Frost, Jr., ed., *The World's Great Sermons* (Garden City, NY: Halcyon House, 1943), p. 121.

29. Whitefield, *Journals*, p. 484.

30. Tracy, p. 239.

31. Ibid., p. 240.

32. Ibid., p. 242.

33. Ibid., p. 248.

34. Ibid., p. 251.

4. *The Evangelical Style*

1. See, for example, Edwin Scott Gaustad, *The Great Awakening in New England* (New York: Harper, 1957); Wesley M. Gewehr, *The Great Awakening in Virginia, 1740–1790* (Durham, NC: Duke Univ. Pr., 1930); C. C. Goen, *Revivalism and Separatism in New England, 1740–1800* (New Haven, CT: Yale Univ. Pr., 1962); Charles H. Maxson, *The Great Awakening in the Middle Colonies* (Chicago: The Univ. of Chicago Pr., 1920).

2. George Whitefield, *George Whitefield's Journals* (London: The Banner of Truth Trust, 1960), p. 477.

3. Thomas Prince, ed., *The Christian History Containing Accounts of the Revival and Propagation of Religion in Great Britain, America, Etc., For the Year 1744* (Boston: S. Kneeland and T. Green, 1745), p. 136.

4. Joseph Tracy, *The Great Awakening: A History of the Revival of Religion in the Time of Edwards and Whitefield* (Boston: Tappan and Dennet, 1842), pp. x–xiii.

5. Leonard W. Labaree and Whitefield J. Bell, Jr., eds. *The Papers of Benjamin Franklin* (New Haven: Yale Univ. Pr., 1960), II, pp. 287–88.

6. Ibid., p. 288.

7. Robert T. Oliver, *History of Public Speaking in America* (Boston: Allyn and Bacon, 1965), p. 39.

8. Orville A. Hitchcock, "Jonathan Edwards," *A History and Criticism of American Public Address*, ed. William Norwood Brigance (New York: McGraw-Hill, 1943), I, pp. 232–33.

9. Goen, p. 30.

10. Jonathan Edwards, *The Works of President Edwards* (New York: Leavitt, Trow, 1808), III, pp. 580–92.

11. Goen, p. 176.

12. Tracy, p. 115.

13. Leonard Labaree, et. al., eds., *The Autobiography of Benjamin Franklin* (New Haven, CT: Yale Univ. Pr. 1964), p. 175.

14. Jonathan Edwards, "Sinners in the Hands of an Angry God," *American Speeches*, ed. Wayland Maxfield Parrish and Marie Hochmuth (New York: Longmans, Green, 1954), p. 82.

15. Tracy, p. 253.

16. Ibid.

17. Goen, p. 179.

18. Tracy, p. ix.

19. Ibid., pp. 413–14.

20. Whitefield, p. 575.

21. Ibid., pp. 575–76.

22. Tracy, p. 138.

23. Parrish and Hochmuth, eds., *American Speeches*, p. 88.

24. William G. McLoughlin, ed., *Lectures on Revivals of Religion by Charles Grandison Finney* (Cambridge, MA: Belknap Pr. of Harvard Univ. Pr., 1960), p. x.

25. William G. McLoughlin, *Modern Revivalism: Charles Grandison Finney to Billy Graham* (New York: Ronald Pr., 1959), p. 11.

26. Edwards, p. 334.

27. Ibid., pp. 334–35.

28. Ibid., p. 335.

29. Ibid., p. 336.

5. *The Ungenteel Style*

1. William Warren Sweet, *Religion in the Development of American Culture 1765–1840* (New York: Scribner's, 1952), p. 53.

2. Wesley M. Gewehr, *The Great Awakening in Virginia, 1740–1790* (Durham, NC: Duke Univ. Pr. 1930), pp. 60–61.

3. Samuel Davies, *Sermons on Important Subjects*, 3rd American ed. (Boston: Lincoln and Edmands, 1811), I, p. 39.

4. A thorough rhetorical analysis of Davies' preaching is to be found in Barbara Ann Larson, "A Rhetorical Study of the Preaching of the Reverend Samuel Davies in the Colony of Virginia from 1747–1759," Diss. Univ. of Minnesota, 1969. See also Barbara Ann Larson, "Samuel Davies and the Rhetoric of the New Light," *Speech Monographs*, 38 (1971), 207–16; Barbara Ann Larson, *Prologue to Revolution: The War Sermons of the Reverend Samuel Davies* (Fall Church, VA: Speech Communication Association, 1976).

5. Gewehr, p. 110.

6. Winthrop S. Hudson, *Religion in America* (New York: Scribner's, 1965), p. 115.

7. Ibid., p. 134.

8. Walter Brownlow Posey, *The Baptist Church in the Lower Mississippi Valley, 1776–1845* (Lexington, KY: Univ. of Kentucky Pr., 1957), pp. 21–22.

9. *The Recollections of a Long Life* (Richmond, VA: Religious Herald Co., 1891), pp. 19–20.

10. Ibid., p. 20.

11. Ibid., p. 23.

12. Peter Cartwright, *The Autobiography of Peter Cartwright*, ed. Charles L. Wallis (Nashville: Abingdon Pr., 1956), p. 38.

13. Ibid., p. 32.

14. Ibid., pp. 207–9.

15. Ibid., pp. 75–76.

16. William Henry Milburn, *Ten Years of Preacher-Life: Chapters from an Autobiography* (New York: Derby and Jackson, 1859), pp. 111–14.

17. James B. Finley, *Sketches of Western Methodism; Biographical, Historical, and Miscellaneous. Illustrative of Pioneer Life*. ed. W.P. Strickland (Cincinnati: Methodist Book Concern, 1854), pp. 540–51.

18. Milburn, p. 218.

19. Lucius Daniel Davis, *Life in the Itinerancy, in its Relations to the Circuit and Station, and to the Minister's Home and Family* (New York: Miller, Orton and Mulligan, 1856), pp. v–vi.

20. Ibid., pp. 128–29.

21. Caroline F. Richardson, *English Preachers and Preaching 1640–1670* (New York: Macmillan, 1928), pp. 80–81.

22. Edward Eggleston, *The Circuit Rider: A Tale of the Heroic Age* (New York: Scribners, 1924), pp. 126–27.

23. Ibid., pp. 262–63.

24. Finley, pp. 243–45.

25. William Henry Milburn, *The Pioneers, Preachers, and People of the Mississippi Valley* (New York: Derby and Jackson, 1860), p. 371.

26. Abel Stevens, *Essays on the Preaching Required by the Times* (New York: Carlton and Phillips, 1855), pp. 128–29.

27. Paul H. Boase, "The Methodist Circuit-Rider on the Ohio Frontier," Diss. Univ. of Wisconsin, 1952, p. 140.

28. Ibid.

29. Howard C. Dunham, "Methodists of the Olden Times," manuscript memoir in the New England Methodist Historical Society Archives.

6. *Nature and the New Birth*

1. William Henry Milburn, *Ten Years of Preacher-Life: Chapters from an Autobiography* (New York: Derby & Jackson, 1859), p. 102.

2. Ibid., p. 284.

3. The controversy within the Methodist denomination in the first half of the nineteenth century over the proper style of preaching reveals the tendency of the writers of books and articles to praise the effectiveness of the circuit riders while urging less shouting, bombast and crudity. The controversy is documented in detail by Paul H. Boase, "The Methodist Circuit-Rider on the Ohio Frontier," Diss. Univ. of Wisconsin, 1952.

4. Milburn's sketch of Cartwright is in Milburn, pp. 38–46.

5. Milburn's sketch of Prentiss is in Milburn, pp. 238–66.

6. William Henry Milburn, *The Pioneers, Preachers, and People of the Mississippi Valley* (New York: Derby & Jackson, 1860), p. 416.

7. Ibid., pp. 414–15.

8. Peter Cartwright, *The Autobiography of Peter Cartwright*, ed. Charles L. Wallis (Nashville: Abingdon Pr., 1956), p. 64.

9. Ibid., p. 64.

10. Milburn, *Pioneers*, p. 401.

11. Ibid., pp. 413–14.

12. Milburn, *Ten Years*, p. 43.

13. Milburn, *Pioneers*, pp. 405–6.

14. Ibid., pp. 410–11.

15. Ibid., pp. 412–13.

16. James B. Finley, *Sketches of Western Methodism, Biographical, Historical, and Miscellaneous. Illustrative of Pioneer Life*. ed. W.P. Strickland (Cincinnati: Methodist Book Concern, 1854), pp. 432–33.

17. Ibid., pp. 430–32.

18. Ibid., p. 325.

19. W. P. Strickland, ed., *The Backwoods Preacher: An Autobiography of Peter Cartwright* (London: Alexander Heylin, 1858), p. vii.

20. Milburn, *Pioneers*, p. 358.

21. Cartwright, p. 236.

22. Ibid., p. 204.

23. Anonymous (Cincinnati: H.M. Rulison, 1856), p. 13.

24. Ibid., pp. 16–17.

25. Frederick Jackson Turner, *The Frontier in American History*, rev. ed. (New York: Holt, 1920).

26. "Address At the Dedication of the Cemetery at Gettysburg," *American Speeches*, ed. Wayland Maxfield Parrish and Marie Hochmuth (New York: Longmans, Green, 1954), p. 307.

27. See, for example, James W. Chesebro, John F. Cragan, and Patricia W. McCullough, "The Small Group Technique of the Radical Revolutionary: A Synthetic Study of Consciousness Raising," *Speech Monographs*, 40 (1973), 136–46. For a study of feminist consciousness raising, see Ernest G. Bormann, "The Symbolic Convergence Theory of communication and the Creation, Raising, and Sustaining of Public Consciousnesses," *The Jensen Lectures: Contemporary Communication Studies*, ed. John I. Sisco (Tampa: Department of Communications, Univ. of South Florida, 1983).

28. See, for example, Harriet Martineau, *Society in America*, 4th ed. (New York: Saunders and Otley, 1837), II, pp. 314–66; Frances Trollope, *Domestic Manners of the Americans*, ed. Donald Smalley (New York: Knopf, 1949), Chap. 8, "Absence of Public and Private Amusement—Churches and Chapels—Influence of the Clergy—A Revival," and Chap. 15, "Camp-Meeting." Of a camp meeting Trollope wrote: "But how am I to describe the sounds that proceeded from this strange mass of human beings? I know no words which can convey an idea of it. Hysterical sobbings, convulsive groans, shrieks and screams the most appalling, burst forth on all sides. I felt sick with horror" (p. 172); Capt. C. B. Marryat, *A Diary in America With Remarks on its Institutions* (London: Longman, Orme, Brown, Green, & Longmans, 1839), II,

pp. 180–89. Of a camp meeting Marryat wrote: "I quitted the spot, and hastened away into the forest, for the sight was too painful, too melancholy" (p. 187).

29. For studies of the effect of severity of admission to a group on cohesiveness, see Elliot Aronson and Judson Mills, "The Effect of Severity of Initiation on Liking for a Group," *Journal of Abnormal and Social Psychology*, 59 (1959), 177–81, and Harold B. Gerard and Grover C. Mathewson, "The Effects of Severity of Initiation on Liking for a Group: A Replication," *Journal of Experimental Social Psychology*, 2 (1966), 278–87. For studies of the effect of competition on cohesiveness see A. Paul Hare, *Handbook of Small Group Research* (New York: Free Press, 1962), pp. 254–63; also Robert E. Dunn and Morton Goldman, "Competition and Noncompetition in Relationship to Satisfaction and Feelings Toward Owngroup and Nongroup Members," *Journal of Social Psychology*, 68 (1966), 299–311.

30. See Boase Diss.

7. The Style of Evangelical Reform

1. Charles Grandison Finney, *Lectures on Revivals of Religion*, ed. William G. McLoughlin (Cambridge, MA: Belknap Pr. of Harvard Univ. Pr., 1960), p. x.

2. Whitney R. Cross, *The Burned-over District: The Social and Intellectual History of Enthusiastic Religion in Western New York: 1800–1850* (New York: Harper Torchbook, 1965), p. 3.

3. James Donnell Brown, "Rhetorical Fantasy in the Webster-Calhoun Debate on the Revenue Collection Bill of 1833," Diss., Univ. of Minnesota, 1977.

4. Gilbert H. Barnes and Dwight L. Dumond, eds., *Letters of Theodore Dwight Weld, Angelina Grimké Weld, and Sarah Grimké, 1822–1844*, 2 vols. (New York: Appleton-Century, 1934), p. 595. The letters will be used extensively in this chapter. They were published in two volumes, but the pages were numbered consecutively. Subsequent references to the letters will note the page number in parentheses in the text following the quotation. In the last part of the chapter, I use the same notation for extensive quotations from Finney, *Lectures on Revivals of Religion*. Whenever the context does not make clear which source is appropriate, I will use footnotes.

5. Benjamin P. Thomas, *Theodore Weld: Crusader for Freedom* (New Brunswick, NJ: Rutgers Univ. Pr., 1950), p. 49.

6. See Paul A. Carmack, "The Lane Seminary Debates," *Central States Speech Journal*, 1 (March 1950), 33–39; Lawrence Thomas Lesick, *The Lane Rebels: Evangelicalism and Antislavery in Antebellum America* (Metuchen, NJ: Scarecrow Pr., 1980).

7. The Tappans fulfilled their commitments to Lane but gave it no further financial support. Instead, they turned their attention to a small school in Oberlin, Ohio, and with Asa Mahan as president and assurances of student freedom for discussion and the admission of qualified Negroes, the Tappans agreed to support Oberlin College. When Charles Finney agreed to come as professor of theology, Weld urged his followers at Cumminsville to enroll at Oberlin and about twenty of the Lane rebels moved to Oberlin in 1935. See Robert S. Fletcher, *A History of Oberlin College*, 2 vols. (Oberlin, OH: Oberlin College, 1943).

8. Theodore Weld to Anne Weston, 23 March 1836. Antislavery collection, Manuscript Division, Boston Public Library.

9. Thomas, pp. 34–35.

10. *The Anti-Slavery Examiner*, No. 6, *The Bible Against Slavery: An Inquiry Into the Patriarchial and Mosaic Systems on the Subject of Human Rights*, 3rd ed. (New York: The American Anti-Slavery Society, 1838), p. 2.

11. In the following analysis I shall use the edition of Finney's *Lectures* edited by William G. McLoughlin. Subsequent references to Finney's lectures will appear in parentheses within the text. Finney's lectures had first appeared in th *New York Evangelist*, subsequently collected into the first edition of *Lectures on Revivals of Religion*, published in 1835. McLoughlin maintains that

when Finney issued a new revised edition in 1868, he made few changes except to rewrite the last two lectures and change "ain't" to "is not" and "can't" to "cannot." McLoughlin concluded that he had "seen no reason to use the later edition (nor any of the English editions). The first edition was the most popular and the most widely read." (p. lviii). McLoughlin described the origin of the lectures as follows:

> Finney did not write out these lectures any more than he ever wrote out his sermons. He merely prepared a brief skeleton or outline and preached extemporaneously from that. Leavitt [editor of the *New York Evangelist* who had asked Finney to prepare the lectures to save the paper from bankruptcy] did not know shorthand, but he had a good ear, a quick pencil, and a retentive memory. He attended every lecture, taking the words down in abbreviated form, and the next morning he would sit down and rewrite the lecture from his notes and rush it off to the printer. Finney did not see the lectures in this form until they appeared in the newspapaer on the following Saturday. However, he always maintained that Leavitt had caught both the spirit and the content of them very well. The only criticism Finney offered was that the lectures averaged "not less than an hour and three quarters in their delivery. But all that he . . . could catch and report could be read probably in thirty minutes" (p. lvii).

If one were interested in using the lectures for a study in rhetorical criticism that required authentic texts, they would need to be carefully evaluated to determine their debt to Leavitt. Since my concern is primarily to reconstruct the rhetorical theory embedded in the lectures and since Finney felt Leavitt caught the spirit and content of the remarks, they serve my purpose quite well.

12. Barnes and Dumond, eds., p. 67.
13. Ibid., p. 319.
14. Thomas, p. 30.
15. Barnes and Dumond, eds., p. vii.

8. The Styles of Antislavery Rhetoric

1. Archibald H. Grimké, *William Lloyd Garrison, The Abolitionist* (New York: Funk and Wagnalls, 1891), pp. 63–64.

2. Ibid., pp. 310–11.

3. Ibid., p. 354.

4. Gilbert Barnes, *The Antislavery Impulse, 1830–1844* (New York: Appleton-Century, 1933), p. 98.

5. Gilbert H. Barnes and Dwight L. Dumond, eds., *Letters of Theodore Dwight Weld, Angelina Grimké Weld and Sarah Grimké, 1822–1844*, 2 vols. (New York: Appleton-Century, 1943), p. viii. The letters of the Welds and Sarah Grimké were published in two volumes, but the pages were numbered consecutively. Subsequent references will be to *Weld-Grimké Letters* and the page numbers.

6. *Liberator*, March 18, 1837, p. 46.

7. Ibid., p. 46.

8. The book ran through many editions. A well-edited version is Kenneth S. Lynn, ed., *Uncle Tom's Cabin or, Life Among the Lowly by Harriet Beecher Stowe* (Cambridge, MA: Harvard Univ. Pr., 1962).

9. "The Brotherhood of Thieves: A True Picture of the American Church and Clergy," *Forerunners of Black Power: The Rhetoric of Abolition*, ed. Ernest G. Bormann (Englewood Cliffs, NJ: Prentice-Hall, 1971), p. 109.

10. From Tract No. 1, New England Anti-Slavery Tract Association (Boston: J.W. Alden Publishing Agent, n.d.). Reprinted in Bormann, pp. 91–92.

11. Barnes, p. 139.

12. (New York: Arno Press, 1968).

13. Gilbert H. Barnes, "The Western Revival Origins," *The Abolitionists: Reformers or Fanatics?*, ed. Richard O. Curry (New York: Holt, Rinehart, 1965), p. 18.

14. Margaret Mitchell, *Gone with the Wind* (New York: Macmillan, 1936).

15. *The Anti-Slavery Examiner*, No. 6, *The Bible Against Slavery: An Inquiry Into the Patriarchal and Mosaic Systems on the Subject of Human Rights*, 3rd ed. (New York: The American Anti-Slavery Society, 1838).

16. *Weld-Grimké Letters*, p. 126.

17. Phillip S. Foner, *The Life and Writings of Frederick Douglass* (New York: International Publishers, 1950), I, p. 40.

18. *Weld-Grimké Letters*, p. 319.

19. *Things for Northern Men to Do: A Discourse Delivered Lord's Day Evening, July 17, 1836, in the Presbyterian Church, Whitesboro, New York* (New York: n.p., 1836). Reprinted in Bormann, p. 81.

20. *Liberator*, March 18, 1837, p. 46.

21. Ibid.

22. *Weld-Grimké Letters*, pp. 67–68.

23. Benjamin P. Thomas, *Theodore Weld: Crusader for Freedom* (New Brunswick, NJ: Rutgers Univ. Pr., 1950), p. 111.

24. Grimké, p. 59.

25. *Weld-Grimké Letters*, p. 310.

26. Grimké, pp. 82–83.

27. *Weld-Grimké Letters*, p. 96.

28. *Weld-Grimké Letters*, p. 99.

29. Martin Luther King, Jr., "I Have a Dream," *Contemporary American Speeches*, ed. Wil A. Linkuel, R. R. Allen, and Richard L. Johannesen, 2nd ed. (Belmont, CA: Wadsworth, 1969), p. 270.

30. Barnes, *The Antislavery Impulse*, p. 103.

31. James A. Thome and J. Horace Kimball, *The Anti-Slavery Examiner*, No. 7, *Emancipation in the West Indies: A Six Months Tour in Antigua, Barbadoes and Jamaica in the Year 1837* (New York: The American Anti-Slavery Society, 1838).

32. *Weld-Grimké Letters*, pp. 425–27.

33. See, for example, Wendell Phillips, "Philosophy of the Abolition Movement," in his *Speeches, Lectures, and Letters* (Boston: Lee and Shepard, 1870), pp. 98–153.

34. Thomas S. Kuhn, *The Structure of Scientific Revolutions*, 2nd ed. (Chicago: Univ. of Chicago Pr., 1970), p. 150.

35. Carl Wayne Hensley, "The Disciples of Christ: A Rhetoric of American Millennialism," Diss. Univ. of Minnesota, 1972.

36. See, for example, Marvin Meyers, *The Jacksonian Persuasion: Politics and Belief* (Stanford, CA: Stanford Univ. Pr., 1957), Chapter 2, "The Restoration Theme."

37. Bormann, pp. 96–97. [The address was originally published in the *Liberator* of July 13, 1838.]

9. *The Rhetorical Vision of Abraham Lincoln*

1. For my analysis of the structure of the persuasive campaign for abolition, I am indebted to Gilbert Barnes' classic study, *The Antislavery Impulse, 1830–1844* (New York: Appleton-Century, 1933). Barnes makes a convincing case for the move from speeches to tracts to

house-to-house canvasses for petition signatures to the Congress, and then to political parties in the campaign for abolition.

2. The campaign of 1844, including these songs, is covered in Betty Fladeland, *James Gillespie Birney: Slaveholder to Abolitionist* (Ithaca, NY: Cornell Univ. Pr., 1955), pp. 227–51.

3. Some clue to the rhetorical style in which Edward Everett participated is given by a letter he wrote to Epes Sargent from Cambridge, Massachusetts, on March 28, 1851. Sargent had asked Everett's advice on what to include in a collection of eloquence he was preparing. Everett furnished Sargent with one of his own speeches for the collection and made this evaluation of the speaking of the day: "I do not remember to have seen in the 'Readers' and 'Speakers' of my day the pathetic Speech of Stafford after his condemnation, nor the sublime passages in Burke's speech on Conciliation with America, nor his allusion to the Queen of France—of more recent brilliant efforts, I recollect nothing more striking than some passages in a speech of Wm. Canning about sending relief to Portugal. . . . I have heard that Mr. C. revised the proofs of that speech four times. I would put into the collection, if I were you, some of the magnificent passages in *Paradise Lost*. They would fill to great advantage a portion of the space occupied by the feeble sentimentalisms of modern times." The letter is in the Manuscript Division of the Boston Public Library.

4. Roy P. Basler, ed., *The Collected Works of Abraham Lincoln*, I (New Brunswick, NJ: Rutgers Univ. Pr., 1953), pp. 291–97.

5. Ibid., pp. 299–303.

6. Ibid., pp. 501–16.

7. Ibid., pp. 108–15.

8. Ibid., p. 113.

9. Paul M. Angle, ed., *Created Equal? The Complete Lincoln-Douglas Debates of 1858* (Chicago: Univ. of Chicago Pr., 1958), p. x.

10. Ibid.

11. Basler, ed., *Collected Works of Abraham Lincoln*, II, p. 276.

12. Angle, p. 1.

13. Ibid., p. 12.

14. Ibid., pp. 163–64.

15. Ibid., pp. 107–8.

16. Ibid., p. 118.

17. Ibid., p. 33.

18. Ibid., pp. 221–22.

19. See, for example, Ernest G. Bormann, "The Eagleton Affair: A Fantasy Theme Analysis," *Quarterly Journal of Speech*, 59 (1973), 143–59.

20. Angle, p. 376.

21. Ibid., p. 356.

22. Ibid., p. 306.

23. Ibid., p. 130.

24. Ibid., p. 393.

25. Ibid.

26. Angle, p. 101. The authenticity of the account has been challenged, but that is beside the point for my argument here since the quotation was widely used in the mass media of the time and since it aptly expresses the Lincoln rhetorical vision.

27. Ibid., pp. 100–101.

28. Ibid., p. 117.

29. Ibid., p. 390.

10. *The Culmination of Romantic Pragmatism*

1. John H. Clifford and Marion M. Miller, eds., *The Works of Abraham Lincoln* (New York: C. S. Hammond, 1908), III, part 1, p. 146. The address has also been widely anthologized.

2. Woodrow Wilson, "War Message," *American Speeches*, ed. Wayland Maxfield Parrish and Marie Hochmuth (New York: Longmans, Green, 1954), pp. 472–81.

3. Clifford and Miller, III, part 1, p. 146.

4. Ibid., III, part 1, p. 183.

5. Ibid., III, part 2, pp. 8–9.

6. Ibid., III, part 1, pp. 223–24.

7. Barbara Ann Larson demonstrates that Samuel Davies used the form of the New England preacher's jeremiad in developing public opinion for the war against the French and Indians: see *Prologue to Revolution: The War Sermons of the Reverend Samuel Davies* (Falls Church, VA: Speech Communication Association, 1977). Perry Miller makes the case that the jeremiad was also widely used to mobilize the colonists for the fight against the mother country during the revolution in the South as well as the North; see Perry Miller, "From the Covenant to the Revival," *Religion in American Life, I: The Shaping of American Religion*, James Ward Smith and A. Leland Jamieson ed. (Princeton, NJ: Princeton Univ. Pr., 1961),p. 346.

The concept of the jeremiad has caught the imagination of a number of scholars who have used it to analyze intellectual and social history as well as communication. In the process, its meaning has been changed and enlarged to encompass a number of different fantasy themes and types and sometimes different rhetorical visions as well. See, for example, David W. Noble, *Historians against History: The Frontier Thesis and the National Covenant in American History* (Minneapolis: Univ. of Minnesota Pr., 1965); Sacvan Bercovitch, *The American Jeremiad* (Madison: Univ. of Wisconsin Pr., 1978); Kurt W. Ritter, "American Political Rhetoric and the Jeremiad Tradition: Presidential Nomination Acceptance Addresses, 1960–1976," *Central States Speech Journal*, 31 (1980), 153–71.

8. Clifford and Miller, III, part 2, pp. 156–57.

9. Ibid., III, part 1, pp. 223–25.

10. Ibid., III, part 2, p. 81.

11. Ibid., III, part 1, p. 225.

12. Dixon Wecter, *The Hero in America: A Chronicle of Hero-Worship* (Ann Arbor: Univ. of Michigan Pr., Ann Arbor Paperbacks, 1963), p. 265.

13. Clifford and Miller, III, part 1, p. 206.

14. Martin Luther King, Jr., "I Have a Dream," *Contemporary American Speeches*, ed. Wil Linkugel, R. R. Allen, and Richard Johannesen, 2nd ed. (Belmont, CA: Wadsworth, 1969), p. 293.

15. Sidney Kraus, ed., *The Great Debates* (Bloomington: Indiana Univ. Pr., 1962).

16. Albert M. Beveridge, "The March of the Flag," *Modern Eloquence*, ed. Thomas B. Reed (New York: American Law Book company, 1903), XI, pp. 224–43.

17. Carl Wayne Hensley, "The Rhetorical Vision of the Disciples of Christ: A Rhetoric of American Millenialism," Diss. Univ. of Minnesota, 1972.

Bibliography 🌿

Manuscript Collections

The following are the chief manuscript collections that were searched for sermon and speech texts, letters, diaries, and journals:

The anti-slavery collection and the papers of numberous Congregational and Unitarian ministers at the Boston Public Library, Boston, MA.

The archives of the Massachusetts Historical Society, Boston, MA.

The archives of the New England Methodist Historical Society, Boston, MA.

The manuscript division of of the Alderman Library of the University of Virginia, Charlottesville, VA.

The archives of the Colonial Williamsburg Corporation, Williamsburg, VA.

The archives of the Virginia State Historical Society, Richmond, VA.

The archives of the Baptist Historical Society, Richmond, VA.

Unpublished Studies

Barton, Fred J. "Modes of Delivery in American Homiletic Theory in the Eighteenth and Nineteenth Centuries." Ph.D. dissertation, State Univ. of Iowa, 1949.

Baxter, Batsell Barrett. "An Analysis of the Basic Elements of Persuasion in the Yale Lectures on Preaching." Ph.D. dissertation, Univ. of Southern California, 1944.

Boase, Paul H. "The Methodist Circuit-Rider on the Ohio Frontier." Ph.D. dissertation, Univ. of Wisconsin, 1952.

Breitlow, John R. "Rhetorical Fantasy at the Virginia Convention of 1788." Ph.D. dissertation, Univ. of Minnesota, 1972.

Brown, James Donnell. "Rhetorical Fantasy in the Webster-Calhoun Debate on the Revenue Collection Bill of 1833." Ph.D. dissertation, Univ. of Minnesota, 1977.

Carmack, Paul. "Theodore Dwight Weld, Reformer," Ph.D. dissertation, Syracuse Univ., 1948.

Emmel, James Robert. "The Persuasive Techniques of Charles Grandison Finney as a Revivalist and Social Reform Speaker, 1820–1860." Ph.D. dissertation, Pennsylvania State Univ., 1959.

Hensley, Carl Wayne. "The Disciples of Christ: A Rhetoric of American Millennialism." Ph.D. dissertation, Univ. of Minnesota, 1972.

Hitchcock, Orville Alban. "A Critical Study of the Oratorical Technique of Jonathan Edwards." Ph.D. dissertation, State Univ. of Iowa, 1936.

Hudson, Roy Fred. "The Theory of Communication of Colonial New England Preachers, 1620–1670." Ph.D. dissertation, Cornell Univ., 1935.

Kelley, Barbara Marie. "A Rhetorical Analysis of Selected Sermons of Gilbert Tennant, 1735–1745." Master's thesis, State Univ. of Iowa, 1951.

Lambertson, Floyd Wesley. "A Survey and Analysis of American Homiletics Prior to 1860." Ph.D. dissertation, State Univ. of Iowa, 1930.

Larson, Barbara Ann. "A Rhetorical Study of the Preaching of the Reverend Samuel Davies in the Colony of Virginia from 1747–1759." Ph.D. dissertation, Univ. of Minnesota, 1969.

Porter, Laurinda Wright. "Drama and Fantasy: A Critical Analysis of Nineteenth-Century American Dreams." Master's thesis, Univ. of Minnesota, 1971.

White, Eugene E. "The Preaching of George Whitefield during the Great Awakening in America." Ph.D. dissertation, Louisiana State Univ., 1956.

Articles

Andrews, James R. "History and Theory in the Study of the Rhetoric of Social Movements." *Central States Speech Journal*, 31 (1980), 274–82.

Aronson, Elliot, and Judson Mills. "The Effect of Severity of Initiation on Liking for a Group." *Journal of Abnormal and Social Psychology*, 59 (1959), 177–81.

Bailey, Raymond. "Building Men for Citizenship." *Preaching in American History*. Ed. DeWitte Holland. Nashville: Abingdon Pr., 1969, pp. 135–49.

Barnard, Raymond H. "The Freedom Speech of Wendell Phillips." *Quarterly Journal of Speech*, 25 (1939), 596–611.

———. "Wendell Phillips's Adaptability as a Speaker." *Western Speech Journal*, 5 (1941), 6–10.

Barnes, Gilbert H. "The Western Revival Origins." *The Abolitionists: Reformers or Fanatics?* Ed. Richard O. Curry. New York: Holt, Rinehart, 1965, pp. 15–24.

Barnhart, Elbert, and Wayne C. Eubank. "N. B. Hardeman, Southern Evangelist." *Southern Speech Journal*, 19 (1953), 98–107.

Berry, Mildred Freeburg. "Abraham Lincoln: His Development in the Skills of the Platform." *A History and Criticism of American Public Address*. Ed. William Norwood Brigance. New York: McGraw-Hill, 1943, II, pp. 828–59.

Beveridge, Albert M. "The March of the Flag." *Modern Eloquence*. Ed. Thomas B. Reed. New York: American Lay Book Company, 1903, XI, pp. 224–43.

Boase, Paul H. "The Education of a Circuit Rider." *Quarterly Journal of Speech*, 40 (1954), 130–36.

Bohman, George V. "Rhetorical Practice in Colonial America." *History of Speech Education in America*. Ed. Karl R. Wallace. New York: Appleton-Century-Crofts, 1954, pp. 60–79.

———. "The Colonial Period." *A History and Criticism of American Public Address*. Ed. William Norwood Brigance. New York: McGraw-Hill, 1943, I, pp. 3–54.

Bormann, Ernest G. "The Eagleton Affair: A Fantasy Theme Analysis." *Quarterly Journal of Speech*, 59 (1973), 143–59.

———. "Ephphatha, or, Some Advice to Stammerers." *Journal of Speech and Hearing Research*, 12 (Sept. 1969), pp. 453–61.

———. "Fantasy and Rhetorical Vision: The Rhetorical Criticism of Social Reality." *Quarterly Journal of Speech*, 58 (1972), 396–407.

———. "Fantasy and Rhetorical Vision: Ten Years Later." *Quarterly Journal of Speech*, 68 (1982), 288–305.

————. "A Fantasy Theme Analysis of the Television Coverage of the Reagan Inaugural and the Hostage Release." *Quarterly Journal of Speech*, 68 (1982), 133–45.

————. "Rhetoric as a Way of Knowing: Ernest Bormann and Fantasy Theme Analysis." *The Rhetoric of Western thought*. Ed. James L. Golden, Goodwin Bergquist, and William E. Coleman. 3rd ed. Dubuque, IA: Kendall/Hunt, 1983, pp. 431–49.

————. "The Symbolic Convergence Theory of Communication and the Creation, Raising, and Sustaining of Public Consciousness." *The Jensen Lectures: Contemporary Communication Studies*. Ed. John I. Sisco. Tampa: Department of Communication, Univ. of South Florida, 1983, pp. 71–90.

Bost, George H. "Samuel Davies Preacher of the Great Awakening." *Journal of Presbyterian Historical Society*, 26 (1948), 65–86.

Braden, Waldo W. "Myths in a Rhetorical Context." *Southern Speech Communication Journal*, 40 (1974), 113–26.

Broadus, J. A. "The American Baptist Ministry 100 Years Ago." *Baptist Quarterly*, 9 (1875), 1–20.

Carmack, Paul. "The Lane Seminary Debates." *Central States Speech Journal*, (March 1950), 33–39.

Cathcart, Robert S. "Defining Social Movements by Their Rhetorical Form." *Central States Speech Journal*, 31 (1980), 267–73.

————. "Movements: Confrontation as Rhetorical Form." *Southern Speech Communication Journal*, 43 (1978), 233–47.

————. "New Approaches to the Study of Movements: Defining Movements Rhetorically." *Western Journal of Speech Communication*, 36 (1972), 82–88.

Chesebro, James W., John F. Cragan, and Patricia W. McCullough. "The Small Group Technique of the Radical Revolutionary: A Synthetic Study of Consciousness Raising." *Speech Monographs*, 40 (1973), 136–46.

Chesebro, James W., and Caroline D. Hamsher. "Contemporary Rhetorical Theory and Criticism: Dimensions of the New Rhetoric." *Communication Monographs*, 42 (1975), 311–34.

Cleveland, Les. "Symbols and Politics: Mass Communication and Public Drama." *Politics: Australasian Political Studies Association Journal*, 4 (1969), 186–96.

Collins, Edward M., Jr. "The Rhetoric of Sensation Challenges the Rhetoric of the Intellect: An Eighteenth-Century Controversy." *Preaching in American History: Selected Issues in the American Pulpit, 1630–1967*. Nashville: Abingdon Pr., 1969, pp. 98–117.

Conrad, Charles. "Agon and Rhetorical Form: The Essence of 'Old Feminist' Rhetoric." *Central States Speech Journal*, 32 (1981), 45–53.

————. "The Transformation of the 'Old Feminist' Movement." *Quarterly Journal of Speech*, 67 (1981), 284–97.

Cotton, John. "God's Promise to His Plantations." *Old South Leaflets*, III, 53, 1–16.

Crocker, Lionel. "Henry Ward Beecher." *A History and Criticism of American Public Address*. Ed. William Norwood Brigance. New York: McGraw-Hill, 1943, I, pp. 268–69.

Dick, Robert C. "Negro Oratory in the Anti-Slavery Societies: 1830–1860." *Western Speech*, 28 (1964), 5–14.

Doyle, J. H. "The Style of Wendell Phillips." *Quarterly Journal of Speech*, 2 (1916), 331–39.

Duncan, Hugh Dalziel. "The Search for a Social Theory of Communication in American Sociology." *Human Communication Theory: Original Essays*. Ed. Frank E. X. Dance. New York: Hold, Rinehart, and Winston, 1967, pp. 236–63.

Dunn, Robert E., and Morton Goldman. "Competition and Noncompetition in Relationship to Satisfaction and Feelings toward Owngroup and Nongroup Members." *Journal of Social Psychology*, 68 (1966), 299–311.

Edwards, Jonathan. "Sinners in the Hands of an Angry God." *American Speeches*. Ed. Wayland Maxfield Parrish and Marie Hochmuth. New York: Longmans, Green, 1954, pp. 73–90.

Emerson, Everett H. "John Udall and the Puritan Sermon." *Quarterly Journal of Speech*, 44 (1958), 282–84.

Ewebank, Henry L., Jr. "Current Interest Topics in the Lyceums, 1832–1837." *Speech Monographs*, 23 (1956), 284–87.

Fletcher, Winona L. "Knight-Errant or Screaming Eagle? E. L. Godkin's Criticism of Wendell Phillips." *Southern Speech Journal*, 29 (1964), 214–23.

Gerard, Harold B., and Grover C. Mathewson. "The Effects of Severity of Initiation on Liking for a Group: A Replication." *Journal of Experimental Social Psychology*, 2 (1966), 278–87.

Griffin, Leland M. "A Dramatistic Theory of the Rhetoric of Movements." *Critical Responses to Kenneth Burke.* Ed. William H. Ruckert. Minneapolis: Univ. of Minnesota Pr., 1969, pp. 462–69.

———. "On Studying Movements." *Central States Speech Journal*, 31 (1980), 225–32.

———. "The Rhetoric of Historical Movements." *Quarterly Journal of Speech*, 38 (1952), 184–88.

Grover, David H. "Elocution at Harvard: The Saga of Jonathan Barber." *Quarterly Journal of Speech*, 51 (1965), 62–67.

Guthrie, Warren. "Rhetorical Theory in Colonial America." *History of Speech Education in America.* Ed. Karl R. Wallace. New York: Appleton-Century-Crofts, 1954, pp. 48–59.

Hahn, Dan F., and Ruth M. Gonchar. "Studying Social Movements: A Rhetorical methodology." *Communication Education*, 20 (1971), 44–52.

Hanson, Robert. "Form and Content of the Puritan Funeral Elegy." *American Literature.* 32 (1960), 11–27.

Heisey, D. Ray. "On Entering the Kingdom: New birth or Nurture." *Preaching in American History: Selected Issues in the American Pulpit, 1630–1967.* Ed. DeWitte Holland. Nashville: Abingdon Pr., 1969, pp. 150–67.

Hitchcock, Orville A. "Jonathan Edwards." *A History and Criticism of American Public Address.* Ed. William Norwood Brigance. New York: McGraw-Hill, 1943, I, pp. 232–33.

Hochmuth, Marie. "Lincoln's First Inaugural." *American Speeches.* Ed. Wayland Maxfield Parrish and Marie Hochmuth. New York: Longmans, Green, 1954, pp. 21–71.

Hoshor, John P. "Lectures on Rhetoric and Public Speaking by Chauncey Allen Goodrich." *Speech Monographs*, 14 (1947), 1–37.

Howell, Wilbur Samuel. "English Backgrounds of Rhetoric." *History of Speech Educaiton in America.* Ed. Karl R. Wallace. New York: Appleton-Century-Crofts, 1954, pp. 3–47.

———. "Ramus and English Rhetoric, 1574–1681." *Quarterly Journal of Speech*, 37 (1951), 299–310.

Hudson, Roy Fred. "Rhetorical Invention in Colonial New England." *Speech Monographs*, 25 (1958), 215–21.

Kennicott, Patrick C. "Black Persuaders in the Antislavery Movement." *Speech Monographs*, 37 (1970), 15–34.

Kerr, Harry P. "The Election Sermon: Primer for Revolutionaries." *Speech Monographs*, 29 (1962), 13–22.

———. "Politics and Religion in Colonial Fast and Thanksgiving Sermons, 1763–1783." *Quarterly Journal of Speech*, 46 (1960), 372–82.

King, C. Harold. "George Whitefield: Commoner Evangelist." *Historical Studies of Rhetoric and Rhetoricians.* Ed. Raymond F. Howes. Ithaca, NY: Cornell Univ. Pr., 1961, pp. 253–70.

———. "George Whitefield: Dramatic Evangelist." *Quarterly Journal of Speech*, 19 (1933), 165–75.

———. "George Whitefield: God's Commoner." *Quarterly Journal of Speech*, 29 (1943), 32–36.

King, Martin Luther, Jr. "I Have a Dream." *Contemporary American Speeches.* Ed. Wil A. Linkugel, R. R. Allen, and Richard L. Johannesen. 2nd ed. Belmont, CA: Wadsworth, 1969, pp. 290–94.

Larson, Barbara Ann. "Samuel Davies and the Rhetoric of the New Light." *Speech Monographs*, 38 (1971), 207–16.

Lazenby, Walter. "Exhortation as Exorcism: Cotton Mather's Sermons to Murderers." *Quarterly Journal of Speech*, 57 (1971), 50–56.

Linkugel, Wil A. "Lincoln, Kansas, and Cooper Union." *Speech Monographs*, 37 (1970), 172–79.

Martin, Howard H. "Puritan Preachers on Preaching: Notes on American Colonial Rhetoric." *Quarterly Journal of Speech*, 50 (1964), 285–92.

———. "Ramus, Ames, Perkins and Colonial Rhetoric." *Western Speech*, 23 (1959), 74–82.

Mather, Increase. "Man Knows Not His Time." *The Puritans*. Ed. Perry Miller and Thomas H. Johnson. New York: Harper Torchbooks, 1963, I, pp. 340–481.

Miller, Perry. "From the Covenant to the Revival." *Religion in American Life, I: The Shaping of American Religion*. Ed. James Ward Smith and A. Leland Jamieson. Princeton, NJ: Princeton Univ. Pr., 1961, pp. 322–68.

———. "Jonathan Edwards' Sociology of the Great Awakening." *The New England Quarterly*, 21 (1948), 50–78.

———. "Solomon Stoddard, 1643–1729." *The Harvard Theological Review*, 34 (1941), 277–320.

Minnick, Wayne C. "The New England Execution Sermon, 1639–1800." *Speech Monographs*, 35 (1968), 77–89.

Mixon, Harold D. "Boston's Artillery Election Sermons and the American Revolution." *Speech Monographs*, 34 (1967), 43–50.

Mohrmann, G. P., and Michael C. Leff. "Lincoln at Cooper Union: A Rationale for Neo-Classical Criticism." *Quarterly Journal of Speech*, 40 (1974), 459–67.

Quimby, Rollin W. "Charles Grandison Finney: Herald of Modern Revivalism." *Speech Monographs*, 20 (1953), 293–99.

Quimby, Rollin W., and Robert A. Billigmeier. "The Varying Role of Revivalistic Preaching in American Protestant Evangelism." *Speech Monographs*, 26 (1959), 217–28.

Reid, Ronald F. "Apocalypticism and Typology: Rhetorical Dimensions of Symbolic Reality." *Quarterly Journal of Speech*, 69 (1983), 229–48.

Ritter, Kurt W. "American Political Rhetoric and the Jeremiad Tradition: Presidential Nomination Acceptance Addresses, 1960-1976." *Central States Speech Journal*, 31 (1980), 153–71.

Schachter, Stanley, and Jerome E. Singer. "Cognitive, Social, and Physiological Determinants of Emotional State." *Psychological Review*, 69 (1962), 379–99.

Shepard, Thomas. "Autobiography." *The Puritans*. Ed. Perry Miller and Thomas H. Johnson. New York: Harper Torchbooks, 1963, II, pp. 471–75.

Smith, Ralph R. "The Historical Criticism of Social Movements." *Central States Speech Journal*, 31 (1980), 298–305.

———. "The Rhetoric of Mobilization: Implications for the Study of Movements." *Southern Speech Communication Journal*, 42 (1976), 1–19.

Smith, Ralph R., and Russell R. Windes. "The Innovational Movement: A Rhetorical Theory." *Quarterly Journal of Speech*, 61 (1975), 140–53.

Taylor, Hubert Vance. "Preaching on Slavery, 1831–1861." *Preaching in American History: Selected Issues in the American Pulpit, 1630–1967*. Ed. DeWitte Holland. Nashville: Abingdon Pr., 1969, pp. 168–83.

Thomas, Ota. "The Teaching of Rhetoric in the United States during the Classical Period of Education." *A History and Criticism of American Public Address*. Ed. William Norwood Brigance. New York: McGraw-Hill, 1943, I, pp. 193–210.

White, Eugene E. "Cotton Mather's *Manuductio ad Ministerium*." *Quarterly Journal of Speech*, 49 (1963), 308–19.

———. "George Whitefield's Preaching in Masachusetts and Georgia: A Case Study in Persuasion." *Southern Speech Journal*, 15 (1950), 249–62.

———. "The Great Awakener: George Whitefield." *Southern Speech Journal*, 11 (1945), 6–15.

———. "The Preaching of George Whitefield during the Great Awakening." *Speech Monographs*, 15 (1948), 33–43.

———. "The Protasis of the Great Awakening in New England." *Speech Monographs*, 21 (1954), 10–20.

———. "Puritan Preaching and the Authority of God." *Preaching in American History: Selected Issues in the American Pulpit, 1630–1967*. Ed. DeWitte Holland. Nashville: Abingdon Pr., 1969, pp. 36–73.

———. "Solomon Stoddard's Theories of Persuasion." *Speech Monographs*, 29 (1962), 235–59.

Whitefield, George. "The Kingdom of God." *The World's Great Sermons*. Ed. S. E. Frost, Jr. Garden City, NY: Halcyon House, 1943, pp. 119–23.

Whitfield, George. "Frederick Douglass: Negro Abolitionist." *Today's Speech*, 11 (1963), 6–8.

Wilkinson, Charles A. "A Rhetorical Definition of Movements." *Central States Speech Journal*, 27 (1976), 88–94.

Wilson, Woodrow. "War Message." *American Speeches*. Ed. Wayland Maxfield Parrish and Marie Hochmuth. New York: Longmans, Green, 1954, pp. 472–78.

Wrage, Ernest J. "Public Address: A Study in Social and Intellectual History." *Quarterly Journal of Speech*, 33 (1947), 451–57.

Books

Abzug, Robert H. *Passionate Liberator: Theodore Dwight Weld and the Dilemma of Reform*. New York: Oxford Univ. Pr., 1980.

Angle, Paul M., ed. *Created Equal? The Complete Lincoln-Douglas Debates of 1858*. Chicago: Univ. of Chicago Pr., 1958.

The Anti-Slavery Examiner, No. 6. The Bible against Slavery: An Inquiry into the Patriarchial and Mosaic Systems on the Subject of Human Rights. 3rd ed. New York: The American Anti-Slavery Society, 1838.

Asbury, Francis. *The Journal of the Rev. Francis Asbury, Bishop of the Methodist Episcopal Church from August 7, 1771, to December 7, 1815*. 3 vols. New York: N. Bangs and T. Mason, 1821.

Auer, J. Jeffrey, ed. *Antislavery and Disunion, 1858–1861: Studies in the Rhetoric of Compromise and Conflict*. New York: Harper and Row, 1963.

Baird, A. Craig, ed. *American Public Addresses: 1740–1952*. New York: McGraw-Hill, 1956.

Bales, Robert F. *Personality and Interpersonal Behavior*. New York: Holt, Rinehart, and Winston, 1970.

Barnes, Gilbert H. *The Antislavery Impulse, 1830–1844*. Gloucester, MA: Peter Smith, 1957.

Barnes, Gilbert H., and Dwight L. Dumond. *Letters of Theodore Dwight Weld, Angelina Grimké-Weld, and Sarah Grimké, 1822–1844*. 2 vols. New York: Appleton-Century, 1934.

Bartlett, Irving H. *Wendell Phillips, Brahmin Radical*. Boston: Beacon Pr., 1961.

Basler, Roy P., ed. *The Collected Works of Abraham Lincoln*. 9 vols. New Brunswick, NJ: Rutgers Univ. Pr., 1953.

Bercovitch, Sacvan. *The American Jeremiad*. Madison: Univ. of Wisconsin Pr., 1978.

———. *The Puritan Origins of the American Self*. New Haven: Yale Univ. Pr., 1980.

Birney, Catherine H. *The Grimké Sisters: Sarah and Angelina Grimké, the First American Women Advocates of Abolition and Woman's Rights*. Boston: Lee and Shepard, 1885.

Black, Edwin. *Rhetorical Criticism: A Study in Method*. Madison: Univ. of Wisconsin Pr., 1978.

Blackwood, Andrew Watterson. *The Protestant Pulpit*. New York: Abingdon-Cokesbury Pr., 1947.

Blau, Joseph L., ed. *American Philosophic Addresses, 1700–1900.* New York: Columbia Univ. Pr., 1946.

Blench, J. W. *Preaching in England in the Late Fifteenth and Sixteenth Centuries: A Study of English Sermons, 1450–1600.* New York: Barnes and Noble, 1964.

Bliss, William Root. *Side Glimpses from the Colonial Meeting-House.* Detroit: Gale Research, 1970.

Bode, Carl. *The American Lyceum: Town Meeting of the Mind.* New York: Oxford Univ. Pr., 1956.

Bormann, Ernest G. *Communication Theory.* New York: Holt, Rinehart, and Winston, 1980.

———. *Discussion and Group Methods: Theory and Practice.* 2nd ed. New York: Harper and Row, 1975.

———, ed. *Forerunners of Black Power: The Rhetoric of Abolition.* Englewood Cliffs, NJ: Prentice-Hall, 1971.

Braden, Waldo. *The Oral Tradition in the South.* Baton Rouge: Louisiana State Univ. Pr., 1983.

Brigance, William Norwood, ed. *A History and Criticism of American Public Address.* 2 vols. New York: McGraw-Hill, 1943.

Brock, Bernard L., and Robert L. Scott. *Methods of Rhetorical Criticism: A Twentieth-Century Perspective.* 2nd ed. Detroit: Wayne State Univ. Pr., 1980.

Brunson, Alfred. *A Western Pioneer.* Cincinnati: Walden and Stowe, 1880.

Burns, Edward McNall. *The American Idea of Mission, Concepts of American Purpose and Destiny.* New Brunswick, NJ: Rutgers Univ. Pr., 1957.

Campbell, Karlyn Kohrs, and Kathleen Hall Jamieson, eds. *Form and Genre: Shaping Rhetorical Action.* Falls Church, VA: The Speech Communication Association, 1978.

Carroll, Andrew. *Moral and Religious Sketches and Collections.* Cincinnati: Methodist Book Concern, 1857.

Cassirer, Ernst. *Language and Myth.* New York: Dover, 1946.

Cathcart, Robert. *Post Communication: Rhetorical Analysis and Evaluation.* 2nd ed. Indianapolis: Bobbs-Merrill, 1981.

Cherry, Conrad, ed. *God's New Israel, Religious Interpretations of American Destiny.* Englewood Cliffs, NJ: Prentice-Hall, 1971.

Cleveland, Catherine C. *The Great Revival in the West, 1797–1805.* Chicago: Univ. of Chicago Pr., 1916.

Clifford, John H., and Marion M. Miller. *The Works of Abraham Lincoln.* 4 vols. New York: Newton and Cartwright, 1907.

Cole, Charles C., Jr. *the Social Ideas of the Northern Evangelists, 1826–1860.* New York: Columbia Univ. Pr., 1954.

Combs, James E., and Michael W. Mansfield, eds. *Drama in Life: The Uses of Communication in Society.* New York: Hastings House, 1976.

Craven, Wesley Frank. *The Legend of the Founding Fathers.* New York: New York Univ. Pr., 1956.

Cross, Whitney R. *The Burned-over District: The Social and Intellectual History of Enthusiastic Religion in Western New York, 1800–1850.* New York: Harper And Row, 1965.

Curry, Richard O., ed. *The Abolitionists: Reformers or Fanatics?* New York: Holt, Rinehart, 1965.

Dance, Frank E. X., ed. *Human Communication Theory: Original Essays.* New York: Holt, Rinehart, and Winston, 1967.

Davies, Horton. *The Worship of the English Puritans.* London: Dacre Pr., 1948.

Davies, Samuel. *Sermons on Important Subjects.* Boston: Lincoln and Edwards, 1811.

Davis, Lucius Daniel. *Life in the Itinerancy, in Its Relations to the Circuit and Station, and to the Minister's Home and Family.* New York: Miller, Orton, and Mulligan, 1856.

Dixon, James. *Methodism in America: Personal Narrative of a Tour through a Part of the United States and Canada with Notices of the History and Institutions of Methodism in America.* New York: Lane and Scott, 1849.

Dumond, Dwight L. *Antislavery: The Crusade for Freedom in America.* Ann Arbor: Univ. of Michigan Pr., 1961.

Earle, Alice Morse. *The Sabbath in Puritan New England.* New York: Charles Scribner's Sons, 1913.

Edelman, Murray. *The Symbolic Uses of Politics.* Urbana: Univ. of Illinois Pr., 1964.

Edwards, Jonathan. *Account of Abigail Hutchinson: A Young Woman, Hopefully Converted at Northampton, Mass. 1734.* Philadelphia: Religious Tract Society of Philadelphia, 1818.

————. *A Faithful Narrative of the Surprising Work of God.* Halifax: Holden and Dawson, 1808.

————. *The Works of President Edwards.* 6 vols. New York: Leavitt, Trow, 1844-1847.

Eggleston, Edward. *The Circuit Rider: A Tale of the Heroic Age.* New York: Charles Scribner's Sons, 1878.

Filler, Louis. *The Crusade against Slavery, 1830–1860.* New York: Harper and Brothers, 1960.

Finley, James B. *Sketches of Western Methodism; Biographical, Historical, and Miscellaneous. Illustrative of Pioneer Life.* Ed. W. P. Strickland. Cincinnati: Methodist Book Concern, 1854.

Finney, Charles Grandison. *Lecture on Revivals of Religion.* Ed. William G. McLoughlin. Cambridge, MA: Belknap Pr. of Harvard Univ. Pr., 1960.

————. *Memoirs of the Rev. Charles G. Finney Written by Himself.* New York: Fleming H. Revell, 1876.

————. *Sermons on Various Subjects.* New York: S. W. Benedict, 1835.

Fladeland, Betty. *James Gillespie Birney: Slaveholder to Abolitionist.* Ithaca, NY: Cornell Univ. Pr., 1955.

Fletcher, Robert S. *A History of Oberlin College.* 2 vols. Oberlin, OH: Oberlin College, 1943.

Flexner, Eleanor. *Century of Struggle: The Woman's Rights Movement in the United States.* Cambridge, MA: Harvard Univ. Pr., 1959.

Foner, Philip S. *The Life and Writings of Frederick Douglass.* Vol. I. New York: International Publishers, 1950.

Foote, William Henry. *Sketches of Virginia: Historical and Biographical.* Richmond, VA: John Knox Pr., 1966.

Foster, Charles I. *An Errand of Mercy: The Evangelical United Front, 1790–1837.* Chapel Hill Univ. of North Carolina Pr., 1960.

Frost, S. E., Jr., ed. *The World's Great Sermons.* Garden City, NY: Halcyon House, 1943.

Gaddis, Maxwell Pierson. *Foot-prints of an Itinerant.* Cincinnati: Methodist Book Concern, 1855.

Gaustad, Edwin S. *The Great Awakening in New England.* New York: Harper and Row, 1957.

Gewehr, Wesley M. *The Great Awakening in Virginia, 1740–1790.* Durham, NC: Duke Univ. Pr., 1930.

Gibbard, Graham S., John J. Hartman, and Richard D. Mann, eds. *Analysis of Groups.* San Francisco: Jossey-Bass, 1974.

Goen, C. C. *Revivalism and Separatism in New England, 1740–1800: Strict Congregationalists and Separate Baptists in the Great Awakening.* New Haven: Yale Univ. Pr., 1962.

Golden, James L., Goodwin Bergquist, and William E. Coleman, eds. *The Rhetoric of Western Thought.* 3rd ed. Dubuque, IA: Kendall/Hunt, 1983.

Green, Beriah. *Things for Northern Men to Do: A Discourse Delivered Lord's Day Evening, July 17, 1836, in the Presbyterian Church, Whitesboro, New York.* n. p., 1836.

Grimké, Archibald H. *William Lloyd Garrison, the Abolitionist.* New York: Funk and Wagnalls, 1891.

Haller, William. *The Rise of Puritanism or, The Way to the New Jerusalem as Set Forth in Pulpit and Press from Thomas Cartwright to John Lilburne and John Milton, 1570–1643.* New York: Harper and Row, 1957.

Hare, A. Paul. *Handbook of Small Group Research.* New York: Free Pr., 1962.

Harlow, Ralph V. *Gerrit Smith, Philanthropist and Reformer.* New York: Holt, 1939.

Hart, A. B. *Slavery and Abolition, 1831–1841.* New York: Harper and Brothers, 1906.

Heimert, Alan. *Religion and the American Mind. From the Great Awakening to the Revolution.* Cambridge, MA: Harvard Univ. Pr., 1966.

Herr, Alan F. *The Elizabethan Sermon: A Survey and Bibliography.* New York: Octagon Books, 1969.

Hochmuth, Marie, ed. *A History and Criticism of American Public Address.* Vol. III. New York: Longmans, Green, 1955.

Holland, DeWitte, ed. *American in Controversy: History of American Public Address.* Dubuque, IA: Wm. C. Brown, 1973.

————. *Preaching in American History: Selected Issues in the American Pulpit, 1630–1967.* Nashville: Abingdon Pr., 1969.

Howell, Wilbur Samuel. *Logic and Rhetoric in England, 1500–1700.* Princeton: Princeton Univ. Pr., 1956.

Howes, Raymond F., ed. *Historical Studies of Rhetoric and Rhetoricians.* Ithaca, NY: Cornell Univ. Pr., 1961.

Hudson, Winthrop S. *Religion in America.* New York: Charles Scribner's Sons, 1965.

Jeter, Jeremiah Bell. *The Recollections of a Long Life.* Richmond, VA: Religious Herald, 1891.

Johnson, Charles A. *The Frontier Camp Meeting: Religion's Harvest Time.* Dallas: Southern Methodist Univ. Pr., 1956.

Jones, James William. *The Shattered Synthesis: New England Puritanism before the Great Awakening.* New Haven: Yale Univ. Pr., 1973.

Kamler, Howard. *Communication: Sharing our Stories of Experience.* Seattle: Psychological Pr., 1983.

Kelly, Regina Zimmerman. *Lincoln and Douglas: The Years of Decision.* New York: Random House, 1956.

Kraus, Sidney, ed. *The Great Debates.* Bloomington: Indiana Univ. Pr., 1962.

Kuhn, Thomas S. *The Structure of Scientific Revolutions.* 2nd ed. Chicago: Univ. of Chicago Pr., 1970.

Kwiat, Joseph J., and Mary C. Turpie, eds. *Studies in American Culture: Dominant Ideas and Images.* Minneapolis: Univ. of Minnesota Pr., 1960.

Labaree, Leonard, et al., eds. *The Autobiography of Benjamin Franklin.* New Haven: Yale Univ. Pr., 1964.

Labaree, Leonard, and Whitefield J. Bell, Jr., eds. *The Papers of Benjamin Franklin.* 7 vols. New Haven: Yale Univ. Pr., 1959–1963.

Larson, Barbara Ann. *Prologue to Revolution: The War Sermons of the Reverend Samuel Davies.* Falls Church, VA: Speech Communication Association, 1978.

Lerner, Gerda. *The Grimké Sisters from South Carolina: Rebels against Slavery.* Boston: Houghton Mifflin, 1967.

Levy, Babette May. *Preaching in the First Half-Century of New England History.* Hartford, CT: American Society of Church History, 1945.

Linkugel, Wil A., R. R. Allen, and Richard L. Johannesen, eds. *Contemporary American Speeches.* 2nd ed. Belmont, CA: Wadsworth, 1969.

Lumpkin, Katherine Du Pre. *The Emancipation of Angelina Grimké.* Chapel Hill: Univ. of North Carolina Pr., 1974.

Lynn, Kenneth S., ed. *Uncle Tom's Cabin or, Life among the Lowly by Harriet Beecher Stowe.* Cambridge, MA: Harvard Univ. Pr., 1962.

McCurdy, Frances Lea. *Stump, Bar, and Pulpit: Speechmaking on the Missouri Frontier.* Columbia: Univ. of Missouri Pr., 1969.

McLoughlin, William G. *Modern Revivalism: Charles Grandison Finney to Billy Graham.* New York: Ronald Pr., 1959.

————, ed. *Lectures on Revivals of Religion by Charles Grandison Finney.* Cambridge, MA: Belknap Pr. of Harvard Univ. Pr., 1960.

McNemar, Richard. *The Kentucky Revival: or, A Short History of the Late Extraordinary Outpouring of the Spirit of God in the Western States of America, etc.* New York: E. O. Jenkins, 1846.

Marryat, Capt. C. B. *A Diary in America with Remarks on Its Institutions.* Vol. II. London: Longman, Orme, Brown, Green, and Longmans, 1839.

Martineau, Harriet. *The Martyr Age of the United States.* New York: Arno Pr., 1969.

—————. *Society in America.* 4th ed. Vol. II. New York: Saunders and Otley, 1837.

Mather, Cotton. *Diary of Cotton Mather.* 2 vols. New York: Frederick Ungar, 1911.

—————. *Manuductio ad Ministerium: Directions for a Candidate of the Ministry.* New York: Columbia Univ. Pr. for the Facsimile Text Society, 1938.

Maxson, Charles. *The Great Awakening in the Middle Colonies.* Chicago: Univ. of Chicago Pr., 1920.

Merrill, W. M. *Against Wind and Tide: A Biography of William Lloyd Garrison.* Cambridge, MA: Harvard Univ. Pr., 1963.

Meyers, Marvin. *The Jacksonian Persuasion: Politics and Belief.* Stanford, CA: Stanford Univ. Pr., 1957.

Milburn, William Henry, *The Pioneers, Preachers, and People of the Mississippi Valley.* New York: Derby and Jackson, 1860.

—————. *The Rifle, Axe, and Saddle-Bags, and Other Lectures.* New York: Derby and Jackson, 1857.

—————. *Ten Years of Preacher-Life: Chapters from an Autobiography.* New York: Derby and Jackson, 1859.

Miller, Perry. *Jonathan Edwards.* New York: William Sloan, 1949.

—————. *The New England Mind: From Colony to Province.* Boston: Beacon Pr., 1961.

—————. *The New England Mind: The Seventeenth Century.* New York: Macmillan, 1939.

—————. *Orthodoxy in Massachusetts, 1630–1650.* Boston: Beacon Pr., 1959.

Miller, Perry, and Thomas H. Johnson, eds. *The Puritans.* 2 vols. New York: Harper and Row, 1963.

Mitchell, Margaret. *Gone with the Wind.* New York: Macmillan, 1936.

Morgan, Irvonwy. *The Godly Preachers of the Elizabethan Church.* London: Epworth Press, 1965.

Morison, Samuel Eliot. *The Founding of Harvard College.* Cambridge, MA: Harvard Univ. Pr., 1935.

—————. *Harvard College in the Seventeenth Century.* Cambridge, MA: Harvard Univ. Pr., 1936.

Murdock, Kenneth B. *Increase Mather, the Foremost American Puritan.* Cambridge, MA: Harvard Univ. Pr., 1925.

—————. *Literature and Theology in Colonial New England.* New York: Harper and Row, 1963.

Mutual Criticism. Syracuse, NY: Syracuse Univ. Pr., 1975.

Nimmo, Dan, and James E. Combs. *Mediated Political Realities.* New York: Longman, 1983.

Noble, David W. *Historians against History: The Frontier Thesis and the National Covenant in American History.* Minneapolis: Univ. of Minnesota Pr., 1965.

Nye, Russel B. *William Lloyd Garrison and the Humanitarian Reformers.* Boston: Little, Brown, 1956.

O'Connor, Lillian. *Pioneer Women Orators: Rhetoric in the Ante-Bellum Reform Movement.* New York: Columbia Univ. Pr., 1954.

Oliver, Robert T. *History of Public Speaking in America.* Boston: Allyn and Bacon, 1965.

Owst, G. R. *Preaching in Medieval England: An Introduction to Sermon Manuscripts of the Period c. 1350–1450.* Cambridge: Cambridge Univ. Pr., 1926.

Parker, E. G. *Golden Age of American Oratory.* Boston: Wittemore, Niles, and Hall, 1857.

Parrish, Wayland Maxfield, and Marie Hochmuth, eds. *American Speeches.* New York: Longmans, Green, 1954.

Phillips, Wendell. *Speeches, Lectures, and Letters.* Boston: Lee and Shepard, 1870.

Plumstead, A. W., ed. *The Wall and the Garden: Selected Massachusetts Election Sermons, 1670–1775.* Minneapolis: Univ. of Minnesota Pr., 1968.

Posey, Walter Brownlow. *The Baptist Church in the Lower Mississippi Valley, 1776–1845*. Lexington: Univ. of Kentucky Pr., 1957.

Prince, Thomas, ed. *The Christian History, Containing Accounts of the Revival and Propagation of Religion in Great Britain, America, etc. for the Year 1744*. Boston: S. Kneeland and T. Green, 1745.

Quarles, Benjamin. *Black Abolitionists*. New York: Oxford Univ. Pr., 1969.

Reed, Thomas B., ed. *Modern Eloquence*. 15 vols. New York: American Law Book Company, 1903.

Richardson, Caroline Francis. *English Preachers and Preaching, 1640–1670*. New York: Macmillan, 1928.

Rosenberg, Bruce A. *The Art of the American Folk Preacher*. New York: Oxford Univ. Pr., 1970.

Rouke, Constance M. *Trumpets of Jubilee*. New York: Harcourt, Brace, 1927.

Ruckert, William H., ed. *Critical Responses to Kenneth Burke*. Minneapolis: Univ. of Minnesota Pr., 1969.

Seaver, Paul S. *The Puritan Lectureships: The Politics of Religious Dissent, 1560–1662*. Stanford, CA: Stanford Univ. Pr., 1970.

Semple, Robert B. *A History of the Rise and Progress of the Baptists in Virginia*. Philadelphia: American Baptist Publication Society, 1894.

Sermons on Miscellaneous Subjects, by the Bishops of the Methodist Episcopal Church, and the Senior Preachers of the Ohio and North Ohio Conferences. Cincinnati: Methodist Book Concern, 1847.

Sisco, John I. *The Jensen Lectures: Contemporary Communication Studies*. Tampa: Department of Communication, Univ. of South Florida, 1983.

Smith, James Ward, and A. Leland Jamieson, eds. *Religion in American Life, 1: The Shaping of American Religion*. Princeton, NJ: Princeton Univ. Pr., 1961.

Smith, Timothy L. *Revivalism and Social Reform in mid-Nineteenth Century America*. Nashville: Abingdon Pr., 1957.

Stanton, Henry B. *Random Recollections*. 2nd ed. New York: Macgowan and Slipper, 1886.

Stevens, Abel. *Essays on the Preaching Required by the Times*. New York: Carlton and Phillips, 1855.

Stowe, Harriet Beecher. *Uncle Tom's Cabin or, Life among the Lowly by Harriet Beecher Stowe*. Ed. Kenneth S. Lynn. Cambridge, MA: Harvard Univ. Pr., 1962.

Strickland, W. P., ed. *The Backwoods Preacher: An Autobiography of Peter Cartwright*. London: Alexander Heylin, 1858.

———, ed. *Sketches of Western Methodism; Biographical, Historical, and Miscellaneous. Illustrative of Pioneer Life. By James B. Finley*. Cincinnati: Methodist Book Concern, 1854.

Sweet, William Warren. *Circuit-Rider Days along the Ohio: Being the Journals of the Ohio Conference from Its Organization in 1812 to 1826*. New York: Methodist Book Concern, 1923.

———. *Methodism in American History*. New York: Abingdon Pr., 1961.

———. *Religion in the Development of American Culture, 1765–1840*. New York: Scribner's, 1952.

———. *Religion on the American Frontier*. 4 vols. *The Presbyterians*. New York: Harper and Brothers, 1936; *The Baptists*. New York: Henry Holt, 1939; *The Congregationalists*. Chicago: Univ. of Chicago Pr., 1939; *The Methodists*. Chicago: Univ. of Chicago Pr., 1946.

———. *Revivalism in America, Its Origin, Growth, and Decline*. New York: Charles Scribner's Sons, 1944.

Thomas, Benjamin P. *Theodore Weld: Crusader for Freedom*. New Brunswick, NJ: Rutgers Univ. Pr., 1950.

Thomas, John L. *The Liberator: A Biography of William Lloyd Garrison*. Boston: Little, Brown, 1963.

Thome, James A., and J. Horace Kimball. *Emancipation in the West Indies: A Six Months Tour in Antigua, Barbados, and Jamaica in the Year 1837. The Anti-Slavery Examiner, No. 7*. New York: American Anti-Slavery Society, 1838.

Thomson, Edward. *Sketches, Biographical and Incidental.* Cincinnati: L. Swormstedt and A. Poe, 1857.

Thonssen, Lester, A. Craig Baird, and Waldo Braden. *Speech Criticism: The Development of Standards of Rhetorical Appraisal.* 2nd ed. New York: Ronald, 1970.

Tract No. 1, New England Anti-Slavery Tract Association. Boston: J. W. Alden Publishing Agent, n.d.

Tracy, Joseph. *The Great Awakening: A History of the Revival of Religion in the Time of Edwards and Whitefield.* Boston: Tappan and Dennet, 1842.

Trinterud, L. J. *The Forming of an American Tradition.* Philadelphia: Westminster Pr., 1949.

Trollope, Frances. *Domestic Manners of the Americans.* Ed. Donald Smalley. New York: Knopf, 1949.

Turner, Frederick Jackson. *The Frontier in American History.* Rev. ed. New York: Holt, 1920.

Tuveson, Ernest Lee. *Redeemer Nation: The Idea of America's Millennial Role.* Chicago: Univ. of Chicago Pr., 1968.

————. *Millennium and Utopia: A Study in the Background of the Idea of Progress.* New York: Harper and Row, 1964.

Wallace, Karl R., ed. *History of Speech Education in America.* New York: Appleton-Century-Crofts, 1954.

Wallis, Charles L., ed. *The Autobiography of Peter Cartwright.* Nashville: Abingdon Pr., 1956.

Walzer, Michael. *The Revolution of the Saints: A Study of the Origins of Radical Politics.* Cambridge, MA: Harvard Univ. Pr., 1965.

Wecter, Dixon. *The Hero in America: A Chronicle of Hero-Worship.* Ann Arbor: Univ. of Michigan Pr., Ann Arbor Paperbacks, 1963.

Weisberger, Bernard A. *They Gathered at the River: The Story of the Great Revivalists and Their Impact upon Religion in America.* Boston: Little, Brown, 1958.

Wendell, Barrett. *Cotton Mather, the Puritan Priest.* New York: Harcourt, Brace, and World, 1963.

White, Eugene E. *Puritan Rhetoric: The Issue of Emotion in Religion.* Carbondale: Southern Illinois Univ. Pr., 1972.

Whitefield, George. *George Whitefield's Journals.* London: Banner of Truth Trust, 1960.

Index 🌿